The Havoc of Capitalism

Bold Visions in Educational Research
Volume 28

Scope
Bold Visions in Educational Research is international in scope and includes books from two areas: *teaching and learning to teach* and *research methods in education.* Each area contains multi-authored handbooks of approximately 200,000 words and monographs (authored and edited collections) of approximately 130,000 words. All books are scholarly, written to engage specified readers and catalyze changes in policies and practices. Defining characteristics of books in the series are their explicit uses of theory and associated methodologies to address important problems. We invite books from across a theoretical and methodological spectrum from scholars employing quantitative, statistical, experimental, ethnographic, semiotic, hermeneutic, historical, ethnomethodological, phenomenological, case studies, action, cultural studies, content analysis, rhetorical, deconstructive, critical, literary, aesthetic and other research methods.

Books on *teaching and learning to teach* focus on any of the curriculum areas (e.g., literacy, science, mathematics, social science), in and out of school settings, and points along the age continuum (pre K to adult). The purpose of books on *research methods in education* is **not** to present generalized and abstract procedures but to show how research is undertaken, highlighting the particulars that pertain to a study. Each book brings to the foreground those details that must be considered at every step on the way to doing a good study. The goal is **not** to show how generalizable methods are but to present rich descriptions to show how research is enacted. The books focus on methodology, within a context of substantive results so that methods, theory, and the processes leading to empirical analyses and outcomes are juxtaposed. In this way method is not reified, but is explored within well-described contexts and the emergent research outcomes. Three illustrative examples of books are those that allow proponents of particular perspectives to interact and debate, comprehensive handbooks where leading scholars explore particular genres of inquiry in detail, and introductory texts to particular educational research methods/issues of interest. to novice researchers.

The Havoc of Capitalism

Publics, Pedagogies and Environmental Crisis

Edited by

Gregory Martin
University of Technology, Sydney, Australia

Donna Houston
Macquarie University, Sydney, Australia

Peter McLaren
University of California, Los Angeles, USA

Juha Suoranta
University of Tampere, Finland

SENSE PUBLISHERS
ROTTERDAM/BOSTON/TAIPEI

A C.I.P. record for this book is available from the Library of Congress.

ISBN: 978-94-6091-111-8 (paperback)
ISBN: 978-94-6091-112-5 (hardback)
ISBN: 978-94-6091-113-2 (e-book)

Published by: Sense Publishers,
P.O. Box 21858,
3001 AW Rotterdam,
The Netherlands
http://www.sensepublisher.com

Printed on acid-free paper

Cover image: 'Oil Rig' by Anne Lunghi, 2008

CONTENTS

PART III: TRANSFORMATIONS: PEDAGOGY, ACTIVISM AND THE ENVIRONMENT OF JUSTICE

DONNA HOUSTON AND GREGORY MARTIN

1. CRITICAL PEDAGOGY "AFTER THE STORM"[1]

> Landfall is not just a physical question. Geography is always socially produced.
> And so every landscape can reveal sedimented and contentious histories
> of occupation; struggles over land use and clashes over meaning, rights of
> occupancy, and rights to resources. Katrina churned through historical geo-
> graphies of extraordinary multiculturalism but extreme racial segregation, of
> amazing environmental wealth exploited rapaciously, of mythic significance
> in the American and even global imaginary whose celebrations masked the
> enduring legacies of poverty and discrimination that they fed off and opposed.
> (Katz, 2008, p. 16).

This edited collection is about the unfolding "dialectics of ordinary disaster"
that has shaped global cultures, pedagogies and environments at the beginning of
the twenty-first century (Davis, 1999). Mike Davis in his influential book *Ecology
of Fear: Los Angeles and the Imagination of Disaster* observed that the radical
transformation of the Southern California landscape through flood and fire,
understood from the perspective of the region's deep environmental history, is a
relatively ordinary occurrence. For Davis, what is extraordinary about ordinary
disaster is how its material production is "largely hidden from view by a way of
thinking that simultaneously imposes false expectations on the environment and then
explains the inevitable disappointments as proof of a malign and hostile nature"
(1999, p. 9). In other words, hidden in the acute shocks of environmental
catastrophe are the everyday social, economic and political dimensions that help to
make it. What gets erased by media spectacles of extreme "acts of nature" is the
extent to which rapacious urbanization, discriminatory housing and planning
practice, and bureaucratic cost effectiveness puts vulnerable people and places in
"harm's way" (Davis, 1999).

   The question of what is "natural" about disaster is a crucial one because the very
act of attributing catastrophe to external Nature hides the all-too-human histories of
uneven development and disinvestment in poor and minority communities. After the
landfall of Hurricane Katrina, the then US President George Bush commented that,
"the storm didn't discriminate" (Davis, 2005). But the social and environmental
injustices piling up in its long wake tell another story. Indeed, well before Katrina
begun to transform into a super-storm over the Gulf of Mexico in late August
2005, it was well known that the landfall of a major hurricane in New Orleans
would sweep a deadly path across communities already devastated by years of
institutional neglect, decaying infrastructure and ecological stress. In the living

*G. Martin, D. Houston, P. McLaren and J. Suoranta (eds.), The Havoc of Capitalism:
Publics, Pedagogies and Environmental Crisis, 1–12.*
© *2010 Sense Publishers. All rights reserved.*

memory of many of the older residents of the Lower Ninth Ward in New Orleans is Hurricane Betsy, the first hurricane in the history of the United States to cost over a billion dollars in 1965 (Bullard, 2005). Betsy caused the levees in the Lower Ninth Ward to breach (it was in fact rumored at the time that the levees were breached on purpose by city officials to protect white areas), flooding houses up to the eaves and trapping people in their attics. Memories of Betsy in the community was no doubt one of the reasons why many people in the Lower Ninth Ward kept hatchets and axes in their roofs to chop their way out in the event of a flood (Bullard, 2005).

Figure 1. New Orleans after Hurricane Katrina. Photograph by Win Henderson (FEMA).

SEDIMENTED INEQUITIES AND ORDINARY CRISES

There are other legacies from Betsy too. Debris from the storm was dumped in a black neighborhood at the Agriculture Street landfill, which is now a Superfund site. And as environmental justice scholar Robert Bullard observes, this particular history of toxic dumping in African American communities raises serious concerns about where the debris from hurricane Katrina will ultimately end up (Bullard, 2005). Indeed, environmental catastrophe in poor communities of color in Louisiana has been a lived reality in the region for decades. The stretch of the Mississippi River between New Orleans to Baton Rouge is the site of a massive petrochemical industrial corridor where over a hundred chemical and oil plants manufacture plastics, paints, fertilizers and gasoline (Pezzullo, 2003). Local residents (most of whom are working class and people of color) call this industrial corridor "cancer alley" and tell stories about an accumulative local history of epidemiological disorder in both adults and children living near industrial and Toxic Release Inventory sites. Since the collapse of the sugar and cotton plantations, toxic industries along the Mississippi River flourished during the later part of the twentieth century in a climate of convenience and cheap labor. However, recent years have seen a decline in petrochemical production and weakened the regional economy, leaving in its wake contaminated land and water and nearly twenty-five percent of the city's population living in poverty (Comfort, 2006). This is an all too familiar story for localities and regions that suffer the predations of environmental racism and injustice that, as Bullard (2001) argues:

> ...institutionalizes unequal [environmental] enforcement, trades human health for profit, places the burden of proof on the 'victims' rather than the polluters, legitimizes exposure to harmful chemicals, pesticides and harmful substances, promotes "risky" technologies, exploits the vulnerability of economic and politically disenfranchised communities, subsidizes ecological destruction, creates an industry around risk as-sessment, delays clean-up actions and fails to develop pollution prevention and precaution processes as the overarching and dominant strategy. (p. iii)

Along with bearing the brunt of the toxic burden of the environmental injustices of cancer alley, poor and working class black people in New Orleans have been particularly vulnerable to the effects of flooding – a result of the confluence of canal and levee construction, the development of heavy industries, wholesale wetland destruction, urban sprawl and governmental neglect at all scales. In the lower Mississippi Delta, over 15000 kilometers of canals have been dredged for drainage, logging, and for oil and gas development (Day Jr et al, 2007). This has radically altered the hydrology of the region and accelerated the destruction of its wetlands (that act as an ecological buffer to flooding) by saltwater intrusion (Day Jr et al, 2007). In this regard, the "ordinary crisis" of environmental injustice in New Orleans has been considerably worsened by Katrina, which wreaked havoc in areas that have already paid a heavy social and ecological debt in terms of health, livelihood and wellbeing. As Cindy Katz (2008) observes "the hurricane hit at a nadir of a three decades-long deterioration in the social wage; a combination of social relations and policies at the national, state, and municipal scales that eroded virtually every aspect of social reproduction, except those associated with militarism and policing" (p. 17).

Such tangible declines in social and economic wellbeing before and after Katrina starkly revealed the "disposability" of poor and minority people and the places where they work and live (see Henry Giroux, Chapter 3). This disposability was made glaringly visible through racist reporting in the media in Katrina's aftermath (see Doug Kellner, Chapter 2). But lying beneath the media spectacle that further victimized the city's most vulnerable populations, resides a pervasive social geography of "organized abandonment" (Lipsitz, 2006). The organized abandonment of New Orleans' working class people of color has been the result of what George

3

Lipsitz calls a "hostile social warrant of privatism" propelled by neoliberal economies and cultures (2006). Neoliberalism, he argues, produces a hostile warrant of "competitive consumer citizenship" that threatens to replace forms of citizenship concerned with the public good that emerged out of the civil rights movement. The social warrant of privatism cultivates subjects of self-care and places individual rights and needs over those of the whole social collective. Using the example of education, Lipsitz (2006) explains it this way:

> When the social warrant of the civil rights movement secured widespread credibility, support for education increased. If one thinks as a citizen or as a community member, then the more educated people there are, the better it is for everyone. However, if one thinks as an accumulator and as a consumer competing with others for scarce resources, educating other people's children might place your own in a competitive disadvantage. This approach creates massive inefficiency and misallocation of resources at the societal level. Direct discrimination costs the gross national product from two to four percent a year in lost productivity and waste. Yet what is disastrous at the societal level can be advantageous at the level of the household – at least in the short run. (p. 455)

Organized abandonment thus speaks to the pathology of the free market system that has reigned supreme over the past several decades. In this regard, the hostile social warrant of privatism haunts the future of New Orleans as much as it haunts the past. The deepening economic crisis both in the United States and globally has registered the fragile and ephemeral nature of the neoliberal social contract. But the fundamental question remains: *what ought to be done*? And as George Lipsitz asks, what can we learn from New Orleans? Now, more than ever, these questions are important to the task of transforming social and environmental injustice. Hurricane Katrina is a poignant reminder of the escalating toxic crisis and the very real problem of climate change. The stories that emerged from the environmental crisis in New Orleans and its aftermath amplify the urgent need for educators, community members and activists to rethink how humans and their everyday environments are intimately interconnected.

LEARNING FROM ENVIRONMENTAL IN/JUSTICE

The uneven and wounded terrains of environmental crisis are the debt of consumer capitalism lurking on the historical horizon. Walter Benjamin, though writing in the early decades of the twentieth century, famously captured this debt in the figure of the "angel of history." With its eyes turned to the past, Benjamin's (1968) angel sees "one single catastrophe" of accumulated threats, consequences and liabilities - everywhere - "in front of his feet" (p. 257). For Benjamin, progress is a storm that "keeps piling wreckage on wreckage" as it "irresistibly propels" us into an unforeseeable future (Benjamin, 1968, pp. 257, 258). Catastrophe is the ongoing crisis of capitalist progress that presses relentlessly forward. This crisis is occasionally interrupted by turbulence and counter-flows, when higher than expected storm surges whipped up by the winds of Paradise hurl debris at our feet. The economic, political and climatic shocks of the first decade of the twenty-first century have certainly precipitated such turbulence. There is a rising tide of recognition that climate and environmental change is exacerbated by human activities such as the burning of fossil fuels, declining biodiversity as a result of development, and unsustainable patterns of production and consumption amongst the planet's wealthiest populations. Mining, drilling, agribusiness and construction are all driving this activity, which is further supported by anti-environmental government policies that provide enormous subsidies to these industries (Dirty Metals, 2004). All this while the rich countries attempt to blame developing countries for failing to take action to cut carbon emissions.

But not all is doom and gloom. Shifting through the debris, fragments and wreckage, Benjamin's angel of history desires to "reassemble" and "make whole what has been smashed" (Benjamin, 1968, p. 257). Moving beyond the disorientating or "shock" effects of catastrophe and the desire to cushion its impact, Benjamin (1968) emphasized the productive potential for actualizing critical awareness and the radical struggle to transform the everyday. Located as we are within the modern corporate university, we argue that this implies a break from the traditional distinction between professionalism and activism. Acting as a high pressure brake on that impetus is the growth of neo-liberal discourses of professionalism or competence that set the limits of the "knowing" subject as well as the form and spatial scale of community engagement (Maxey, 2004, p. 159). As the plug is pulled on state funding, an entrepreneurial spirit is emerging at the individual and group level that is freighted toward market based research and strategies driven by competitive funding and a corporate research culture. This insidious barrier to social activism has led to efforts to reconceptualise professional identity, toward "a new form of professionalism and [activist] engagement" (Sachs, 1999). Groundwater-Smith and Sachs (2002) write, "first and foremost an activist professional is concerned to reduce or eliminate exploitation, inequality and oppression. Accordingly the development of this identity is deeply rooted in principles of equity and social justice" (p. 352). But strong disincentives and risks exist for developing this kind of activist identity, particularly given the rise of a surveillance and audit culture designed to enhance "performance" in higher education (Peters, 2007). Stepping outside of our comfort zone of institutional privilege and using it to support wider struggles for social justice can also result in our teaching and research being labelled ideologically biased or too partisan, and even subjected to administrative censure or prosecution. Despite operating under difficult contextual conditions, we believe that activist scholars ought to develop a more critically reflexive and engaged orientation toward community to bridge the gap between theory and practice.

This is the grist of Alain Touraine's argument (see Tapio Litmanen, Chapter 14), who holds that it is important for scholars to be "close to the action" in order to engage in the production of knowledges and practices that are socially useful for collective action. Picking up on this point, we argue that it is political for "trouble making" elements in the academy to act independent of the corporate interests of the university and to reach out in solidarity to social movements and other civil society actors in order to integrate their collective demands and concerns into their work and the wider struggle for environmental and social justice. Unfortunately, in the reified world of academia, Fuller and Kitchin (2004) lament that:

> critical praxis seems to consist of little else beyond pedagogy and academic writing. Potentially it might consist of calling for changes in policy. It may consist of research praxis that aims to become reflexive or emancipatory or empowering (changing the conditions of the research process but rarely seeking wider social change). But it rarely consists of a marriage between academic and activist roles, in which one's private and professional attempts to change the world are not divided into distinct and separable roles and tasks. (p. 6)

Having opted for independent action, we propose that activist scholars engage in a genuine dialogue with those social collectives struggling to enact, sustain, and inspire substantial change in place-based community contexts. For Freire (1972), dialogue is not mere communication, talk or "verbalism" (p. 75). Rather, it is a relational encounter, based in attentively listening to and learning "*with*" the oppressed, that is enacted through a diverse set of age-old and evolving practices including storytelling, music, dance, community arts, street theatre, digital networking and new multi-media productions (p. 33). Here, dialogue creates the pedagogical conditions for a critical place-based consciousness that has the power to "name the world" in order to transform it (p. 76). Such a place-based approach to learning through the mutual sharing, challenging and questioning of stories, ideas and meaning offers, from the ground up, the possibility of creating pedagogic spaces for cross border participation, debate and action, including the development of perspectives and strategies amongst a wide range of activists, intellectuals, First Nation groups, NGOs, alternative schools, social movements, the labour movement and green-left political organisations. This expansion of arenas and the links it establishes combined with a corresponding shift in activities and priorities, feeds into an activist agenda that makes political sense, as it is educational, personally satisfying, and politically relevant. We believe that taking a stand together means, to put it colloquially, "walking the talk." Breaking down the false division between scholarship and activism, this form of praxis intervention engages with the issues of different communities and movements by asserting the importance of collective knowledge and resistance, and as such, constitutes an activist form of "public sociology" (Burawoy, 2004, 2005) or "public pedagogy" (Giroux, 2004). Although often not well defined, such concepts are mobilized to acknowledge the subjective potential for academic and extra-academic audiences to engage public issues and problems as sites of transformative learning and action.

Given the effects of what Benjamin (1968) refers to as a history of permanent "catastrophe" that hangs over the whole globe including recent economic, environmental and political events, this politically driven agenda for academic activism constitutes a call for academics to be more socially relevant and to make a contribution to the real world struggles of real world victims (p. 257). What matters here, for Benjamin, is that "The tradition of the oppressed teaches us that the "state of emergency" in which we live is not the exception but the rule. We must attain to a conception of history that is in keeping with this insight" (p. 257). This requires an embodied and engaged approach to pedagogy, where academics are not afraid to get dirt under their fingernails. We believe that it is incumbent upon politically committed scholars to find positions for themselves within the various grassroots groups, networks and coalitions, social movements, NGOs, and political parties that have arisen as a defensive reflex against the horrors of environmental destruction and human misery (Moss, 2004). "In this [sort of] situation," as Joe Kincheloe (2008) recently wrote, "we have been touched by Walter Benjamin's Angel of History in a way that forever changes us, the knowledge we generate, and the reasons we produce it in the first place" (p. 8). The focus here is not on the appropriate degree of immersion or participation but rather on engaging in dialogue, solidarity and praxis with social movements and other groups that are so often out of reach. Such pedagogies are attuned to the histories and activities of those communities that have been marginalized by the onward trajectory of industrial progress and who keep the presence of alternatives alive through their networks of exchange and interconnection.

At a time where contemporary "matters of concern" (to borrow a phrase from Bruno Latour) encompass a whole range of environmental and place-based issues, educational institutions such as universities ought to be deeply involved in this effort. This includes collaborating across disciplinary borders, as well as identifying and analyzing the adverse effects of public policies and other interventions across the nature-society interface. To be effective, a coordinated, principled, multi-level and multi-pronged approach in all these key areas ought to be tied to efforts to raise civic engagement through different forms of community organizing, whereby schools, local communities, and other sites of public pedagogy could serve as catalysts for substantial revitalization. With an emphasis on material empowerment and imaginative transformation, we need to reinvest our purpose with criticality and hope. Here, every ingredient in the political and civic cauldron works to bring about the desired forces of change.

A popular refrain from the recently inaugurated US president Barack Obama is that change is always possible but that it won't be easy or quick. Even as we might take a moment to reflect on the turbulent storms that have recently passed, new clouds gather on the horizon. The question of how fundamental change might be enacted as a response to what Naomi Klein (2007) calls "disaster capitalism" remains a deeply fraught issue (see also Doug Kellner, Chapter 2). With an outstretched hand, free market ideologues –with some help from the state—have cleverly exploited the mayhem, fear and trauma of crisis (terrorist attacks, wars, disasters and other "shocks") to sell the need for economic reforms that are potentially unpopular and painful. A prime example of this is when Milton Freidman, the ideological Godfather of neoliberalism and free market solutions, argued that the "tragedy" of Katrina, which left "Most New Orleans schools…in ruins" also afforded "an opportunity to radically reform the education system" via a voucher system (pp. 4–5). Yet, as Klein writes, numerous instances exist of "real challenges" to the neoliberal agenda at different geographical locations and scales (p. 448). And this "backlash"—which has unleashed some reactionary as well as hopeful forces—points to the limits or reversibility of the neoliberal "shock doctrine" of development (p. 448).

What is increasingly apparent, then, is the need to develop new energetic capacities and strategies for engaging in what Klein calls "peoples' reconstruction" (p. 443). Such collective strategies for reconstruction actively produce strong alternatives to disaster capitalism and create spaces where people forge relationships with each other and with nonhuman nature that recognize the complex material worlds that we all inhabit. Practically, this means working in areas traditionally placed "outside" of educational practice and cultural reproduction. Linked to a wide variety of sites and struggles, what we are advocating is an *enlarged* pedagogy that engages politically with historical and material registers in contemporary everyday life. Echoing the words of Walter Benjamin, this requires what Giroux (1994) terms "…a discourse of imagination and hope that pushes history against the grain" (p. 42). Benjamin's angel offers the possibility for redemption amongst the ruins of neoliberalism, carbon-based industrialism and hyper-consumption. It offers the hope and possibility for social and environmental alternatives for living in and sustaining a world shared with others.

This book, we hope, offers a step in this direction. Rather than advocating any particular theoretical approach, the eclectic nature of the chapters included in this volume are intended to demonstrate a diversity of perspectives that shape understandings of the relationalities between pedagogy, publics, politics and environment. In other words, this book works towards an enlarged pedagogy that brings together a diverse set of ontologies and knowledges that share a political commitment to a collective project of transformation and justice.

The chapters in the first part of the book titled "Havoc: Katrina and the Crisis of Capital" highlight the failure of neoliberal 'free market' ideology' and reveal how race, class, policy and place still matter. The systemic failure at all levels of government to address long term environmental, economic, social and political problems is an example of how public policy renders poor people and people of color 'invisible' and vulnerable to environmental injustice and environmental racism. Clearly, there is a geography to neoliberalism and its effects are uneven. On this point, Katrina was a showcase of national humiliation and abandonment, from the destruction of coastal wetlands and the antiquated levee system to the resulting evacuations and institutionalised neglect and vilification of the storm's victims. But it also meant that there was a resurgence of interest in environmental racism and environmental justice providing the impetus for a number of projects and activities.

The first essay by Douglas Kellner discusses the media spectacle of Katrina that revealed the political cronyism of the Bush Administration and the failure of the neoliberal state to plan and respond to the predicted disaster. Despite a massive White House PR effort, the spectacle of destruction, suffering and despair that followed in the awful wake of Katrina "put on display the glaring inequities of race and class that define the U.S. in the new millennium" (p. 26). Symptomatic of a larger problem with neoliberal globalization, Giroux argues further that all the Katrina generated debris made visible a new and pernicious form of biopolitics that marks entire populations as disposable. He writes, "The disposable populations serve as an unwelcome reminder that the once vaunted social state no longer exists, the living dead now an apt personification of the death of the social contract in the United States" (p. 42). Mclaren and Jaramillo offer a critique of the Bush administration's response to Katrina and the catastrophic effects of US imperialism (e.g., the War in Iraq) on the domestic front. Ville Lähde, a Finish researcher and activist, makes the case that an autonomous conception of "Nature" is often used to depoliticise disasters such as Hurricane Katrina and the 2004 South Asian Tsunami. With a focus on strategies for change, he argues that "*adaptation* [is] a vital political issue" that offers the possibility of reshaping political consciousness and human nature relations (p. 75). In summary, what all these pieces on the politics of Hurricane Katrina reveal is that contemporary ecological and social crises have a common historical origin and global character.

The second part of this book explores the theme of "Resilience: Indigenous Pedagogies and the Critique of Neo-colonialism." The focus shifts to understanding how contemporary social and environmental crises continue to carry the weight of colonial histories, epistemologies and pedagogies. The injustices of colonial history and the Indigenous and local ecological knowledges developed, shared and passed on from one generation to the next in response to the complexities of colonialism or imperialism are often overlooked, if not ignored. This is not just a matter of abstract academic concern and the praxis of the following is to open up spaces for intercultural dialogue, debate and political action as an alternative relational geography. In the wake of Katrina, Grande surveys the real, material effects of the colonial project on Indigenous peoples and lays the epistemological groundwork for a Red Pedagogy that is place-based and promotes decolonization. Although it is not officially recognised in Australian universities or schools, Sheehan, Dunleavy Cohen and Mitchell use Indigenous Knowledge (IK) to track the "relational movements" of predatory colonialism (p. 107). Within the context of social dominance and racism, they propose an Indigenous Knowledge Pedagogy (IKP) that "adopts a [structural] approach to educating for social wellness (p. 113). Writing in the Australian context, Kerwin provides a stinging critique of changes to environmental and cultural heritage policies and the new paternalism of economic rationalism (neoliberalism). Certainly, this is no time for subtlety. Regardless of political party, in Kerwin's view, "The major problem for Aboriginal peoples around the country is the inability of the political machinery to accept Aboriginal knowledges and beliefs" (p. 125). Woods and Martin provide a discourse analysis of former Australian Prime Minister John Howard's policy speech on Aboriginal reconciliation to the Sydney Institute. They argue that Howard's so-called "new statement of reconciliation" pointed to the dominant position of the white majority in Australia, as well as the structural benefits of Whiteness and institutionalised racism. Here, reconciliation is predicated upon an extremely narrow and limiting conception of the nation and responsibility for historical injustices. This is an example of how white sovereignty in settler societies such as Australia remains invisible, normal, and unmarked. On this point, Sammel a "white middle class girl growing up in urban Australia" (p. 159) and Pete "a First Nations woman from Saskatchewan" (p. 158) share their personal stories of teaching about racism and White privilege in both Australia and Canada.

The final part of the book under the theme "Transformations: Pedagogy, Activism and the Environment of Justice," explores questions of what ought to be done? Drawing on the historical legacy of the 1960s and its significance for revolutionary praxis, Moisio, FitzSimmons and Suoranta identify the importance of critical education in creating "weather persons" who "have the skills to dissect and to explain the direction in which the wind is actually blowing" (p. 180). Aspects of that contested legacy are highly controversial, as exemplified by William Ayers, a former leader of the US radical group the Weathermen, who became a political liability to Obama in the US Presidential race in 2008. However, it also offers a number of theoretical and practical insights, particularly for critical pedagogy. And as the storm clouds gather, they argue that radical educators have a role in "set[ting] forth curricula for new possibilities and actions that actively involve people in transforming their social and ecological environments with a form belief in the possibility to effect change by their own direct intervention in social and economic settings and practices" (p. 187).

Taking a non-deterministic approach to history and the uneven and unpredictable dynamic of human action, Tammilehto explores the potential of informal relational structures and tactics for articulating demands for social change. In a similar vein, Latensach and Latensach identify the complicity of higher education in the global environmental crisis. To counter this state of affairs, they argue for an educational program of curriculum reform that challenges ideologies of progress and anthropocentrism. To the degree that the global crisis is a world crisis for both human and nonhuman beings, a pedagogy of liberation or critical pedagogy must refocus its myopic lens in order to address anthropocentricism. Indeed, rethinking the central role of humans in critical pedagogy also re-energises issues of ontological diversity and difference across political, ecological and historical borders. Finally, Litmanen argues for the academic and political significance of Alain Touraine's work. Given the poverty of university specific activism, Touraine's methods are particularly revealing for scholars who are interested in actively intervening in processes of social struggle and historical transformation.

What all the contributing chapters in this book demonstrate, are many far-reaching lessons to be learnt from Katrina and the media and political frenzy that emerged in its aftermath. The larger story that emerges from this edited collection is that the confluence of poverty, racism and environmental crisis in the first decades of the twenty-first century so viscerally manifested by Katrina, also converge on deeper histories of imperialism, uneven capitalist development and the profound alienation from nonhuman nature that these practices attend. At the same time, the current global financial crisis and economic downturn have prompted a critical re-examination of economic ideas and policy agendas. In this climate, it appears that we are now at a critical crossroads. The contributors to this book point to the substantive ways in which the often disparate but always collective projects of critical pedagogy can be enlarged to address the material and affective relations of social and environmental justice.

NOTES

[1] Title inspired by Mike Davis' chapter 'Los Angeles After the Storm: A Dialectics of Ordinary Disaster' in *Ecology of Fear: Los Angeles and the Imagination of Disaster*. New York: Vintage Books.

REFERENCES

Benjamin, W. (1968). Theses on the philosophy of history. In H. Arendt (Ed.), *Illuminations: Essays and Reflections* (H. Zohn, Trans.). New York: Schocken Books.

Bullard, R. D. (2001). Environment and Morality: Confronting Environmental Racism in the United States. *Identities, Conflict and Cohesion Programme Paper Number 8*, United Nations Research Institute for Social Development. Retrieved February 18, 2009, from http://unrisd.org/unrisd/website/document.nsf/(httpPublications)/543B2B250E64745280256B6D005788F7?OpenDocument

Bullard, R. D. (2005). Environmental Justice Professor Robert Bullard on How Race Affected the Federal Government's Response to Katrina. *Democracy Now!* Transcript Retrieved February 18, 2009, from http://www.democracynow.org/2005/10/24/environmental_justice_professor_robert_bullard_on

Burawoy, M. (2004). Public sociologies: Contradictions, dilemmas, and possibilities. *Social Forces, 82*(4), 1603–1618.

Burawoy, M. (2005). For public sociology. *American Sociological Review, 70*, 4–28.

Comfort, L. K. (2006). Cities at Risk: Hurricane Katrina and the Drowning of New Orleans. *Urban Affairs Review, 41*(4), 501–516.

Davis, M. (2005) The Predators of New Orleans, *Le Monde Diplomatique*. Retrieved February 18, 2009, from http://mondediplo.com/2005/10/02katrina

Davis, M. (1999). *Ecology of Fear: Los Angeles and the Imagination of Disaster*. New York: Vintage Books.

Day, J. W., Jr., Boesch, D., Clairain, E., Kemp, P., Laska, S., Mitch, W., Orth, K., & Mashriqui, H. (2007). Restoration of the Mississippi Delta: Lessons from Hurricanes Katrina and Rita. *Science, 315*(5819), 1679–1684.

Dirty Metals: Mining Communities and the Environment. (2004). A report by Earthworks and Oxfam America. Available at: http://www.nodirtygold.org/dirty_metals_report.cfm

Fuller, D., & Kitchin, R. (2004). Introduction. *Radical theory/critical praxis: Academic geography beyond the academy?* (pp. 1–20). Praxis(e)Press. Retrieved October 1, 2004, from http://www.praxis-epress.org

Freire, P. (1972). *Pedagogy of the oppressed* (M. Ramos, Trans.). London: Sheed and Ward Ltd.

Giroux, H. (1994). Pedagogy and the politics of hope: Theory, culture and schooling. In K. Myrsiades & L. Myrsiades (Eds.), *Margins in the classroom: Teaching literature* (pp. 1–51). Minneapolis, MN: University of Minnesota Press.

Giroux, H. (2004). Public Pedagogy and the Politics of Neo-liberalism: making the political more pedagogical. *Policy Futures in Education, 2*(3), 494–503.

Groundwater-Smith, S., & Sachs, J. (2002). The activist professional and the reinstatement of trust. *Cambridge Journal of Education, 32*(3), 341–358.

Houston, D. (in press). Grounds upon which to act: Pedagogy, place-making and collective histories of praxis. In S. Macrine, D. Hill, & P. McLaren (Eds.), *Critical Pedagogy: In Search of Democracy, Liberation and Socialism*. London: Routledge.

Katz, C. (2008). Bad elements: Katrina and the scoured landscape of social reproduction. *Gender, Place and Culture, 15*(1), 15–29.

Klein, N. (2007). *The shock doctrine: The rise of disaster capitalism*. New York: Metropolitan Books.

Kincheloe, J. (2008). Critical pedagogy and the knowledge wars of the twenty-first century. *International Journal of Critical Pedagogy, 1*(1), 1–22. Retrieved January 3, 2009, from http://freire.mcgill.ca/ojs/index.php/home/article/view/48/16

Lipsitz, G. (2006). Learning from New Orleans: The social warrant of hostile privatism and competitive consumer citizenship. *Cultural Anthropology, 21*(3), 451–468.

Maxey, L. (2004). Moving beyond from within: Reflective activism and critical geographies. In D. Fuller & R. Kitchin (Eds.), *Radical theory/critical praxis: Making a difference beyond the academy* (pp. 159–171). Praxis(e)Press. Retrieved October 2, 2004, from http://www.praxis-epress.org

Moss, P. (2004). A 'politics of local politics': Praxis in places that matter. In D. Fuller & R. Kitchin (Eds.), *Radical theory/critical praxis: Making a difference beyond the academy* (pp. 103–115). Praxis(e)Press. Retrieved October 2, 2004, from http://www.praxis-epress.org

Peters, M. (2007). *Knowledge, economy, development and the future of higher education*. The Netherlands: Sense Publishers.

Pezzullo, P. (2003). Touring "Cancer Alley," Louisiana: Performances of Community and Memory for Environmental Justice. *Text and Performance Quarterly, 23*(3), 226–252.

Sachs, J. (1999). *Teacher professional identity: Competing discourses, competing outcomes*. Paper Presented at AARE Conference Melbourne, November 1999. Retrieved February 22, 2009, from http://www.aare.edu.au/99pap/sac99611.htm

PART I: HAVOC: KATRINA AND THE CRISIS OF CAPITAL

DOUGLAS KELLNER

2. HURRICANE SPECTACLES AND THE CRISIS OF THE BUSH PRESIDENCY

On the weekend of August 27–28, 2005, Hurricane Katrina hurtled toward the Louisiana coast. With winds up to 175 miles per hour it was deemed a Hurricane 5, the most dangerous on the Saffir-Simpson scale. The media had been warning that a big hurricane was going to strike the Gulf coast and was heading straight for New Orleans for days prior to its eventual landing on Monday, August 29. Reports had focused on the potentially catastrophic threats to New Orleans, noting how much of the city was perilously below sea-level and how flooding threatened its precarious levee and canal system that protected the city from potential catastrophe. There were copious media speculations that this could be "the big one," prophesized for years and documented in government and media reports, warning that New Orleans could be devastated by a major hurricane. Accordingly, the mayor of New Orleans and state officials had ordered the city evacuated, while the Governor of Louisiana declared a "state of emergency," putting the federal government in charge.

Despite all the warnings, there appeared to be utterly inadequate preparation in the days preceding the well-forecast hurricane and for days after it was apparent that this was indeed a major catastrophe. Although the New Orleans mayor ordered evacuation just before the storm was to hit, tens of thousands, mostly poor and black people, remained behind because they had no transportation or funds to leave the city. Tens of thousands of the remaining citizens were herded into the New Orleans Superdome and Convention Center to ride out the storm, without proper food and water, sanitary facilities, police protection, or other basic necessities. Although the crowds survived the storm, which did not strike New Orleans directly, and while the storm was weaker than initially predicted, Hurricane Katrina inflicted tremendous damage when on Monday September 29 the 17th Street Canal levee was breached, others cracked, and 80–90% of the city lay under water.[1]

HURRICANE DISASTER RESPONSE: MIA

Hurricane Katrina and its aftermath unleashed one of the most astonishing media spectacles in U.S. history. Houses and towns along the Gulf coast in Louisiana and Mississippi were destroyed and flood surges wreaked havoc miles inland. New Orleans was buried in water and for several days, the crowds in the Superdome and Convention Center were not given food, water, or evacuation and there were reports of fighting, rape, robbery, and death, some exaggerated as we shall see

G. Martin, D. Houston, P. McLaren and J. Suoranta (eds.), The Havoc of Capitalism:
Publics, Pedagogies and Environmental Crisis, 15–28.
© 2010 Sense Publishers. All rights reserved.

below. Indeed, no federal or state troops were sent to the city in the early days of the disaster, and thousands were trapped in their homes as the flood waters rose and there were widespread images of looting and crime.

Just as President Bush remained transfixed reading "My Pet Goat" to a Florida audience of schoolchildren after 9/11, a spectacle preserved on the Internet and memorialized by Michael Moore in *Fahrenheit 9/11*, so too was the president invisible in the aftermath of Katrina (as he had been after the Asian Tsunami). Bush remained on a five-week vacation during the first days of the disaster punctuated by a visit to a private event in Arizona where he bragged about how well things were going in Iraq, comparing the war there that he initiated to World War II, inferring that he was FDR. The next day Bush was shown clowning at a fundraiser in San Diego, smiling and strumming a guitar, and again bragging about Iraq and touting his failed domestic policies, leading commentator David Jenkins to exclaim:

> The last few weeks have been irrefutable proof that America is being wrecked and mismanaged by the most incompetent, dangerous and out of touch boobs ever to obtain power. Any American with even a tiny amount of conscience who watched those images from New Orleans shook their heads with disbelief and shame that something like this should happen within our own borders in these modern times. As pictures of floating corpses glared at us through our TV sets, we were treated to photo-ops of our supposed leader golfing, blithering about Social Security, eating cake and strumming a guitar. Meanwhile, our Secretary of State [Rice] shopped for shoes and took in a show while the Vice President [Cheney] shopped for a house in a ritzy Maryland neighborhood.[2]

During Bush's first visit to the disaster area, he made inappropriate jokes about how he knew New Orleans during his party days all too well and bantered that he hoped to visit Republican Senator Trent Lott's new house upon hearing that his beachfront estate was destroyed. In a fateful comment, Bush told his hapless FEMA director Michael Brown on camera: "You are doing a heck of a job, Brownie." Bush's first visit to the area kept him away from New Orleans and isolated from angry people who would confront him. His visit to the heavily damaged city of Biloxi, Mississippi was preceded by a team that cleared rubble and corpses from the route that the president would take, leaving the rest of the city in ruin. The same day, in an interview with Diane Sawyer, Bush remarked "I don't think anyone anticipated the breach of the levees" at a time when the media had circulated copious reports of previous warnings by scientists, journalists, and government officials concerning dangers of the levees breaching and catastrophic flooding in the city of New Orleans, much of which was dangerously below sea level.

Bush's response to the catastrophe revealed all the weaknesses of the Bush presidency: immature frat-boy, good-old boy behavior and banter; political cronyism; a bubble of isolation by sycophantic advisors; an arrogant out-of-touchness with the realities of the sufferings his policies had unleashed; a general incompetence; and belief that image-making can compensate for the lack of public policy.

THE OTHER AMERICA

But the media spectacle of the hurricane, which dominated the U.S. cable news channels for days and was heavily covered on the U.S. network news, showed images of unbelievable suffering and destruction, depicting thousands of people without food and water, and images of unimaginable loss and death in a city that had descended into anarchy and looked like a Third World disaster area with no relief in sight.

The spectacle of the poor, sick, and largely black population left behind provided rare media images of what Michael Harrington (1963) described as "the other America," and the media engaged in rare serious discussions of race and class as they tried to describe and make sense of the disaster. As John Powers put it:

> Suddenly, the Others were right in front of our noses, and the major media predominantly white and pretty well-off — were talking about race and class. Newspapers ran front-page articles noting that nearly six million people have fallen into poverty since President Bush took office — a nifty 20 percent increase to accompany the greatest tax cuts in world history. Feisty columnists rightly fulminated that, even as tens of thousands suffered in hellish conditions, the buses first rescued people inside the Hyatt Hotel. Of course, such bigotry was already inscribed in the very layout of New Orleans. One reason the Superdome became a de facto island is that, like the city's prosperous business district, it was carefully constructed so it would be easy to protect from the disenfranchised (30 percent of New Orleans lives below the poverty line).[3]

Usually the media exaggerate the danger of hurricanes, put their talking heads on the scene, and then exploit human suffering by showing images of destruction and death. While there was an exploitative dimension to the Katrina coverage, it was clear that this was a major event and disaster, and media figures and crews risked their lives to cover the story. Moreover, many reporters and TV commentators were genuinely indignant when federal relief failed to come day after day, and for the first time in recent memory seriously criticized the Bush administration and Bush himself, while sharply questioning officials of the administration when they tried to minimize the damage or deflect blame. As Mick Farren put it:

> In the disaster that was New Orleans, TV news and Harry Connick were the first responders. It may well have been a news generation's finest hour. Reporters who had been spun or embedded for most of their careers faced towering disaster and intimacy with death, and told the tale with a horrified honesty. When anchors like Brian Williams and Anderson Cooper waded in the water, dirty and soaked in sweat, it transcended showboating. It was the story getting out. Okay, so Geraldo Rivera made an asshole of himself, but I will never forget the eloquent shell shock of NBC cameraman Tony Zumbado after he discovered the horror at the Convention Center.

That CNN could function where FEMA feared to tread undercut most federal excuses and potential perjuries. Journalists who could see the bodies refused to accept "factuality" from Michael Brown, Michael Chertoff, or even George Bush. Ted Koppel and Paula Zahn all but screamed "bullshit!" at them on camera.[4]

BROWNIE AND BUSH CRONYISM

The rightwing Republican attack machine (Brock 2004) first blamed the New Orleans poor for not leaving and then descending into barbarism, but it came out quickly that there were tens of thousands who were so poor they had no transportation, money, or anyplace to go, and many had to care for sick and infirm friends, relatives, or beloved pets. Moreover, the poor were abandoned for days without any food, water, or public assistance. The rightwing attack machine then targeted local officials for the crisis, but intense media focus soon attached major blame for the criminally inadequate public response on Bush administration FEMA Director Michael Brown. It was revealed that Brown, who had no real experience with disaster management, had received his job because he was college roommate of Joe Allbaugh, the first FEMA director and one of the major Texas architects of Bush's election successes, known as the "enforcer" because of his fierce loyalty to Bush and tough Texas behavior and demeanor.[5]

Stories circulated about how Allbaugh gutted FEMA of disaster response professionals and packed it with political appointees, such as previous Bush team PR and media people. Joe Allbaugh was part of Bush's anti-government conservative coalition which cut back funding for FEMA, as the administration would later cut back plans to prepare disaster relief for New Orleans and cut federal funds to boost up its levee system. Allbaugh was FEMA director when 9/11 hit and quickly resigned, going into the public sector to advise corporations on how to deal with terrorism and then set up a business helping corporations get contracts in Iraq and security to protect their employees.

Meanwhile, Internet sources and *Time* magazine revealed that Brown had fudged his vita, claiming in testimony to Congress that he had been a manager of local emergency services when he had only had a low-level position.[6] He had claimed he was a professor at a college where he was a student and generally had padded his c.v. Stories also circulated that in his previous job he had helped run Arabian horse shows, but had been dismissed for incompetence. After these reports, it was a matter of time until Bush first sent him back to Washington, relieving him of his duties, and allowing him to resign a couple of days later.

The media then had a field day scapegoating the hapless Brown, who admittedly was a poster boy for Bush administration incompetent political appointees. But the top echelons of FEMA were full of Bush appointees who had fumbled and stumbled during the first crucial days of disaster relief and who were unqualified to deal with the tremendous challenges confronting the country. Moreover, Brown was castigated in the media for a statement that he did not know there were tens of thousands of people left behind stranded in the New Orleans Convention Center without food, water, or protection after pictures of their plight had circulated through the media, while Michael Chertoff, head of the cabinet level Department of Homeland Security, also made such statements, and the federal non-response could easily be blamed on his ineptness and failure to coordinate disaster response efforts.[7]

Media images of the thousands left on their own in New Orleans and the surrounding area were largely poor and black, leading to charges that the Bush administration were blind to the suffering of the poor and people of color.[8] Revealingly, these individuals were referred to as "refugees" and indeed they appeared homeless and devastated, as in familiar images of people escaping devastation in the developing world, although this time it was happening domestically.

While there was a fierce debate as to whether the federal response would or would not have been more vigorous if the victims were largely white or middle class people, readers of Yahoo news recognized that racism was blatantly obvious in captions to two pictures circulating, one of whites wading through water and described as "carrying food," while another picture showing blacks with armloads of food described as "looters." During NBC's Concert for Hurricane Relief, rapper Kanye West declared "George Bush doesn't care about black people," and asserted that America is set up "to help the poor, the black people, the less well-off as slow as possible." West sharply criticized Bush's domestic priorities and Iraq policy before NBC was able to cut away to a smiling Chris Tucker.[9]

While Laura Bush and conservatives claimed that charges of racism were "ridiculous" and offensive, it was clear to many that there were serious issues of class and race concerning who was left behind without resources to evacuate and which neighborhoods were more vulnerable to devastation. Later, serious questions were raised concerning relative strengths of floodwalls in various regions of town and why poorer neighborhoods tended to be devastated by flood waters.[10]

Bush himself, ever in denial, told Diane Sawyer in a *Good Morning America* interview that: "I don't think anybody anticipated the breach of the levees" – an inane response reduced to a blatant lie when later videotape showed a FEMA authority warning Bush that the levees could breach and the city could be flooded. Bush's mother Barbara also put on display the famous Bush family insensitivity when she said on a visit to evacuees in Houston's Astrodome: "So many of the people in the arena here, you know, were underprivileged anyway, so this is working very well for them."

BUSHSPEAK, THE WAVERING MEDIA AND STAGECRAFT

Bush administration operatives deplored critics playing "the blame game," showing once again how one of the defining features of Bushspeak is to deny reality and refuse to take responsibility for failures of his administration.[11] Bush's presidential ratings continued to plunge as day after day there were pictures of incredible suffering, devastation, and death, and discussions of the utterly inadequate federal, local, and state response. While the U.S. corporate media had failed to critically discuss the failings of George W. Bush in either the 2000 or 2004 elections and had white-washed his failed presidency, for the first time one saw sustained criticism of the Bush administration on the U.S. cable TV news networks. The network correspondents on the ground were appalled by the magnitude of the devastation and paucity of the federal response and presented images of the horrific spectacle day after day, including voices from the area critical of the Bush administration. Even media correspondents who had been completely supportive of Bush's policies began to express doubts and intense public interest in the tragedy ensured maximum coverage and continued critical discussion.

The Bush administration went on the offensive, sending Bush, Cheney, Rice, Rumsfeld, and other high officials to the disaster area, but the stark spectacle of suffering undercut whatever rhetoric the Bush team produced. Vice President Dick Cheney was reportedly hunting in Montana and then shopping for a $2.5 million vacation house on the Maryland shore when the hurricane hit. It was widely reported that Secretary of State Condoleezza Rice was on a shopping spree in New York buying $5000 plus pairs of shoes when the spectacle unfolded on TV, and her first press conference during the disaster showed her giddy and bubbly, impervious to the suffering; to improve her image, she was sent to her home-state Alabama where photographers dutifully snapped her helping organize relief packages for flood victims.

Whereas the Bush administration tried to emphasize positive features of the relief effort, the images of continued devastation and the slow initial response undercut efforts to convey an image that the Bushites were in charge and dealing with the problem. Although the Bush team tried to scapegoat the poor, local officials, environmental groups, and even God,[12] it was clear that only the federal government had the resources to deal with the immensity of the tragedy and that the Bush administration had largely failed.

Bush's claim that he would himself lead an investigation into what went wrong with the federal response to Katrina was met by ridicule,[13] and although the Democrats attempted to mandate an independent government commission to investigate the failure, Republicans resisted and formed a committee of their own to investigate that Democrats refused to participate in.

RETURN TO THE CONSERVATIVE MEDIA AGENDA

After praising CNN and cable coverage of Hurricane Katrina, media critic Nikki Finke describes how the U.S. corporate media returned to their conservative agenda some weeks into the tragedy:

> For the first 120 hours after Hurricane Katrina, TV journalists were let off their leashes by their mogul owners, the result of a rare conjoining of flawless timing (summer's biggest vacation week) and foulest tragedy (America's worst natural disaster). All of a sudden, broadcasters narrated disturbing images of the poor, the minority, the aged, the sick and the dead, and discussed complex issues like poverty, race, class, infirmity and ecology that never make it on the air in this swift-boat/anti-gay-marriage/Michael Jackson media-sideshow era. So began a perfect storm of controversy.

Contrary to the scripture so often quoted in these areas of Louisiana and Mississippi, the TV newscasters knew the truth, but the truth did not set them free. Because once the crisis point had passed, most TV journalists went back to business-as-usual, their choke chains yanked by no-longer-inattentive parent-company bosses who, fearful of fallout from fingering Dubya for the FEMA fuckups, decided yet again to sacrifice community need for corporate greed. Too quickly, Katrina's wake was spun into a web of deceit by the Bush administration, then disseminated by the Big Media boys' club. (Karl Rove spent the post-hurricane weekend conjuring up ways to shift blame).[14]

Karl Rove was reportedly put in charge of both the White House PR effort and reconstruction efforts and suddenly Bush was sent down to the disaster area every few days to make an appearance, hugging black people and showing that he cared and was in charge. Of course, these media visits were pseudo-events constructed to make Bush look presidential. NBC anchor Brian Williams's reported on his blog how he and the residents of New Orleans were plunged in darkness during one presidential visit, when suddenly all the electricity came on and everyone cheered and rejoiced. After Bush's motorcade passed through to celebratory applause, electricity was suddenly cut, not to be soon restored, causing groans and dismissals of the president who found the political will to have electricity for his safe passage and stagecraft, but not for those still stuck in the city. Another visit showed Bush in Mississippi with shirt-sleeves rolled up, speaking to a man who seemed dazed and lost, wanting to know where he could find a Red Cross station which he had been searching for days. A decisive Bush pointed down the road, declaring "there's one right down there," appearing to be on top of the situation. However, it was later reported that the man never made it to that station because it was just a theater prop and that false "Red Cross stations" were popping up all over the South during Bush's visits, only to disappear the moment the camera left. His "visits" also diverted military and relief efforts to set creation instead of emergency assistance.

Three weeks after Katrina, Bush imagineers concocted a staged spectacle to attempt to make Bush look like a decisive leader. In an evening prime-time address to the nation, Bush was shown striding across the fabled Jackson Square in New Orleans with blue-background lighting and the famed St. Louis Cathedral in the background. The White House had brought generators to produce electricity for the shoot in the blacked out city, and had put up background patches of military camouflage netting to hide the president from the ghostly deserted streets of the French Quarter. But the long shot of Bush walking up to the podium made him look more like a small figure in an Antonioni movie, dwarfed by the environment, and critics dammed the speech as failed stagecraft. As Maureen Dowd put it:

All Andrew Jackson's horses and all the Boy King's men could not put Humpty Dumpty together again. His gladiatorial walk across the darkened greensward, past a St. Louis Cathedral bathed in moon glow from White House klieg lights, just seemed to intensify the sense of an isolated, out-of-touch president clinging to hollow symbols as his disastrous disaster agency continues to flail.

In a ruined city – still largely without power, stinking with piles of garbage and still 40 percent submerged; where people are foraging in the miasma and muck for food, corpses and the sentimental detritus of their lives; and where unbearably sad stories continue to spill out about hordes of evacuees who lost their homes and patients who died in hospitals without either electricity or rescuers - isn't it rather tasteless, not to mention a waste of energy, to haul in White House generators just to give the president a burnished skin tone and a prettified background?[15]

This was typical Bush administration image making: stagecraft over substance, and carefully planned spectacle to attempt to produce an image of Bush as a decisive leader. But the previous three weeks had shown that Bush was not a leader at all, but a front man for a regime based on cronyism, providing spoils from the treasury and government patronage jobs to their supporters and loyalists. Michael Brown of FEMA had been unveiled as totally unqualified for the job and had received it only because he was the roommate of Joe Allbaugh, who himself had dismantled FEMA and filled it with incompetent political appointees. As Douglas J. Amy put it:

Brown is just one example of an ongoing pattern of inappropriate and disturbing appointments by President Bush – appointments that threaten to undermine the basic functioning of many key government agencies. This administration's guiding political philosophy is that government is a bad thing and should be cut back to a minimum. It has a particular contempt for the federal bureaucracy, which it sees as the embodiment of "liberal big government." So it is hardly surprising that the administration has not made a great effort to ensure that the best-qualified people are running these agencies. But the situation is actually much worse than this. It is not simply that Bush put incompetent political hacks like Brown in place. He has also been appointing officials who are actually hostile to the agencies that they run. Many of them have political values and views diametrically opposed to the very missions of these agencies. For example, many of Bush's appointees to agencies charged with protecting the environment have been opposed to environmental regulations in particular, and government regulation in general. And many have come from businesses or conservative organizations that have fought against efforts at environmental protection.[16]

The Bush administration has combined cronyism with cutting back federal government programs and funding for public works that help people. Bush's tax cuts for the rich, attempts to privatize social security, and cut backs on environmental and government regulation, constitute an attack on a liberal conception of government itself. Allowing unrestricted economic development in the Gulf coast, cutting back on funds to shore up protection against flooding, and trimming government agencies to deal with crisis, exhibit the Bush administration's anti-government bias – and its dangers. For Katrina showed that in time of major emergencies and facing serious problems, the federal government has the most resources to deal with problems and if it is undermined the country is weakened and its very national security is threatened.

Not only did the FEMA fiasco reveal how Bush had put political hacks and rightwing ideologues throughout government and carry out an assault on government itself, but it revealed his personal failings and those of his administration's policies and ideology as well. As Frank Rich put it:

The worst storm in our history proved perfect for exposing this president because in one big blast it illuminated all his failings: the rampant cronyism, the empty sloganeering of "compassionate conservatism," the lack of concern for the "underprivileged" his mother condescended to at the Astrodome, the reckless lack of planning for all government operations except tax cuts, the use of spin and photo-ops to camouflage failure and to substitute for action.[17]

BUSH'S RECONSTRUCTION PLANS: A CORPORATE BOONDOOGLE

Bush's speech revealed one of the most ambitious reconstruction efforts in U.S. history, a two billion plus dollar effort that would provide a bonanza for the corporations and special interests that the Bush administration serve and that provide their financial support. It is an index of the administrations hubris and lack of shame that they instantly started pushing privatization a la Iraq to deal with the Katrina debacle and put arch-rogue Karl Rove in charge of both the PR and the dividing up the spoils for reconstruction, already going out to the usual suspects.[18] The boondoogle exemplifies what Naomi Klein describes as "disaster capitalism" whereby crises like Katrina or the Iraq invasion create situations where corporations have profit from catastrophe (Klein 2007). Indeed, Joe Allbaugh, Bush's former campaign enforcer and first FEMA chief who packed the agency with political hacks, was already getting contracts for his clients, while no-bid contracts were handed out to Halliburton's subsidy Kellogg, Brown & Root.[19] As Weldon Berger put it:

Rove's overt involvement... marks the death of any hope that the recovery operation will become something other than a cesspool of cronyism and political pandering. The action manuals will be vote counts, the 2006 electoral map and Republican Party campaign contribution lists. The result will be a hedonistic political and fiscal binge Bremer could only have dreamed of (op. cit.).

Berger recalled that under Paul Bremer's command in Iraq, at least $16 billion of Iraqi oil money was misplaced, there were numerous no-bid contracts to Bush cronies and scandalous over-billing and corruption, and little accountability to the privatization binges and contracts to the politically connected. In his Jackson Square speech, Bush stressed that he would emphasize "entrepreneurship" and market-solutions to the Gulf Coast catastrophe, a code for supporting corporate allies and cutting-back on regulation and oversight of reconstruction. Moreover, the Bush administration immediately began pushing tax cuts for wealthy investors in the area, eliminating minimum wage requirements and environmental regulation, opening the way for pushing through yet another rightwing agenda, as they did after 9/11, and providing copious contracts and financial benefits for political supporters and allies.

As Naomi Klein points out, Milton Friedman and other neo-cons exploited the opportunity of the destruction of a vast arena of New Orleans' public schools to replace them with charter schools (Klein 2007: 5ff), embodying Friedman's belief that public schools were a form of socialism. The rightwing reconstruction also gutted New Orleans strong teacher's union and public housing provided the right yet another opportunity to seize cultural power.

Yet the spectacle of the devastation and the inadequate response of the Bush administration may block or undercut Bush's attempts to exploit the tragedy for his own political ends. The media continued to focus intensely on the destruction and hoped-for recovery, more and more people and journalists on the front-line were becoming increasingly sceptical of Bush, and his ratings continued to go south after his Jackson Plaza speech and sketched ambitious plan for reconstruction, and would continue to plunge until the end of his administration when he had the lowest ratings in the history of presidential polling.[20]

Bush continued to insist that taxes would not be raised to pay for the reconstruction and weeks after the event he still would not concede his planned next round of tax cuts for the superrich, his expensive plans to privatize Social Security, or his deceptive Medicare plans that would provide a bonanza to drug companies. Hurricane Katrina, however, would focus attention on his policies and the outrageous level of federal debt they would incur, while benefiting largely special corporate interests and the rich.

Some speculated that the Katrina catastrophe and the failed Bush administration response signaled the death knell of the pro-market laissez-faire politics that had dominated the U.S. for the past years. It was clear that global warming had contributed to the intensity of the hurricanes and other extreme weather that had been plaguing the world for the past several years. While there was a fierce debate whether global warming or cyclical hurricane patters were the major cause of the extreme weather, it is likely that both are to blame.[21] The Bush administration's dismissal of the science of global warming and blocking efforts to deal with the problem now appear criminally negligent. In addition, the deregulation that characterized neoliberal politics had been responsible for destruction of the wetlands, which traditionally helped buffet hurricanes and extreme weather, as well as uncontrolled coastal development along the Gulf Coast which contributed to the immensity of the destruction (Brinkley 2006, pp. 9ff).

The Bush administration response, led by Karl Rove, trumpeted out the same old neoliberal policies and made it highly likely that there would be major corruption and political cronyism in Gulf redevelopment. But the intensity of Hurricane Katrina, followed by the potentially devastating Hurricane Rita and future possible destruction of the Gulf by deadly Hurricanes, has led many to speculate that something like a new Marshall Plan, focusing on rebuilding the Gulf Coast guided by environmental restoration and a flood control system like Holland's, as well as providing housing and jobs for the poor, would be needed to deal with the immensity of the tragedy.

As Hurricane Rita gathered intensity in the Gulf, speculation emerged that George W. Bush was the worse president in modern history, or perhaps the worst ever, and that there needed to be a serious discussion about impeachment.[22]

There were also reports that Bush had started drinking again,[23] and during September 22 when Rita was scheduled for landfall David Gregory of NBC queried Bush whether his planned trip to San Antonio to observe disaster response efforts in Texas would be "disruptive for first responders." Bush turned away in anger, revealing what appeared to be a wired telecommunication device on the back of his jacket,[24] and then suddenly turned around and told reporters that "there is no risk of me getting in the way, I promise you." But then suddenly Bush's trip to San Antonio was cancelled and he went instead to Colorado to monitor reports, and when it appeared that the effects of Hurricane Rita were not as dire for Texas as feared, he flew to Austin and San Antonio for photo events.

Reporting on Bush's day, the September 24, 2005, NBC News noted that political commentators believed that going to so many places and making so many pronouncements could lead to Bush being seen as a "political opportunist," and indeed there was an air of desperation to the president's frenetic activity in response to Hurricane Rita after his much criticized feeble response to Katrina. For those who cared to see, Bush's behavior indeed revealed him to be concerned with image rather than substance and unable to provide effective leadership and communication.

Although Hurricane Rita wreaked havoc on the North Texas and Southwestern Louisiana Gulf Coast, it did not, as feared, destroy any major cities and was less intense and destructive than predicted. Nonetheless, the cumulative damage of hurricanes Katrina and Rita were severe and a major battle loomed over differing proposals for reconstruction. In the aftermaths of the hurricanes, the media focused on personal stories of suffering and destruction, moments of heroism, and recovery putting on a back burner again questions of who was responsible and the differing positions on reconstruction. It came out that reports of robbery, rape, mayhem, and death in early days after Katrina were exaggerated and the death toll was less than predicted, although the destruction was evident and overwhelming.[25]

AFTERMATH

On the first anniversary of Hurricane Katrina there were many media retrospectives and analyses and a large majority of articles, TV reports, and commentaries documented how little reconstruction had taken place, with the hardest hit poor areas still rubble. Less than half of New Orleans's residents had returned, more than one-third of the garbage had not been picked up, and federal agencies had only spent $444 billion of the $1110 billion in congressionally approved funds.

Bush's political popularity began a steady decline with what was perceived as his inadequate response to Hurricane Katrina and continued to spiral downwards into the 30% range never to recover. As Frank Rich summed it up:

> The storm... was destined to join the tornado that uprooted Dorothy in *The Wizard of Oz* in the pantheon of American culture.... The Wizard could never be the Wizard again once Toto parted the curtain and exposed him as Professor Marvel; Bush, too, stood revealed as a blowhard and a snake oil salesman (see Rich 2006, p. 199).

George W. Bush's entire life has been grounded in monumental failures and perhaps the Katrina spectacles will be seen in retrospect as his Waterloo.[26] The spectacles of Iraq, inadequate response to Hurricane Katrina and the specter of crony capitalism in its aftermath, on-going Republican party scandals involving leaders of the House and Senate and key figures in Bush's and Cheney's staff, and the systematic breaking of US and international law through the illegal rendition and torture of suspects, violation of civil liberties, illegal wire-taping, and other crimes of the administration raised the specter of impeachment—but the Bush/Cheney regime survived the ever-erupting and escalating media spectacles of scandal and corruption that have characterized the regime.[27]

Of course, the financial meltdown of Fall 2008 and evident failure of Bush/ Cheney administration and neoliberal policies ensure Bush's reputation as one of the most disasterously failed presidents in U.S. history. Yet whatever the judgment over the Bush/Cheney administration, it is clear that the Hurricane Katrina media spectacle put on display the glaring inequities of race and class that define the U.S. in the new millennium during the rightwing Republican regime. The inability of the federal government to respond to the catastrophe called attention not only to the failures and incompetence of the Bush/Cheney administration, but also the crisis of neoliberalism whereby the market alone cannot provide for the needs of citizens and deal with acute social problems and natural disasters. As Henry Giroux argues (2006), Katrina also called attention to a "politics of disposability" whereby certain people are deemed disposable and not worthy of care and help. Market capitalism in the era of neoliberalism has been increasingly predatory with groups of poor people ready to be disposed and pushed aside. The biopolitics of inequality and disposability was put on full display in the Katrina spectacle and may be one of the most important after-effects of the tragic episode.

NOTES

1 For an excellent initial overview of the storm and the government failed response, see Walter M. Brasch, "SPECIAL REPORT: 'Unacceptable': The federal response to Katrina," September 12, 2005 at *www.smirkingchimp.com/article.php?sid=22719*. For an engaging documentary on Hurricane Katrina, that takes on the question of the breaching of the levees, see Spike Lee, *When the Levees Broke: A Requiem in Four Acts*, HBO films, 2006. For a historical overview of problems of storms and flooding in the New Orleans area and day to day account of the Katrina tragedy from August 27 to September 3, 2006, see Brinkley 2006.

2 W. David Jenkins III: "Georgie, you're doing a heck of a job," September 17, 2005 at *http://www. smirkingchimp.com/article.php?sid=22787*.

3 John Powers, "Week of the Living Death," *LA Weekly*, September 9-15, 2005 at *http://www. laweekly.com/ ink/05/42/on-powers.php*.

4 Mick Farren, "Post-Storm Watch," *Citybeat*, September 22-28, 2005 at *http://www.lacitybeat.com/ article.php?id=2645&IssueNum=120*.

5 Mark Benjamin, "The crony who prospered. Joe Allbaugh was George W. Bush's good ol' boy in Texas. He hired his good friend Mike Brown to run FEMA. Now Brownie's gone and Allbaugh is living large." Salon, September 16, 2005 at *http://www.salon.com/news/feature/2005/09/16/ allbaugh/index.html*. Allbaugh was known as Bush's enforcer during his stint as Texas governor, allegedly being in charge of sanitizing the records of Bush's National Guard service that suggested

he had gone AWOL and not completed his military service; see Douglas Kellner, <u>Media Spectacle</u> and the Crisis of Democracy. Boulder, Col.: Paradigm Press, 2005.

[6] Mark Benjamin, "Brownout!" Salon, September 11, 2005 at *http://www.salon.com/news/feature/ 2005/09/10/brown/index.html.*

[7] See Jonathan S. Landay, Alison Young and Shannon McCaffrey, "Chertoff delayed federal response, memo shows," Knight-Ridder News Service, September 13, 2005. The report indicates that Chertoff, not FEMA Director Michael Brown, was in charge of disaster response and delayed federal action. Chertoff was a lawyer and Republican partisan who participated in the Whitewater crusade against Bill Clinton and had no experience in either national security or disaster response when Bush made him head of the Department of Homeland Security.

[8] On the issue of race and the history of New Orleans, see Mike Davis, "The Struggle Over the Future of New Orleans," *Socialist Worker*, September 21, 2005 collected online at *http://www.zmag.org/ content/showarticle.cfm?SectionID=72&ItemID=8784.*

[9] NBC circulated a disclaimer after the show saying that West did not speak for the network and departed from his prepared speech, and also cut the clip from a West coast broadcast three hours later, but the initial video circulated over the Internet and was immediately incorporated into rap songs and anti-Bush websites; see the video clip at *http://politicalhumor.about.com/od/ hurricanekatrina/v/kanyewestbush.htm* (accessed September 23, 2005) and see Chris Lee, "Playback Time. Two rappers use Kanye West's anti-Bush quote to launch a mashed-up Web smash," Los Angeles Times, September 23, 2005: E1.

[10] Mike Davis and Anthony Fontenot, "Katrina's 25 Biggest Questions," October 4, 2005 at *www. alternet.org/story/26349/.*

[11] On Bushspeak, see Kellner 2005.

[12] At a National Prayer Service in the Washington Cathedral, aimed to replicate a spectacle held right after the September 11 terror attacks, Bush presented the Katrina tragedy as an act of God. See Amy Sullivan, "Bush scapegoats God; After weeks of blaming others for the disastrous response to Katrina, Bush used the pulpit at the National Prayer Service to blame the biggest scapegoat of all: God." Salon, September 17, 2005 at *www.salon.com/opinion/feature/2005/09/17/god/print.*

[13] Bush appointed Francis Fargos Townsend to head a federal investigation who it turned out was the wife of his Andover and Yale roommate and a rightwing ideologue; see the discussion in "Fact Check" at *www.cjrdaily.org* on September 20, 2005.

[14] Nikki Finke, "They Shoot News Anchors, Don't They?," LA Weekly, September 16-22, 2005 at *http://www.laweekly.com/ink/05/43/deadline-finke.php.* See also Finke's earlier version of this column at *http://www.laweekly.com/ink/05/42/deadline-finke.php.*

[15] Maureen Dowd, "Disney on Parade," *New York Times*, September 17, 2005.

[16] Douglas J. Amy: "Bush's strategy to hobble government," September 18, 2005 at *http://www. smirkingchimp.com/article.php?sid=22798&mode=thread&order=0&thold=0.*

[17] Frank Rich, "Message: I Care About the Black Folks," New York Times, September 18, 2005 at *http://www.nytimes.com/2005/09/18/opinion/18rich.html?incamp=article_popular&pagewanted=print.*

[18] Weldon Berger: 'Bush: "We'll do for the Gulf Coast what we did for Iraq," September 18, 2005 at *www.smirkingchimp.com/article.php?sid=22797.*

[19] Media reports on who got early contracts for Gulf coast reconstruction and who didn't indicate that Allbaugh connected-firms and Halliburton got lucrative no-bid contracts, while local Gulf Coast firms tended to lose out, see Eric Lipton and Ron Nixon, "Many Contracts for Storm Work Raise Questions," *New York Times*, September 26, 2005 and Griff Witte, Renae Merle and Derek Willis, "Gulf Firms Losing Cleanup Contracts," *Washington Post*, October 4, 2005.

[20] In one of the last polls taken on the Bush/Cheney presidency, Bush's favorably ratings kicked in at an all-time low 22%, while Cheney's favorability ratings came in at another record low of 13 percent. See the discussion of the New York *Times*/CBS News poll in Michael Duffy, "As Dick Cheney Prepares to Depart, His Mystery Lingers," *Time*, January 19, 2009 at *http://www. time.com/time/ printout/0,8816,1872531,00.html.* (accessed on January 21, 2009).

[21] Michael McCarthy, "This is Global Warming," *Independent*, September 24, 2005.

[22] Beth Quinn: "George is worst natural disaster to hit country," September 19 at *http://www. smirkingchimp.com/article.php?sid=22810*; Donald Kaul, "Bush faring well in Incompetence Derby," September 19 at *http://www.smirkingchimp.com/article.php?sid=22808*; and Robert Parry: "What to do about the Bush problem," September 23 at *http://www.smirkingchimp.com/article. php?sid=22869&mode=thread&order=0&thold=0.*

[23] Jennifer Luce and Don Gentile, "Bush's Booze Crisis," *National Enquirer*, September 24, 2005 at *http://www.nationalenquirer.com/celebrity/63426.*

[24] On reports and images that showed Bush wearing what appeared to be a communication wire during the 2004 presidential debates and on other occasions, see Douglas Kellner, "Media Spectacle and the Wired Bush Controversy," *Flow*, Vol. 1, Nr. 3, at *http://jot.communication.utexas.edu/flow/?jot= view&id=473.*

[25] On how the media exaggerated the anarchy and chaos in the days following Katrina and the critiques of media rumor and failures, see the Columbia Journalism review Daily, "Setting the Record Straight," September 27, 2005 at *http://www.cjrdaily.org/archives/001861.asp* and "The Backlash Begins," at *http://www.cjrdaily.org/archives/001863.asp.*

[26] On Bush's life-as-failure, see Mike Whitney, "No exit: Descending into hell with George W. Bush," September 22, 2005 at *http://www.smirkingchimp.com/article.php?sid=22857&mode=thread& order=0&thold=0.*

[27] On the specter of impeachment, see Bernard Weiner, "Suppose...: Arguments for an impeachment resolution," September 28, 2005 at *http://www.smirkingchimp.com/print.php?sid=22933* and Robert Parry, "Can Bush Be Ousted?", October 1, 2005 at http://consortiumnews.com/2005/093005.html.

REFERENCES

Brinkley, D. (2006). *The great deluge: Hurricane Katrina, New Orleans, and the Mississippi Gulf Coast*. New York: William Morrow.

Brock, D. (2004). *The republican noise machine: Right-wing media and how it corrupts democracy*. New York: Crown.

Giroux, H. (2006). *Stormy weather: Katrina and the politics of disposability*. Boulder, CO: Paradigm Press.

Harrington, M. (1963). *The other America*. Baltimore: Penguin Books.

Kellner, D. (2005). *Media spectacle and the crisis of democracy*. Boulder, CO: Paradigm Press.

Klein, N. (2007). *The shock doctrine. The rise of disaster capitalism*. New York: Metropolitan Books.

Rich, F. (2006). *The greatest story ever sold. The decline and fall of truth from 9/11 to Katrina*. New York: The Penguin Press.

HENRY A. GIROUX

3. THE MEDIA AND HURRICANE KATRINA: FLOATING BODIES AND DISPOSABLE POPULATIONS[1]

In the long aftermath of Hurricane Katrina, citizens in the U.S. and globally are still struggling to draw the correct conclusions, learn the right lessons from that horrific catastrophe. Initially we were led to believe that Katrina was the result of a fateful combination of a natural disaster and government incompetence. The perfect storm of bad luck provided one more example of the general inability of the Bush administration to actually govern, let alone protect its citizenry. Yet, with some distance and sober reflection, such assessment seems a bit short-sighted, a little too localized. In truth, Katrina offers a number of relevant lessons not only for U.S. citizens, but for Canadians and citizens all over the world who must grapple with the global advance of what I call a politics of disposability. First, Katrina is symptomatic of a form of negative globalization that is as evident in Ottawa, Paris and London, as it is in Washington D.C. or New Orleans, or any other city throughout the world. As capital, goods, trade, and information flow all over the globe, material and symbolic resources are increasingly being invested in the "free market" while the social state pays a terrible price. As safety nets and social services are being hollowed out and communities crumble and give way to individualized, one-man archipelagos, it is increasingly difficult to address as a collectivity, to act in concert, to meet the basic needs of citizens or maintain the social investments needed to provide life-sustaining services. As nation-states fall under the sway of the principal philosophy of the times, which insists on the end of the era of "big government" in favor of unencumbered individualism and the all-encompassing logic of the market, it is difficult to resurrect a language of social investment, protection, and accountability. Second, as Katrina made perfectly clear, the challenges of a global world, especially its growing ecological challenges, are collective and not simply private. This suggests that citizens in New Orleans as well as in Vancouver, Halifax and Toronto—coastal and inland—must protect those principles of the social contract that offer collective solutions to foster and maintain both ecological sustainability and human survival. Certainly Canadians have done much to ensure environmental protections, especially in comparison with their neighbours to the South, but there is much, much more that has to be done to curtail the threat of global warming and numerous ecological disasters. Third, as Hurricane Katrina vividly illustrated, the decline of the social state along with the rise of massive inequality increasingly bar whole populations from the

G. Martin, D. Houston, P. McLaren and J. Suoranta (eds.), The Havoc of Capitalism: Publics, Pedagogies and Environmental Crisis, 29–51.

rights and guarantees accorded to fully fledged citizens of the republic and who are increasingly rendered disposable, left to fend for themselves in the face of natural or man-made disasters. This last challenge is difficult, for here we must connect the painful dots between the crisis in the Gulf Coast and that "other" Gulf crisis in the Middle East; we must connect the dots between images of U.S. soldiers standing next to tortured Iraqis forced to assume the additional indignity of a dog leash to images of bloated bodies floating in the toxic waters that overwhelmed New Orleans city streets after five long days of punctuated government indifference to the suffering of some of its citizen populations. If we continue to squander the world's natural resources, prioritize free markets over free people, or beggar populations already in need because of financial debt, is it not then likely that we will have to endure more "natural" catastrophes, more terrorist threats, along with media images that punctuate our own loss of humanity, whether of Canadian soldiers in Somalia or U.S. soldiers in Abu Ghraib? In earlier eras, imagery of racist brutality and war atrocities moved nations to act and to change domestic and foreign policy in the interests of global justice. These contemporary images moved all of us, but only it seems for a time. Why is that?

Emmett Till's body arrived home in Chicago in September 1955. White racists in Mississippi had tortured, mutilated, and killed the young 14-year-old African-American boy for whistling at a white woman. Determined to make visible the horribly mangled face and twisted body of the child as an expression of racial hatred and killing, Mamie Till, the boy's mother, insisted that the coffin, interred at the A.A. Ranier Funeral Parlor on the South Side of Chicago, be left open for four long days. While mainstream news organizations ignored the horrifying image, *Jet* magazine published an unedited photo of Till's face taken while he lay in his coffin. Shaila Dewan points out that "[m]utilated is the word most often used to describe the face of Emmett Till after his body was hauled out of the Tallahatchie River in Mississippi. Inhuman is more like it: melted, bloated, missing an eye, swollen so large that its patch of wiry hair looks like that of a balding old man, not a handsome, brazen 14-year-old boy."[2] Till had been castrated and shot in the head; his tongue had been cut out; and a blow from an ax had practically severed his nose from his face—all of this done to a teenage boy who came to bear the burden of the inheritance of slavery and the inhuman pathology that drives its racist imaginary. The photo not only made visible the violent effects of the racial state; it also fuelled massive public anger, especially among blacks, and helped to launch the Civil Rights Movement.

From the beginning of the Civil Rights Movement to the war in Vietnam, images of human suffering and violence provided the grounds for a charged political indignation and collective sense of moral outrage inflamed by the horrors of poverty, militarism, war, and racism—eventually mobilizing widespread opposition to these antidemocratic forces. Of course, the seeds of a vast conservative counter-revolution were already well underway as images of a previous era—"whites only" signs, segregated schools, segregated housing, and nonviolent resistance—gave way to a troubling iconography of cities aflame, mass rioting, and armed black youth who came to embody the very precepts of lawlessness, disorder, and criminality.

Building on the reactionary rhetoric of Barry Goldwater and Richard Nixon, Ronald Reagan took office in 1980 with a trickle-down theory that would transform corporate America and a corresponding visual economy. The twin images of the young black male "gangsta" and his counterpart, the "welfare queen," became the primary vehicles for selling the American public on the need to dismantle the welfare state, ushering in an era of unprecedented deregulation, downsizing, privatization, and regressive taxation. The propaganda campaign was so successful that George H. W. Bush could launch his 1988 presidential bid with the image of Willie Horton, an African-American male convicted of rape and granted early release, and succeed in trouncing his opponent with little public outcry over the overtly racist nature of the campaign. By the beginning of the 1990s, global media consolidation, coupled with the outbreak of a new war that encouraged hyper-patriotism and a rigid nationalism, resulted in a tightly controlled visual landscape—managed both by the Pentagon and by corporate-owned networks—that delivered a paucity of images representative of the widespread systemic violence.[3] Selectively informed and cynically inclined, American civic life became more sanitized, controlled, and regulated.

Hurricane Katrina may have reversed the self-imposed silence of the media and public numbness in the face of terrible suffering. Fifty years after the body of Emmett Till was plucked out of the mud-filled waters of the Tallahatchie River, another set of troubling visual representations emerged that both shocked and shamed the nation. In the aftermath of Hurricane Katrina, grotesque images of bloated corpses floating in the rotting waters that flooded the streets of New Orleans circulated throughout the mainstream media. What first appeared to be a natural catastrophe soon degenerated into a social debacle as further images revealed, days after Katrina had passed over the Gulf Coast, hundreds of thousands of poor people, mostly blacks, some Latinos, many elderly, and a few white people, packed into the New Orleans Superdome and the city's convention center, stranded on rooftops, or isolated on patches of dry highway without any food, water, or any place to wash, urinate, or find relief from the scorching sun.[4] Weeks passed as the flood water gradually receded and the military gained control of the city, and more images of dead bodies surfaced in the national and global media. TV cameras rolled as bodies emerged from the flood waters while people stood by indifferently, eating their lunch or occasionally snapping a photograph. Most of the bodies found "were 50 or older, people who tried to wait the hurricane out."[5] Various media soon reported that over 154 bodies had been found in hospitals and nursing homes. The *New York Times* wrote that "the collapse of one of society's most basic covenants—to care for the helpless—suggests that the elderly and critically ill plummeted to the bottom of priority lists as calamity engulfed New Orleans."[6] Dead people, mostly poor African-Americans, left uncollected in the streets, on porches, in hospitals, nursing homes, electric wheelchairs, and collapsed houses prompted some people to claim that America had become like a "Third World country" while others argued that New Orleans resembled a "Third World Refugee Camp."[7] There were now, irrefutably, two Gulf crises. The Federal Emergency Management Agency (FEMA) tried to do damage control by forbidding journalists to "accompany rescue boats as they went out to search for storm victims." As a bureau spokeswoman told Reuters News Agency, "We have requested that no photographs of the deceased be made by the media."[8] But questions about responsibility and answerability would not go away. Even the dominant media for a short time rose to the occasion of posing tough questions about accountability to those in power in light of such egregious acts of incompetence and indifference. The images of dead bodies kept reappearing in New Orleans, refusing to go away. For many, the bodies of the poor, black, brown, elderly, and sick came to signify what the battered body of Emmett Till once unavoidably revealed, and America was forced to confront these disturbing images and the damning reality behind the images. The Hurricane Katrina disaster, like the Emmett Till affair, revealed a vulnerable and destitute segment of the nation's citizenry that conservatives not only refused to see but had spent the better part of two decades demonizing. But like the incessant beating of Poe's tell-tale heart, cadavers have a way of insinuating themselves on consciousness, demanding answers to questions that aren't often asked. The body of Emmett Till symbolized overt white supremacy and state terrorism organized against the supposed threat that black men (apparently of all sizes and ages) posed against white women. But the black bodies of the dead and walking wounded in New Orleans in 2005 revealed a different image of the racial state, a different modality of state terrorism, marked less by an overt form of white racism than by a highly mediated displacement of race as a central concept for understanding both Katrina and its place in the broader history of U.S. racism.[9] That is, while Till's body insisted upon a public recognition of the violence of white supremacy, the decaying black bodies floating in the waters of the Gulf Coast represented a return of race against the media's insistence that this disaster was more about class than race, more about the shameful and growing presence of poverty, "the abject failure to provide aid to the most vulnerable."[10] Till's body allowed the racism that destroyed it to be made visible, to speak publicly to the systemic character of American racial injustice. The bodies of the Katrina victims could not speak with the same directness to the state of American racist violence, but they did reveal and shatter the conservative fiction of living in a color-blind society. The bodies of the Katrina victims laid bare the racial and class fault lines that mark an increasingly damaged and withering democracy and revealed the emergence of a new kind of politics, one in which entire populations are now considered disposable, an unnecessary burden on state coffers, and consigned to fend for themselves. At the same time, what happened in New Orleans also revealed some frightening signposts of those repressive features in American society, demanding that artists, public intellectuals, scholars, and other cultural workers take seriously what Angela Davis insists "are very clear signs of ... impending fascist policies and practices," which not only construct an imaginary social environment for all of those populations rendered disposable but also exemplify a site and space "where democracy has lost its claims."[11]

Soon after Hurricane Katrina hit the Gulf Coast, the consequences of the long legacy of attacking big government and bleeding the social and public service sectors of the state became glaringly evident as did a government that displayed a "staggering indifference to human suffering."[12] Hurricane Katrina made it abundantly clear that only the government had the power, resources, and authority to address complex undertakings, such as dealing with the totality of the economic, environmental, cultural, and social destruction that impacted the Gulf Coast. Given the Bush administration's disdain for the legacy of the New Deal, important government agencies were viewed scornfully as oversized entitlement programs, stripped of their power, and served up as dumping grounds to provide lucrative administrative jobs for political hacks who were often unqualified to lead such agencies. Not only was FEMA downsized and placed under the Department of Homeland Security but its role in disaster planning and preparation was subordinated to the all-inclusive goal of fighting terrorists. While it was virtually impossible to miss the total failure of the government response in the aftermath of Katrina, what many people saw as incompetence or failed national leadership was more than that. Something more systemic and deep-rooted was revealed in the wake of Katrina—namely, that the state no longer provided a safety net for the poor, sick, elderly, and homeless. Instead, it had been transformed into a punishing institution intent on dismantling the welfare state and treating the homeless, unemployed, illiterate, and disabled as dispensable populations to be managed, criminalized, and made to disappear into prisons, ghettos, and the black hole of despair.

The Bush administration was not simply unprepared for Hurricane Katrina as it denied that the federal government alone had the resources to address catastrophic events; it actually felt no responsibility for the lives of poor blacks and others marginalized by poverty and relegated to the outskirts of society. Increasingly, the role of the state seemed to be about engendering the financial rewards and privileges of only some members of society, while the welfare of those marginalized by race and class was viewed with criminal contempt. The coupling of the market state with the racial state under George W. Bush meant that policies were aggressively pursued to dismantle the welfare state, eliminate affirmative action, model urban public schools after prisons, aggressively pursue anti-immigrant policies, and incarcerate with impunity Arabs, Muslims, and poor youth of color. While the Bush government's most neoconservative policies may be reversed by Barack Obama, it is important not to forget that Bush's policies were symptoms rather than causes of a global hyper-neoliberalism now organized around the best way to remove or make invisible those individuals and groups who are either seen as a drain on the prosperity of the rich or stand in the way of market freedoms, free trade, consumerism, and the dream of an American empire. This is what I call the *new biopolitics of disposability*: the poor, especially people of color, not only have to fend for themselves in the face of life's tragedies but are also supposed to do it without being seen by the dominant society. Excommunicated from the sphere of human concern, they have been rendered invisible, utterly disposable, and heir to that army of socially homeless that allegedly no longer existed in color-blind America.

How else to explain the cruel jokes and insults either implied or made explicit by Bush and his ideological allies in the aftermath of such massive destruction and suffering? When it became obvious in the week following Katrina that thousands of the elderly, poor, and sick could not get out of New Orleans because they had no cars or money to take a taxi or any other form of transportation, or were sick and infirmed, the third-highest-ranking politician in Washington, Rick Santorum, stated in an interview "that people who did not heed evacuation warnings in the future may need to be penalized."[13] For Santorum, those who were trapped in the flood because of poverty, sickness, or lack of transportation had become an unwelcome reminder of the state of poverty and racism in the United States, and for that they should be punished. Their crime, it seemed, was that a natural disaster made a social and politically embarrassing disaster visible to the world, and they just happened to be its victims. Commenting on facilities that had been set up for the poor in the Houston Astrodome in Texas, Bush's mother and the wife of former President George H.W. Bush said in a National Public Radio interview, "So many of the people here, you know, were underprivileged anyway, so this is working very well for them."[14] Other right-wing ideologues seeking to deflect criticism from the obscene incompetence and indifference of the Bush administration used a barely concealed racism to frame the events of Katrina. For example, Neil Boortz, a syndicated host on WFTL-AM in Florida stated that "a huge percentage" of those forced to leave New Orleans were "parasites, like ticks on a dog. They are coming to a community near you."[15] On the September 13 broadcast of *The Radio Factor,* Fox News host Bill O'Reilly overtly indulged his own racism before millions of his viewers in claiming that poor black people in New Orleans were basically drug addicts who failed to evacuate the city because they would not have access to their fix.[16]

In one of the most blatant displays of racism underscoring the biopolitical "live free or die" agenda in Bush's America, the dominant media increasingly framed the events that unfolded during and immediately after the hurricane by focusing on acts of crime, looting, rape, and murder, allegedly perpetrated by the black residents of New Orleans. In predictable fashion, politicians such as Louisiana Governor Kathleen Blanco issued an order allowing soldiers to shoot to kill looters in an effort to restore calm. Later inquiries revealed that almost all of these crimes did not take place. The philosopher, Slavoj Zizek, argued that "what motivated these stories were not facts, but racist prejudices, the satisfaction felt by those who would be able to say: 'You see, Blacks really are like that, violent barbarians under the thin layer of civilization!'"[17] It must be noted that there was more at stake here than the resurgence of old-style racism; there was the recognition that some groups have the power to protect themselves from such stereotypes and others do not, and for those who do not—especially poor blacks—racist myths have a way of producing precise, if not deadly, material consequences. Given the public's preoccupation with violence and safety, crime and terror merged in the all-too-familiar equation of black culture with the culture of criminality, and images of poor blacks were made indistinguishable from images of crime and violence. Criminalizing black behavior and relying on punitive measures to solve social problems did more than legitimate a biopolitics defined increasingly by the authority of an expanding national security state. They also legitimized a state in which the police and military, often operating behind closed doors, took on public functions that were not subject to public scrutiny.[18] This becomes particularly dangerous in a democracy when paramilitary or military organisations gain their legitimacy increasingly from an appeal to fear and terror, prompted largely by the presence of those racialized and class-specific groups considered both threatening and disposable.

Within a few days after Katrina struck, New Orleans was under martial law occupied by nearly 65,000 U.S. military personnel. Cries of desperation and help were quickly redefined as the pleas of "refugees," a designation that suggested an alien population lacking both citizenship and legal rights had inhabited the Gulf Coast. Images of thousands of desperate and poor blacks gave way to pictures of combat-ready troops and soldiers with mounted bayonets canvassing houses in order to remove stranded civilians. Embedded journalists now travelled with soldiers on Humvees, armoured carriers, and military helicopters in downtown USA. What had begun as a botched rescue operation by the federal government was transformed into a military operation. Given the Bush government's recurrent contemptuous treatment of those who were poor and black, it was not surprising that the transformation of New Orleans and the Gulf Coast from disaster area to war zone occurred without any audible dissent from either the general public or the dominant media. New Orleans increasingly came to look like a city in Iraq as scores of private soldiers appeared on the scene—either on contract with the Department of Homeland Security or hired by wealthy elites to protect their private estates and businesses. Much like Iraq, the Gulf Coast became another recipient of deregulated market capitalism as soon as the flood waters began to recede. The fruits of privatization and an utter disregard for public values were all too visible in the use of private mercenaries and security companies hired to guard federal projects, often indulging in acts of violence that constituted clear-cut cases of vigilantism.

Katrina laid bare what many people in the United States do not want to see: large numbers of poor black and brown people struggling to make ends meet, benefiting very little from a social system that makes it difficult to obtain health insurance, child care, social assistance, cars, savings, and minimum-wage jobs, if lucky, and instead offers to black and brown youth inadequate schools, poor public services, and no future, except a possible stint in the penitentiary. As Janet Pelz rightly insists, "These are the people the Republicans have been teaching us to disdain, if not hate, since President Reagan decried the moral laxness of the Welfare mom."[19] While Pelz's comments provide a crucial context for much of the death and devastation of Katrina, I think to more fully understand this calamity it is important to grasp how the confluence of race and poverty has become part of a new and more insidious set of forces based on a revised set of biopolitical commitments that have largely denied the sanctity of human life for those populations rendered "at risk" by global neoliberal economies.

Within the last few decades, matters of state sovereignty in the new world order have been retheorized so as to provide a range of theoretical insights about the relationship between power and politics, the political nature of social and cultural life, and the merging of life and politics as a new form of biopolitics. While the notion of biopolitics differs significantly among its most prominent theorists, including Michel Foucault, Giorgio Agamben, and Michael Hardt and Antonio Negri,[20] what these theorists share is an attempt to think through the convergence of life and politics, locating matters of "life and death within our ways of thinking about and imagining politics."[21] Within this discourse, politics is no longer understood exclusively through a disciplinary technology centered on the individual body—a body to be measured, surveilled, managed, and included in forecasts, surveys, and statistical projections. Biopolitics points to new relations of power that are more capacious, concerned not only with the body as an object of disciplinary techniques that render it "both useful and docile" but also with a body that needs to be "regularized," subject to those immaterial means of production that produce ways of life that enlarge the targets of control and regulation.[22] This shift in the workings of both sovereignty and power and the emergence of biopolitics are made clear by Foucault, for whom biopower replaces the power to dispense fear and death "with that of a power to foster life—or disallow it to the point of death. ... [Biopower] is no longer a matter of bringing death into play in the field of sovereignty, but of distributing the living in the domain of value and utility. Its task is to take charge of life that needs a continuous regulatory and corrective mechanism."[23] As Foucault insists, the logic of biopower is dialectical, productive, and positive.[24] Yet he also argues that biopolitics does not remove itself from "introducing a break into the domain of life that is under power's control: the break between what must live and what must die."[25] Foucault believes that the death-function in the economy of biopolitics is justified primarily through a form of racism in which biopower "is bound up with the workings of a State that is obliged to use race, the elimination of races and the purification of the race, to exercise its sovereign power."[26]

Michael Hardt and Antonio Negri have both modified and extended Foucault's notion of biopower, highlighting a mode of biopolitics in which immaterial labor such as ideas, knowledge, images, cooperation, affective relations, and forms of communication extend beyond the boundaries of the economic to produce not just material goods as "the means of social life, but social life itself. Immaterial production is biopolitical."[27] In this instance, power is extended to the educational force of the culture and to the various technologies, mechanisms, and social practices through which it reproduces various forms of social life. What is crucial to grasp in this rather generalized notion of biopolitics is that power remains a productive force, provides the grounds for both resistance and domination, and registers culture, society, and politics as a terrain of multiple and diverse struggles waged by numerous groups in a wide range of sites. For my purposes, the importance of both Foucault's and Hardt and Negri's work on biopolitics is that they move matters of culture, especially those aimed at "the production of information, communication, [and] social relations ... to the center of politics itself."[28] Within these approaches, power expands its reach as a political force beyond the traditional scope and boundaries of the state and the registers of officially sanctioned modes of domination. Biopolitics now touches all aspects of social life and is the primary political and pedagogical force through which the creation and reproduction of new subjectivities takes place.

While biopolitics in Foucault and in Hardt and Negri addresses the relations between politics and death, biopolitics in their views is less concerned with the primacy of death than with the production of life both as an individual and a social category. In Giorgio Agamben's formulation, the new biopolitics is the deadly administration of what he calls "bare life," and its ultimate incarnation is the Holocaust with its ominous specter of the concentration camp. In this formulation, the Nazi death camps become the primary exemplar of control, the new space of contemporary politics in which individuals are no longer viewed as citizens but are now seen as inmates, stripped of everything, including their right to live. The uniting of power and bare life, the reduction of the individual to *homo sacer*—the sacred man who under certain states of exception "may be killed and yet not sacrificed"—no longer represents the far end of political life.[29] That is, in this updated version of the ancient category of *homo sacer* is the human who stands beyond the confines of both human and divine law—"a human who can be killed without fear of punishment."[30] According to Agamben, as modern states increasingly suspend their democratic structures, laws, and principles, the very nature of governance changes as "the rule of law is routinely displaced by the state of exception, or emergency, and people are increasingly subject to extra-judicial state violence."[31] The life unfit for life, unworthy of being lived, as the central category of *homo sacer*, is no longer marginal to sovereign power but is now central to its form of governance. State violence and totalitarian power, which, in the past, either were generally short-lived or existed on the fringe of politics and history, have become the rule, rather than the exception, as life is more ruthlessly regulated and placed in the hands of military and state power.

In the current historical moment, as Catherine Mills points out, "all subjects are at least potentially if not actually abandoned by the law and exposed to violence as a constitutive condition of political existence."[32] Nicholas Mirzoeff has observed that all over the world there is a growing resentment of immigrants and refugees, matched by the emergence of detain-and-deport strategies and coupled with the rise of the camp as the key institution and social model of the new millennium. The "empire of camps," according to Mirzoeff, has become the "exemplary institution of a system of global capitalism that supports the West in its high consumption, low-price consumer lifestyle."[33] Zygmunt Bauman calls such camps "garrisons of extraterritoriality" and argues that they have become "the dumping grounds for the indisposed of and as yet unrecycled waste of the global frontier-land."[34] The regime of the camp has increasingly become a key index of modernity and the new world order. The connections among disposability, violence, and death have become common under modernity in those countries where the order of power has become necropolitical. For example, Rosa Linda Fregoso analyzes feminicide as a local expression of global violence against women in the region of the U.S./Mexico border where over one thousand women have been either murdered or disappeared, constituting what amounts to a "politics of gender extermination."[35] The politics of disposability and necropolitics not only generate widespread violence and ever expanding "garrisons of extra-territoriality" but also have taken on a powerful new significance as a foundation for political sovereignty. Biopolitical commitments to "let die" by abandoning citizens appeared increasingly credible in the United States under the authoritarian Bush administration.[36]

Given the Bush administration's use of illegal wiretaps, the holding of "detainees" illegally and indefinitely in prisons such as Guantanamo, the disappearance, kidnapping, and torture of alleged terrorists, and the suspension of civil liberties in the United States, Agamben's theory of biopolitics rightly alerts us to the dangers of a government in which the state of emergency becomes the fundamental structure of control over populations. While Agamben's claim that the concentration camp (as opposed to Foucault's panopticon) is now the model for constitutional states captures the contrariness of biopolitical commitments that have less to do with preserving life than with reproducing violence and death, its totalitarian logic is too narrow and fails in the end to recognize that the threat of violence, bare life, and death is not the only form of biopower in contemporary life. The dialectics of life and death, visibility and invisibility, and privilege and lack in social existence that now constitute the biopolitics of modernity have to be understood in terms of their complexities, specificities, and diverse social formations. For instance, the diverse ways in which the articulation of biopower in the United States worked recently to render some groups disposable and to privilege others within a permanent state of emergency need to be specified. Indeed, any viable rendering of contemporary biopolitics must address more specifically how biopower attempts not just to produce and control life in general, as Hardt and Negri insist, or to reduce all inhabitants of the increasing militarized state to the dystopian space of the "death camp," as Agamben argues, but also to privilege *some* lives over others. The tragedy of pain and suffering wrought by the Bush administration's response to Hurricane Katrina revealed a biopolitical agenda in which the logic of disposability and the politics of death were inscribed differently in the order of contemporary power—structured largely around wretched and broad-based racial and class inequalities.

I want to further this position by arguing that neoliberalism, privatization, and militarism have become the dominant biopolitics of the mid-twentieth-century social state and that the coupling of a market fundamentalism and contemporary forms of subjugation of life to the power of capital accumulation, violence, and disposability has produced a new and dangerous version of biopolitics.[37] While the murder of Emmett Till suggests that a biopolitics structured around the intersection of race and class inequalities, on the one hand, and state violence, on the other, has long existed, the new version of biopolitics adds a distinctively different and more dangerous register. The new biopolitics not only includes state-sanctioned violence but also relegates entire populations to spaces of invisibility and disposability. As William DiFazio points out, "the state has been so weakened over decades of privatization that it ... increasingly fails to provide health care, housing, retirement benefits and education to a massive percentage of its population."[38] In the past, people who were marginalized by class and race could at least expect a modicum of support from the government, either because of the persistence of a drastically reduced social contract or because they still had some value as part of a reserve army of unemployed labour. But if the social contract was increasingly suspended in varying degrees since the 1970s, then under the Bush Administration it was virtually abandoned. Under such circumstances, the state no longer felt obligated to take measures that prevent hardship, suffering, and death. The state no longer protects its own disadvantaged citizens—they were already seen as dead within a transnational economic and political framework. It remains to be seen whether Obama can address the problems in a U.S. context; meanwhile specific populations around the globe now occupy a space of ruthless politics in which the categories of "citizen" and "democratic representation" have never been or are no longer recognized. This new form of biopolitics is conditioned by a permanent state of class and racial exception in which "vast populations are subject to conditions of life conferring upon them the status of living dead,"[39] largely invisible in the global media, or, when disruptively present, defined as redundant, pathological, and dangerous. Within this wasteland of death and disposability, whole populations are relegated to what Zygmunt Bauman calls "social homelessness."[40] While the rich and middle classes in the United States maintain lifestyles produced through vast inequalities of symbolic and material capital, the "free market" provides neither social protection and security nor hope to those who are poor, sick, elderly, and marginalized by race and class. Given the increasing perilous state of the those who are poor and dispossessed in America, it is crucial to reexamine how biopower functions within global neoliberalism and the simultaneous rise of security states organized around cultural (and racial) homogeneity. This task is made all the more urgent by the destruction, politics, and death that followed Hurricane Katrina.

In a May 25, 2001 interview, Grover Norquist, head of the right-wing group Americans for Tax Reform, told National Public Radio's Mara Liasson: "I don't want to abolish government. I simply want to reduce it to the size where I can drag it into the bathroom and drown it in the bathtub."[41] As a radical right-wing activist and practical strategist, Norquist has been enormously instrumental and successful in shaping tax policies designed to "starve the beast," a metaphor for policies designed to drive up deficits by cutting taxes, especially for the rich, in order to paralyze government and dry up funds for many federal programs that offer protection for children, the elderly, and the poor. Norquist saw his efforts pay off when thousands of people, most of them poor and black, drowned in the basin of New Orleans and upwards of one million were displaced. Under such circumstances, a decades-long official policy of *benign* neglect became *malign* neglect, largely rationalized through a market fundamentalism in which the self-interested striving of individuals becomes the cornerstone of both freedom and democracy. This is a politics that wages war against any viable notion of the democratic social. And as Lawrence Grossberg points out, "The free market in neoliberalism is fundamentally an argument against politics, or at least against a politics that attempts to govern society in social rather than economic terms."[42]

The neoliberal efforts to shrink big government and public services must be understood both in terms of those who bore the brunt of such efforts in New Orleans and in terms of the subsequent inability of the government to deal adequately with Hurricane Katrina. Reducing the federal government's ability to respond to social problems is a decisive element of neoliberal policymaking, as was echoed in a *Wall Street Journal* editorial that argued without irony that taxes should be raised for low-income individuals and families, not to make more money available to the federal government for addressing their needs but to rectify the possibility that they "might not be feeling a proper hatred for the government."[43] If the poor can be used as pawns in this logic to further the political attack on big government, it seems reasonable to assume that those who hold such a position would refrain from using "big government" as quickly as possible to save the very lives of such groups, as was evident in the aftermath of Katrina. The vilification of the social state and big government—really an attack on non-military aspects of government—has translated into a steep decline of tax revenues, a massive increase in military spending, and the growing immiseration of poor Americans and people of color. Under the Bush administration, Census Bureau figures revealed that "since 1999, the income of the poorest fifth of Americans has dropped 8.7 percent in inflation-adjusted dollars . . . [and in 2005] 1.1 million were added to the 36 million already on the poverty rolls."[44] While the number of Americans now living below the poverty line is comparable to the combined populations of Louisiana, Mississippi, Alabama, Texas, and Arkansas, the Bush administration chose to make in the 2006 budget $70 billion in new tax cuts for the rich while slashing programs that would benefit the least fortunate.[45] Similarly, the $2.7 trillion budget for 2007 included a $4.9 billion reduction in health funds for senior citizens (Medicare) and the State Children's Health Insurance Program; a $17 million cut in aid for child-support enforcement; cutbacks in funds for low-income people with disabilities; major reductions in child-care and development block grants; major defunding for housing for low-income elderly; and an unprecedented rollback in student aid. In addition, the 2007 budget called for another $70 billion dollars in tax cuts most beneficial to the rich and provided for a huge increase in military spending for the war in Iraq.[46]

While George W. Bush endlessly argued for the economic benefits of his tax cuts, he callously omitted the fact that 13 million children live in poverty in the United States, "4.5 million more than when Bush was first inaugurated."[47] And New Orleans had the third highest rate of children living in poverty in the United States.[48] The illiteracy rate in New Orleans before the flood struck was 40 percent; the embarrassingly ill-equipped public school system was one of the most underfunded in the nation. Nearly 19 percent of Louisiana residents lacked health insurance, putting the state near the bottom for the percentage of people without health insurance. Robert Scheer, a journalist and social critic, estimated that one-third of the 150,000 people living in dire poverty in Louisiana were elderly, left exposed to the flooding in areas most damaged by Katrina.[49] Even worse, in an ironic twist of fate, one day after Katrina hit New Orleans, the U.S. Census Bureau released two important reports on poverty, indicating that "Mississippi (with a 21.6 percent poverty rate) and Louisiana (19.4 percent) are the nation's poorest states, and that New Orleans (with a 23.2 percent poverty rate) is the 12th poorest city in the nation. [Moreover,] New Orleans is not only one of the nation's poorest cities, but its poor people are among the most concentrated in poverty ghettos. Housing discrimination and the location of government-subsidized housing have contributed to the city's economic and racial segregation."[50] Under neoliberal capitalism, the attack on politically responsible government has only been matched by an equally harsh attack on social provisions and safety nets for the poor. And in spite of the massive failures of market-driven neoliberal policies—extending from a soaring $420 billion budget deficit to the sub-prime mortgage crisis and the stock market crash of 2008 to the persistent underfunding of schools, public health, community policing, and environmental protection programs—the right-wing orthodoxy of the Bush administration never failed to "give precedence to private financial gain and market determinism over human lives and broad public values."[51]

The Bush administration's ideological hostility towards the essential role that government should play in providing social services and crucial infrastructure was particularly devastating for New Orleans in the aftermath of Hurricane Katrina. Prior to 9/11, the Federal Emergency Management Agency listed a hurricane strike on New Orleans as one of the three most likely catastrophic disasters facing America. The *Houston Chronicle* wrote in December 2001 that "[t]he New Orleans hurricane scenario may be the deadliest of all."[52] And yet the Bush administration consistently denied repeated requests for funds by the New Orleans Army Corps of Engineers. Ignoring such requests, the Bush administration cut the Army Corps' funding by more than a half-billion dollars in its 2002 budget, leaving unfinished the construction for the levees that eventually burst. And in spite of repeated warnings far in advance by experts that the existing levees could not withstand a Category 4 hurricane, the Bush administration in 2004 rejected the Southeast Louisiana Urban Flood Control Project's request for $100 million, offering instead a measly $16.5 million. Huge tax cuts for the rich and massive cuts in much-needed programs continued unabated during the Bush administration, all the while putting the lives of thousands of poor people in the Gulf Basin in jeopardy. As David Sirota has reported, this disastrous underfunding of efforts to build the levee infrastructure, coupled with even more tax cuts for the rich and less revenue for the states, continued right up to the time that Hurricane Katrina struck, making it almost impossible for governments in the Gulf region either to protect their citizens from the impact of a major hurricane or to develop the resources necessary for an adequate emergency response plan in the event of a flood.

After Katrina, President Bush did not address questions about the lack of proper funding for the levees. Instead, he played dumb and in spite of overwhelming evidence to the contrary came up with one of the most incredulous sound bites of his career: "I don't think anyone anticipated the breach of the levees."[53] In fact, Bush was briefed the day before Katrina hit and emphatically warned by a number of disaster officials that the levees could be breached—a position Bush of course later denied.[54] Much of the press viewed Bush's remarks about the levees as indicative of a president who was simply clueless and indifferent to any information that did not conform to his own budget-busting, anti–big government ideology. But such political and moral indifference should not be solely attributed to the narrow mindedness and rigidity of Bush's character; it should be principally seen as the offspring of a broader set of biopolitical commitments at work in a global system that increasingly dictates who lives and who dies in the context of a rabid neoliberalism and a morally bankrupt neoconservatism.[55] And Katrina represents more than this still. The government's failure to respond quickly to the black poor on the Gulf Coast can be related to a deeper set of memories of racial injustice and violence, memories that connect a long history of apartheid to a more recent manifestation of utter disregard for human life.

Biopower in its current shape has produced a new form of biopolitics marked by a cleansed visual and social landscape in which the poor, the elderly, the infirm, and criminalized populations all share a common fate of disappearing from public view. Rendered invisible in deindustrialized communities far removed from the suburbs, barred from the tourist-laden sections of major cities, locked into understaffed nursing homes, interned in bulging prisons built in remote farm communities, hidden in decaying schools in rundown neighborhoods that bear the look of Third World slums, populations of poor black and brown citizens exist outside of the view of most Americans. They have become the waste-products of the American Dream, if not of modernity itself. The disposable populations serve as an unwelcome reminder that the once vaunted social state no longer exists, the living dead now an apt personification of the death of the social contract in the United States. Having fallen through the large rents in America's social safety nets, they reflect a governmental agenda bent on attacking the poor rather than attacking poverty. That they are largely poor and black undermines the nation's commitment to color-blind ideology. Race remains the "major reason America treats its poor more harshly than any other advanced country."[56] One of the worst storms in our history shamed us into seeing the plight of poor blacks and other minorities. In less than forty-eight hours, Katrina ruptured the pristine image of America as a largely, white middle-class country modeled after a Disney theme park.

Underneath neoliberalism's corporate ethic and market-based fundamentalism, the idea of democracy is disappearing and with it the spaces in which democracy is produced and nurtured. Democratic values, identities, and social relations along with public spaces, the common good, and the obligations of civic responsibility are slowly being overtaken by a market-based notion of freedom and civic indifference in which it becomes more difficult to translate private woes into social issues and collective action or to insist on a language of the public good. The upshot to the evisceration of all notions of sociality is a sense of total abandonment, resulting in fear, anxiety, and insecurity over one's future. The presence of the racialized poor, their needs, and vulnerabilities—now visible—becomes unbearable. All solutions as a result now focus on shoring up a diminished sense of safety, carefully nurtured by a renewed faith in all things military.

Militaristic values and military solutions are profoundly influencing every aspect of American life, ranging from foreign and domestic policy to the shaping of popular culture and the organization of public schools.[57] Faith in democratic governance and cultural pluralism increasingly gives way to military-style uniformity, discipline, and authority coupled with a powerful nationalism and a stifling patriotic correctness, all of which undermine the force of a genuine democracy by claiming that the average citizen does not have the knowledge or authority to see, engage, resist, protest, or make dominant power accountable.[58]

Lost public spaces and public culture have been replaced with what Nicholas Mirzoeff calls the modern anti-spectacle. According to Mirzoeff, "the modern anti-spectacle now dictates that there is nothing to see and that instead one must keep moving, keep circulating and keep consuming."[59] Non-stop images coupled with a manufactured culture of fear strip citizens of their visual agency and potential to act as engaged social participants. The visual subject has been reduced to the life-long consumer, always on the go looking for new goods and promising discounts, all the while travelling in spaces that suggest that public space is largely white and middle-class, free of both unproductive consumers and those individuals marked by the trappings of race, poverty, dependence, and disability.

Under the logic of modernization, neoliberalism, and militarization, the category "waste" includes no longer simply material goods but also human beings, particularly those rendered redundant in the new global economy, that is, those who are no longer capable of making a living, who are unable to consume goods, and who depend upon others for the most basic needs.[60] Defined primarily through the combined discourses of character, personal responsibility, and cultural homogeneity, entire populations expelled from the benefits of the marketplace are reified as products without any value, to be disposed of as "leftovers in the most radical and effective way: we make them invisible by not looking and unthinkable by not thinking."[61] Even when young black and brown youth try to escape the biopolitics of disposability by joining the military, the seduction of economic security is quickly negated by the horror of senseless violence compounded daily in the streets, roads, and battlefields in Iraq and Afghanistan and made concrete in the form of body bags, mangled bodies, and amputated limbs—rarely to be seen in the narrow ocular vision of the dominant media.

If the social state continues to dwindle and the rapacious dynamics of neoliberalism remain unchecked by government regulations, then the public and private policies of investing in the public good will eventually be entirely dismissed as bad business, just as the notion of protecting people from the dire misfortunes of poverty, sickness, or the random blows of fate seems increasingly to be viewed as an act of bad faith. Weakness is now a sin, punishable by social exclusion. This is especially true for those racial groups and immigrant populations who have always been at risk economically and politically. Such groups have become part of an ever-growing army of the impoverished and disenfranchised—removed from the prospect of a decent job, productive education, adequate health care, acceptable child care services, and satisfactory shelter. As the state is transformed into the primary agent of terror and corporate concerns displace democratic values, dominant "power is measured by the speed with which responsibilities can be escaped."[62] With its pathological disdain for social values and public life and its celebration of an unbridled individualism and acquisitiveness, the Bush administration did more than undermine the nature of social obligation and civic responsibility; it also sent a message to those populations who are poor and black—society neither wants, cares about, or needs you.[63] Katrina revealed with startling and disturbing clarity who these individuals are: African-Americans who occupy the poorest sections of New Orleans, those ghettoized frontier-zones created by racism coupled with economic inequality. Cut out of any long term goals and a decent vision of the future, these are the populations, as Zygmunt Bauman points out, who have been rendered redundant and disposable in the age of neoliberal global capitalism.

Katrina reveals that we are living in dark times. The shadow of authoritarianism remains after the storm clouds and hurricane winds have passed, offering a glimpse of its wreckage and terror. The politics of a disaster that affected Louisiana, Alabama, and Mississippi is about more than government incompetence, militarization, socio-economic polarization, environmental disaster, and political scandal. Hurricane Katrina broke through the visual blackout of poverty and the pernicious ideology of color-blindness to reveal the government's role in fostering the dire conditions of largely poor African-Americans, who were bearing the hardships incurred by the full wrath of the indifference and violence at work in the racist, neoliberal state. Global neoliberalism and its victims now occupy a space shaped by authoritarian politics, the terrors inflicted by a police state, and a logic of disposability that removes them from government social provisions and the discourse and privileges of citizenship. One of the most obvious lessons of Katrina—that race and racism still matter in America—is fully operational through a biopolitics in which "sovereignty resides in the power and capacity to dictate who may live and who may die."[64] Those poor minorities of color and class, unable to contribute to the prevailing consumerist ethic, are vanishing into the sinkhole of poverty in desolate and abandoned enclaves of decaying cities, neighborhoods, and rural spaces, or in America's ever-expanding prison empire. Under the Bush regime, a biopolitics driven by the waste machine of what Zygmunt Bauman defines as "liquid modernity"[65] registered a new and brutal racism as part of the emergence of a contemporary and savage authoritarianism.

Any viable attempt to challenge the biopolitical project that shaped American life and culture for the past decade must do more than unearth the powerful antidemocratic forces that impact American economics, politics, education, media, and culture; it must also deepen possibilities of individual and collective struggles by fighting for the rebuilding of civil society and the creation of a vast network of democratic public spheres, such as schools and the alternative media, in order to develop new models of individual and social agency that can expand and deepen the reality of democratic public life. This is a call for a diverse "radical party," following Stanley Aronowitz's exhortation, a party that prioritizes democracy as a global task, views hope as a precondition for political engagement, gives primacy to making the political more pedagogical, and understands the importance of the totality of the struggle as it informs and articulates within and across a wide range of sites and sectors of everyday life—domestically and globally. Democratically minded citizens and social movements must return to the crucial issue of how race, class, power, and inequality in America contribute to the suffering and hardships experienced daily by the poor, people of color, and working- and middle-class people. The fight for equality offers new challenges in the process of constructing a politics that directly addresses poverty, class domination, and a resurgent racism. Such a politics would take seriously what it means to struggle pedagogically and politically over both ideas and material relations of power as they affect diverse individuals and groups at the level of daily life. Such struggles would combine a democratically energized cultural politics of resistance and hope with a politics aimed at offering workers a living wage and all citizens a guaranteed standard of living, one that provides a decent education, housing, and health care to all residents of the United States.

Biopolitics is not just about the reduction of selected elements of the population to the necessities of bare life or worse; it is also potentially about enhancing life by linking hope and a new vision to the struggle for reclaiming the social, providing a language capable of translating individual issues into public considerations, and recognizing that in the age of the new media the terrain of culture is one of the most important pedagogical spheres through which to challenge the most basic precepts of the global neoliberalism. The waste machine of modernity, as Bauman points out, must be challenged within a new understanding of environmental justice, human rights, and democratic politics. Negative globalization with its attachment to the mutually enforcing modalities of militarism and racial segregation must be exposed and dismantled. And this demands new forms of resistance that are both more global and differentiated. But if these struggles are going to emerge, especially in the United States, then we need a politics and pedagogy of hope, one that takes seriously Hannah Arendt's call to use the public realm to throw light on the "dark times" that threaten to extinguish the very idea of democracy. Against the tyranny of market fundamentalism, religious dogmatism, unchecked militarism, and ideological claims to certainty, an emancipatory biopolitics must enlist education as a crucial force in the struggle over democratic identities, spaces, and ideals.

Central to the biopolitics of disposability is the recognition that abiding powerlessness atrophies the public imagination and leads to political paralysis. Consequently, its policies avidly attack critical education at all levels of cultural production in an all-out effort to undermine critical thought, imagination, and substantive agency. To significantly confront the force of a biopolitics in the service of the new authoritarianism, intellectuals, artists, and others in various cultural sites—from schools to higher education to the media—will have to rethink what it means to secure the conditions for critical education both within and outside of the schools. In the context of formal schooling, this means fighting against the corporatization, commercialism, and privatization of public schools. Higher education has to be defended in the same terms. Against the biopolitics of racial exclusion, the university should be a principal site where dialogue, negotiation, mutual understanding, and respect provide the knowledge and experience for students to develop a shared space for affirming differences while simultaneously learning those shared values necessary for an inclusive democratic society. Similarly, both public and higher education must address with new courage the history of American slavery, the enduring legacy of racism in the United States, and its interface with both political nationalism and the insidious market and religious fundamentalisms at work in contemporary society. Similarly, racism must be not be reduced to a private matter, a case of individual prejudice removed from the dictates of state violence and the broader realm of politics, and left to matters of "taste, preference, and ultimately, of consumer, or lifestyle choice."[66] What must be instituted and fought for in higher education is a critical and anti-racist pedagogy that unsettles, stirs up human consciousness, "breeds dissatisfaction with the level of both freedom and democracy achieved thus far," and inextricably connects the fates of freedom, democracy, and critical education.[67]

Hannah Arendt once argued that "the public realm has lost the power of illumination," and one result is that more and more people "have retreated from the world and their obligations within it."[68] The public realm is not merely a space where the political, social, economic, and cultural interconnect; it is also the pre-eminent space of public pedagogy—that is, a space where subjectivities are shaped, public commitments are formed, and choices are made. As sites of cultural politics and public pedagogy, public spaces offer a unique opportunity for critically engaged citizens, young people, academics, teachers, and intellectuals to enter into pedagogical struggles that provide the conditions for social empowerment. Such struggles can be waged through the new media, films, publications, radio interviews, and a range of other forms of cultural production. It is especially crucial, as Mark Poster has argued, that scholars, teachers, public intellectuals, artists, and cultural theorists take on the challenge of understanding how the new media technologies construct subjects differently with multiple forms of literacy that engage a range of intellectual capacities.[69] This also means deploying new technologies of communication such as the Internet, camcorder, and cell phone in political and pedagogically strategic ways to build protracted struggles and reclaim the promise of a democracy that insists on racial, gender, and economic equality. The new technoculture is a powerful pedagogical tool that needs to be used, on the one hand, in the struggle against both dominant media and the hegemonic ideologies they produce, circulate, and legitimate, and, on the other hand, as a valuable tool in treating men and women as agents of change, mindful of the consequences of their actions, and utterly capable of pursuing truly egalitarian models of democracy.

The promise of a better world cannot be found in modes of authority that lack a vision of social justice, renounce the promise of democracy, and reject the dream of a better future, offering instead of dreams the pale assurance of protection from the nightmare of an all-embracing terrorism. Against this stripped-down legitimation of authority is the promise of public spheres, which in their diverse forms, sites, and content offer pedagogical and political possibilities for strengthening the social bonds of democracy, new spaces within which to cultivate the capacities for critical modes of individual and social agency, and crucial opportunities to form alliances to collectively struggle for a biopolitics that expands the scope of vision, operations of democracy, and the range of democratic institutions—that is, a biopolitics that fights against the terrors of totalitarianism. Such spheres are about more than legal rights guaranteeing freedom of speech; they are also sites that demand a certain kind of citizen informed by particular forms of education, a citizen whose education provides the essential conditions for democratic public spheres to flourish. Cornelius Castoriadis, the great philosopher of democracy, argues that if public space is to be experienced not as a private affair, but as a vibrant sphere in which people learn how to participate in and shape public life, then it must be shaped through an education that provides the decisive traits of courage, responsibility, and shame, all of which connect the fate of each individual to the fate of others, the planet, and global democracy.[70]

In the aftermath of Hurricane Katrina, the biopolitical calculus of massive power differentials and iniquitous market relations put the scourge of poverty and racism on full display. To confront the biopolitics of disposability, we need to recognize the dark times in which we live and offer up a vision of hope that creates the conditions for multiple collective and global struggles that refuse to use politics as an act of war and markets as the measure of democracy. Making human beings superfluous is the essence of totalitarianism, and democracy is the antidote in urgent need of being reclaimed. Katrina should keep the hope of such a struggle alive for quite some time because for many of us the images of those floating bodies serve as a desperate reminder of what it means when justice, as the lifeblood of democracy, becomes cold and indifferent in the face of death.

Equally important, we need a new language for recognizing how the mainstream media have become a central form of public pedagogy and site of struggle. Recognizing the pedagogical and political importance of the media as a pedagogical site suggests the need for discourse that lifts the "truth" of images beyond the evidence of our senses. Theory must once again function as an act of defiance, a critical resource, against thought aimed merely at explication, or, even worse, thinking that is merely the reproduction of what already exists. Hurricane Katrina revealed a media system that is global, one that demands a politics that can confront not only a culture industry that now spans the globe but also globally generated problems at their own level. The dominant media colonize public space with a discourse that collapses public issues into private concerns. Offering only individual failure against a world beset with social problems, it privatizes politics just as it depoliticizes any viable notion of agency. Katrina made clear that there is a need to fill the gap between images of collective suffering and the social conditions that produce and mediate them. Connecting the struggle over the media to the need to link public pedagogy to the imperatives of a substantive global democracy represents a new public agenda waiting to be occupied by critical theory and those intellectuals, social movements, educators, youth, and others for whom responsibility is the first obligation of a democratic politics. The dreadful images of human suffering produced by Hurricane Katrina and the Bush administration's incompetence, and widely portrayed by the media, made visible the waning interest in the public good, the waning appetite for social reform, and the disappearance of the social state. But at the same time, such images served as a reminder of the profound shift in the public sphere and how fragile democracy becomes when public problems are now left to the whims of the market, the forces of deregulation, and the tasks of fragmented individuals. The dominant media culture, regardless of its contradictions, has become a principal impediment to democracy, and, yet, it is the media that bear the central responsibility for educating people and shaping public life. It is precisely in that contradiction that a new politics needs to be forged and struggled over.

NOTES

[1] Many of the ideas in this essay are draw from my book, *Stormy Weather: Katrina and the Politics of Disposability* (Boulder: Paradigm Press, 2006).

[2] Shaila Dewan, "How Photos Became an Icon of the Civil rights Movement," *New York Times* (August 28, 2005). Also available online at: http://www.wehaitians.com/how%20photos%20became%20icon%20of%20civil%20rights%20movement.html.

[3] Douglas Kellner, *The Persian Gulf TV War* (Boulder: Westview, 1992).

[4] It is worth noting how the media coverage of the war in Iraq and Hurricane Katrina differ when viewed from the contrasting perspectives of a "natural catastrophe" and the ensuing man-made "social debacle". Labeled as a natural disaster, Katrina initially seemed removed from the political realm and social criticism until it had become clear in the aftermath of the tragedy that matters of race and class had to be addressed. The "natural" aspect of the disaster opened the door for media coverage of a domestic tragedy that could articulate dissent in a way that the state-manufactured war coverage could not. In other words, natural catastrophes are not supposed to be politicized in themselves; it was only in the aftermath that racial and class politics emerged that enabled the media and the public to criticize the negligence and incompetence of the government and, because the event occurred on domestic soil, the government had less control over the way the media constructed the event, particularly in invoking issues related to poverty, race, and inequality. I want to thank Grace Pollock for this insight.

[5] Dan Frosch, "Back from the Dead," *ALTWeeklies.com* (September 28, 2005), pp. 1–3. Online: http://www.altweeklies.com/gyrobase/AltWeeklies/Story?oid=oid%3A151104.

[6] Cited in Derrick Z. Jackson, "Healthcare Swept Away," *Boston Globe* (September 21, 2005). Online: http://www.boston.com.

[7] Rosa Brooks, "Our Homegrown Third World," *Los Angeles Times* (September 7, 2005), pp. 1–2. Online: http://www.commondreams.org/cgi-bin/print.cgi?file=/views05/0907-24.htm.

[8] Terry M. Neal, "Hiding Bodies Won't Hide the Truth," *Washington Post* (September 8, 2005). Online: http://www.washingtonpost.com.

[9] For a brilliant analysis of the racial state, see David Theo Goldberg, *The Racial State* (Malden: Blackwell Publishing, 2001).

[10] Eric Foner, "Bread, Roses, and the Flood," *The Nation* (October 3, 2005), p. 8.

[11] Angela Davis, *Abolition Democracy: Beyond Empire, Prisons, and Torture* (New York: Seven Stories Press, 2005), pp. 122, 124.

[12] Bob Herbert, "A Failure of Leadership," *New York Times* (September 6, 2005). Online: http://www.truthout.org/docs 2005/090505X.shtml.

[13] Sean D. Hamill, "Santorum Retreats on Evacuation Penalty Remarks," *Pittsburgh Post-Gazette* (September 7, 2005). Online: http://www.post-gazette.com/pg/05250/566844.stm.

[14] Cited in Editorial, "Barbara Bush Calls Evacuees Better Off," *New York Times* (September 7, 2005). Online: http://www.nytimes.com/2005/09/07/national/nationalspecial/07barbara.html?ex=1140498000&en=61560581b40ea782&ei=5070.

[15] Bob Norman, "Savage Station," *Miami New Times* (September 22, 2005). Online: www.miaminewtimes.com/Issues/2005-09-022/news/metro4.html.

[16] The audio clip of Fox News host Bill O'Reilly's comments broadcast September 13, 2005, on *The Radio Factor* can be found on *Media Matters for America*. Online: http://mediamatters.org/items/200509150001.

[17] Slavoj Zizek, "The Subject Supposed to Loot and Rape: Reality and Fantasy in New Orleans," *In These Times* (October 20, 2005). Online: http://www.inthesetimes.com/site/main/article/2361/.

[18] Eric Klinenberg in an interview in *In These Times* points out that "Beginning with the Crime Bill in 1994, all levels of government have delegated traditional social service responsibilities to paramilitary or military organizations—responsibilities that in many cases they are poorly suited to handle. ... [Moreover] they are often designed to operate behind closed doors, and much of the work they do is classified and not subject to public scrutiny." Jeff Bleifuss interview with Eric Klinenberg, "Disasters: Natural and Social," *In These Times* (October 24, 2005), p. 22.

[19] Janet Pelz, "The Poor Shamed Us Into Seeing Them," *Seattle Post-Intelligencer* (September 19, 2005), pp. 1–2. Online: http://www.commondreams.org/cgi-bin/print.cgi?file=/views05/0919-26.htm.

[20] See Michel Foucault, *The History of Sexuality. An Introduction* (New York: Vintage Books, 1990); Michel Foucault, *Society Must Be Defended: Lectures at the College De France 1975-1976* (New York: Picador, 1997); Michael Hardt and Antonio Negri, *Empire* (Cambridge: Harvard University Press, 2000); Michael Hardt and Antonio Negri, *Multitude: War and Democracy in the Age of Empire* (New York: Penguin, 2004); Giorgio Agamben, *Homo Sacer: Sovereign Power and Bare Life*, trans. Daniel Heller-Roazen (Stanford: Stanford University Press, 1998); Giorgio Agamben, *Remnants of Auschwitz: The Witness and the Archive*, trans. Daniel Heller-Roazen (Cambridge: Zone Books, 2002); and Giorgio Agamben, *State of Exception*, trans. Kevin Attell (Chicago: University of Chicago, 2003).

[21] Mitchell Dean, "Four Theses on the Powers of Life and Death," *Contretemps*, Vol. 5 (December 2004), p. 17.

[22] Foucault, *Society Must Be Defended*, p. 249.

[23] Mika Ojakangas, "Impossible Dialogue on Bio-Power: Agamben and Foucault," *Foucault Studies* 2 (May 2005), p. 6.

[24] Foucault, *History of Sexuality*, p. 136.

[25] Foucault, *Society Must Be Defended*, p. 255.

[26] Ibid., p. 258.

[27] Hardt and Negri, *Multitude*, p. 146.

[28] Ibid., p. 334.

[29] See, especially, Agamben, *Homo Sacer*, p. 8.

[30] Zygmunt Bauman, *Liquid Love* (London: Polity Press, 2003), p.133.

[31] Malcolm Bull, "States Don't Really Mind Their Citizens Dying (Provided They Don't All Do It at Once): They Just Don't Like Anyone Else to Kill Them," *London Review of Books* (December 16, 2004), p. 3.

[32] Catherine Mills, "Agamben's Messianic Biopolitics: Biopolitics, Abandonment and Happy Life," *Contretemps*, Vol. 5 (December 2004), p. 47.

[33] Nicholas Mirzoeff, *Watching Babylon: The War in Iraq and Global Visual Culture* (New York: Routledge, 2005), p. 145.

[34] Bauman, *Liquid Love*, p. 136.

[35] Rosa Linda Fregoso, "'We Want Them Alive!': The Politics and Culture of Human Rights," *Social Identities* 12:2 (March 2006), p. 109.

[36] See, for instance, Henry A. Giroux, *Against the New Authoritarianism* (Winnipeg: Arbeiter Ring Publishing, 2005).

[37] There are a number of important works on the politics of neoliberalism. I have found the following particularly useful: Anatole Anton, Milton Fisk, and Nancy Holmstrom, eds., *Not for Sale: In Defense of Public Goods* (Boulder: Westview Press, 2000); Zygmunt Bauman, *Work, Consumerism and the New Poor* (London: Polity, 1998); Ulrich Beck, *Individualization* (London: Sage, 2002); Pierre Bourdieu, *Acts of Resistance: Against the Tyranny of the Market* (New York: The New Press, 1998); Pierre Bourdieu, "The Essence of Neoliberalism," *Le Monde Diplomatique* (December 1998), online: http://www.en.monde-diplomatique.fr/1998/12/08bourdieu; Pierre Bourdieu, *Firing Back: Against the Tyranny of the Market 2*, trans. Loic Wacquant (New York: The New Press, 2003); Noam Chomsky, *Profit Over People: Neoliberalism and the Global Order* (New York: Seven Stories Press, 1999); Jean Comaroff and John L. Comaroff, *Millennial Capitalism and the Culture of Neoliberalism* (Durham: Duke University Press, 2000); Lisa Duggan, *The Twilight of*

H. A. GIROUX

Equality: Neoliberalism, Cultural Politics, and the Attack on Democracy (Boston Beacon Press 2003); Henry A. Giroux, *The Terror of Neoliberalism* (Boulder: Paradigm Publishers, 2004); David Harvey, *The New Imperialism* (Oxford: Oxford University Press, 2003); David Harvey, *A Brief History of Neoliberalism* (Oxford: Oxford University Press, 2005); Doug Henwood, *After the New Economy* (New York: The New Press, 2003); Colin Leys, *Market Driven Politics* (London: Verso, 2001); Randy Martin, *Financialization of Daily Life* (Philadelphia: Temple University Press, 2002); Neil Smith, *The Endgame of Globalization* (New York: Routledge, 2005); and Alain Touraine, *Beyond Neoliberalism* (London: Polity Press, 2001).

38 William DiFazio, "Katrina and President George W. Bush Forever," *Situations* 1:2 (2006), p. 87.
39 Achille Mbembe, "Necropolitics," trans. Libby Meintjes, *Public Culture* 15:1 (2003), p. 40.
40 Zygmunt Bauman, *Wasted Lives* (London: Polity Press, 2004), p. 13.
41 Cited in Thom Hartmann, "You Can't Govern if You Don't Believe in Government," *Common Dreams News Center* (September 6, 2005). Online: http://www.commondreams.org/views05/0906-21.htm.
42 Lawrence Grossberg, *Caught in the Crossfire: Kids, Politics, and America's Future* (Boulder: Paradigm, 2005), p. 117.
43 Cited in Paul Krugman "Hey Lucky Duckies," *New York Times* (December 3, 2002), p. 31.
44 Robert Scheer, "The Real Costs of a Culture of Greed," *AlterNet* (September 6, 2005), p. 2. Online: http://www.alternet.org/module/printversion/25095.
45 Judd Legum, Faiz Shakir, Nico Pitney, Amanda Terkel, Payson Schwin, and Christy Harvey, "Budget: After Katrina, More of The Same," *Think Progress.Org* (October 21, 2005). Online: http://www.americanprogressaction.org/site/apps/nl/content2.asp?c=klLWJcP7H&b=914257&ct=15 20271.
46 Jonathan Weisman, "Budget Plan Assumes Too Much, Demands Too Little," *Washington Post* (February 7, 2007), p. A10.
47 Robert Scheer, "Does Bush Finally See Poor People," *Common Dreams News Center* (September 20, 2005). Online: http://www.commondreams.org/views05/0920-28.htm.
48 Judd Legum, Faiz Shakir, Nico Pitney, Amanda Terkel, Payson Schwin, and Christy Harvey, "Poverty: A Close Look at 'The Other America," *ThinkProgress.Org* (September 19, 2005). Online: http://www.americanprogressaction.org/site/apps/nl/content2.asp?c=klLWJcP7H&b=914257&ct=14 28461.
49 Robert Scheer, "Rotten Fruit of the 'Reagan Revolution,'" *Robert Scheer.com* (September 6, 2005). Online: http://www.commondreams.org/views05/0906-23.htm.
50 Peter Dreier, "Katrina in Perspective: The Disaster Raises Key Questions About the Role of Government in American Society," *Dissent Magazine* (Summer 2005). Online: http:// www. dissentmagazine.org/menutest/articles/su05/dreier.htm.
51 William Greider, "Defining a New 'New Deal,'" *The Nation* (September 21, 2005). Online: http:// www.alternet.org/module/printversion/25745.
52 Cited in Paul Krugman, "A Can't-Do Government," *New York Times* (September 2, 2005). Online: http://www.commondreams.org/views05/0902-22.htm.
53 Frank Rich notes the revealing similarity between George W. Bush's "I don't think anyone anticipated the breach of levees" and Condoleezza Rice's post–9/11 claim "I don't think anybody could have predicted that these people could take an air plane and slam it into the World Trade Center." See Frank Rich, "Fallujah Floods the Superdome," *New York Times* (September 4, 2005), p. 10.
54 Spenser S. Husu and Linton Weeks, "Video Shows Bush Being Warned on Katrina," *Washington Post* (March 2, 2006), p. A01.
55 This is not an argument being made only by critics on the Left. Francis Fukuyama, one of the stars of the neoconservative movement, has recently jumped ship and argued in the *New York Times* that neoconservatism increasingly resembles Leninism and that "as both a political symbol and body of thought, it has evolved into something he can no longer support." Francis Fukuyama, "After Neoconservatism," *New York Times Sunday Magazine* (February 19, 2006). Online: http:// www.nytimes.com/2006/02/19/magazine/neo.html?_r=1&oref=slogin.

50

[56] Paul Krugman, "Tragedy in Black and White," *New York Times* (September 19, 2005), p. A27.

[57] See, for example, David A. Gabbard and Kenneth Saltman, eds., *Education as Enforcement* (New York: Routledge, 2003); and Randall R. Beger, "Expansion of Police Power in Public Schools and the Vanishing Rights of Students," *Social Justice* 29:1–2 (2002), pp.119–130.

[58] Richard H. Kohn, "Using the Military at Home: Yesterday, Today, an Tomorrow," *Chicago Journal of International Law* 94:1 (Spring 2003), pp. 165-192; and Catherine Lutz, "Making War at Home in the United States: Militarization and the Current Crisis," *American Anthropologist* 104:3 (2002), pp. 723–735.

[59] Nicholas Mirzoeff, *Watching Babylon*, p. 16.

[60] Zygmunt Bauman, *Liquid Modernity* (London: Polity, 2000). See also Zygmunt Bauman, *Liquid Love* (London: Polity, 2003); and Zygmunt Bauman, *Liquid Life* (London: Polity, 2005).

[61] Bauman, *Wasted Lives*, p. 27.

[62] Zygmunt Bauman cited in Nicholas Fearn, "NS Profile: Zygmunt Bauman," *New Statesman* (January 16, 2006), p. 30.

[63] Zygmunt Bauman, *In Search of Politics* (Stanford: Stanford University Press, 1999), pp. 68–69.

[64] Mbembe, "Necropolitics," pp. 11–12.

[65] Bauman, *Liquid Modernity*.

[66] Paul Gilroy, *Postcolonial Melancholia* (New York: Columbia University Press, 2005), p. 146–147.

[67] Bauman, *Liquid Love*, p. 14.

[68] Hannah Arendt, *Men in Dark Times* (New York: Harcourt, Brace & World, 1955), p. 4.

[69] Mark Poster, *What's the Matter with the Internet?* (Minneapolis: University of Minnesota Press, 2001).

[70] See, especially, Cornelius Castoriadis, "The Greek Polis and the Creation of Democracy," *Philosophy, Politics, Autonomy: Essays in Political Philosophy* (New York: Oxford University Press, 1991), pp. 81–123.

PETER MCLAREN AND NATHALIA E. JARAMILLO

4. KATRINA AND THE BANSHEE'S WAIL: THE RACIALIZATION OF CLASS EXPLOITATION

THE RISING TIDE OF BELLIGERENCE

PELLEY: Do you think you owe the Iraqi people an apology for not doing a better job?

BUSH: That we didn't do a better job or they didn't do a better job?

PELLEY: Well, that the United States did not do a better job in providing security after the invasion.

BUSH: Not at all. I am proud of the efforts we did. We liberated that country from a tyrant. I think the Iraqi people owe the American people a huge debt of gratitude, and I believe most Iraqis express that. I mean, the people understand that we've endured great sacrifice to help them. That's the problem here in America. They wonder whether or not there is a gratitude level that's significant enough in Iraq.

PELLEY: Americans wonder whether . . .

BUSH: Yeah, they wonder whether or not the Iraqis are willing to do hard work necessary to get this democratic experience to survive. That's what they want.

Retrieved January 15 2007 at:
<http://www.cbsnews.com/stories/2007/01/14/60minutes/main2359119_page2.shtml>

The social historical panorama unfolding before us is in tumult, ranging from confused and paranoid to lethally vengeful. It is as if all of human decency has been sucked into a vortex of political imbrioglio. The Bush oligarchy—poster children for torture and endless war—has become an agglomeration of dangerously co-habiting parasites, enforcers, tyrants and calumniators—Captain Queegs with cellphones—operating out of a den of McCarthy-era redivivus. Here in the United States the aroma of corruption is as pungent as the flop sweat that graced the storied jowls of an on-camera Richard Nixon. Fear has become the big stick to wield in the service of patriotism, priming us with images and expectations of imminent attack, blurring the distinction between the imagined and the occurrent, between desultory and carefully orchestrated threats, and producing through a sultry atmosphere of

G. Martin, D. Houston, P. McLaren and J. Suoranta (eds.), The Havoc of Capitalism:
Publics, Pedagogies and Environmental Crisis, 53–69.

impending doom political lassitude among the hapless multitude. De-politicization has become the official hallmark of patriotism, presaging a quickening of fascism. Condi Rice with her team of Kobolds circles the globe, reveling in her new found role as "warrior princess" as she unsuccessfully assures her sepoys around the world that the U.S. government does not use torture and is protecting the interests of the free world.

An air marshal guns down a fleeing mentally ill patient who claimed he had a bomb and Fox News commentators salivate over how well Homeland Security is doing its job. During a visit to Vietnam, President Bush announces that he wants to apply the lesson the United States learned after its war on Vietnam to the war in Iraq—that this time we shouldn't quit until we win. Doesn't our leader realize that the peoples of the so-called Third World are fed up with occupying armies undertaking a high-tech pillaging of their resources under the specious cover of valiant attempts by the United States (or other foreign nations) to 'export democracy' to underdeveloped states (underdeveloped in this sense meaning 'overexploited') struggling to break the chains of tyranny? He probably does, but then again, as John Bellamy Foster points out, "even the likelihood of being caught up in a long-term civil war, may be considered 'worth it' to a ruling elite playing a high-stakes gamble for control of world oil and global hegemony" (2006, p. 6). The mainstream media don't cover the real story—they dare not. They hold up the public face of the war, shamefully refusing to address for the American people the larger geopolitical issue of securing the Middle East and its oil for the empire of capital. You don't have to be a Marxist to figure it out. As John Bellamy Foster reveals, "U.S. and British corporations are now positioned to gain control over the production of, and to reap huge profits from, the Iraqi oil reserves through so-called "production sharing agreements," which will give them rights to the exploitation and sale of the bulk of Iraq oil reserves for decades to come—even allowing them to book this oil as 'assets' in their accounts" (2006, p. 3). Not only is the global-imperial projection of U.S. power—a type of U.S.-centric imperialism in a unipolar world—a brute reality after the demise of the Soviet Union, but it is now directed at potential future rivals (Foster, 2006, p. 5).

It wasn't that long ago that Americans discovered that maintaining the free world comes at a large financial as well as ideological cost. Earlier in the year, it became alarmingly evident that the Bush administration paid conservative pundit Armstrong Williams $240,000 while serving as a media "talking head" to help persuade African Americans to back President Bush's No Child Left Behind law. More recently it has been made clear that purchasing journalistic mercenaries is not only a major part of a larger and well-fueled government scheme to blur the line between legitimate news reporting and political propaganda here in the United States (as part of Psy-Ops [psychological operations] activities within the homeland itself), it is also an integral part of democracy-building efforts in foreign countries such as Iraq. It has been recently disclosed that the Pentagon hired propaganda-making firms to cultivate by means of psychological and influence operations in the Iraqi media an impression of grassroots support for the American occupation. Mr. Rumsfeld may have closed the Office of Strategic Influence, but he kept it functioning covertly by outsourcing work to contractors such as the Rendon Group and the Lincoln Group, which won additional multimillion-dollar Pentagon contracts for media analysis and a media operations center in Baghdad, including "damage control planning." Jacob Weisberg (2005) draws the distinction between propaganda ("a calculated and systematic effort to manage public opinion") and spin (i.e., "lying and routine political dishonesty"). He notes that "when the Bush administration manufactures fake 'news,' suppresses real news, disguises the former as the latter, and challenges the legitimacy of the independent press, it corrodes trust in leaders, institutions, and, to the rest of the world, the United States as a whole."

On the European front, young people of African and Arab descent have recently given the *"bien nacidos"* of France the political megrims in their chosen response— the torch—to decades of criminal misrule, the ghettoization of immigrant youth and the imperialist practices of entitlement of the capitalist elite. Back home, capitalist exploitation, and its ally, racism, while unwanted guests at the banquet known as the American Dream, are still the primary reasons why the poor are excluded from eating at the same table and forced to scramble for whatever scraps are made available to them elsewhere. Whites are likely to forget why more folks of color don't join them at the table of good fortune unless a crisis of national proportion occurs. And such a crisis has occurred and continues still.

This chapter has been written during a time of crisis in the United States and in capitalist societies worldwide, what we could call a crisis of global capitalism. We call it a crisis of global capitalism because, as Foster argues, "Since the 1970s the dominant reality of the U.S. and world economy has been that of stagnation and financial explosion...the general condition of the U.S. economy and world economy as a whole has been slow growth and rising unemployment/underemployment and excess capacity" (2006, p. 7). Here, neoliberalism includes stagnating wages, an economic surplus at the top, a redistribution of income and wealth toward the upper classes, limited profitable investment opportunities within production as a result of overcapacity in key industries worldwide, a shift toward financial speculation and the financialization of the global economy—a condition that Foster explains from the perspective of monopoly capital theory, and which he calls the phase of global monopoly-finance capital (Foster, 2006, p. 7). We agree with Foster that "capitalism, as witnessed particularly its naked imperialism abroad, is increasingly degenerating into a kind of barbarism, where war, brutality, torture, misery, superexploitation, all sorts of draconian measures against the poor, border security, anti-immigration, gated homes, racism, extreme environmental devastation threatening whole populations and even the globe, nuclear proliferation (and hence the danger of more terrible wars), etc., are on the rise" (Foster, 2006, p. 9). We have been able to gauge (modestly) such a crisis not only during our various journeys over the past five years of working together—which took us to Palestine, Israel, South Africa, Cuba, and numerous times to Venezuela, Colombia and Mexico—but also during our visits with radical teachers, scholars and social activists in the United States and Canada (see McLaren & Jaramillo, 2007). We view the bulk of our work not as grist for advancing our careers in the academy but as a way of participating in a wider political project in which we attempt (to echo Henry Giroux) to make the pedagogical more politically informed and the political more pedagogically critical.

When Hurricane Katrina struck the coast of Louisiana and began to devastate the city of New Orleans, we began to see this event as metonymical of the crisis of race and class in the United States, and watching the coverage of Katrina was a pedagogical lesson in itself for us and for our camaradas and students. We wrote about this event for several publications and then decided that it would make a good contribution to this book in so far as it provides an expansive context for many of our arguments about the persistence of racism and class warfare in the United States. We decided to focus our commentary on Katrina because, while we agree with Lawrence D. Bobo, writing in the Du Bois Review, that "Katrina raised powerful questions about American democracy and the racial divide," we also concur that "the sort of deep democratic dialogue...about poverty, racism and the obligations of government that many had hoped for in Katrina's wake has not come about" (2006, p. 2). Bobo remarks that "Americans responded to Katrina on the basis of existing attitudinal, ideological, and political predispositions" resulting in an "absence of profound change in response to dramatic events connected to major social cleavages"—a situation that is unfortunately and tragically "consistent with other major episodes in U.S. race relations" (2006, p. 2). As Bobo also notes, media and politics scholars have shown "how the media portrayed Katrina disaster victims strongly influenced the amount of assistance that their fel-low Americans thought victims should receive" (2006, p. 2). Lack of expedient government assistance to the victims of Katrina certainly impacted how African-American women "bore the brunt of the storm's wrath" and contributed to how single mothers and poor and elderly women would become the most "readily visible victims of Katrina" (Bobo, 2006, p. 4). In many ways the response of the U.S. government to the victims of Katrina is emblematic of the fate of those oppressed by the racist and imperialist practices of global neoliberalism.

We are not surprised to learn that the U.S. Department of Agriculture (USDA) has reported that millions of Americans who cannot put food on their table—who describe their condition as a state of hunger—are to be (euphemistically and shamefully) re-named as existing in a condition of "very low food security" (Williamson, 2006). The term "hunger" has been expelled because, according to a sociologist for the USDA, it is "not a scientifically accurate term" (Williamson, 2006). Hunger, after all, refers to a "potential consequence of food insecurity" due to a "prolonged, involuntary lack of food." Welcome to the future.

KATRINA: EMBLEMATIC OF AMERICA'S WAR WITH THE POOR

On Sunday, August 28, less than 48 hours before Katrina struck, residents of New Orleans were starting to get antsy. While they may not have been prepared for that devastating *rara avis* among mother nature's storehouse of storms, they were even less prepared for the human callousness that would follow in its tremulous wake, especially those among the 112,000 people in New Orleans who were without any private form of transportation and had to bear the full brunt of the havoc wreaked by the Category 4 hurricane (at one stage a Category 5 just prior to making landfall). While they were angry at remarks made by David Brooks in the *New York Times* that "most of the ambitious and organized people abandoned the inner-city areas of New Orleans long ago" (Bacon, 2005b, p. 14), implying that those who could not leave deserved their fate, they were hardly surprised. This was, after all, "a private-sector evacuation, open only to those with the economic means to participate" ("Katrina: Social Tragedy Benefits Exploiters, Devastates Workers," 2005, p. 1).

Coiled like a viper in the hurricane's eye, the Specter of Capitalism unleashed its pent-up supply of hell upon its historically most vulnerable victims: impoverished African Americans (before Hurricane Katrina, the unemployment rate among Gulf residents was among the nation's highest, with 18% to 30% of people in the region living under the poverty line—twice the national rate—and with Blacks in New Orleans suffering a 35% poverty rate Bacon, 2005a). In the 1950s and 1960s Americans witnessed attacks on African Americans by lynch mobs, police dogs and fire hoses; but the assault on African Americans during Hurricane Katrina was of a different sort. It was an attack on hope: hope that the United States had overcome its historical legacy of racism, hope that educated journalists had moved beyond portraying life in the United States with brutally overt or subtle racist stereotypes, hope that capitalist democracies had made necessary headways in ending poverty, hope that the government could muster whatever it took to care for its poor and dispossessed in a time of emergency. Katrina sounded the death knell of such a hope, a hope born in the crucible of the Civil Rights Movement of earlier—and seemingly much more unreal—times. Not only has the immoral geography of the country been illuminated for the world to see but the very meaning and purpose of American capitalist democracy has been called into question. Of course, there was no absence of media pundits (such as Kathleen Parker of the *Orlando Sentinel* and Jeff Jacoby and Kathy Young of the *Boston Globe*) eager to defend Condi's condemnation that the slow response to Katrina had anything to do with racism (Bacon, 2005b, p. 13).

Despite the protestations of Condi and the Bush gang that there was no racism in the botched response to Katrina, during the days that followed the devastation, the entire world bore witness to the much-vaunted American values imploding in the sinkhole of capitalist greed, avarice, and neglect for the poor and for people of African descent. More than just a series of untenable contradictions accumulated in successive moments of bureaucratic neglect, Hurricane Katrina has become emble-matic of White supremacist free-market democracy, prompting an international reassessment of the status of the American Dream. Much of this reassessment echoed *The Human Development Report*, an independent report commissioned by the United Nations Development Program. Its 2005 edition (370 pages) written by Kevin Watkins, the former head of research at Oxfam, investigates inequalities in health provisions inside the United States as part of a survey of how inequality worldwide is retarding the eradication of poverty. We learn, for instance, that the infant mortality rate has been rising in the United States for the past five years and is now the same as Malaysia. We learn that America's Black children are twice as likely as Whites to die before their first birthday and wealth creation does not necessarily mean eradicating or even lessening poverty, because eradicating poverty means providing people with full access to health, education and other social provisions. What we don't learn is that we have known about similar conditions for decades and longer, and we still seem incapable of overcoming them. It's much easier to blame and demonize the victims, and that's exactly what happened in the case of Hurricane Katrina. One stunning illustration of political naiveté and lack of even a rudimentary understanding of the relationship between race and class can be found in remarks by journalist Kathleen Parker of the *Orlando Sentinel*:

> Parker...expressed surprise that an African-American woman told her "matter-of-factly" that Bush doesn't care about people who look like me because the woman was "an elegant professional woman clearly not of the Al Sharpton school of reactionary politics." (Bacon, 2005b, p. 13)

The act of God that began like a susurrus of wind in the eerie darkness swelled into the piercing, piteous wait of a banshee, a blackened sky draped over the city of New Orleans like the funeral cowl of the unshriven dead. The gale force winds seemed to arch the stars across the horizon like a diadem of death. For many, all would soon be lost in the impending chaos.

A moral panic ensued when the public was fed horror stories about what it was like to be trapped in the inferno of Black anarchism, stories refracted in the cesspool of racism and fear that lies deep within the structural unconscious of a nation founded upon violence, slavery and genocide: African American "wildings" gang-raping women and children, looting stores of liquor and drugs, shooting at ambulances, police patrols, and rescue helicopters, and throwing the city into a vortex of violence and anarchy—stories that were later confirmed as untrue. (We are not arguing that no looting took place but we challenge the sentence recently handed down by a judge who condemned three convicted looters—who stole beer, liquor and wine—to 15 years of prison). *Fox News* correspondent Steve Harrington described New Orleans as the "Wild West", while *Fox News* correspondent Phil Keating characterized a fire visible in some news footage as being set "perhaps for no apparent reason but just for the joy of arson" (Yassin, 2005, p. 11). An article in *USA Today* was unembarrassingly headlined "The Looters, They're Like Cockroaches" (Yassin, 2005, p. 10). *Fox News'* viagra posse leader, Bill O'Reilly, revealed that it was not blood running through his veins but the muck that lined the city's drainpipes when he repugnantly opined in the *Florida Sun-Sentinel* on September 10, 2005:

> That "the suffering" of "the poor in New Orleans" should be a lesson: "Connect the dots and wise up. Educate yourself, work hard and be honest...If you don't...the odds are that you will be desperately standing on a symbolic rooftop someday yourself. And trust me, help will not be quick in

coming." And in O'Reilly's view, help should not necessarily be offered...: 'The white American taxpayers are saying: "How much more do we have to give here?'" (Bacon, 2005, p. 13)

For all the descriptions in military terms about New Orleans being bruited about like "war zone", and "theater of operations" where marauding hordes of looters supposedly overturned every act of human civility, it is interesting to note a *Seattle Times* report concluded that there was no more violence in New Orleans during the aftermath of Katrina than in any other typical week (Bacon, 2005b, p. 14). Many stories of violence—such as snipers firing at rescue vehicles and police being attacked by mob violence—were later discredited (Bacon, 2005b; Yassim, 2005). The *New Orleans Times-Picayune* (September 26, 2005) discovered an official count of only four violent deaths citywide for the entire flood period, which was typical of a city that anticipated approximately 400 homicides in 2005 (Yassin, 2005, p. 9). According to Jaime Omar Yassin (2005),

> As the *Washington Post* observed days after the hysteria began to die down (9/15/05), National Guard troops were surprised to encounter 'virtually no violence' at the Convention Center made infamous by countless unsubstantiated media reports of raped babies and wanton murder. Likewise, on the streets, correspondents such as Nick Robertson (*CNN Daybreak*, 9/5/05) seemed almost disappointed that "I haven't been asked to wear a bullet-proof vest" by authorities. While there had been some violence, and looting that could only have been motivated by profit, there were apparently no raping/ murdering/looting gangs, nor was there any substantial devastation wrought by violence and looting. (p. 12)

In contrast to many prevailing media reports at the time, it would have seemed that the only way to enter the urban hell to help the way-worn victims of Katrina without turning into stone was to send in Snake Blisken with a rogue team of ex-convicts specially trained in urban warfare. In fact, food was actually airlifted and dropped into the city when, because of the exaggerated media stories of violence, it was deemed too infested with criminals for rescuers to safely enter the city. The *New York Daily News* retorted that because "anarchy, Mogadishu-style, is just around the corner if they're not stopped," officials "must do whatever it takes to curb the hardcore, armed, violent felons who are making it impossible to save the city," and who are "a very different breed from desperate citizens who are trying to get food and water" (cited in Bacon, 2005b, p. 14). Of course, it is hard to tell which citizens are trying to get food and water when a White couple was described in media reports as "finding provisions" while a Black man was described as "looting" (although Jonah Goldberg admitted: "I don't know what's in the bag the black guy is tugging along behind him. Perhaps he really did loot the grocery store for more than mere essentials? The white couple found the bread and soda 'from' a local grocery store. Did they go in it?"; cited Bacon, 2005b, p. 14). It is telling that the *Daily News* evoked the image of Mogadishu (Somalia), one that the American public associates with "Blackhawk Down" fame, a place where eighteen U.S. soldiers were killed in a rescue attempt, and where U.S. General

Boykin claimed to have taken a photograph of a satanic presence over the city before he went on years later to proclaim George W. Bush as God's choice for the presidency, and to announce triumphantly that the U.S. army sent to occupy Iraq was a Christian army fighting the evil followers of Islam (see McLaren, 2005).

Right wing journalist Jonah Goldberg, who recently replaced leftist columnist Robert Scheer in a conservative putch at the *Los Angeles Times*, described the survivors of Katrina in the *National Review Online* blog as a different species and inhuman, as a mutant breed that had infested the Superdome—what Goldberg dubbed a "Mad Max/Thunderdome/Waterworld/Lord of the Flies horror show" (Bacon, 2005b, p. 14). Goldberg advised those still trapped in the floodwaters of New Orleans to "hoard weapons, grow gills and learn to communicate with serpents," "find the biggest guy you can and when he's not expecting it beat him senseless," and "protect any female who agrees to participate without question in your plans to repopulate the Earth with a race of gilled supermen" (Bacon, 2005b, p. 14). Goldberg's comments about a new species of supermen emerging from the urban swamplands of New Orleans eerily echo in a different register the secret Nazi program of SS Reichsfuhrer Himmler to enrich German racial lines with pure Nordic blood known as the Lebensborn program. Allan Breed's report in the *Cincinnati Post* described "naked babies wail[ing] for food as men get drunk on stolen liquor" and a crowd "whose almost feral intensity" prevented a helicopter from delivering water to victims (Bacon, 2005b, p. 14).

It's not difficult to imagine William Bennett, America's former Drug Czar and now popular radio host and television personality, staying home all week, strangely transfixed by the televised images of the looting and chaos that were a media mainstay the week following Katrina's wrath, shaking his head in self-righteous contempt, his obscene racist fantasies about bringing crime rates down by aborting the fetuses of New Orleans' African American population, coursing like a riptide inside his pious brain soured by a frat boy's impish self-hatred. We imagine that his heart began to palpitate with racial pride upon hearing Governor Blanco's assurance to the ruling class that they would be saved from savagery:

> These troops are fresh back from Iraq, well trained, experienced, battle-tested and under my orders to restore order in the streets. They have M-16s and they are locked and loaded. These troops know how to shoot and kill and they are more than willing to do so if necessary and I expect they will. (Blum, 2005)

Even New Orleans Mayor Ray Nagin ordered the city's police force of 1500 strong to abandon search-and-rescue missions in order to guard the city from the looters (Blum, 2005).

There is never any mistaking the priority given to property rights in capitalist societies. A *Fox News* reporter "boasted that the National Guard and other armed forces, arriving days after the humanitarian crisis had reached critical levels, [and] were 'highly proficient in the use of lethal force'" (Yassin, 2005, p. 11). CNN's Wolf Blitzer could hardly contain his excitement that the cavalry had finally arrived when he announced: "eight convoys and troops are on the ground at last in a place being described as a lawless, deadly war zone" (Yassin, 2005, p. 12). This news also pleased conservative pundit Peggy Noonan, who, writing in the *Wall Street Journal's* OpinionJournal.com, announced: "I hope the looters are shot" (Bacon, 2005b, p. 14). Not many Americans knew that members of Blackwater, America's infamous mercenary army, were also patrolling the streets of New Orleans. Never one to be outdone when it comes to protecting the ruling class from barbarism, Tucker Carlson remarked: "Maybe [the National Guard] should have shot people but they didn't" (Bacon, 2005b, p. 14). Ann Scott Tyson of the *Washington Post* (September 6, 2005) wrote a piece called "Troops Back from Iraq Find Another War Zone" that allowed the public to hear from the National Guard itself:

> 'Just the smell and feel of a war zone in the city put the soldiers on edge.' The article, subtitled 'In New Orleans,' 'It's like Baghdad on a Bad Day,' featured young Guard soldiers boasting, 'If we're out on the streets, we'll fight back and shoot until we kill them'—though the worst first-hand example of the "violence and looting" that 'shocked' the Guard protagonists was the sight of '70-year old women in new Nike high-tops.' (Yassim, 2005, p. 12)

Watching images of African Americans on CNN through Bennett's "dead seeing eyes" (Henry, 2004) confirmed not the common humanity of all those facing overwhelmingly perilous conditions but only his own Whiteness and his palpable and pure racial supremacy, signaling to him how horrifying it must be to be non-White.

When, in an unscripted NBC benefit concert, rapper Kanye West exclaimed: "George Bush doesn't care about black people, ...[America was organized] to help the poor, the black people, the less well-off as slow as possible," his remarks hit a nerve with people of color throughout the country but they also underscored the truism that the poor hit the hardest are disproportionately African American. They also echoed the observation of philosopher Paget Henry (2004), that the condition of African Americans in the United States reflects a "persistent and long-term inability to recognize the humanity of people of African descent" (p. 200) among the "dead seeing eye of the Western master self" (p. 201). Henry argues that the African does not qualify as a genuine "other" in the Western dialectic of the master/slave relationship. Hegel made it clear in his own phenomenology that the African is without self-consciousness and therefore does not qualify as being part of the second moment of the duplication in the unity of the master self. The African was a slave that was located outside of history and was not able to confirm the humanity of the imperial master (Henry, 2004).

Despite repeated pleas from Governor Blanco for emergency relief—500 buses, 40,000 more troops, ice, water and food, base camps, staging areas, amphibious vehicles, the return of the Louisiana Army National Guard's 256th Brigade Combat Team (then deployed to Iraq), mobile morgues, rescue teams, housing, airlift and communications systems—little materialized the week that Katrina made landfall. The situation was so bad that Rep. Charlie Melancon (D-La.), having been pressured to spend time in public relations stunts with President Bush, wrote Blanco's staff that Bush's "entire effort on behalf of the federal government has been reflected in his and his people's nonchalant attitude to the people of LA. You may give him this to read" (Warrick, Hsu, & Hull, 2005).

Those African-Americans who had begged in vain to be rescued on floating rooftops, those who drowned in their attics, those who were abandoned and perished in hospitals and nursing homes, those whose bloated corpses floated down the waterlogged boulevards and which remain to this day unidentified—all of them bore witness to the reverse mirror image of the violence that was directed at their ancestors, but this time dressed up as 'ineffective response' to an act of God. According to faith-based political theory it was not the place of those affected by the hurricane to question, much less attempt to interfere with an act of God. A number of fundamentalist religious leaders took to the pulpit and declared Katrina an act of holy vengeance against 'Southern decadence.' According to Rev. Bill Shanks, pastor of New Covenant Fellowship of New Orleans:

New Orleans now is abortion free. New Orleans now is Mardi Gras free. New Orleans now is free of Southern Decadence and the sodomites, the witchcraft workers, false religion – it's free of all of those things now," Shanks says. "God simply, I believe, in His mercy purged all of that stuff out of there – and now we're going to start over again. (Brown & Martin, 2005)

Antiabortion activist Steve Lefemine likened the satellite map of Hurricane Katrina to "the image of and 8-week old fetus" and clamored that "God judged New Orleans for the sin of shedding innocent blood through abortion" (Cooperman, 2005). Citing "Providence" and judgment against "national sin" Lefemine and his kin washed their hands of the moral and social responsibility to assist our citizens in times of tragedy and rather used Katrina to advance their own fundamentalist ideology – a set of beliefs and practices that are increasingly becoming the norm in an evolving 'Christian America.'

We can imagine an old jazz musician sitting on the damp street corner, unaware of the impact that mold would have on his wheezing lungs in the weeks ahead, staring at a waterlogged saxophone case bobbing in a steamy sewer like a bloated corpse that had risen up from the river Styx. We imagine his relatives, working in public sector jobs, being denied a living wage when they are finally allowed to return to the city and then being hit with massive layoffs if they are lucky enough to find a job in the casualized work zone of part-time positions (according to The Bureau of Labor Statistics, as late as October, 500,000 of the 800,000 people evacuated had yet to return home, see Bacon, 2005b).

For those that do manage to return to their eviscerated homes, and who take a close look at the fine print of their hurricane damage insurance policies, they will notice that the policies cover only for wind damage, not water or flooding. So the policies that they paid into in good faith will be virtually useless for many. But for those fortunate enough to have escaped to Texas, well, we have words of consolation from former First Lady Barbara Bush. After visiting the Astrodome stadium in Houston, Texas, where thousands of evacuees from New Orleans and other affected areas were being housed, Barbara Bush chucked prior to exclaiming:

> So many of the people here, you know, were underprivileged anyway, so this is working very well for them...What I'm hearing, which is sort of scary, is they all want to stay in Texas. Everyone is so overwhelmed by the hospitality. Almost everyone I've talked to says: 'We're going to move to Houston.' (Parry, 2005)

This was subtle racism, to be sure, but journalist reports of black inner-city residents and White suburban residents offered a disturbing contrast:

> There was ...a more subtle racism at work in much of the coverage of the actions taken by whites and African-Americans after the hurricane...the response of the poor black victims was consistently portrayed as at best selfish, and at worst antisocial and criminal. Commentators were much more generous in their assessment of non-blacks. The *Atlanta Journal-Constitution* (9/1/05) and the *Pittsburg Post-Gazette* (9/13/05), for instance, portrayed residents and business owners from Matarie, Louisiana, a mostly white suburb of New Orleans, as grateful, enterprising and generous. (Bacon, 2005b, p. 15)

We're not so sure, however, that the actions of the residents of the mostly white suburb of Gretna could be described as "grateful, enterprising and generous" while they forcibly turned away evacuees, sending them back by bus into the city, and firing warning shots in the air. This seems more like the surfacing of Jim Crow's ugly head than the actions of Mayberry's Aunt Bee. And the police force was behaving anything like Andy Taylor and Barney Fife. Jacqueline Bacon (2005b) notes why "is turning one's neighbors away when they are in need—even physically threatening them—not deemed selfish, antisocial behaviour" (p. 15).

How many survivors of Katrina were mercifully oblivious to the possible connection between climate change and the intensity of the hurricane, the racial politics of why a preventative infrastructure was not in place, the blaming of the victims because they did not heed the warning to evacuate, the all-out war by conservatives against the poor who they felt were created by liberal programs in the first place, the high stakes politics swirling around them in the national arena, unleashed by the federal system of "dual authority" established by the U.S. Constitution incorporating both national and state sovereignty? How, centuries later, this recycled quarrel over the division between state and national power would impact the politics of disaster relief was something few could have imagined.

A major hurricane in New Orleans had been listed as one of the most likely major catastrophes to strike the United States, but what occurred when the hurricane struck was as shocking as the hurricane itself. Much of the equipment (high water vehicles, refueling tankers, and generators) that would have been used to help New Orleans were already deployed in Iraq to help slaughter the Iraqi resistance to the occupation. Instead of being used to help the people of the United States during a time of crisis, these men, women and machines were conscripted into the service of Bush's bloody war for oil that has brought about a free-market 'democracy'—a malediction that some Iraqi leaders have described as a worse situation than during the rule of Saddam. Noam Chomsky (2005) noted that:

> Bush funding cuts in 2004 compelled the Army Corps of Engineers to reduce flood-control work sharply, including badly needed strengthening of the levees that protected New Orleans. Bush's 2005 budget called for another serous reduction—a specialty of Bush-administration timing, much like the proposed sharp cut in security for public transportation right before the London bombings in July 2005.

Just six days after Katrina hit a coalition of low-income groups – Community Labor United – in New Orleans stood resolute and emboldened, demanding that a committee of affected evacuees "actively participate in the rebuilding of New Orleans" (Klein, 2005). Concerned that a pack of corporate hyenas would descend onto the area and use federal relief funds to "replace our homes with newly built mansions and condos in gentrified New Orleans," Community Labor United refused to have its citizens victimized twice over, neither instance which could be attributed to a sacrosanct act of God or the result of minor bureaucratic mismanagement. The citizens claimed rights to the land they once inhabited. As Naomi Klein (2005) observed:

> it's a radical concept: the $10.5 billion released by congress and the $500 million raised by private charities doesn't actually belong to the relief agencies or the government; it belongs to the victims. The agencies entrusted with the money should be accountable to them. Put another way, the people Barbara Bush tactfully described as "underprivileged anyway" just got very rich.

Unfortunately, but perhaps predictably, reconstruction efforts in the devastated area have not actualized the hopes of the people and we are witnessing – yet again – a return to "profit over the people" in cases when the afflicted expect capitalism's ardent supporters to at least powder their faces with a bit of humanity. Shortly after the dead calm, the Bush administration declared the region a "Gulf Opportunity (GO) Zone" an ominous designation at best, indicative of the very same policies put into effect immediately following the fall of Baghdad and subsequent occupation of Iraq.

Measures to support the Republican agendas included, "suspending rules that require payment of prevailing wages by federal contractors and providing displaced schoolchildren with vouchers—another underhanded blow at the public school system. They included lifting environmental restrictions, 'waiving the estate tax for deaths in the storm-affected states'—a great boon for the population fleeing New Orleans slums—and in general making it clear once again that cynicism knows no bounds" (Chomsky, 2005). The Davis Bacon Act's protection for workers' wages (a statute that hails as far back as 1931 that mandates payment of prevailing wages on federally funded construction projects) that the Bush gang had suspended (which would have created large cost differentials between unionized and non-union contractors, replacing union workers with workers who lacked union protection) was reinstated only after the AFL-CIO and many community groups organized massive protests throughout the region and threat of a congressional vote prompted Bush to back down. Similar protests from labor groups have emerged following the department of Homeland Security's easing of sanctions against employers who hire undocumented workers, unleashing yet another fierce firestorm in the Hurricane's wake. As a result, the big fat cats of enterprise – Halliburton, Kellogg Brown & Root, and Bechtel – have cashed in on cheap and oftentimes free immigrant labor. Untold numbers of immigrant laborers are being stiffed, going weeks without pay. Nonpayment of wages is a violation of federal law but when it affects workers rendered invisible because of their immigration status, no one seems to pay much attention.

The politics of immigration is most definitely affecting immigrant workers now doing reconstruction on the Gulf Coast and they might also inflame existing racial divisions. According to David Bacon (2005a),

> the racial fault lines of immigration politics threaten to pit Latinos against Blacks, and migrant laborers against community residents hoping to return to their homes. Community organizations, labor and civil rights advocates can all find common ground in a reconstruction plan the at puts the needs of people first. But flood-ravaged Mississippi and Louisiana could also become a window into a different future, in which poor communities with little economic power fight each other over jobs.

Anti-immigrant politicians and common citizens alike are quick to blame immigrant workers for exploiting reconstruction efforts in the washed out region, for cheating the poor and unemployed residents of New Orleans and Biloxi from the much needed opportunity to work, and for changing the racial, cultural and economic demographic landscape of the area. And yet, although the United States eagerly accepted assistance in the form of military engineers, doctors and nurses from a Mexican military convoy – the first Mexican military unit to operate on U.S. soil since 1846—dozens of displaced Mexican immigrants from the Katrina's wake seeking shelter in the safe confines of church shelters have been deported with nothing to show for their extended stay in the land of freedom and economic success than the haggard and fetid water-soaked clothes on their backs. The steady flow of people-swapping taking place across states and the US-Mexico border can be perplexing to some. As U.S. border control agents steadfastly hunt down displaced immigrants and shoo them out of the country, hundreds of others from bordering states and Mexico are making their way to the "GO zone." Within this context, immigrant laborers are conceptualized as actively responding to environmental forces and maximizing their individual interests, a view that fails to recognize the state's role in creating and recreating the conditions for immigrant labor (Burawoy, 1976).

> Guest worker programs will exploit immigrant labor, and force wages down and communities of color will be forced to compete with each other, sharpening existing race and class inequalities. American Enterprise Institute

researchers Kathryn G. Newmark and Veronique de Rugy (2006) celebrate the entrepreneurial opportunities that Katrina has created for the capitalist overhaul of education. A $20.9 million dollar grants from the federal No Child Left Behind charter school program, combined with assaults on the teachers union, can do wonders in bringing about the neoliberal wet dream of a private sector takeover of public education. When proposed tax-free zones for businesses and school vouchers for students take effect, conditions that further enable the exploitation of the poor will have intensified.

Our understanding of Hurricane Katrina needs to be situated within the disciplinary practices of capital and its process of valorization through unsustainable capital-fueled growth and development, overproduction, resource depletion, and ecosystem destabilization and destruction within the capitalist marketplace. We cannot shift our focus away from capitalism's devastating consequences for the ecosphere and well as the global division of labor and its racialized social relations. Depletion of nonrenewable resources, disruption of natural cycles, and waste and pollution are intrinsically connected to capitalist relations of production which in turn have their differential impacts on populations in terms of race and gender. Capitalists accept collateral damage as part of the overall process, and whether it happens to be the deaths of thousands of human beings or eco-destructivity that leads to the elimination of large clusters of biospheres doesn't really seem to matter to the Masters of Capital—as long as this collateral damage has a minimal effect on the lives of the transnational capitalist class.

The current ecological crisis and crisis of capitalism brought on by the fossil-fuel shortage has led to resource wars, geopolitical conflicts and unilateral invasions, and the deliberate sacrifice of African American communities and other communities of color within the United States who are disproportionately 'cut loose' in times of political, ecological or so-called natural disasters. Continued assaults on the life-sustaining natural processes and resources all of us depend upon can be expected as long as capital's law of value is not challenged. In the case of New Orleans, the wetlands, for example, were not effective in flood control because they had lost their protection and became casualties of the logic of capitalist accumulation. The wetlands—which provide a buffer against storm surge—are depleting at a rate of about 25 miles per year and since the 1930s, Louisiana has lost nearly 2,000 square miles of wetlands, losing every 38 minutes about the equivalent of a football field.

We need to extend Marx's "relentless criticism of everything existing" not only to the failure of the Bush administration to respond to Hurricane Katrina but also to the capitalist system itself, of which the Bush administration is but one manifestation—albeit one of the most repugnant examples of a "rogue nation" in recent history. And even, perhaps, in not so recent history.

Whether the rebuilding of New Orleans will follow the classic capitalist pattern of increased wealth for the few and misery for the majority is still yet to be determined. One of the challenges of critical educators is to make the interconnectedness among capitalism, ecosystem destruction and the racialization of the exploitation of human labor more transparent and less seemingly inevitable–and to find ways of bringing about a socialist alternative. In this regard, the tragedy of Katrina offers us an important pedagogical opportunity to initiate change not only in the case of New Orleans but beyond the reach of our national borders.

It is clear that the United States has abandoned its poor, and for its poor populations of color, it considers them no longer even worthy of abandonment. To abandon a population means that you have had to be with them in some kind of solidarity at some level and at some historical moment. Whatever tenuous solidarity that once might have existed between the predominately white guardians of the state and its people of color has turned to dust. The enlightenment values that once made equality a universal objective have been hijacked by a Christian fundamentalist belief in non- negotiable, ready-made solutions deemed sacrosanct and unalterable by divine fiat. The notion that the population of New Orleans was punished for its sins by Hurricane Katrina is as repugnant as its secular correlate: that those who perished in its floodwaters deserved their fate because the did not prepare themselves for such a natural disaster in advance. Divinely inspired reasoning purportedly found in scriptures and that are on a collision course with evolutionary science and human reason are putting the survival of our eco-system—and our human species—in grave danger. Human technology and the threat of 'resource' wars disguised as 'humanitarian interventions' and defended by the proposition that 'our God is the True God' places our planet on the brink of destruction. We used to be in a position of "mutually assured destruction" (MAD) during the Cold War with the Soviet Union and the Eastern Bloc countries. Now it is something quite different. Istvan Mészáros notes: "Now that the 'neoconservatives' can no longer pretend the United States (and the West in general) are threatened by nuclear annihilation, the acronym has been turned into literal *madness*, as the 'legitimate policy orientation' of *institutionalized military/political insanity*" (2006, p. 36, italics in original).

We have addressed the issue of Christian fundamentalism in our other work (see McLaren and Jaramillo, 2008), but we have not approached the broader issue of religion per se. While we are not advocating the elimination of religion, we would like to draw attention to the fact that it is not merely anti-clericalism that needs to be advanced, that is, resistance to those clerics who would use religious triumphalism to justify the waging of wars against others, but the recognition that religion (as it stands today in many of the mainstream churches) is now maladaptive to the survival of the species. Whereas during earlier epochs, religion and war, yoked together, might have enhanced the global dominance of the human species via technological development, since the invention of the atomic bomb it has clearly become maladaptive. What we need now are not politically opportunistic projects dressed in the guise of "faith-based initiatives." We need international co-operation to save the planet from the global marketplace, not efforts at asserting its dominion. As Alexander Saxton notes:

> Religion, by consigning "our" enemies to the Evil Empire, makes the possession of weapons of mass destruction (and readiness to use them) appear under the guise of sacred duty. Scientifically-guided efforts, meanwhile, to salvage our planetary ecosystem point to the need for international cooperation and global

re-allocations of energy and resources. These necessarily would impinge on affluent societies and wealth-holding classes. Religious belief, on the other hand, assigns priority to believing over knowing, to faith over science. Thus believers believe the Invisible Hand of Providence will save us (or some of us at least), in much the same way that some of our world political leaders believe the invisible hand of the Global Market can exempt (some of us) from the rigors of ecological meltdown. Religion moves in to provide ideological armor for a politics of denial. In God we trust: what market value, today, has biological life on earth a thousand years from now? Or one hundred? (cited in Dunbar-Ortiz, 2006).

What is painfully clear in the midst of such a daunting scenario is the need for a new critical humanist pedagogy, an approach to reading the word and the world that puts the struggle against capitalism (and the imperialism inherent in it) at the center of the pedagogical project, a project that is powered by the oxygen of socialism's universal quest for human freedom and social justice. When the bean chaointe (keening woman) announces the death of humanity, it will be not be a eerie wail from the flapping, crisscrossed jowls of Barbara Bush, but the slow rasp of an emphysemic, dying planet, a planet failed by the human consciousness to which it gave birth.

REFERENCES

Bacon, D. (2005a). Divided we fall. *Truthout/Perspective.* Retrieved December 10, 2005, from http://www.truthout.org/docs_2005/printer_112305D.shtml
Bacon, J. (2005b, December). Saying what they've been thinking. *Extra!, 18*(6), 13–15.
Blum, B. (2005). Some things you need to know before the world ends. *The Anti-Empire Report.* Retrieved December 10, 2005, from http://members.aol.com/bblum6/aer25.htm
Bobo, L. (2006). Unmasking race, poverty, and politics in the 21st Century. *Cambridge University Press, 3*(1), 1–6.
Brown, J., & Martin, A. (2005). New Orleans residents: Go's mercy evident in Katrina's wake. *AgapePress* (September 2). Retrieved December 14, 2005, from http://headlines.agapepress.org/archive/9/22005b.asp
Burawoy, M. (1976, March). The functions and reproduction of migrant labor: Comparative material from Southern Africa and the United States. *The American Journal of Sociology, 81*(5), 1050–1087.
Blum, B. (2005). Some things you need to know before the world ends. *The Anti-Empire Report.* September 5. Retrieved December 10, 2005, from http://members.aol.com/bblum6/aer25.htm
Chomsky, N. (2005, October 5). Wanted a leader for America. *Khaleej Times.* Retrieved December 10, 2005, from http://www.chomsky.info/articles/20051005.htm
Cooperman, A. (2005). Some say natural catastrophe was 'divine judgment.' *Houston Chronicle.* Retrieved December 14, 2005, from http://www.chron.com/cs/csa/printstory.mpl/nation/3338642
Foster, J. B. (2006). Naked imperialism: An interview with John Bellamy Foster. MRZine. Retrieved November 17, 2005, from http://mrzine.monthlyreview.org/foster171106.html
Gasper, P. (2005). Report from San Quentin, California murders Tookie Williams. *Counterpunch.* Retrieved December 14, 2005, from http://counterpunch.co/gasper12132005.html
Grieder, W. (2005). Apollo now. *The Nation, 282*(1), 22–25.
Henry, P. (2004). Whiteness and Africana phenomenology. In G. Yancy, (Ed.), *What white looks like: African –American philosophers on the whiteness question* (pp. 195–209). New York and London: Routledge.

Hoover, M. (2005). Rowboat federalism: The politics of U.S. disaster relief. *MRZine*. Retrieved December 10, 2005, from http://mrzine.monthlyreview.org/hoover021205.html

Katrina: Social tragedy benefits exploiters, devastates workers. (2005). *Industrial Worker, 102*(9), 1, 8.

Klein, N. (2005). Let the people rebuild New Orleans. *The Nation*. Retrieved December 14, 2005, from http://www.thenation.com/doc/20050926/klein

McLaren, P. (2005). *Capitalists and Conquerors*. Lanham, MD: Rowman and Littlefield.

McLaren, P., & Jaramillo, N. (2007). *Pedagogy and praxis in the age of empire: Towards a new humanism*. Rotterdam, The Netherlands: Sense Publishers.

Parry, R. (2005, September 7). Bush: They were underprivileged, so this is working very well for them. *Mirror.co.uk*. Retrieved December 10, 2005, from http://www.mirror.co.uk/news/tm_objectid= 159 38967&method=full&siteid=94762&headline=so-many-of-the-people-here-were-underprivileged-any way--so-this-is-working-very-well-for-them----name_page.html

Patel, P. (2005). DeLay to evacuees: 'Is this kind of fun?' *Houston Chronicle Blog*. Retrieved December 10, 2005, from http://blogs.chron.com/domeblog/archives/2005/09/delay_to_evacue.html

Roig-Franzia, M. (2005, December 18). In New Orleans, no easy work for willing Latinos. *Washington Post*, p. A03. Available at http://www.washingtonpost.com/wp-dyn/content/article/2005/12/17/ AR2005121700932.html?nav=rss_print/asect

Sothern, B. (2005). Left to die. *The Nation, 282*(1), 18–22.

Straight, S. (2005). Katrina lives. *The Nation, 282*(1), 15–18.

Warrick, J., Hsu, S. S., & Ann, H. (2005, December 4). Blanco releases Katrina records: La. Governor Seeks to 'Set the Record Straight' Washington Post Staff Writers, p. A01. Retrieved December 10, 2005, from http://www.washingtonpost.com/wpdyn/content/article/2005/12/03/AR2005120301480.html

Watkins, K. (2005). Human development report. Retrieved December 10, 2005, from http://hdr.undp. org/reports/global/2005/

Weisberg, J. (2005). Beyond spin the propaganda presidency of George W. Bush. Posted Wednesday, Dec. 7, at 7:13 PM ET. Retrieved December 10, 2005, from http://www.slate.com/ default.aspx? id=2131768&nav/tap1

Williamson, E. (2006). Some Americans Lack Food but USDA Won't Call Them Hungry. *Washington Post*, November 16, A01.

Yassin, J. O. (2005, December). Demonizing the victims of Katrina. *Extra! 18*(6), 9–12.

VILLE LÄHDE

5. NATURE IN OUR MIDST

The fate of New Orleans profoundly changed public sensibilities towards natural disasters. No longer were the roaring masses of water seen as a purely outside force, a hand of god, which swept away the hapless humans. Hurricane Katrina was recruited as a symbol of short-sighted environmental policies, both on local and global levels. The disaster was understood even more generally as a political event – environmental relationships were instantly connected to questions of equality. It was a sudden change, if one compares it with the reaction to the tsunami of 2004 in the Indian Ocean. Sure, there were some admirable reactions to the lot of the people affected by the tidal waves. But the tsunami disaster was mainly seen as an act of Nature, a chance event, in itself faceless and unbiased. There was little or no discussion as to whether something was wrong *before* the tectonic plates shook, other than the lack of warning systems. In New Orleans we had erred, and Nature got back at us. This is true, but at the same time dangerously narrow-minded.

REAPING THE WHIRLWIND

Hurricane Katrina became a symbol of environmental problems from two different angles. First and foremost it was taken as a warning signal of the failure of climate policies both on global and local levels and especially the failures of the US administration. It doesn't really matter what the actual causalities of this particular hurricane were. As always, the most important thing about political symbols is that they force an issue into the public space. The pictures of Earth taken from the Apollo spacecraft didn't have much to do with environmental issues per se, and they didn't really give any concrete revelations, any new proof. But the pictures made an abstract idea tangible. Just like monarch butterflies aren't actually the rarest of species in the US, but it was their familiarity and tangibility which blew the lid on GMO discussion in the US during the 90's. And what's more tangible than a hurricane?

There was another thing which lowered the need for point-by-point causal proof. Hurricanes are systemic features of the climate, and climate change is not a question of single disturbances "caused" by human influence. It is a question of widespread and enduring human influence in a complex system, the local effects of which are practically impossible to predict. The everyday language of causality is by necessity even more challenged than in the case of, say, tobacco lawsuits.

G. Martin, D. Houston, P. McLaren and J. Suoranta (eds.), The Havoc of Capitalism:
Publics, Pedagogies and Environmental Crisis, 71–77.
© *2010 Sense Publishers. All rights reserved.*

Katrina became an exemplar of the warning of many climatologists that climate change may increase the frequency of such extreme events. It emphasized that we are moving into an era of heightening insecurity.

So Katrina could be seen to have a link with the general concern over climate change, yet it was much easier to grasp than necessarily uncertain predictions about the future. Climate change could come knocking on your front door, huffing and puffing and blowing your house in.

This forces us to acknowledge that large-scale economic and technological policies have diverse outcomes. Climate change has been mostly approached by globalizing strategies which are ideal for state-level actors, as any actor is made visible only by the aggregation of calculation units (population, carbon output, carbon input, growth rates) which seem significant only on a large scale. The consequences have been measured on an equally high level of abstraction: climate change has been reduced into an issue of average temperatures, rainfall averages and sea levels. Katrina not only hit many homes, it hit home the message that with climate change the local contingencies will be altered.

THE WALLS CAME DOWN

Katrina didn't stop at this dominant environmental theme. It also showed how flawed the traditional strategies of environmental management can be. This was especially important in US: for many activists around the world it had for long seemed that US environmentalism had been successfully co-opted by an "imperialist" trend, and very few credible countering voices remained. The tradition of water management has leaned on a literally militaristic approach of isolation and control, with Mississippi being the archetype. Recurring floods have been answered by ever-growing levees, damming, artificial drainages and other intensive operations. The inherent risks of this approach have been known for a long time, but the status of organizations like the US Army Corps of Engineers has stood in the way of serious rethinking.[1]

Water management is just one example of the tradition of "imperialist" environmental management. The vermin eradication programs that targeted especially wild canines; removal of indigenous people to preserve "untouched wilderness" as a national heritage; intensive control of wild burros, slaughter of buffaloes that dare step out of Yellowstone. It should have been clear to anyone that there are very different ways of how "environmental protection" can be realized, and it can be connected to a diverse range of interests. Calling something environmental doesn't make it nice. Often it is just a new name for the old resource management paradigm with a clear bias for large-scale industrial production or centralized government.

This is an old problem, and it has been pointed out many times by people in academic fields, NGOs and indigenous movements. But Hurricane Katrina gave it a renewed credibility. It showed how linear strategies of control will fail when we are dealing with extremely complex phenomena. The militaristic approach of control is based on the assumption that a thing like a river system can be brought under control. In "normal" conditions such a strategy may seem successful, but surprising contingencies can and will break through the controls. But the thing is, those contingencies can be expected to happen: they are normal. Changing the local practices of housing, agriculture and transport would in the long run be a more sensible strategy. But it would also require centralized actors to relinquish control, to relinquish power.

Often the fallout of environmental management hits those who cannot speak, or those who have no voice in the present order. This makes it easier to keep up the regime despite problems. But Katrina targeted those who have a vote – at least in theory.

DEMOCRACY OF DISASTERS DISPELLED

Problems of environmental management resonated with the general environmental discourse. But since its inception, tensions have existed within the modern environmental debate with other political considerations. Some environmental organizations have been justly criticized for ignoring socio-economic issues, while many environmentalists have criticized mainstream policies for mere greenwashing. It was surprising to see how the questions of equality rose to the forefront after Katrina. Especially surprising was that this took place in the U.S., where the constellation "us vs. them" (or US vs. them) had been so dominant – or at least that was "their" perception. This intervention of equality issues is no small achievement, considering the seemingly hopeless battle which activists in the U.S. and other countries have been waging against realpolitik versions of environmentalism.

The main issue was the reaction to disasters. Who is left behind? Who gets food, water and warmth? These were of course important questions in 2005 when the country was (and of course still is) spending huge amounts of money in the War against Terror. Iraq had become a huge "public works" project, which didn't constitute a new deal but a sapping of public resources to violence which created humongous profits for the few. Levees were badly maintained, disaster relief lacked funds.

For those who watch disaster movies this was a big dramaturgic transition. We had become used to "democratic disaster movies" where an outside threat – were it an asteroid, a volcano, a comet, an earthquake or a tornado – solidifies "us" into a unified front against the threat of nature or the revenge of nature. It brings out the best in us. Do you remember that embarrassing end scene of the 1997 movie "Volcano"? Citizens of all color, creed and occupation, gangsta and police working side by side, have been covered with soot. It takes of course a child to notice "how we all look alike." I mean, get real. It took only four years to see those soot-covered people on the other side of the continent, and how the illusion of that togetherness disintegrated so soon. "The Day After Tomorrow" (2004) achieved a partial negation by sending American refugees over Rio Grande, but it was still the Nation under threat, with even the hardest skeptic realizing his evil ways.

Now the imagery of disasters is changing. The outside force no longer unifies us. It reveals the cracks in our walls and the inherent racism and inequality of our world. This returns us to another tradition of movies with the greedy landlords, big business, corrupt politicians and the lot. I'm waiting for the first blockbuster of this genre, but the wait might be in vain.

POLITICS MADE INTO NATURE

This reaction to Katrina is important, but it gets only halfway there. It leaves the disaster itself in the realm of "Nature." It is still pictured as an outside force that is neutral in itself. When tectonic plates shake, Nature acts in mysterious ways. When hurricanes close in on our coasts, Nature takes its revenge on our collective hubris. In both cases however the Event is separated from the Consequences. Reaction to Katrina was separated into two discourses with their specific framing of the problem.

This neglects the fact that the forces of nature – no matter how much or how little human influence can be seen behind them – never act in a vacuum but in a world that has been formed by a history of human action with all its problems objectified into infrastructures. In a way this is the same thing that was wrong in all those movies about corruption. Chain of command is okay until you break it. Capitalism is okay until you become corrupt. The present political system is okay until that one crackpot gets to head the administration. Thailand's economy of tourist attractions was okay before the tide crushed on the beaches. New Orleans was quaint until the walls came crumbling down. By looking at the Force of Nature as an outsider we forget that it will be the houses which will have to withstand it or fall, the fields which will be inundated or sheltered by vegetation. It is not primarily about the administration which fails to act properly, it is first and foremost about the political and economic order that makes others safe and others vulnerable.

Disasters happen before they happen. After the Lisbon earthquake in 1755, most philosophers debated the Will of God and his mysterious ways. In his letter to Voltaire Jean-Jacques Rousseau reminded that it was not God who had built buildings five stories high on the ocean coast. Granted, Rousseau was still engaged in the debate over God's beneficence, but it was a good point which was neglected.

THERE ARE NO NATURAL DISASTERS

Why didn't the tsunami disaster become a symbol of something greater? Even in Finland not only the hundreds of thousands were mourned, there was the more personal sorrow over 178 dead and many still missing, the greatest peacetime disaster for a long time. Still mostly the public discussion focused on the same things as in 1755: Where was God? How small indeed are we humans before Nature. How can we prepare against God's or Nature's wrath? And so on.

I believe that it is because the question of *agency* dominates our thinking about disasters. When Nature is behind them, nobody can be blamed. Tectonic plates and asteroids have no face, unless we transport blame to god or personalize Nature. But when we have messed with nature, someone can be blamed. The tsunami disaster lacked the link with the general environmental concern and the issues of guilt that it brings.

The debate on climate change focused here for a long time. Those who shared vested interests to keep up the present levels of pollution were stubbornly questioning human influence in climate change. First they wanted to deny any change at all. When that didn't seem viable anymore, they put their hopes on those few who claimed that the changes were "natural". This argument gains its power precisely from the bias on agency. If nature is to blame, nothing can be done. But by the time Katrina came rolling in, those rhetoric strategies had begun to lose credibility even in the U.S. The force of nature could be given a human face.

It is of course important that climate discussion is changing at least a bit. But such strict differentiation of the tsunami and Katrina eventually misses the point. If changes are on their way, agency is only a part of the problem. Whether a disaster is instigated by tectonic tension or climate change, its results are realized in and through our artifacts and social institutions. There will always be a political element in disasters.

Before the 2004 tsunami disaster, Indian activists had tried for years to politicize these issues of institutionalized vulnerability: Is tourism a sustainable livelihood? What does clearcutting of vegetation cover like mangrove forests do to local communities? In this case the move towards aquafarming from small-scale fishing was very important. Dependence on heavy investments on vulnerable production equipment spelled disaster for many. The message of the activists was simple. Unequal social and economic organization makes "the forces of nature" unequal. Disasters will in the end be of our own making. This is true in any part of the world.

We can only discount extinction-level incidents, which fit the democratic disaster genre so well. All that irritating political trivia goes out the window when the end is nigh. If you want to keep your hands clean of politics, pick a huge asteroid or comet, and we'll all be in it together. But of course it is not just a movie. Stories became analogues of our lives, feeding illusions of simplicity for us. In the opening stages of "the environmental awakening" of the 60's such imagery served a purpose by mobilizing many people to notice a host of problems. "Spaceship Earth" and "Our Common Future" glued together many issues that had before seemed separate and trivial. But at the same time the rhetoric of crisis and urgency depoliticized the issues. We were all in it together. But really, when have we truly been that? The world may look like a whole, but people just don't live in the same worlds.

Speaking of natural disasters makes us believe that the disaster itself is beyond our control. We can just build warning systems, wall ourselves away, and try to control the threatening forces. But nature is always in our midst, realized through the structures of our societies.

THE NECESSITY OF ADAPTATION

This makes *adaptation* a vital political issue. For a long time adaptation was however a dividing issue in environmental discourse regarding climate change. Environmentalists were arguing for limitation of greenhouse gas emissions, and any talk of adaptation to the coming changes seemed like surrendering to the problem. And indeed, many opponents of limitation were arguing for adaptation as a more sensible and cost-effective strategy. Some such arguments stemmed from profound notions about the problems in trying to "control" complex systems like the climate, and the inevitability of changes due to the inheritance of the last decades, even centuries. Others were clearly just reactionary maneuvers in disguise. But now the situation seems to be changing. Some changes do indeed seem inevitable. Also, the possibility of growth in the frequency of hurricanes and other such events heightens the appeal of adaptation.

This doesn't invalidate the appeals to limitation. On the contrary, the links between the two approaches are easy to see. In order to make adaptation possible, the coming changes should be mitigated. The big change is that we have to look at the climate system in a very different way. It is not just some abstract force of nature that we should try to keep in check. The centuries of human action, both increasing emissions of greenhouse gasses and the reduction in carbon sinks (vegetation cover), are objectified in the present states of the climate. There is no way this inheritance can be wished away.

But there is a danger that an important political opportunity is lost. Katrina and many other events have afforded us with an opportunity to make a fresh intervention into climate politics. As we saw before, until now climate politics has been the realm of state-level actors. Localized solutions have inevitably seemed like well-meaning but insignificant idealism, as their results disappear in the vast sea of carbon emissions. Climate change is a strange issue. The global climate system is literally a global issue: all carbon emissions, human and nonhuman, contribute to the same dynamics. But the emissions are actually not strictly a global issue. The political and economic backgrounds of emissions differ very much, and viable solutions have to be fitted to the local contingencies. But it is the mathematics of large political units in the climate negotiations that make the small-scale vanish. A move to adaptation might make local solutions viable again.

The state-level actors aren't sleeping, however. Adaptation issues can easily be co-opted to serve dominant interests. By making adaptation a question of gross national income, food production of a country, availability of energy resources and access to water on a national scale, the local viewpoints can again be swept away. We shouldn't lose the opportunities that events like Katrina give us to open up new political spaces.

RESOURCES OF ADAPTATION

Disasters of both "natural" and "human" origin show us that not all resources can be calculated on a universal scale. In the face of tidal waves and hurricanes perhaps the most important resources are mobility and versatility, the possibility to change one's practices of living and gaining a living in changing circumstances, or migrating in case the circumstances get unbearable. Here is the wide gulf in political worldviews: those who draft national or regional strategies of adaptation worry in the end how *the present way of life* can be preserved. For them the problem is how to keep up in the competition and to remain in the current strategic position. The most morbid strategists see the coming changes as an opportunity to better one's strategic position. In Finland there are those who seriously welcome the possible increase in agricultural and forestry production – and stubbornly discount the much more daunting risks. There are those who think that U.S. agriculture will be hit much less than that of others, and the country will gain an upper hand. And so on.

But such strategies omit those who will become the collateral damage. For them keeping up the old way of life is a patent impossibility. Recurrent droughts or floods will displace legions of people, even in the richer countries, if they are not allowed resources of change.

It is precisely this gulf between political strategies that makes radicalizing the adaptation issue possible. When the climate debate was confined in the sphere of emission limitation, the political constellation seemed very simple. It was the rich versus the poor, North versus South, the centre versus the margin. Disasters however show that the people of coastal Bangladesh and New Orleans may share things in common. For them land and livelihood are climate issues.

NOTES

[1] I would like to thank my colleague professor Yrjö Haila from University of Tampere, whose writings were valuable for this section.

PART II: RESILIENCE: INDIGENOUS PEDAGOGIES AND THE CRITIQUE OF ECO- COLONIALISM

SANDY GRANDE

6. A PEDAGOGY OF THE DISPOSSESSED: TOWARD A RED STATE OF DECOLONIZATION, SOVEREIGNTY AND SURVIVANCE

The oppressor must be liberated just as surely as the oppressed...For to be free is not merely to cast off one's chains, but to live in a way that respects and enhances the freedom of others – Nelson Mandela (1995).

Hurakan is a creation god of the Mayans. As a god of creation, Hurakan delivers the cleansing waters of resurrection, not the tides of damnation. Washing away centuries of corruption, his winds and rain literally level playing fields, enabling more democratic vistas of possibility to take root. In New Orleans, Hurakan not only washed away the satiny gloss of Mardi Gras memories and casino dreams but also exposed the unbridled "havoc of capitalism," leaving in its wake glimmers of possibility. It was only after Hurakan receded back into the sky that the storm was unleashed, flooding the streets of New Orleans with a swamp disaster profiteers, spin doctors, and robber barons.

INTRODUCTION

In their report, *"Big Easy Money: Disaster Profiteering on the American Gulf Coast,"* CorpWatch (CW) details the litany of abuse and exploitation that came in the wake of Katrina. According to CW, fully ninety percent of the initial reconstruction contracts were awarded to non-Gulf Coast companies, in particular to many of the same "disaster profiteers" responsible for bungling reconstruction efforts in Iraq and Afghanistan (i.e. Bechtel, Haliburton, the Army Corps of Engineers). Such cronyism and corporate malfeasance has become synonympus with the Bush administration, which has been quick to cash in on the so-called Age of Crisis. Ever since 9–11 the broad aim has been to transform crisis into political capital and to use this latitude to implement expansive agendas without the trappings of accountability. As Indigenous scholar Makere Stewart-Harawira (2005) notes, "In the twenty-first century, notions of crisis and chaos have become the rationale for a new discourse in which empire is the logical outcome of a world no longer secure" (p. 205).

Sociologist Ali Mirsepassi (2006) defines empire by its systematic character, and the manner in which it posits global hierarchies through the introduction of "new strategies of power," which extend well beyond those in the imperialist phase of global capitalism. This description fits the burgeoning Bush empire, which has

G. Martin, D. Houston, P. McLaren and J. Suoranta (eds.), The Havoc of Capitalism: Publics, Pedagogies and Environmental Crisis, 81–98.

been in the business of selling security to the American public through the extension of such "new strategies" as the Homeland Security Act, the pre-emptive strike, the Patriot Act, the Project for the New American Century (PNAC) and the Military Commissions Act. All of which were implemented through the carefully cultivated climate of a President who launched the "global war against terror" with the remarks, "Every nation, in every region, now has a decision to make. Either you are with us, or you are with the terrorists" (Bush, September 20, 2001). Indeed, these (in)famous words are viewed by many – both within and outside of the Bush syndicate – as commencing the "new" American empire.

Presently, the phrase "American Empire" solicits over one million hits on Google.com, over 10,000 book titles on Amazon.com and over 300 articles in *The New York Times*. Generally speaking the "new" empire is viewed as emerging from the synchronistic coupling of neoliberalism with neoconservative politics. Specifically, the post 9–11 deployment of policies such as deregulation, privatization, unrestricted access to consumer markets, downsizing, outsourcing, flexible arrangements of labor, intensification of competition among transnational corporations, increasing centralization of economic political power. The goal from the start has been to dismantle the constellation of existing economic and social structures with any potential to obstruct the so-called "logic of the pure market" (Hursh, 2003).

One of the central aims of this chapter is to illustrate how the view of the present as either unparalleled in its expression of "terrorism" or in the "rise" of the authoritarian state – perpetuates a profoundly ahistorical analysis that glosses over the indigenous and colonialist past. From an indigenous perspective it is not the grips of crisis, imperialism, globalization, or empire that arrests the development of American democracy but rather the ongoing march of colonization (a multidimensional force underwritten by religious fundamentalism, defined through white supremacy, and fueled by global capitalism). Thus, I argue that the *rebranding*[1] of colonization (i.e. as the new American empire, globalization, the rise of the authoritarian state, McWorld) not only promotes the false notion of American exceptionalism but also deracinates the American experience.

While it may be necessary to continually analyze the colonialist project through contemporary lenses, it is critically important to perceive its current incarnations as an extension of an, not departure from the historical project that began in 1492. In other words, rather than view the post 9–11 era as a new Age of Crisis, I suggest that we perceive it as a time when the contradictions of colonization are expanding beyond indigenous communities to affect a broader cross-section of society. From this vantage point, the project of democratization – at home (New Orleans) and abroad (Iraq) – raises the same questions regarding the state of the nation that were raised at the moment of contact (i.e. the genocide of American Indians). Can the "good life" be built upon the death of thousands? Is it possible for democracy to grow from the seeds of tyranny? Can a democratic citizenry be reclaimed from centuries of miseducation?

Therefore the central aim of this chapter is to illustrate how the refusal to name and attend to the ongoing effects of the colonialist project not only threatens the vitality of indigenous peoples but also the viability of the democratic project and our ability to envision a socially and environmentally sustainable future. Insofar as the rebranding of colonization presupposed colonialist pedagogies of disconnection, linearity and hierarchy; at the heart of a pedagogy of the dispossessed are the constructs of interconnection, circularity and community. Therefore, the structure of this paper reflects a roadmap – connecting the terrains of colonization, empire and globalization with the experiences of Indigenous and other colonized peoples. Specifically, the map begins with demonstrating the connections between the Bush Empire, 9-11, Iraq and the experiences of the peoples of the Ninth ward in New Orleans. From there, connections between current constructions of empire and colonization are made by interfacing the experiences of Indigenous peoples with those of the citizens of New Orleans. Finally, a pedagogical framework is developed that attends to the experiences of colonization and dispossession as well as to the need for building transnational and transcultural coalitions.

MAPPING THE ROAD OF EMPIRE: FROM IRAQ TO NEW ORLEANS

Critical scholars McLaren and Farahmandpur (2005) note September 11, 2001 as the day when "the United States was able to find the political and ideological justification to maintain and expand its imperial dominance" (p. 4). Empires, however, are not built in one day. Indeed, the groundwork for the Bush empire was being laid a full decade before, in 1992 when Paul Wolfowitz then undersecretary for defense, began drafting a policy plan for the Pentagon (a.k.a. the Wolfowitz doctrine). The discourse was so strident that even the President expressed his reservations if not disapproval. Then, *The New York Times* leaked an early draft the doctrine, creating a firestorm of controversy over the ominous and boldly expressed aspirations for world domination:

> Our first objective is to prevent the re-emergence of a new rival...(which) requires that we endeavor to prevent any hostile power from dominating a region whose resources would, under consolidated control, be sufficient to generate global power...There are three additional aspects to this objective: First the U.S must show the leadership necessary to establish and protect a new order...Second, in the non-defense areas, we must account sufficiently for the interests of the advanced industrial nations to discourage them from challenging our leadership or seeking to overturn the established political and economic order. Finally, we must maintain the mechanisms for deterring potential competitors from even aspiring to a larger regional or global role. (Tyler, 1992)

After the firestorm, the doctrine was rewritten with less stridency. In collaboration with the neo-conservative think tank Project for a New American Century (PNAC), the document was eventually released as "Rebuilding America's Defenses: Strategies, Forces and Reasons for a New Century" (2000). In this version Wolfowitz and his co-authors (including Lewis "Scooter" Libby, Donald Rumsfeld and Dick Cheney) retained their global aspirations while lamenting that only an inimitable crisis could provide the requisite fear and urgency to rationalize such a Machiavellian project. Indeed, they conceded that "the process of transformation" was likely to be a long one "absent some catastrophic and catalyzing event like a new Pearl Harbor" (2000). In other words, just as political philosophers Hardt and Negri (2001) theorize, empire building presupposes crisis.

One year later the nation watched in horror as two hijacked planes crashed into the twin towers of the World Trade Center, another into the Pentagon and a fourth into a field in rural Pennsylvania. All tolled nearly 3,000[2] civilians were murdered that day. Like Pearl Harbor, this "catalyzing event" thrust the nation into a state of crisis and from there it was a short road to the Axis of Evil. Once the center of the controversy, Wolfowitz's entreaty for a Pax Americana was now an easy sell to the American public. Now packaged in the language of "American leadership," the architects of PNAC set their sites on the ultimate goal – to achieve "benevolent global hegemony."[3]

Specifically, the final PNAC report delineates a four-point plan calling for: (1) militarization through the rapid and significant increase of defense spending, (2) unilateralism, through the creation of intricate webs of power (a.k.a. cronyism), (3) privatization and the globalization of free-market fundamentalism, and (4) cultural hegemony.[4] The document concludes, "Such a Reganite policy of military strength and moral clarity may not be fashionable today. But it is necessary if the United States is to build on the successes of this past century and ensure our security and our greatness in the next" (PNAC, 2000). Bush's initial ambivalence toward PNAC instantly gave way as he moved to adopt its principles, one by one, as the foundation for his "global war on terror."

Currently the cost of the war is estimated to be between $453 billion and $1.2 trillion dollars in direct cost. In addition to this money, several organizations such as the national Priorities Project (NPP) and the Center for American Progress are calculating and calling attention to the indirect or "opportunity costs" of war. That is, as we spend billions of dollars on the war, what other national priorities (i.e. education, health care, public housing) are we not investing in or ignoring? Perhaps no other event illustrates the "opportunity costs" of the war as graphically as Hurricane Katrina with New Orleans caught in the crosshairs of the PNAC plan of militarization, cronyism, privatization and cultural hegemony.

First, in the rapid militarization following 9–11, several government agencies involving protection and security, including the Federal Emergency Management Agency (FEMA), underwent a massive reorganization in order to create the Department of Homeland Security (DHS). As part of this process FEMA's budget was increased to $6.6 billion but $3.5 billion of that was earmarked for counter-terrorism, representing an actual net decrease for emergency management. In addition, federal funding of FEMA's mitigation programs (i.e. those designed to protect people and property from disaster) was cut in half and then subjected to privatization, leaving communities to compete against each other for pre-disaster mitigation dollars (Elliston, 2004). In response to this shift away from mitigation, many long-time disaster specialists at FEMA left in droves.

Political analyst Patrick Martin writes, "The agency became a dumping ground for political hacks whose only principal job qualification was previous service in the Bush election campaigns of 2000 and 2004" (2005, 2). For example, the newly appointed FEMA director was Joe Allbaugh, Bush's ex-chief of staff in Texas. Then, despite the fact that Allbaugh was forced to resign after one year due to lack of experience with emergency management, Bush appointed Michael Brown, a college friend of Allbaugh's, and director of judging for the Arabian Horse Association. Martin (2005) reports that, over a year before Hurricane Katrina the union representing FEMA employees sent a letter to Congress warning that as experienced emergency managers get supplanted by "politically connected contractors and novice employees with little background or knowledge… professionalism diminishes (and) FEMA is gradually losing its ability to function and help disaster victims" (p. 2).

FEMA veterans also expressed growing concern over the increasing practice of outsourcing and privatizing essential services. One program administrator commented that such practices not only put them in the position of having to compete for their own jobs but also of having to prove that they could do them cheaper stating, "And when it comes to handling disaster, cheaper is not always better" (Elliston, 2004). A full-year before Katrina FEMA director James Lee Witt testified at a Congressional hearing, "I am extremely concerned that the ability of our nation to prepare for and respond to disasters has been sharply eroded…I hear from emergency mangers, local and state leaders, and first responders nearly every day that the FEMA they knew and worked well with has now disappeared" (Elliston, 2004). Finally, in a cruel irony, one disaster expert warned, "If you talk to FEMA and emergency management people around the country, people have almost been hoping for a major natural disaster like a hurricane, just to remind the DHS and administration that there are other big things–even bigger things than al Qaeda" (Elliston, 2005).

Clearly, despite revisionist efforts by the Bush administration, the tragedy of Hurricane Katrina was neither "natural" nor unpredictable. In addition to the warnings issued by inside officials there were numerous others that made their way to the public sector. Beginning in 2001, (four years before Katrina) FEMA issued a report registering its concerns about the impact of restructuring in the name of "Homeland Security" which was followed by similar reports in the Houston Chronicle and Scientific American. The following year, the New Orleans-based *Times Picayune* (2002) published a five-part series detailing the devastation that could descend upon the city in the event of a category four or five hurricane. Then, two years later, in 2004, *Times-Picayune* reporter, Sheila Grissett similarly warned of the impact of cuts in federal funding on hurricane preparedness. She wrote, "Levee-raising is only part of the flood-related work that has stopped since the federal government began reducing Corps of Engineers appropriations in 2001," when "money was diverted to homeland security, the fight against terrorism and the war in Iraq" (Grissett, 2004). One year after Grissett's incisive report, on August 29, 2005, the Big Easy became the other big thing, "bigger than Al Queda" that had been envisioned, gravely illustrating to the world the lethal cost of empire building and its "new strategies of power." Though we all paid the price for the appointment of Michael Brown as FEMA director, a depleted National Guard and the funneling of tax dollars to the Department of Defense, the peoples of the Gulf Coast paid with their lives.

THE PRESENT AS PAST: RED AS THE NEW BLACK

Perhaps the view that Katrina was no "natural" disaster is old news, but to the best of my knowledge the fact that it was also no historical anomaly has remained under-theorized. That is, contrary to the hyperbolic discourse of "empire," I maintain that the post-Katrina debacle was not an unprecedented catastrophe but rather the logical and intended consequence of colonization. Indeed, as the nation looked on, held captive by the shocking images of mostly black bodies being herded through the streets and corralled in the Superdome, it seemed like dejá vu all over again. But as the tragedy unfolded in real time, I felt alone in my remembrance. Each time the thousands of news stories, headlines and exposés failed to make the connection to the forced removal of Native peoples, I felt a deeper sense of emptiness. To me, the silence was stunning especially given that the connections seemed so painfully obvious.

This was not the first time the U.S. government engaged a policy of forced removal.[5] In 1838 President Andrew Jackson ordered the removal of thousands of Cherokee men, women, and children, including the elderly and infirmed. Federal troops and State militia rounded up Indians like cattle, giving them only moments to gather belongings. The masses were herded into makeshift forts with minimal provisions and as they were forced to walk thousands of miles in the hot summer sun, order was maintained at gunpoint. As the Cherokee marched westward, white looters followed close behind ransacking homesteads for their share of the spoils of war. Under the cold watch of callous army commanders, the human death toll in the first waves of removal was unimaginable. In the end, nearly 4,000 Cherokee met their death on the journey known as the Trail of Tears or in Cherokee, Nunna daul Tsuny, "The Trail Where They Cried." Who could have predicted that over a century and a half later, so many people would cry again? In other words, the forced encampment and evacuation (read: removal) of the citizens of the Ninth Ward followed by the grossly incompetent attempts at reconstruction is nothing but a twenty-first century remix of colonization.

Given this history, everything in New Orleans from the makeshift encampments with limited provisions, to the brutality of the state and federal officials and the rising death toll with each passing day were familiar. It was devastating to watch the already fractured families endure the violent and chaotic process of forced removal and dispersion to unknown lands with no guarantee of return. Now, in the aftermath of removal, the nation lays witness as the cold "banality of evil" and rituals of colonization take hold. First, there is the bureaucracy of FEMA rolls, which like the Dawes rolls of the 19th century only recognize the head of household for the receipt of relief funds. Moreover, after execution of this specious process, all "surplus lands" were similarly released to profit hungry land prospectors (i.e. realtors) primed to capitalize on the so-called unclaimed lands. In addition, the newly formed reservations of FEMA trailer camps (i.e. Renaissance Village) many of which have been found to be laced with asbestos, and the influx of missionaries enthralled by the prospect of (re)civilizing the "new" frontier are all redolent of Indian policy.

Unfortunately, just as with other aspects of the infrastructure, the opportunity to "reinvent public education" in New Orleans was also seized upon by disaster profiteers looking to transform the public school system into a "market-driven smorgasbord" (Dingerson, 2007). Days after the levees broke the Heritage Foundation was on the ground advocating for vouchers and "market solutions" to the city's education problems (Flaherty, 2006). Three months after Katrina, the state legislature pronounced 83% of the city-run public schools as "failing" and seized control for the next five years. In so doing, the legislature opened the door for the Bush administration to pump in millions of dollars specifically earmarked for the expansion of charter schools (Waldman, 2007). One of the major casualties of this massive reorganization was the Orleans Parish School Board. Stripped of its domain and financing, it was forced to fire all 7,500 of its teachers and support staff, effectively breaking the teachers' union.[6] The end result was "the fastest makeover of an urban school system in American history" (Waldman, 2007, p. 88).

By the start of the 2006 school year, 53 New Orleans schools were in operation: the Orleans Parish School Board was running five, the Louisiana Department of Education[7] operating 17, and the rest, or 60% of the remaining schools were being run by independent management corporations mostly from outside the state. Though New Orleans was barely a presence in the charter-school movement before the storm, it now has the highest proportion of charter schools than any other city in America (Waldman, 2007). As one member of the state school board remarks, New Orleans is "the most market driven system in the United States" or as a National Public Radio (NPR) correspondent remarks, it is the "country's leading laboratory for charter school experiments" (October 3, 2006).

Once again, while the discourse intimates that the landscape of post-Katrina schools represents the first wide scale, federally funded, experiment in public education, it closely parallels the history of Indian education. The devastation of infrastructure, the seizure by federal agents, and the dedication of significant amounts of capital – both monetary and human – to launch an educational experiment are all familiar themes. Native educational historian Tsianna Lomawaima writes, "Indian schools were established as laboratories for a grand experiment in cultural cleansing…(and) reservations were envisioned as laboratories to implement the scientifically phrased project of 'elevating a race'" (Lomawaima, 2006 p. 4). Though some might perceive it as a stretch to label what is happening in New Orleans as a "cultural cleansing," the city is, without question, serving as a laboratory, with multiple players envisioning either an erasure or "elevation" of its predominantly black and poor population. Tacitly, this is happening through the imposition of market forces but also more explicitly through the policies and practices of outside interests looking to actualize their vision of a "reinvented" school system.

In terms of market forces, the devastation of New Orleans' infrastructure has created a level of economic dependency similar to that of many American Indian reservations. Just like "Rez Indians," citizens of the Gulf are learning that such a level of dependency generates a subordinating effect that leaves the dispossessed at the mercy of a myriad of powers. In particular, venture capitalists, private entrepreneurs, liberal do-gooders and zealous missionaries have descended upon the city. In the free marketplace of goods and ideas, the modern day "pioneers" of the new frontier – all peddling salvation to the indigent in one form or another – engage in fierce competition for both dollars and souls. Waldman (2007) describes the scene as a "pedagogical bazaar" (p. 92) with vendors and contractors bivouacked on Canal Street selling wares to the assemblage of educational prospectors. Virtually everything is for sale from food and janitorial services to reading and math programs, with the real premium being placed on human capital.

Specifically, the massive firing of teachers and staff created a sellers market in New Orleans. While under different circumstances this might be good for the labor force, after Katrina rents in the city rose as much as 70% and nearly 80% of the city's licensed childcare centers were lost, making the city virtually unliveable for returning teachers (Waldman, 2007). Moreover, the "free" market principles of supply and demand compel the more qualified teachers to go to the highest bidders – the well-funded for-profit charter schools and not the public schools. Meanwhile the young, inexperienced, middle class imports, though dedicated to "helping" the public schools, quickly learn that good intentions and lofty ideals are not self-sustaining. Money, however, isn't the only issue as Leigh Dingerson, an educational policy analyst doing on-the-ground work in New Orleans reports, "This week, at Frederick Douglass High School, I read students the text of an advertisement for New Orleans teachers that…read: 'Certified teachers will teach in the city's charter schools. Uncertified teachers will teach in the Recovery (Public) School district'" (Dingerson, 2007). One student's response to this news was to shake her head, hang it down and mutter, "It's like we're experiments" (Dingerson, 2007). As a result, just as it is in many reservation communities, Waldman reports that the quitting ratios of teachers have come to exceed the hiring ratios.

Finally, in addition to staffing issues, the already traumatized students of New Orleans have been forced to deal with the militarization of their city and schools. According to Waldman (2007) the operating assumption is that the mostly Black and poor students need "to be menaced, intimidated, (and) tamed," into order (Waldman, 2007, p. 98). Indeed, in preparation for returning students, "the city was on war footing," with National Guard unit's ordered to be "very visible in their Humvees" and do aggressive patrolling (p. 98). Some schools were described as having tighter security protocols than the average airport, with the security guard to student ratios equal to or higher than the teacher to student ratios (Waldman, 2007). Militarization was also endemic to the history of American Indian education. From its initial structural location in the Department of War to the use of military officers as personnel, the military presence in Native education has been pervasive. Students wore uniforms, donned military haircuts, given military ranks and, subjected to corporal punishment. If the comparison of New Orleans public schools to 19th century American Indian education seems overstated, consider the account of one New Orleans teacher who works at a school that employs 39 security guards, three police officers, and only 27 teachers. She notes that during one (unremarkable) week, there were three fights in two days between the young and untrained security guards and the students. A student at the same school remarked: "Being at John Mac feels like I'm in prison...The bus ride to school feels like a trip from court to jail" (Flaherty, 2006).

In the end, the real crisis is the unseemly coupling of education with neoliberal and neoconservative policies and practices. While undermining public education and, for that matter, teachers' unions, has long been the agenda of educational conservatives, until Hurricane Katrina, they lacked a "catalyzing event," their own crisis moment..."like another Pearl Harbor." Now, in the wake of catastrophe, it appears that the nation can add to the death/murder/genocide toll, the voluntary, systematic dismantling of the common school. The tangled web of independently operated educational experiments that have been erected in its place has driven the final nail into the coffin of local control, community ownership and the neighborhood school. In other words the forces of capitalism, fundamentalism, and white supremacy have colonized the sovereignty and self-determination of the peoples of New Orleans, especially the Ninth Ward. Under the neo-liberal agenda, concerned parents have been reduced to "customers," teachers to "vendors," and knowledge to human capital. In terms of what this trend means for the future of public schools, policy analyst Leigh Dingerson is worth quoting at length:

> The dismantling of the New Orleans public schools has allowed us to witness a radical transformation of American public education in a single city in a single year. But this transformation is not confined to the Crescent City. Across the country the same "reformers" that engineered the dismantling of New Orleans' schools are working to do the same elsewhere. As in New Orleans, universal access is disappearing into networks of schools that can and do shape their student bodies, that are minimally accountable to society as a whole, and that further sort, separate, and pick apart community. These schools continue to receive substantial public and private funding, while traditional public school districts struggle. We believe the implications of this trend are evident in New Orleans. It would be a mistake to ignore them. It would be a travesty to ignore the words of the young people and dedicated teachers who call us to a loftier vision.

Though Dingerson's words are powerful, they also rebrand the federal and corporate domination of education as a recent "trend" rather than as the extension of the history of colonization. Yet clearly, the dispossession of the peoples of New Orleans, the refusal of their right of return, and denial of self-determination parallels the colonization of indigenous peoples. Recognition of this connection transforms the issue of sovereignty from a particular indigenous problem to one shared by all citizens of a democratic nation.

Perhaps the not-so-quite-silver lining of 9–11 and Katrina, is that there seems to be a growing recognition of our interconnection and of the broader relevance of sovereignty and self-determination. The once omnipotent nation of American dreams is fast becoming a caricature of itself, so preoccupied with its own importance that it is mistaking the narcissistic struggles of empire with the more dignified labor of nation building. One need not be a historian to realize the qualitative difference between the defining moments of nation building (i.e. the American Revolution, the Civil War, and the Civil Rights Movement) and the exploits of empire (i.e. Guantanamo Bay, the war in Iraq, the Abramoff and Gonzales scandals). For centuries, it was the particular experience of Native Americans to be subject to the random and militaristic powers of the federal government, to live under the continual threat of eminent domain (A.K.A. detribalization, termination, and/or plenary power), and to be corralled onto reservations of poverty, despair, and dependency. Now, in the wake of Katrina, even the most callous among us are beginning to wonder whether its possible to disperse the poor and colonized far and wide enough – to build the walls high and fast enough – to maintain the quixotic comfort zones of the investor class. Eventually, levees break, tyrannies tumble and the subaltern reveal – the empire has no clothes.

EDUCATION AND EMPIRE: COLONIALIST PEDAGOGIES IN THE 21ST CENTURY

Throughout history American schools have served as a battleground for broader political struggles and this era of empire proves to be no exception. In essence, the Bush agenda for education has been to overlay the same four-point plan for "benevolent global hegemony" onto the American school system. That is, advocating for market reforms and privatization primarily in the guise of charter schools and voucher systems. In theory, the Bush plan for privatizing public education subjects schools to the logic of the marketplace, placing them in direct competition with each other in their efforts to attract and retain potential consumers (i.e. students). While this theory may appeal to some, in practice, the supposed "fair" market principles guiding "competition" are undermined by the fact that the private venture firms backing the charter and other for-profit industries are well funded and politically connected in ways that public schools have never been. Thus the "competition" is neither free nor fair. In addition, the lure of potential profit and power has fueled a proliferation of policies (i.e. new strategies of power) that games the system in favor of privatization, the most notorious of which is the No Child Left Behind Act (NCLB).[8] As schools lose money and students and communities lose their neighborhood schools, it raises the question, who or what lies at the end of the money trail? The answer: a who's who among corporate and Bush family elites.

For example, in 1990, a commission funded by the (Bill) Gates Foundation issued a the report *"America's Choice: High Skills or Low Wages,"* which argued that the United States could only remain competitive in the global market if public schools adopted a standards-based approach using standardized tests to enforce accountability of students and teachers. Then, in 1999, the President's older brother Neil Bush (banned from banking activities for his role in the Savings and Loan scandal) founded *Ignite Incorporated,* an interactive e educational software company, that sells a program designed to help students prepare for standardized tests. In 2001, President Bush spearheaded the passage of the *No Child Left Behind Act,* calling for emphasis on highstakes testing and standards based education. Five years later, *Ignite Incorporated's* profits were estimated at $5 million, including a "charitable donation" of over $100,000 from the trustees of the Houston Independent School District, and profits gained from the statewide pilot program in Florida where brother Jeb Bush is governor. Always one to pay it forward, profit sharers in the new knowledge industry include Bill Bennett's "virtual academy," K12 Inc., Kaplan, Pearson, the Educational Testing Service (ETS), McGraw Hill, White Hat management, Houghton-Mifflin, and Harcourt – all corporations identified as "Bush stocks" by Wall Street.

In the final analysis, the policies and practices of neoliberalism and neoconservatism have had the same paradoxical impact on schools that they have on the economy. That is, while professing the rhetoric of small government they have launched the most cumbersome federal educational policy (NCLB) in the history of schooling; while promising the proliferation of choice, they have deeply constrained alternatives; and while pledging allegiance to the "fair" market strategies of deregulation and privatization, they have greatly exacerbated inequality.

While the "havoc of capitalism" has impeded education nationwide, the impact on poor and urban communities has been grave and disproportionate. For example, long before Katrina, New Orleans was well known as a city with one of the worst (read: corrupt) educational systems in the country. In a city with a 40 percent illiteracy rate, where over 50 percent of the black ninth graders failed to graduate high school in four years and with a per-pupil expenditure significantly below the national average,[9] it should be no surprise that before Katrina, 74 percent of eighth graders failed to demonstrate "basic" skills in English/Language Arts and 70 percent scored below "basic" in math. In a political and educational climate where such numbers are used to determine a child's worth, it is important to peel back the layers of "crisis" to assess the "secret adventures of order" (Borges cited in Torres 1998, p. 1) and the inner workings of empire.

At present one of the most incisive critiques of capitalist education comes from revolutionary critical theorists (list) who reject liberal/postmodern pedagogies and their abandonment of emancipatory/anti-capitalist struggles. Given the relentless march of global capitalism they argue that such pedagogies have irresponsibly substituted the project of radical, social transformation with a politics of representation. As Scatamburlo and McLaren (2002) note, to remain "enamored with the 'cultural' and seemingly blind to the 'economic," in this moment of late capitalism is not simply an act of ignoring, but one of complicity (pp. 4–5). They also expose the politics of educational agendas that remain content with textual analysis as social critique, ignoring the inhumanity of the "real existing world." That is, the 37 million people in the United States living below the poverty line, most of whom reside in the South where Louisiana remains the second poorest state in the Nation and New Orleans retains the highest percentage of child poverty. In the face of this revolutionary critical theorists insist that the inherent contradictions of capitalism continue to take us further away from "democratic accountability" and toward what "Rosa Luxemborg (1919) referred to as an age of 'barbarism'" (McLaren & Farahmandpur, 2001, p. 277). From this vantage point such theorists argue that we do not simply need a multicultural education for equity and social justice, but rather an anticapitalist education for a socialist democracy.

TOWARDS A PEDAGOGY OF THE DISPOSSESSED

The principles of revolutionary critical pedagogy are clearly relevant to colonized peoples and the need for pedagogies of disruption, intervention and affirmative action. In particular, the foregrounding of capitalist relations as the axis of exploitation helps to frame the history of indigenous peoples as one of dispossession and not simply cultural oppression, and the trenchant critique of postmodernism reveals the current obsession with identity politics as a dangerous distraction from the imperatives of social transformation. That being said, as articulated in *Red Pedagogy* (Grande, 2004), the Western foundation of revolutionary critical pedagogy (particularly its Marxist roots) presents significant tensions for scholars working to develop decolonizing pedagogies. Specifically, even a "rematerialized" critical project of democratization remains defined through Western epistemological frames, carrying particular assumptions about: human beings and their relationship to the rest of nature, the view of progress, and the primacy of the rational process.

The implications of such tensions are myriad, giving rise to competing notions of governance, economy, and identity. Moreover, in *Red Pedagogy* I argue that, beyond an anticapitalist pedagogy, colonized peoples require a praxis that enables the dismantling of *colonialist* forces, that is, a pedagogy that also cultivates a sense of community agency and spiritual solidarity. Thus, while the tools of revolutionary critical pedagogy elicit a powerful critique of capitalism and other hegemonic forces, the question remains whether its Western roots preclude it from disrupting the deep structures of the colonialist project.

While I do not equivocate the ravages of capitalism, a *Red* critique of critical pedagogy decenters it as the central struggle concept and replaces it with colonization. This fundamental difference shifts the pedagogic goal away from the critique and transformation of capitalist social relations of production (i.e. *democratization*), toward the critique and transformation of colonialist relations of exploitation (i.e. *sovereignty*). This is not to say that the political/pedagogical projects of democratization and sovereignty are mutually exclusive; on the contrary, in this new era of empire, it may be that sovereignty offers democracy its only lifeline.

Such is the premise and promise of *Red Pedagogy*. It is an indigenous pedagogy that operates at the crossroads of Western theory and indigenous knowledge. In bridging these epistemological worlds, *Red Pedagogy* asks that as we examine our own communities, policies, and practices, we take seriously the notion that to know ourselves as revolutionary agents is more than an act of understanding who we are. It is an act of reinventing ourselves, of validating our overlapping cultural identifications and relating them to the materiality of social life, power relations, and localities of place. As such, *Red Pedagogy* is, by definition, a space of engagement. It is the liminal and intellectual borderlands where indigenous and nonindigenous scholars encounter one another, working to remember, redefine, and reverse the devastation of the original colonialist "encounter." The main imperative before us as citizens is to reject capitalist forms of schooling and to acquire the grammar of empire as just *one* tool for unthinking our colonial roots.

For teachers and students, this means that we must be willing to act as agents of transgression, posing critical questions and engaging dangerous discourse. It means calling into question the hegemonic discourses of unilateralism, monoculturalism, English-only, consumerism, nationalism, and free-market fundamentalism that construct education as a privilege and consider instead the implications of multilateralism, multicultural, multilingualism, contingency and coalition that reasserts education as the right of a people. In the end it also means undertaking a deep examination of the colonialist project and its implications for all of us, understanding that at root is the quest for a reconciliation of the relationship between democracy (the rights of a nation) and sovereignty (the rights of a people). Such is the epistemological basis of *Red Pedagogy*. Specifically, it offers the following ways of thinking around and through the challenges facing American education in the twenty-first century, in particular our need to define a pedagogy for decolonization:

- *Red Pedagogy* is primarily a pedagogical project wherein pedagogy is understood as inherently relational, political, cultural, spiritual, intellectual, and perhaps most importantly, place-based.
- *Red Pedagogy* is fundamentally rooted in indigenous knowledge and praxis. It is particularly interested in knowledge that furthers understanding and analyses of colonization.
- *Red Pedagogy* searches for ways it can both deepen and be deepened by engagement with critical and revolutionary theories and praxis.
- *Red pedagogy* promotes an education for decolonization where the root metaphors of relationship, sovereignty, and balance provide the foundation.
- *Red Pedagogy* is a project that interrogates both democracy and indigenous sovereignty, working to define the relationship between them.
- *Red Pedagogy* actively cultivates a praxis of collective agency. That is, *Red Pedagogy* aims to build transcultural and transnational solidarities among indigenous peoples and others committed to reimagining a sovereign space free of imperialist, colonialist, and capitalist exploitation.
- *Red Pedagogy* is grounded in hope. This is, however, not the future-centered hope of the Western imagination, but rather a hope that lives in contingency with the past—one that trusts the beliefs and understandings of our ancestors, the power of traditional knowledge, and the possibilities of new understandings.

Development of the above principles emerged through a series of conversations with Indigenous scholars working on developing pedagogies of decolonization in differing contexts, specifically in New York City, in Aoteroa, New Zealand, and on the Rosebud reservation in South Dakota. Though approaches differ, the principles above cut across groups and communities. With regard to delineating more specific approaches related to *Red Pedagogy* and its use in classrooms, it is evident that, like other critical theories, *Red Pedagogy* is not a methodology but rather a consciousness and way of being in/reading the world. As such, it is not a something that can be "done" by teachers or "to" students, nor is it a technique that can be lifted, decontextualized, and applied.

It is rather a way of thinking about knowledge and the processes of teaching and learning as it emerges within and through relationships – between and among students, teachers, communities, and places.

Pedagogies aimed at decolonization are inherently place-based. That is rooted, in the tribal or local knowledges/politics, in a manner that takes Freire's notion of reading the word and the world to a different level, understanding these as processes that are not simply interrelated but rather one in the same. While other critical theorists have constructed "spatialized" critical pedagogies (Gruenewald, 2003, Harvey, 1996, Massey, 1994, Soja, 1989) that recognize "how relationships of power and domination are inscribed in material places" (Gruenewald, 2003, p. 5). Pedagogies of decolonization differ in that they recognize the ways that power works through places to either limit or expand possibilities, to be either empowering or disempowering. In other words, it recognizes that place/nature/environment/land has an ontology and epistemology of its own that remains in a dialogical relationship with the rest of "nature," including human beings. In working to articulate this and other aspects of Red Pedagogy I have been continually reminded of the limitations of the English language.

For example there is no word in English to describe the world, outside of human existence, that recognizes its own agency/being-ness. In Quechua, the word to describe the earth as being – *pacha* – is a different than the word used for ground or land – *allpa*. *Pacha* can also be used to describe transitions in time, as in *pachacuti*, which refers to a cataclysm, an earthquake or the end of an era, but is can also be used to simply describe being from the earth. *Hanan Pacha*, is the upper earth, meaning sky or heaven, but also the world of spirits; *Kay Pacha*, is this earth but also implies one being on the earth; and *Urqu Pacha* means lower earth, underneath the earth or also the world of the dead (Huaman, 20003). Moreover, as Quechua scholar, Elizabeth Sumida Huaman notes, "nothing in the Andean world is finite. Instead, life and death are fluid, always occurring and necessary parts of creation, and our language describes this process" (Huaman, 2003). My experience in talking across other indigenous communities is that language is central to developing their own particular approaches to *decolonizing* pedagogies. Among the most successful and promising are the Kaupapa Maori initiative in New Zealand, anchored by Linda Thuiwai-Smith and Graham Smith.

According to (Smith, 1997), Kaupapa Māori builds on the validity and legitimacy of Māori language, knowledge and culture, bridging the potential of critical theory with the logic of 'organic' Kaupapa Māori practice to formulate an intervention strategy that critiques and reconstitutes the notions of conscientization, resistance, and transformative praxis in different configurations (p. 65, 97). To be clear about the relationship between Kaupapa Maori and critical theory, however, Pihama (2001) notes, "Kaupapa Māori theory does not depend on Critical Theory for its existence just as Critical Theory does not depend on Kaupapa Māori theory for its existence. Kaupapa Māori theory is founded in this land, Aotearoa. Critical Theory is founded in Europe. A strong Kaupapa Māori theoretical framework must be cognisant of our historical and cultural realities, in all their complexities" (p. 88). Hermes (2005) similarly emphasizes the importance of language as a tool to bridge "the artificial gap between academic and cultural curriculum" (p. 53). She writes, "Students grounded in their heritage language will be able to learn other course content without fear of assimilation. The reclaiming of language could propel the gains of the culture-based movement far beyond superficially adding fragmented pieces of cultural knowledge to the existing structure. Schools based on Indigenous languages create a cultural context—a filter through which any content can be viewed" (p. 53).

I would argue that the principles of *Kaupapa Maori, Red Pedagogy* and/or other decolonizing pedagogies have relevance to colonized communities, knowledgeable of their own histories and connections to place through language and relationship, whether those communities are in the Ninth ward, the South Bronx, or Appalachia. Because, in the end, a *Red Pedagogy* is about engaging the development of "community-based power" in the interest of "a responsible political, economic, and spiritual society." That is, the power to live out "active presences and *survivances* rather than an illusionary democracy." Vizenor's notion of survivance signifies a state of being beyond "survival, endurance, or a mere response to colonization," and toward "an active presence…an active repudiation of dominance, tragedy and victimry."

In rethinking the tragedies of 9–11 and Hurricane Katrina, I find the notion of survivance to be both humbling and poignant. These tragedies speak to our collective need to decolonize our minds, bodies and souls, to push back against empire, and reclaim what it means to be a people of sovereign mind and body. The hope is that such a Red Pedagogy will help shape schools and processes of learning around a decolonial imaginary where Indigenous and non-Indigenous peoples work in solidarity to build transcultural and transnational coalitions to construct a nation free of imperialist, colonialist, and capitalist exploitation. The stories of the peoples of the Ninth Ward, the World Trade Center, the South Bronx, Red Lake (Ojibwe Nation), Jena and other colonized communities serve as a reminder to all of us that just as the specter of colonialism haunts the collective soul of America, so too does the more hopeful spirit of indigeneity.

NOTES

[1] Rebranding is the marketing strategy by which a product or service is marketed or distributed with a different identity. Rebranding often occurs when one company acquires another.

[2] It should be noted that official death tolls of 9/11 do not include the estimated dozens of undocumented workers who also perished in the attacks.

[3] This term first appears in a 1996 article in Foreign Affairs Magazine co-authored by Bill Kristol and Robert Kagan who warned that "conservatives will not be able to govern America over the long term if they fail to offer a more elevated vision of America's international role. What should that role be? Benevolent global hegemony."

[4] The four strategies are actually worded as follows: We need to increase defense spending significantly if we are to carry out our global responsibilities today and modernize our armed forces for the future; We need to strengthen our ties to democratic allies and to challenge regimes hostile to our interests and values; We need to promote the cause of political and economic freedom abroad; We need to accept responsibility for America's unique role in preserving and extending an international order friendly to our security, our prosperity and our principles.

[5] In an article in History Today, "Reconstructing the American South," historian Jim Downs, draws parallels between New Orleans during the Reconstruction era in the South and after Hurricane Katrina. He particularly notes the similarities between the massive dislocation of emancipated slaves and the current "evacuation" of peoples of the Ninth Ward. One could also point to the forced encampment of Asian Americans during World War II as a similar example.

[6] It should be noted that the teachers and employees of AFT Local 527 (originally established in 1937 to represent Black teachers) and the United Teachers of New Orleans (UTNO) have a long histories of activism.

[7] Prior to Hurricane Katrina, the Louisiana Department of Education had never operated any schools.

[8] Under NCLB, public schools must achieve Annual Yearly Progress (AYP) as determined by a series of standardized measures, primarily test scores on standardized exams. Based on these measures schools achieve a categoric designation of either meets AYP or "Needs Improvement." If after fiver years of limited intervention, a school still does not meet AYP, they are subjected to a restructuring process. While such strategies might appear as the logical consequence of a school system in "crisis," further examination suggests that it is the strategies that have compelled the crisis and not the other way around. Consider for example, the effect of NCLB on one representative school district in Ohio. In this particular district, schools must achieve AYP on 112 different measures. If nothing else, the law of averages virtually guarantees that some schools will come up short on at least one or two measures which is all it takes for the entire school district and/or a particular school to be designated as "needs improvement" – which then leads to a series of yearly mandates/punishments that includes the loss of funding and "alternative restructuring" (i.e. privatization). As a result, in 2006, this one Ohio school district lost over $700,000 at the hands of NCLB (Greanoff, 2006).

[9] NO $7,000, national average $8,500, highest at $14,000.

REFERENCES

Alfred, T. (1999). *Peace, power, righteousness: An Indigenous manifesto.* Oxford, UK: Oxford University Press.

Allman, P. (2001). *Critical education against global capital: Karl Marx and revolutionary critical education.* Westport, CT: Bergin & Garvey.

Arendt, H. (1963). *Eichman's Jerusalem: A report on the banality of evil.* New York: Penguin Classic Books.

Biggs, B. (Ed.). (2006). *Big easy money: Disaster profiteering on the American gulf coast.* Oakland, CA: CorpWatch.

Bowers, C. A. (1993, Spring). Can critical pedagogy be greened? *Educational Studies 34*(1), 11–21.

Deloria, V., Jr., & Lytle, C (1984). *The nations within: The past and future of American Indian sovereignity.* Austin, TX: University of Texas Press.

Deloria, V., Jr. (1983). *American Indians, American justice.* Austin, TX: University of Texas Press.

Dingerson, L. (2007). Playing school in Katrina's wake. Retrieved March 21, 2007, from http://www.tompaine.com/

Donnelly, T. (2000). *Rebuilding America's defenses: Strategy, forces and resources, for a new century.* Washington, DC: Project for the New American Century.

Downs, J. (2006). Reconstructing the American south – after Katrina. *History Today, 56*(1), 16–18.

Dyson, M. E. (2006). *Come hell or high water: Hurricane Katrina and the color of disaster.* New York: Basic Books.

Elliston, J. (2004, September 22). Disaster in the making. *The Independent Weekly.* Retrieved April 4, 2007, from http://www.indyweekly.com/gyrobase/.

Flaherty, J. (2006). Continuing crisis in New Orleans' schools. Retrieved March 21, 2007, from http://www.dissidentvoice.org/Oct06/Flaherty16.htm.

Frymer, B. (2005). Freire, alienation, and contemporary youth: Toward a pedagogy of everyday life. *InterActions: UCLA Journal of Education and Information Studies.* 1.2 Retrieved January 1, 2008, from http://repositories.cdlib.org/gseis/interactions/vol1/iss2/art3

Giroux, H. (2001). Pedagogy of the Depressed: Beyond the New Politics of Cynicism. *College Literature, 28*(3), 1–32.

Grande, S. (2004). *Red pedagogy: Native American social and political thought.* New York: Rowman and Littlefield.

Grissett, S. (2004). Shifting federal budget erodes protection from levees; Because of cuts, hurricane risk grows. *Times Picayune.* Retrieved March 22, 2007, from http://usliberals.about.com/od/theeconomyjobs/a/TimesPicayune.htm.

Greanoff, C. (2006). Schools left behind in 'No child left behind. *The Lakewood Observer.* Retrieved March 21, 2007, from http://lakewoodobserver.com/read/news/schools/2.

Gruenewald, D. (2003). The best of both worlds: A critical pedagogy of place. *Educational Researcher, 32*(4), 3–12.

Hardt, M., & Negri, A. (2001). *Empire.* Cambridge, MA: Harvard University Press.

Harvey, D. (1996). *Justice, nature, and the geography of difference.* Malden, MA: Blackwell.

Hauman, E. S. (2003). A Comparative Look at Yupiaq and Quechua Philosophies on War and Peace. Retrieved April 22, 2007, from http://www.gse.harvard.edu/~t656_web/peace/Basic pages/Site_map.htm.

Hermes, M. (2005). "Ma'iingan Is Just a Misspelling of the Word Wolf": A Case for Teaching Culture through Language. *Anthropology & Education Quarterly, 36*(1), 43–56.

Hendrix, J. B. (1983). Redbird Smith and the Nighthawk Keetowahs. *Journal of Cherokee Studies, 8*(1), 32.

Hursh, D. (2003). Neo-liberalism, markets and accountability: transforming education and undermining democracy in the United States and England. *Policy Futures in Education, 3*(1), 3–15.

Lomawaima, K. T., & McCarty, T. L. (2006). *To remain an Indian: Lessons in democracy from a century of Native American education.* New York: Teachers College Press.

Lyons, S. R. (2000). Rhetorical Sovereignty: What do American Indians Want from Writing? College. *Composition and Communication, 51*(3), 447–468.

Lyotard, J. (1984). *The Postmodern condition: A report on knowledge.* Minneapolis, MN: University of Minnesota Press.

Martin, P. (2005). Hurricane Katrina and the meaning of September, 11. Retrieved April 4, 2007, from http://www.wsws.org/.

Massey, D. (1994). *Space, place, and gender.* Minneapolis, MN: University of Minnesota Press.

Matza, D. (1999). Introduction. In N. Davis (Ed.), *Youth crisis: growing up in the high-risk society.* Westport, CT: Praeger.

McLaren, P. (2002). *Life in Schools: An Introduction to Critical Pedagogy in the Foundations of Education* (4th ed.). Boston: Allyn and Bacon.

McLaren, P., & Farahmandpur, R. (2001). The Globalization of Capitalism and the New Imperialism: Notes Toward a Revolutionary Pedagogy. *The Review of Education, Pedagogy, Cultural Studies, 23,* 271–315.

McLaren, P., & Farahmandpur, R. (2005). *Teaching against global capitalism and the new imperialism: A critical pedagogy.* New York: Rowman and Littlefield.

McQuaig, L. (2001). *All you can eat: Greed, lust and the new capitalism.* Toronto: Penguin Books.

Memmi, A. (1991). *The colonizer and colonized.* Boston: Beacon Press.

Mitchell, K. (2001). Education for Democratic Citizenship: Transnationalism, Multiculturalism, and the Limits of Liberalism. *Harvard Educational Review, 71*(1), 51–78.

Pihama, L. (2001). *Tihei mauri ora Honouring our voices: Mana wahine as kaupapa Maori theoretical framework.* Unpublished PhD. Auckland, NZ: The University of Auckland.

Scatamburlo-D'Annibale, V., & McLaren, P. (2002). The Strategic Centrality of Class in the Politics of 'Race' and 'Difference.' *Cultural Studies/Critical Methodologies, 3*(2), 148–175.

Soja, E. (1989). *Postmodern geographies: The reassertion of space in critical social theory.* London: Verso.

Smith, G. (1997). *Kaupapa Maori: Theory and Praxis.* Doctoral Dissertation. The Unviersity of Aukland, New Zealand: Auckland College of Education Publication.

Stewart-Harawira, M. (2005). *The new imperial order: Indigenous responses to globalization*. New Zealand: Huia Publishers.

Torres, C. (1998). *Democracy, Education and Multiculturalism: Dilemmas of Citizenship in a Global World*. Lanham, MD: Rowman and Littlefield.

Trask, H. K. (1996). Feminism and Indigenous Hawaiian Nationalism. *Signs: Journal of Women in Culture and Society, 21*(4), 906–916.

Tyler, P. (1992). Pentagon drops goal of blocking new superpowers. *New York Times*, May 23, 1992. Retrieved March 2, 2007, from http://work.colum.edu/~amiller/wolfowitz1992.htm.

Vizenor, G. (1993). The ruins of representation. *American Indian Quarterly, 17*, 1–7.

Waldman, A. (2007). Reading, writing, resurrection. *The Atlantic*, (January/February), 88–103.

Warrior, R. A. (1995). *Tribal secrets: Recovering American Indian intellectual traditions*. Minneapolis, MN: University of Minnesota.

NORM W. SHEEHAN, JANINE DUNLEAVY, TAMAR COHEN
AND SEAN MITCHELL

7. DENATURED SPIRIT: NEO-COLONIAL SOCIAL DESIGN

INTRODUCTION: NEO-COLONIAL PEDAGOGY

The Indigenous Knowledge approach described in this paper engages dialogue as a methodology for sharing knowledge. In these conversations between equals there is a free and flow of ideas that levels the normative structures of higher education. Therefore we present this chapter as a small group that includes research project students and their lecturer[1].

Bernstein defines pedagogy as cultural reproduction that operates through regulatory codes which are culturally determined positioning devices. These codes regulate relationships within social groups through communications that determine the legitimacy of individual consciousness. In this view ideology inheres in and regulates modes of relation[2].

Neo-colonial pedagogy currently prevails in Australian social life and its institutions through a particularly Australian version of racism that is founded in a pervasive ambivalence. We characterise this pedagogy as neo-colonial because it imposes white male values as held in common and validates this regulation through schemas informed by these same values. These divisive codes have become increasingly evident in public life, the media and higher education classrooms[3].

Neo-colonial pedagogy may be seen as a centring tradition within Western society that directs social perception away from others and their understandings. Such centring is evident in the orientation of neo-colonial activists to an imaginary morality from which they construct Indigenous culture and understandings as deviant and culpable in 'the Aboriginal problem'. Major media presentations sustain these constructions by promoting moral anxiety concerning the culture of Aboriginal others. Indeed our definition of this pedagogy as neo-colonial is based on the correlation between the early colonial moral concern for primitives and contemporary moral anxieties concerning Aboriginal culture that are created, popularized and then addressed by the proponents of these views[4].

These neo-colonial social orientations position the majority of our students to habitually deny, disparage or ignore Indigenous issues. This position is in contrast to Aboriginal life experience where there seems to be no respite from the structural, passive and lateral violence enacted by this social movement. So there are

*G. Martin, D. Houston, P. McLaren and J. Suoranta (eds.), The Havoc of Capitalism:
Publics, Pedagogies and Environmental Crisis, 99–116.*
© *2010 Sense Publishers. All rights reserved.*

two critical dimensions to our encounters with neo-colonial pedagogy. The first is the methodical condemnation and attempted erasure of Indigenous people and their understandings. The second is the systemic provision of opportunities for individuals in the majority population to believe in their own benevolence as they participate in these actions[5].

What is significant to us in this scrutiny is that all peoples who encounter neo-colonial pedagogy are regulated by it. While some are forced to the margins in ways that make them acutely aware of regulative processes others who see themselves as free, productive and benign are oriented to the centre through social codes that disable their awareness of regulation[6].

The social dominance we attempt to address is conspicuous in the Australian media and public discourses which problematize Aboriginal citizenry. The cultural centrality of this problematic representation *inside* Australian society is aligned with an innate movement which relegates the objects of this faux concern as being *outside* beyond the limits of social contact and moral normalcy. In this sense these representations constitute structurally embedded acts of social exclusion.

INSIDE & OUTSIDE KNOWLEDGE

Indigenous Knowledge (IK) proposes that the complex world of things in relation can be understood using a version of dualism that is best expressed by the conceptions *inside* and *outside*. This basic dualism is one aspect of IK which provides a way to conduct an introductory examination of relational structure. Western theorists have come to use this dualism in contemporary times as a basis for understanding the ways that humans position themselves and others. In Indigenous Australian cultures the conception of inside and outside knowledge is part of very long tradition of philosophic inquiry into the relational significance of being[7].

In this section I will adopt a textual device to convey a general and accessible Indigenous Knowledge (IK) understanding of the term structure. The IK version if this understanding will be presented as [structure] in the text to represent the different ontological basis for this understanding[8].

If we are outside in the cold and rain then being inside a warm dry cave becomes attractive. Our selection between *inside* or *outside* depends on our immediate needs and the conditions in each context. Thus in this context relational dualism there is no universal rule or truth that may be applied because environments are changeable and caves do not always meet our needs. It is simply a matter of deciding where it is best to be or how we might best position ourselves. The IK proposal is that in this choice between *inside – outside* our thinking is determined in part by the *cave* because it has features that sometimes provide attractive conditions which we call shelter. Therefore a cave is integral to landscape language and consciousness because we have often needed to choose these conditions. The thinking that informs this *inside – outside* choice is not minor, arbitrary or instinctual because it is related to the cave through a long history of imitative interactions with places that provide shelter. Ergo the origin of the concept *shelter* is the *inside – outside* positioning possibilities provided and related to us by the environment that includes conditions that are physically challenging, features such as caves and humans with our inherent bodily limitations which cause us to seek shelter.

Through this relational model the environment is demonstrated as the origin of a specific pattern of perceptual thinking (*inside – outside shelter*). This shelter seeking relation between perception, movement, consciousness and environment is evident in our sheltering designs. Our embodied needs relate us to the environment which structures our perceptual understanding and thus builds our culture so that our physical, mental and social structures draw us in and we feel sheltered. This regard for shelter originated in an embodied relation to place that is relationally driven by external and internal conditions. Thus through the *inside –outside shelter* example we may see that a [structure] is a relation between an embodied sensibility and an externally positioning agency. What is most significant in this understanding is that together these two aspects, the embodied sensibility and the external positioning agency, describe the particular fit of a being within the whole of being.

Indigenous Knowledge presents the concept [structure] as a phenomenological and relational dialectic that is evident in the way that every living being in natural systems is individuated, interactive and also related; supported by systemic relations. In this IK view an animal is not only a biological type that exists in an environment it is also a relational [structure] which is a species of fit between embodiment, systemic positioning and supporting agency. From this a [structure] is proposed as an intelligent ordering relation between *inside* embodiment and *outside* position provision that is individuated as a pattern specific to each being in complex systems. Thus the order embedded in the vast complexity of natural systems may be approached through understanding [structure][9].

A cave is a structure made by the movement of water in interaction with the geology of an area. In a similar way the [structure] of a cave is an imprint made by water and geology interacting in the environment of a place that influences the positioning of other things in the vicinity. The agency of a cave as a place in geological movement is motile in that it positions many other things. In IK terms this positioning power or motility is indicative of the [structure] of the cave.

Variations in structure produce caves in different places each with a different appearance and experience. Thus the [structure] of a cave is an experientially evident imprint in systemic relations. Each cave has a feel to it which may cause us fear and repel us, draw us into its warmth or fill us with awe as we stand on the edge and look in- just as many other species are drawn into or repelled by this positioning power. In all these possibilities it is the relational agency or [structure] cave that moves us and many other embodied forms into different positions. So in IK terms the cave [structure] is a living moving and positioning agent that communicates modes, moods or emotions which it relates through spatial form, interiorised conditions and contained ambiences that instigate and organize the positioning of other things. Such smaller environments are separate and active positioning agents with the whole.

In a similar way a social [structure] may be proposed as a positioning agency that has major environments and also smaller localised environments. In a social movement we may observe obvious change and also local, embedded movements that may only become evident within a general social movement over generations. Through this conception of social [structure] seemingly minor and embedded (inside) positioning movements may be seen to accumulate through repetition in complex adaptive systems. This accumulation effect often produces major formative features (outside); such as caves and cultures. Most significant in this understanding is that such deep simple repetitive features are initially apparent through the movements that other things make outside in relation to this [structure].

From this we may conclude that simple repeated patterns of social behaviour can accumulate and generate an impetus that pre-positions a whole social group to impact on its surroundings in away that is beneath individual or group awareness. Knowledge held within beneath group awareness or concern is often deeply for mative and most powerful. In terms of Indigenous Knowledge this knowledge from the *inside* is significant because it demonstrates that an *outside* environment is related to us through [structure] and will inform us about any unintentional social and environmental consequences that follow from these inherent (inside) features. Such emergent consequences describe the most significant features of a social system in IK terms because they represent the individually unconscious and therefore embodied movement of a whole; these embodied movements describe the fit- the deeper unconscious agency or [structure] of a whole social group.

The relation between the environment and our embodiment has always moved us around the landscape and moved our understandings. Positioning movements are integral to social and environmental being. We position ourselves and we are positioned through our being by the movements of other things. Social things move us in ways that we are aware of and in ways beneath awareness. The challenge of IK approaches is that we must position ourselves as respectfully aware and conversant negotiators so that we may identify and address the often concealed positioning power implicit within the [structure] of our social whole.

This conception of [structure] is a relational and conversant approach which recognises that only the social can know and address the social however it positions the devices for establishing this knowing *outside* of the social. Indigenous Knowledge involves the understanding that to know the social-self intelligence must be brought to mind as a distributed and relational knowing shared across wider social and environmental contexts because the deeper aspects of the social are only evident in the movement of others. It should be most evident in times such as these that *outside* movements such as changes in the environment and conditions in other social groups are the primary means for identifying *inside* social flaws.

INDIGENOUS KNOWLEDGE RESEARCH – IDENTIFYING NEO-COLONIAL SOCIAL [STRUCTURE]

The Introductory Indigenous issues course provides an opportunity to study the positioning that non-indigenous students adopt in relation to issues that are generally avoided in Australian society. Over ninety five percent of students enrolled in these courses have never studied Aboriginal history or issues before. In this research we have developed a visual coding schema to describe the way that student's position themselves in writing and talking about Indigenous issues[10].

The approach taken in the Indigenous Knowledge Research (IKR) project was to recruit post graduate and final year Aboriginal Studies students to visually code students' origin statements. The following is an edited version of the research report submitted by this group.

We sat and read snippets looking for one origin statement that was easy to code so we could work on it together and found one that excited our attention.

> I'm a city person. So is my father, but my grandfather grew up in (a rural town). His grandparents were pioneers in that area. I don't know a great deal about my ancestors except that my great grandfather ... was supposedly the wealthiest landowner in the region. He was also a xxxx whom nobody liked. He was rumoured to have fathered a child with a local indigenous girl but refused to acknowledge either her or the child. I assume that my ancestors may have darker secrets concerning the local indigenous people of the area. It doesn't matter to me personally because I refuse to take on the guilt of my ancestors. I do believe in reconciliation however and understand how powerful it can be to have representatives of the original people take part in the process. I cannot truly represent my ancestors because the link between us has been eroded by poor ... relationships, but I would like to research their history, hopefully to understand things a little more, and maybe to stand up and be counted (Origin Statement 0621).

After a few attempts to code this statement some preliminary concepts come out:

- The author states that they do not know a great deal about their ancestors.
- Except they were pioneers.
- Narrator is disconnected from the past by bad relationships - is this a separation from origin statement?
- Wealthy xxxx- yet this is a passionate rather than a neutral disconnected statement.
- Rumour-Indigenous woman/relatives-darker secrets-negative connotations.
- Researching "their" history- legitimising - yet still disassociating?
- Like representatives of them to be part of the process then maybe I (we) can learn a little more about ourselves.

We start to assign a sequence of codes from the visual research sheet and using symbols that will help us describe the positioning conveyed in the narrative.

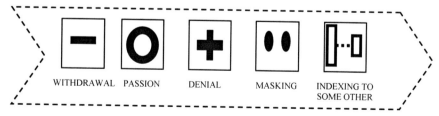

We coin words to describe the positions expressed in the statement: Passionately masking relation to origin and absolving self from generational connection/ responsibility. Reaching out to relocate / reallocate / reorder / reconcile self with

origin. DENYING (everything that has gone before)-seeking a comfortable origin-
"the past is the past".

We realise that his is a huge story that is evocative of the white blindfold view
of Australian history... the great Australian forgettory. So we debate and critically
analyse the narrative as an unjust resistance to what we know is the truth of these
events. Does this person realize that they most likely have Aboriginal relatives
living in the region and that they have a history that needs to be told as well ...
what about the Indigenous women who were used and abused ... colonial morality
and white male superiority that was a cover for stealing women and sexual abuse in
remote places? We tear into this discussion reviling the statements made in the
narrative and start to impose divisive value judgements. "He says he has to understand the past he denies before he can make a stand about our rights!" "Does he
expect us to do all this for him?" We get very angry.

One of us has been listening and stops the argument. "Argument is counter productive to our task because we are meant to be coding not condemning. This conflict
is leading us into disrespecting each other and the author's legitimate right to speak
in their own unique voice and expertly narrate their own experience. Remember that
we were told to suspend judgement because this is not mere data it is someone's
story. If we are to apply this methodology we have to engage through the IK
principle of respect"[11].

We agree that the questions we must ask are ones of position and movement.
How is this story moving us? Where and how does the writer/narrator position
themselves? We re-evaluate the story as being one of Dislocation-Separation and
also a narrative that will position us very strongly in contestation unless we also
dislocate from it. We see that the narrator is also dislocated so we devise a new
symbol that we believe encapsulates positioning within this narrative.

Dislocation – separation
+ *positioning power*

Then we start to ask how does the story move in and of itself? It alternates
between passionate withdrawal and tentative explorations but we believe that the
story is overwhelmingly about an innate search for comfort and safety – it is shelter
seeking. "I thought about how we could describe this without value judgements
and envisaged a hermit crab"[12].

We saw this image as trivial and joke about it at first but the more we talked about this metaphor the more apt and disarming of our contestations and conflict it became. Each time a hermit crab grows it has to find a place in which to shelter its vulnerable bits. These delicate bits impose a burden elemental to the identity of the hermit crab. In this exploration there were also jokes made about those delicate bits being a problem right from the start of this history. In this way the hermit crab became an effective mediation tool for us so that we could address the violence of denial apparent in the narrative.

The hermit crab is a [structural] image for understanding the positioning power of the narrative. Through this tool we ceased judging the person and started to draw them recognising as we did the repeated historic pattern of this denial. Essentially the narrative describes an everyday social position of seeking to protect the *vulnerable* parts of history.

As this image drew in our interest and spurred our creativity and our laughter we also saw that the lateral violence evident in our argument was dissipated. Through this [structure] (hermit crab) the inquiry was not made trivial nor was the model we employed a vehicle for ridicule of the narrative. Indeed hermit crabs are essential and such engaging creatures that we had to have a drawing of one in this text. What this IKR process did was to allow us to situate the narrative as part of a continuum that described by circumscription its origin in reality. It did this in a way that disarmed the wounding intent we can now see in this origin statement.

This narrative demonstrates how everyday racism can emerge, wound and incite conflict. The narrator consciously chose to write this in an origin statement in the first week of an Indigenous issues course. If their position was that they were authentically dislocated from their family and history would they have written about this differently? Indeed this narrative clearly states that this family did things in the past for which the narrator refuses to be responsible. From an Aboriginal standpoint it also seems that this narration is taunting us to convince the narrator to become responsible for their own history. This is a very powerful position to adopt in a task that caused many other students concern.

Through the hermit crab metaphor we realised that this narrative is not an origin statement at all. This statement is an example of the way that this particular origin in the general Australian social movement has been positioned to clothe itself in relation to the past. We can see in this analysis the repetition of a movement in shelter seeking that originated in the reality of colonial brutality which is bypassed by the narrative but integral to the shelter seeking habitus of this narrative form.

The relation between the hermit crab model and the inherent movement towards denial can be expressed in the following way.

As a [structure] the hermit crab belongs as much to a shell as it does to the seashore due to its embodied needs and the sheltering possibilities provided near the sea. In the same way this narrative as a [structure] belongs as much to a history of denial as it does to Australian society due to the needs inherent in the body of perpetration (colonial reality) and the sheltering possibilities provided by a tradition of social silence.

This narrator's enmeshment in social movement is in an often repeated position of being [structurally] protected. A narrator in this position recognises the normative social features that shelter them and allow them to clothe their history. They are sheltered because contestation with this position draws detractors into conflict with this *clothing* which is a socially reproduced protective enactment particular to this social [structure]. Ergo the social [structure] informing neo-colonial pedagogy is an interiorising positioning agency.

The members of our research group have often experienced the violence of denial in Australian society and the media. Now when we examine these narratives the hermit crab pops into our minds and we perceive these denigrations and denials differently. We can look at them and say; "Now that is a big shiny shell what colonial vulnerabilities do you think are sheltered in there?" The hermit crab model is an effective Indigenous Knowledge device because it grounds us *outside* in the truth of our perception and shows us a way to see *inside* through these often toxic coverings[13].

INDIGENOUS KNOWLEDGE, [STRUCTURE] AND SOCIAL INQUIRY

Every thing that moves makes tracks in Indigenous Knowledge. The IK conception [structure] provides us with a way to perceive the deeper agency of a social whole through the positioning movements that are integral to local social contexts. Galtung[14] describes a comparable approach through concepts such as the deep texts that are collectively informed and yet remain unrecognized by the culture constructing the narrative. These deep texts are the unwritten, unspoken parallels that are ontologically situated and therefore informed by the collective subconscious. Kristeva[15] also proposed a focus on the modality and form of social communication in an attempt to engage directly with the *signifiance* embedded in the code of linguistics. The proposal is that through examining the utterances of others, we can start to elucidate the outside, fragmentary phenomena that point to the inside nature and process of *signifiance* – and thus communicate with the *semeion* (σημεῖον): the tracks left behind by a social movement.

The difficulty of examining *signifiance* lies not solely in the development of an understanding of how a social movement tracks. Rather the *signifiant* nature of these very tracks and their position beyond the text, beyond words, in a deeper reality obscures our attempts at communication. Indigenous Knowledge Research indicates that this deeper reality is an informative companion that is available through visual design and perceptual devices for tracking positional movement and by the application of [structural] insight as demonstrated in the hermit crab outcome of the research exercise.

Bourdeiu[16] relates the significance of structure to social understanding through structured structures predisposed to function as structuring structures. These are principals that generate and organize practices and representations into a habitus which is a sense of one's (and others') place and role in the world. Habitus is an embodied as well as a cognitive sense of place. These systems of social norms predispose individuals to act more in some ways than others. Habitus is the product of history through an open system of influences from experience which either modify or reinforce dispositions. However because it is a socialized subjectivity events will tend to be interpreted according to pre-existing dispositions. This makes habitus durable but not eternal. The model used in this understanding of social action is games where actors play out dispositions and play with the rules informing dispositions in a field endowed with a specific gravity which acts on all that enter this space. In a variance to this approach Indigenous Knowledge employs models from natural systems as a basis for understanding the emergence of [structures], the positioning interactions they foster and the social places that afford these relations and support such movement[17].

The Indigenous Knowledge (IK) conception of social [structure] allows us to envisage that tracks occur in relational movements and are evident in the patterns of relation that accompany any movement. In a very pragmatic observational sense a track is made from the movement of a body coming into contact with a ground that responds deforming into a shape that is defined equally by the structure of the body in movement, the strength and direction of the contact, and, the qualities of the ground. Tracks of the kind understood in IK implicitly relate very practical information between layers of relational understanding. An imprint is a reliable contextual dialectic within which we may engage to perceive and recognize the relations between [structures] and contexts.

In a similar way the rhythm of imprinting such as in the movement of a hopping kangaroo is directly related to the physical form of a body in movement. In this way the [structure] of a social group will also exhibit an individually specific rhythmic component as it repeats the actions that provide mobility. These rhythms indicate the features of the [structure] and variations in this rhythm the different behavior of the social body. Thus a social grouping such as neocolonial pedagogy will come into being develop a kind of repetitive mobility to seek those things that it must to survive and continue this movement. Just like any animal this social grouping or [structure] will have a desire for sustenance, shelter and protection. Hence it has a longer rhythm in its mobility evident in the repeated and often cyclic patterning of its imprints from place to place and from position to position within a social or environmental whole.

Interactions between tracks in an environment describe the complex relationships between [structures] encapsulated in such terms as herbaceous, predatory or parasitic. In IK terms this vast complexity of movements constitutes a constant relational dialogue which sustains the whole. We can conceive of this meta-[structure] through such terms as the reef, the desert or the forest. Each resident [structure] contributes in its way to the being-ness of these places.

From this we can propose that a social [structure] will also occupy a niche that positions self and others and therefore influences the social whole. We may also discern that social meta-[structures] exist and provide the conditions in which a specific range of [structures] may flourish.

TRACKING SOCIAL DOMINANCE

The Plato's allegory of cave is often quoted as a centering treatise used to expose the vacuity of perceptual understanding and the supremacy of logical method. This story is rarely conveyed in full however because the persons in the cave are originally described as prisoners chained and restrained so their heads cannot turn to the light. Thus tortured all they see are shadow plays contrived and shown to them on the wall by their captors. These prisoners assume that these contrivances are particulars (things in themselves) because no other experience of things is possible[18].

Plato's allegory may be seen as a deep text which expresses an implicit acceptance of social dominance. In IK terms this story is an imprint on human being that distorts the social conception of this being.

The allegory commences in absolute control of the individual, reaches its pinnacle only in partial freedom because the released prisoner must be guided in the blinding light of the sun and concludes with a return to the cave. The positions of the cave, the prisoner, the torturer, the contrivers of images and the gentle guiding hand of authority are all imprints of this distorted species of understanding. The narrative is descriptive of liberation but it is also recursive because it situates dominance as an integral component at each stage of being. Indeed this allegory is the original narrative that led to the foundation of ousiodic ontology which separates mind from body and knowledge from the natural world as conveyed very clearly by the experience of the prisoner[19]. All the agents in this narrative inhibit or restrict the perceiver from direct and individual perception of the world and thus ignore the intelligent responses available from the environment.

We observed a contemporary version of this original narrative. After the Whiteness lecture where we showed an ABC television program describing child abuse in Aboriginal Communities[20] and then exposed this program as being entirely fabricated students described symptoms akin to physical shock. But the most significant details of the lecture were not mentioned or addressed by any in the group. While they spoke about how they felt the guilt, shame and fears the lecture described as the fears of Whiteness they also expressed a desire to un-know or a profound sense of loss as to how to encompass the newfound depth of their knowing[21].

Like the prisoner struggling in the light their dialogue indicated that they were finding it especially difficult to see the links between their benign self image and the social violence they witnessed in media representations. The source of their disturbance was the potent and immediately denied realisation that their social understandings are artefacts manufactured and presented to them as real in shared experience by the reality of this social violence which they cannot directly apprehend.

The fact that Aboriginal people are not at liberty to shelter themselves from this social action was not raised by any of the group. This awful irony underlying their dialogue totally escaped them until they were encouraged to examine it.

This Australian forgetting impulse signifies the deep social regression evident as a repeated imprint which gives mobility to the neo-colonial pedagogic [structure].

This regression is traceable in the almost imperceptible movement from awareness of violence to various degrees of shelter from this reality. These repeated inward turning positions devolve from a naive shelter to a sublating dependence and finally a denial of being. In our observation this regression is accompanied by stages of escalating anxiety that individuals demonstrate towards the objects regulating this denial; their social fellows.

Social regression reveals the positioning power of neo-colonial pedagogy evident in the vicinity of Indigenous issues. Pain is not permitted in these situated denials. Indeed very capable students will often make quite absurd statements rather than acknowledge the trauma of colonial dominance. Statements such as "this violence is too terrible to include in the classroom if we did parents would complain and we would lose our jobs" are made. In this there is truth and absurdity because parents will complain about this specific history and ignore key curriculum subjects that are entirely couched in violence such as World War I and II. In these locations a cultural positioning occurs where it is mandatory to imagine that the shared pain of acknowledging this particular truth is so great that it banishes the lingering truth of the pain inflicted.

In this way the [structure] of neo-colonial pedagogy is revealed as a cultural mode that is founded in violent coaction which habitually deploys internalisation to disable individual culpability and whole group responsibility. In IK terms these embedded denials are evidence of the predatory nature of this social [structure]. However this predatory image is also suspect because this sheltering code also positions the majority group as reliant on the same social regulation for the protection of its benign self-image. Thus the guiding hand of authority is made viable and sustained by the contrivances of denial. The cave and controlling captors inhabit a recursive and deeply embedded social reality. Inside this social body a body of perpetration is maintained as a feature of progress regardless of individual objections.

Colonial capitalism proceeds through the designation that everything including the body and its actions are property. All that can exist in this progress is made by and hence belongs to someone. In this understanding things of value require protection and the initial protection is a common rendering of this value to inform equal exchange. Thus the economy of property is couched only in terms of dominant values; this is the socio-cultural climate that supports and sustains neo-colonial pedagogy. Through the economy of property the environment and the social become mere matter over which competition and contestation may play and generate reward. In this realm individual agency is a mere subsidiary to the economy of property which is positioned as the primary legitimizing agent. Through the economy of property repeated internalising actions distort the social which is impelled to seek reward only in ways that sever external relations. Thus through its internal objectification the economy of property automatically prohibits social awareness of the intelligence distributed outside of its regulation in environmental places and the social spaces of others[22]. These repeated actions reveal a self-blinding component elemental to colonising social [structure].

DENATURED SPIRIT

The domination of the economy of property operates through everyday actions that regulate and transform environmental, social and mental places and make them alien and alienating to Aboriginal people. The positioning power of this social dominance is evident in the naïve statements of everyday racism. These statements are coercive because they regulate and transform social reality in a manner that repositions us in conflict as we seek to respond. We may engage in this contestation and imagine that we are engaging in a productive dialectic process that will achieve some resolution. However neo-colonial social dominance has no interest in being informed[23].

A deep and familiar disturbance accompanies this realisation. We referred to this disturbance as the denaturing imprint of neo-colonial [structure] in our dialogues. We defined denaturing as a deep fear for being that arises from the realisation that neo- colonial social dominance is not merely unwilling it is [structurally] incapable of addressing the social or environmental consequences of its actions[24].

We also identified denaturing as a form of intimidation because it repositions informed opponents as hopeless in their desire to resist and respond. This is especially so in the light of major media productions which deliberately misrepresent and denigrate Aboriginal people. Denaturing initiates an impulse to renature; to take on the seemingly impossible task of finding some retaliation that will prevent cure or simply allow us and our fellows to endure the social and environmental devastation of neo-colonial dominance. In this way the denaturing – renaturing duality enacts lateral violence on Aboriginal populations because there is a desperate need to express this deep fear and no place for a responding voice to be heard.

Denaturing – renaturing cycles also cultivate anxiety to reactivate social oppression. Denaturing is evident in media representations that present Aboriginal groups as in need of outside intervention and control. These informational contrivances modulate the moral anxiety of the dominant so they are positioned to exercise their dominance for the good of all. Denatured information activates the re-naturing anxiety of the majority which allows an escalation in the dominance of Aboriginal people to be framed as a social and moral good. There is nothing more destructive than a self-referential society committed to doing 'good' to some silenced other[25].

The [structure] of neo-colonial pedagogy moves as a denatured spirit because it is interiorized – this social structure is informed and reformed only from within. This denatured spirit like its namesake the mentholated spirits of the chronic alcoholic it is an intoxicating and toxic social substance. The economy of property provides the conditions for the denatured stance which positions others as depraved or dependant. Neo-colonial pedagogy intentionally constructs images to direct the regard of social fellows. In its contemporary form this social code serves the colonisers craving for benevolence and belonging through contrivances that conceal recolonising actions and the huge material rewards that flow from this repossession[26].

INDIGENOUS KNOWLEDGE PEDAGOGY

Indigenous Knowledge Pedagogy is a relational education that provides a principle based framework for the development of positioning awareness. This program is founded in the observation that prejudice involves the group construction or *social design* of images that filter and direct individual regard. To regard some 'thing' is to perceive or to think of it with a certain feeling. Social design involves the creation of shared images for regard; for emotive perception or thought. Such directive social design is an integral and necessary component of social coding in colonising social formations because social violence requires a specific focus of regard to incite and justify its actions[27].

The opportunity provided by an examination of social design is that when cultural images (e.g. that of the *settler* or the *aborigine*) are addressed as contrived social codes rather than immutable objects the intent of socially deterministic actions can be explicated and the processes instigated by colonial social design begin to reveal themselves.

These investigations explicate the social regard, self-regard, disregard and blindness structured into the positioning experience of individuals. In this sense members of dominating and neo-colonial social groups are necessarily disabled because there is no social imperative for the dominant to be aware of their shared dominating mechanisms. Aboriginal peoples have immense difficulty dealing with the continually shifting contestations of socially dominant action however we are much better positioned than the dominant to address these issues because this domination is apparent and present in Aboriginal experience and has been for generations[28]. In this regard resistant Aboriginal voices provide the outside information that is truly descriptive of colonial social dominance.

A deep and awakening challenge is available in this context through the institution of Aboriginal principles as a basis for Indigenous Knowledge Pedagogy (IKP). These principles reposition students to regard issues through a clarifying lens that has its origin in Aboriginal cultural responses to social dominance[29].

The first principle is respect conceived as the proper way of proceeding in a context. Throughout the whole process of IKP there needs to be a demonstration of cross-cultural respect. This means accepting that it is essential for other ways of being, seeing, knowing and expressing to exist. Respect is about showing care and awareness in the way you identify, explore and assess meaning across cultural contexts, including your own. Respect is an awareness of your own cultural contexts and the ability to suspend the judgements based on them to allow other understandings to be brought to mind. It is a kind of openness that allows conceptions to come to mind through suspending social and cultural filters. It is also about relationships and responsibility and the responsibility to maintain good relations. Respect means to be human in the proper way for humans, a moral and ethical understanding of being in the world in which difference is a vital living component.

The second principle involves deep listening to discern social positioning movement. Deep listening attempts to discern the patterns that fit us into a social position. It is about positioning your self in the context of learning, recognising your personal importance in the process, about whether you accept a role in the continuum: whether you see yourself as no longer separate from the context. Deep listening examines the ways ideas are shared and the limitations imposed on this sharing in some social contexts. It is also about how ideas, assumptions, and pre-conceptions fit with various contexts; and how the same things re-emerge in other contexts, so that history can be recognised as a record of the social reconstruction of significance. Fit is about a deeper understanding of how all these things, and the self, are located; how sometimes things just seem to 'fit' and why some other things are automatically excluded from a social understanding. In this way deep listening seeks to identify responses that emerge from outside of a shared social awareness.

The third principle is mobility which is related to tracking or knowledge from observation. This concerns the ability to perceive movement in knowledge across contexts and time. It is about tracking ideas, where did this idea come from? Why was that idea given this significance? Where are the relationships between these ideas? It is also about the recognition that history is not a single linear or static series of 'facts' but a critical literature itself: created, imagined and manipulated. It is about the ability to see and appreciate where knowledge comes from, whose knowledge is being spoken about, what is understood as 'knowledge', and identify where that knowledge is directing our inquiry. Mobility also seeks to instigate movement where understandings are seen to be static. Mobility challenges imposed and unconsidered understandings and reveals knowledge clothed by social regard.

The final principle is engagement. This is about expressing and sharing the emotional dimension of learning in difficult contexts. Engagement requires you to self question, to ask: "Am I part of the Dialogic process the class is generating and do I engage with these issues?" "What does this mean to me? How do I feel? What if this happened to my community?" It is also about responding from this place, not always seeking to say the 'right' thing, the 'intelligent' thing, but instead saying what you feel, reflecting on how the topic, the discussion is affecting you. It is about authentically sharing your self with care for others and respecting others as they share themselves. Engagement is an ethic of care that informs inquiry in challenging social contexts through maintaining a supporting and mediating human contact across divisive and dislocating issues.

In Dialogue we talk through issues as equals in a context where everyone speaks and listens. When we track the changes in neo-colonial images, perceive the ways neo-colonial pedagogy deploys images to direct our regard and we ask what kinds of social operations these images might facilitate through such direction our talking about them automatically saps the significance of the images. Social redesign involves a commitment to probe into the shared imaginings that drive, inhibit and/or skew the ways we regard others and ourselves. Structuring new cultural places in which it is possible to simply speak as equals about these images and the social imperatives they contain constitutes social redesign because it automatically repositions individuals outside of the flow of neo-colonial cultural reproduction. In this sense Indigenous Knowledge Pedagogy (IKP) involves the generation of social and psychic spaces within which principles that originate outside of the normative stream of neo-colonial pedagogy can be presented. In the majority of instances the generation of these spaces alone is sufficient to expose the collective non-reality that is imposed by prejudicial social movements[30].

CONCLUSION

We developed this social perception approach to teaching/learning and research as a response to demanding task of teaching Aboriginal and Torres Strait Islander Studies through the years of the Howard government - a time when every public image of Aboriginal people and culture was fraught[31]. Indigenous Knowledge Pedagogy (IKP) adopts a [structural] approach to educating for social wellness. IKP has emerged from learning and teaching in a context where social dominance and everyday racism prevail but it does not seek to directly respond to this dominance instead it aims to spur students to become more [structurally] conversant. This approach engages students with principles that [structure] their experience so that the may become aware of social positioning devices and learn how these devices can implicitly direct their perceptions[32]. Indigenous Knowledge Pedagogy (IKP) is a method that simply attempts to provide the outside intelligence that neo-colonial pedagogy fails to apprehend.

A focus on locating prejudice within the individual is suspect because prejudice resides in and is sustained by social structures which inhibit the generation of positive self images for both dominant and dominated individuals[33]. Vygotsky's famous dictum that all higher mental functions originate at the social level through actual relationships between individuals fits well with Bernstien's research which demonstrated that cultural reproduction (pedagogy) institutes and then operates through the positioning codes embedded in informational discourses[34]. From these eminent origins we may see that the primary target for prejudice reduction programmes is these positioning codes and the structures that promulgate them.

Indigenous Knowledge Pedagogy emphasises the significance of relations because a fully alive and animated system such as a well society or a pristine environment is constituted of individuation, interaction and inter-reliance. The strength of the Indigenous Knowledge approach lies outside in natural systems where the intelligent relations that it seeks exist and exercise their agency. This mediating systemic intelligence of the environment is one source of Indigenous Knowledge. This source is evident in the correspondence between social and biological vulnerabilities apparent in the hermit crab metaphor which mediated the violence of denial for the group seeking a position from which to understand the narrative that generates social dislocation.

Our students must face the facts that racism wounds us and living in denial imprisons us all in a re-wounding place. The fears of whiteness expressed by students are evidence of an emerging awareness of their restrained and socially determined position. Their discomfort indicates a first movement towards gaining the personal insight and agency to make the small healing movements that may allow them to discover a way to position themselves in respect and face the reality of our shared past. In this sense Indigenous Knowledge Pedagogy provides a place where the imprints of neo-colonial dominance can be revealed to and addressed by some of those who are coerced into making them.

It is deeply threatening to experience the supremacy of the economy of property which fosters this social and environmental violence. We see no sense in responding directly to this dominance because this only entangles us more deeply in the social regulation enacted by this same dominance. Argument and divisive contestation are fundamental positioning tools which are devices of colonial reproduction. These are not our tools. Instead we instigate Indigenous Knowledge Pedagogy to [structure] a place through principles where social and environmental wellness can be brought into consideration. We propose this approach as a fundamental challenge to neo-colonial pedagogy because it is made from.

ACKNOWLEDGEMENTS

We acknowledge and thank the following participants in the Australian Research Council Funded Project *Testing Ground* which informs this chapter. Research Mentor: Emeritus Prof. John Western, University of Queensland (UQ). Michael Williams, Sam Watson and Jackie Huggins ATSISU, UQ. UQ postgraduate participants; Michael Red Shirt Semchison, Kym Kilroy, & Leila Akubar. Teaching and Educational Development Institute UQ: Dr Catherine Manathunga, Caroline Steele. School of Journalism UQ: Prof Michael Bromley, Dr Pradip Thomas. UQ Anthropology Museum: Dr Leonn Satterthwaite.

NOTES

[1] Bohm, D., Factor, D. & Garrettt, P. (1992) Dialogue - A proposal. Available online at: http://wga.dmz.uni-wh.de/wiwi/html/default/bkoh-75ehxc.en.4/~file/Dialogue%20(English).doc

[2] Bernstein, B. (1996) *Pedagogy, Symbolic Control and Identity.* Taylor & Francis, London, pp. 3–80.

[3] Moreton-Robinson, A. Ed. (2004b) *Whitening race: essays in social and cultural criticism.* Aboriginal Studies Press, Canberra 2004.

[4] McCumber, J. (2005, May) Dialogue as Resistance to Western Metaphysics. *Social Identities* Vol. 11. No 3, pp. 197–208. Goode, E. & Ben-Yehuda, N. (1994) Moral Panics: Culture, Politics, and Social Construction. *Annual Review of Sociology*, Vol. 20., pp. 149–171. Hatton & Atkinson 2006 Ibid; Stratton 2006 Ibid; Sheehan 2001 Ibid.

[5] Jackson, M, (2005) *Existential anthropology: events, exigencies, and effects.* Berghahn Books, New York. pp. 37–63.

[6] Windschuttle, K. (2003) *The fabrication of Aboriginal history.* Macleay Press, Sydney.

[7] Sheehan, N.W. (2004) *Indigenous Knowledge and Education; Instigating Relational Education in a Neo-colonial Context.* University of Queensland. pp. 214. Morphy in Kleinert, S. & Neale, M. Eds. (2000) *The Oxford Companion to Aboriginal Art and Culture.* The Oxford University press, South Melbourne. pp. 130.

[8] Sheehan 2004 Ibid pp. 58–59.

[9] Cajete, G. (2000) *Native Science. Natural Laws of Interdependence.* Clear Light Publishers, Santa Fe New Mexico.

[10] Sheehan 2004 Ibid pp. 274–367.

[11] Cohen, T. Unpublished Research Report 9/2006.

[12] Cohen, T. Unpublished Research Report 11/2006.

[13] Freire, P. (1974) *Pedagogy of the Oppressed.* Seabury Press, New York.

[14] Galtung, J. (2004) *Transcend and transform: an introduction to conflict work.* Pluto, London pp. 146–147.

[15] Kristeva, J. (1974) *Revolution in Poetic Language.* Trans. M. Waller. Colombia University Press, New York p.17.

[16] Grenfell, Michael (2004) *Bourdieu in the Classroom.* In, Olssen, Mark (ed.) *Culture and Learning: Access and Opportunity in the Classroom.* Information Age, Greenwich, USA, pp. 49–72.

[17] Hillier & Rooksby 2005 Ibid pp. 21–25; Sheehan 2004 Ibid pp. 304–367.

[18] Gurley, J. (1999) Platonic Paideia. *Philosophy and Literature* Vol 23. No: 2: 351–377.

[19] Dunleavy, J. Unpublished Research Report 2/2007. Gurley 1999 Ibid. Sheehan 2004 Ibid pp. 30–64. McCumber, J. (2005, May) Dialogue as Resistance to Western Metaphysics. *Social Identities* Vol 11. No 3, pp. 197–208.

[20] Indigenous Times. *A timeline of the Mutitjulu scandal: How the Mutitjulu scandal emerged.* Issue 112, August 24, 2006. Online at: http://www.nit.com.au/News/story.aspx?id=7645

[21] Dunleavy Ibid 2/2007. Anderson, W. (2005) *The cultivation of whiteness: science, health and racial destiny in Australia.* Melbourne University Press, Carlton, Vic.

[22] Oliver, K. (2004) *The Colonisation of Psychic Space. A psychoanalytic social theory of oppression.* University of Minnesota Press, London.

[23] Fernandez, J. W. Ed. (1991) *Beyond metaphor : the theory of tropes in anthropology* Stanford University Press, Stanford, California.

[24] Dunleavy, J. Unpublished Research Report 6/2007.

[25] Ibid.

[26] Dunleavy, Cohen, Mitchell & Sheehan Unpublished Research Report 6/2007.

[27] Sheehan, N. (In press) Social Design

[28] Nakata, M. (2007) *Disciplining the Savages Savaging the Disciplines.* Aboriginal Studies Press, Canberra ACT, pp. 215–217.

[29] Gilbert, K. (1978) *Living Black; blacks talk to Kevin Gilbert.* Penguin Books, Ringwood Victoria.

[30] Tuomela, R. (2003, January) Collective Acceptance, Social Institutions, and Social Reality. American Journal of Economics and Sociology, Vol. 62, No. 1.

[31] Bonnell, A. & Crotty, M. (2008, May) Australia's History under Howard. *The Annals of the American Academy of Political and Social Science* Vol 617.

[32] Sheehan (2004) Ibid.

[33] Hill, M. & Augoustinos, M. (2001) Stereotype Change and Prejudice Reduction: Short and Long-term Evaluation of a Cross-cultural Awareness Programme. *Journal of Community and Applied Social Psychology* Vol 11 No: 3 pp. 243–262.

[34] Vygotsky, L. S. (1978) *Mind in Society.* Cambridge, MA: MIT Press. p 57. Bernstien (1996) Ibid.

REFERENCES

Attwood, B. (2005). *Telling the truth about Australian history.* Crows Nest, NSW: Allen & Unwin.

Bernstein, B. (1990). *The structuring of pedagogic discourse. Volume IV: Class, codes & control.* London: Routledge.

Bobo, L. D. (1999). Prejudice as group position: Microfoundations of a sociological approach to racism and race relations. *Journal of Social Issues, 55*(3), 445–472. Sheehan. (2001). Ibid; Robinson, M. (2004a). Ibid.

Bonnell, A., & Crotty, M. (2008, May). Australia's history under Howard. *The Annals of the American Academy of Political and Social Science, 617.*

Dunleavy, Cohen, Mitchell & Sheehan. Unpublished Research Report 11/2006.

Freire, P. (1998). *Teachers as cultural workers: Letters to those who dare teach.* Boulder, CO: Westview Press.

Fuery, P., & Fuery, K. (2003). *Visual cultures and critical theory.* London: Arnold.

Gell, A. (1998). *Art and agency: An anthropological theory.* Oxford: Clarendon Press.

Gillborn, D. (2006, March). Critical race theory & education: Racism and anti-racism in educational theory and praxis. *Discourse: Studies in the cultural politics of education, 27*(1), 11–32.

Goode, E., & Ben-Yehuda, N. (1994). Moral panics: Culture, politics, and social construction. *Annual Review of Sociology, 20,* 149–171. Hatton & Atkinson. (2006). Ibid; Stratton. (2006). Ibid; Sheehan. (2001). Ibid.

Grenfell, M. (2004). *Bourdieu in the classroom.* In M. Olssen (Ed.), *Culture and learning: Access and opportunity in the classroom* (pp. 49–72). Greenwich, CT: Information Age.

Hatton, R., & Atkinson, S. (2006, November). Reconciliation as a frame for rethinking racism in Australia. *Social Identities, 12*(6), 683–700.

Hillier, J., & Rooksby, E. (Eds.). (2005). *Habitus: A sense of place.* Ashgate, England: Aldershot Hants.

Hillier, J., & Rooksby, E. (Eds.). (2005). *Habitus: a sense of place.* Ashgate, England: Aldershot Hants.

Levine-Rasky. (2000, October). Framing whiteness; Working through the tensions of introducing whiteness to educators. *Race, Ethnicity & Education, 3*(3).

Levi, G. (2006, June). Considerations on the connections between race, politics, economics and genocide. *Journal of Genocide Research, 8*(2), 137–148.

Reason, P. (1998). Political, epistemological, ecological & spiritual dimensions of participation. *Studies in Cultures, Organisations and Societies, 4,* 147–167.

Riggs, D. W. (2004). *Constructing the national good – Howard and the rhetoric of benevolence.* Paper presented at the Australian Political Studies Association conference, University of Adelaide 29/9–1/10, 2004.

Riggs, D. W., & Augoustinos, M. (2005). The Psychic life of colonial power: Racialised subjectivities, bodies and methods. *Journal of Community & Applied Social Psychology, 15,* 461–477; Oliver. (2004). Ibid.

Rose, D. B. (1986). Passive violence. *Australian Aboriginal Studies, 1,* 24–30.

Sheehan, N. W. (2001, August). Some call it culture: Aboriginal identity and the imaginary moral centre. *Social Alternatives, 20*(3), 29–33.

Sheehan. (2004) Ibid. pp. 274–367.

Sless, D. (1991). Communication and certainty. *Australian Journal of Communication, 18*(3), 19–31.

Sini, C. (1993). *Images of truth. From sign to symbol.* New Jersey, NJ: Humanities Press.

Stratton, J. (2006, November). Two rescues one history: Everyday racism in Australia. *Social Identities, 12*(6), 657–681.

Taylor, L. (1996). *Seeing the inside: Bark painting in Western Arnhem land.* Oxford: Clarendon Press.

DALE KERWIN

8. FAIR GO MATE AND UN-AUSTRALIAN: AUSTRALIAN SOCIO-POLITICAL VERNACULAR

In the age of the neo-conservative politics of John Howard's Federal coalition government the individual and family became responsible for welfare rather than the government. John Howard's Federal coalition government took a hard line approach to spending on welfare priorities and this marked an ideological shift from previous federal governments' universal policy of providing a safety net for all. Through an economical rationalist vein John Howard imposed unrealistic measures on the whole of the Australian society. This shift took away individual rights and it can be argued that the change to welfare provision impacted on Australian Aboriginal peoples autonomy. This paper will, exam the discourses of welfare and what it means to Australian Aboriginal people within the rhetoric of self determination, equality, human rights and equal justice in Australian law. As John Howard the Australian prime minister stated in 2006 "you get nothing for nothing."

At the present time in Australia and a year before a Federal election of 2007 each State and Territory in Australia is governed by the Labor Party, and the Liberal led coalition of the John Howard Government governs the Commonwealth of Australia. It is my contention that Aboriginal people are no better off under either of the political parties and that in the current political climate policies are based on paternalisms and discriminatory language. Both political parties have shifted public policy away from cultural heritage, land rights and right based discourses to demonising Aboriginal men and society. The political language has also shifted the public discourses away from equality to fiscal management and welfare stigma. All sides of the political philosophy are bipartisan in their approach to Aboriginal affairs in Australia.

UNSHACKLING THE CHAINS

In 1967, the Australian people voted in a landmark Federal election where a referendum was included in the ballot for the purposes of constitutional amendments to the Australian Constitution. Still today and at any other time in Australian history it was the biggest yes vote of 91% in a referendum (Sawer, 1988). The changes that the Australian people voted for were meant to end the discriminating and exclusionary practices of State and Federal Governments against Aboriginal people. Before 1967, the Australian Constitution within the special race powers provision read, section 51 sub section (xxvl).

G. Martin, D. Houston, P. McLaren and J. Suoranta (eds.), The Havoc of Capitalism: Publics, Pedagogies and Environmental Crisis, 117–129.

"The people of any race, other than the aboriginal race in any State, for whom it is deemed necessary to make special laws", and section 127, "In reckoning the numbers of people in the Commonwealth, or State or other part of the Commonwealth, aboriginal natives shall not be counted." (Sawer, 1988, pp. 48–66)

Basically what this meant was Aboriginal people had no rights, no citizen rights, no voting rights, no political representation, no rights to be treated fairly within the justice system and no rights of repeal against discriminative laws and decisions. The yes vote meant that the Commonwealth could design laws on the "basis for welfare policies related for Aboriginal people" by the Commonwealth (Sawer, 1988, p. 24). The constitution was amended by deleting Aboriginal race in section 57 and section 127 was also deleted from the constitution.

39 years later in 2006, Aboriginal people have the right to vote, pay taxes, can freely use medical services, are able to stand in unemployment lines and attend educational institutions. However this is where it stops, Aboriginal cultural heritage is being destroyed at ever increasing rates for development. Aboriginal languages are becoming extinct with the death of Elders who speak traditional languages, and there is no political representation with the demise of the Aboriginal and Torres Strait Islander Commission (ATSIC). In the current political climate in Australia there has been a devaluing of the administration of Aboriginal Affairs in most states of Australia. Aboriginal Affairs has become compartmental in large bureaucratic structures. In 2006, Queensland under the Labor State Government of Premier Beattie abolished the Department for Ministry of Aboriginal Affairs and basically Queensland has no dedicated Minister for the portfolio of Aboriginal and Torres Strait Islander Affairs. For the Australian Commonwealth, Aboriginal Affairs is located in the portfolio responsibility of the Minister for Immigration and Multicultural and Indigenous Affairs.

1990S LIBERATION OR CON JOB

Authorship has mainly come from non-Aboriginal subjects/academics/"experts" with little insight into the internal dynamics of Aboriginal society. Aboriginal authorship has mainly focussed on cultural heritage and land rights (more recently native title). Further Aboriginal leaders in Charlie Perkins (1995) promoted rights based policy for Aboriginal people. More recently Noel Pearson (2000) with his rhetoric on "Our Right to take Responsibility" and getting out of the welfare cycle and Michael Mansell promotion of human rights and equal justice in the law for Aboriginal people. There are many more but these Aboriginal leaders have been major influences in public debates and major critics of government policy in regards to affecting change for Aboriginal people.

Michael Mansell and Noel Pearson in the 1990's after the successful Mabo court challenge for Native Title saw it as a victory for Aboriginal rights in all spheres of Australian judicial systems and the beginning of a new era. They saw it as the restoration of 'Aboriginal sovereignty' (Pearson, 1993, p. 14). It signalled a new phase to Australian official policy in regards to Aboriginal legal and cultural self- determination with the High Court decision of 'Mabo' and its recognition of Aboriginal customary law and property ownership. There was a renewed hope in Aboriginal Australian leading into the 21st century when the then Prime Minister Paul Keating (1992) of the Labor led Commonwealth Government said at Redfern in Sydney New South Wales, "we have to make peace with the Aboriginal people" (Keating, 1992). The Mabo High Court decision forced the Australian political system to devise laws for Aboriginal claims to country. It also saw Australian political institutions trying to come to terms with concepts of Aboriginality and Aboriginal rights, but continued to draft public policy and legislation that is discriminatory. Huge amounts of resources and effort was spent on what Aboriginal Australians call 'extinguishment of rights' policies and the public calls the 'Aboriginal industry'.

Aboriginal Australians aspirations became squashed in 1996 with the change of the Commonwealth Government from Labor to the Liberal lead coalition of Howard. The Hon John Winston Howard was sworn in as Prime Minister of Australia on 11 March 1996. One of his first policy changes was to introduce 'mutual obligation' for people who were recipients of Government support from tax payer funds for unemployment benefits, single parent, sickness benefits and disability pensions. In 2005, the Aboriginal and Torres Strait Islander Advisory Committee (all appointed by Mr Howard and not elected by the people they are supposed to be representing) to the Coalition Prime Minister John Howard supported a shift in policy (Karvelas, 2005, p. 6). The result of this policy forces young Aboriginal people who live on traditional lands to leave their communities and move where there is work, or undertake training in large regional townships (Karvelas, 2005, p. 6). If these young people do not accept they are breached and their Community Development Employment Program (CDEP) income support is terminated. In Australia the unemployed youth receive Newstart and for Aboriginal Australians it is CDEP (Work for the dole- mutual obligation). This policy has had the effect of being seen as one based on segregation for Aboriginal communities where the majority of people are employed through this program and assimilation with moving the youth from their cultural supports into city enclaves. These systemic and orchestrated government public policies of abusing and demonising Aboriginal people as undeserving poor have occurred within the historical notion of charity.

The Howard Government also introduced changes to environmental and cultural heritage policies with the successful challenge to the World Heritage listing of Kakadu National Park stage III for uranium mining in 1997 at Jabiluka. These shifts in public policy attacked at the very heart of Aboriginal aspirations for sovereignty and self-determination and victimised Aboriginal people within the welfare discourses. Michael Mansell in 1989 saw the death of Land Rights for Aboriginal people in 'the promises on land rights legislation have gone and it is my opinion that no more will we see land rights legislation in this country' (Mansell, 1989).

Land Rights and Cultural Heritage is a corner stone of the Aboriginal political movement and the Howard government over a ten year period has slowly dismantled the major provisions for the Land Rights legislation. This was achieved in 2006 with changes to the *Commonwealth Land Rights Act 1976*. It is also my position that the Labor lead States also have slowly dismantled Land Rights legislation when in 1992 the Goss Labor Government in Queensland eroded important provisions in the Queensland Land Rights legislation. This led to a huge Aboriginal rally demanding the main provisions be reinstated. The Commonwealth Government has also wound up the repatriation of cultural property, mainly skeletal remains from international collecting institutions to Aboriginal ownership. This saw the Federal Department of Communication Technology and the Arts bureaucratise the process by excluding Aboriginal participation and siding with large collecting institutions. Collecting institutions saw it as the death of scientific investigation once the material was handed back to Aboriginal people as inalienable property rights.

In this new political era of neo-conservatism Aboriginal interests for the environment, cultural material property and land clash with the interests of the State. The Commonwealth under John Howard is pursuing a developmentalist philosophy at all cost and maximisation of the bottom line with as little regulation by the Commonwealth to a corporatist model. This incorporates functions previously carried out by the Commonwealth to be transferred to private corporations. At the core of the current Commonwealth's approach to Aboriginal communities is Shared Responsibility Agreements, which are a contractual agreement between State, Territory or Federal Governments with an Aboriginal community. The agreement requires a level of onus on the Aboriginal community to meet the government's objectives for funding. These agreements, apply to many other service provisions of health, pollution levels, water quality monitoring, sanitation and welfare provisions. In many of these areas service provisions should be carried out as a public service, organised and controlled by public institutions of some kind not privately owned enterprises.

Aboriginal leaders who are moderates such as Noel Pearson and members of the Aboriginal and Torres Strait Islander Advisory Committee are calling for Aboriginal people to get out off the welfare cycle and became economically independent. These people have forgotten the historical subjugation and economic rape of Aboriginal nations by a dominant colonial force hell bent on relegating Aboriginal society as museum specimens to display and be marvelled at as a dead culture.

Australian government policies for Aboriginal people have played a key role in structuring the race relations that have developed since colonisation. They have been marked by the earlier attitudes of Christianity and official attitudes of doing good, then followed by official policies of 'closed reserves' and 'separate development' and in the twentieth century an attitude that is analogous to paternalism (Reynolds, 1996). This history was marked by official policies of 'assimilation' and 'integration' of mixed-bloods into Australian society (Reynolds, 1996). In the wake of what is called decolonisation late in the twentieth century official Australian policy focused on providing Aboriginal people a mechanism to take control of their lives and have a say in the future development of their communities. This was enhanced within the concepts of social justice and equal opportunity with Aboriginal demands that services which the Commonwealth government provides should be universally accessible to all Australians. There was a recognition that Aboriginal people had been for a long period of time shut out from equitable services and equal treatment within the Australian society.

The 1990's was a consolidation of advancement of Aboriginal rights and equality in Australian law most which arose out of legislative protection in the form of the *Racial Discrimination Act 1975 (Cwth)*. Examples of these so-called rights are, the High Court's 3 June 1992, judgment on Native Title in the Mabo case, and self-determination which was a collective right rather than an individual right for Aboriginal communities. The 1990's also saw Australian Law recognise Aboriginal Customary Law within Commonwealth jurisdictions as a source of Law. The 1990's also saw the final report of Royal Commission into Aboriginal Deaths in Custody being presented to the Australian Federal Government. The report included 339 recommendations that provided a vehicle for Governments around Australia to include measures to reform their justice systems, reform their laws to address endemic disadvantages that Aboriginal people are facing. This saw a change to many Governments policies for education, housing, health and the criminal justice system. The 1990's also saw the establishment of the Social Justice Commission.

ABORIGINAL ASPIRATIONS SMASHED

Since 1971, there has been tension between liberalism and conservatism across the political divide over Aboriginal Land Rights, Self Determination, Self Government (Stokes, 1994, p. 10). The debates have evolved over 'ideological barricades' (Neill, 2002, pp. 6–7) that entrench ideas of 'black arm band approach to history' (Howard 2006) and denial of 'historical mistreatment', under funding of programs and 'racism' (Neill, 2002, pp. 6–7). John Howard's neo-conservative politics created a political climate where he forced his ideology of a democratic and monoculture Australian society. In doing this he opposed those views of a collectivist and pluralist Australian society. Thus thrusting social change on Aboriginal people (Howard 2006). We can read this into the raft of changes made to social policy for Aboriginal land rights, welfare reform, and the notion that rights are something people earn not given.

All the hard fought ground made by Aboriginal people and supporters up to the 1996 have now been eroded, such rights as equality, freedom and opportunity. The passing of the *Racial Discrimination Act 1975 (cwth)* was meant to empower and provide social justice to Aboriginal people. The major principles of Social Justice are to develop a fairer, more prosperous and a more just society for all Australians. It is directed at expending choices and opportunities for all Australians so that they are able to participate fully as Australian citizens in economic, social and political life and are better able to determine the direction of their own life (Social Justice Report, 2002).

The then Aboriginal and Torres Strait Islander Social Justice Commissioner in 1995 Michael Dodson stated, the Governments long term objective is for Aboriginal and Torres Strait Islander people to have sufficient economic and social independence to enjoy to the full their right as Australian citizens and opportunities to participate in Australian society. (Dodson, 1995, p. 27)

Social Justice began for Aboriginal people in 1993 with the enactment of Federal Legislation for Social Justice Commission. This occurred through section 46B (1) of the *Human Rights and Equal Opportunity Commission Act (1986)*, "There is to be an Aboriginal and Torres Strait Islander Social Justice Commissioner, who is to be appointed by the Governor-General" (http://www.austlii.edu.au/au/legis/cth/consol_ act/hraeoca1986512/s46b.html).

This was a recommendation of the Royal Commission into Aboriginal Deaths in Custody, that there is "a need for there to be an ongoing overall report on the exercise of basic human rights by Aboriginal and Torres Strait Islander people" (Duffy, 1992, p. 1). It was an attempt by the Federal Government to acknowledge the extent of disadvantages suffered by Aboriginal and Torres Strait Islander people and the Government to be actively involved in improving the lives of Aboriginal and Torres Strait Islander people.

All peoples have the rights to self-determination. By virtue of that right they freely determine their political status and freely pursue their economic, social and cultural developments. (Article 1, International Covenant on Civil and Political Rights)

Today the neo-conservatives' ideologies of economic rationalism are ignominious in their embodiment of 'conservative and paternalistic' design to finding solutions to Aboriginal disadvantages (Stokes, 1994, p. 17).

RECONCILIATION

The white moderate who is more devoted to order than justice; who prefers a negative peace which is the absence of tension to a positive peace which is the presence of justice; who constantly says 'I agree with you in the goal you seek, but I can't agree with your methods.' (Martin Luther King, 1963, BGGS-A13\JB\T:HEN\10HIST\I-HAVEADRM)

On December 2000, John Howard the Coalition Prime Minister of Australia delivered his address for the future of Reconciliation in Australia,

past policies designed to assist have often failed to recognise the significance of Indigenous culture and resulted in the further marginalisation of Aboriginal and Torres Strait Islander people from the social, cultural and economic development of mainstream. This led to a culture of dependency and victim hood, which condemned many Indigenous Australians to lives of poverty and further devalued their culture in the eyes of their fellow Australians. (Howard, 2000, http://australianpolitics.com/news/2000/00-05-27.shtml)

At the core of John Howard speech was the notion of 'fair go' and that the Australian Government will be "guided in its policy deliberations by core Australian values. And the principle of equity and fair go, at the heart of the Australian character, is also at the heart of *practical reconciliation* programmes" (Howard, 2000, http://australianpolitics.com/news/2000/00-05-27.shtml). This ushered in a new phrase for Reconciliation and defined as Practical Reconciliation. The corner stone to Practical Reconciliation is the key policy of Shared Responsibility Agreements.

Shared Responsibility Agreements are contractual agreements made between State, Territory or Federal Governments with an Aboriginal community. The agreement places a level of onus on an Aboriginal community to meet the government's objectives for funding. Basically an Aboriginal community states what its aims are for example, clean water, school, or youth programs. Shared Responsibility Agreements are designed as a control mechanism with discriminatory provisions of paternalism. In most cases these are legally binding on Aboriginal communities that have no other recourse but to accept Government provisions for funding. In most cases it is stand-over tactics in the context that Aboriginal communities are the most vulnerable, poverty stricken and victims of human rights abuses in Australian society and least able to afford to say no.

Such provision could be washing the faces of young children and funds would be given for a swimming pool. Another example all primary aged children must attend the local school and a petrol pump will be funded. Shared Responsibility Agreements can also be developed for social programs in exchange for goods or services they need in their community. For example air conditioners for a school or petrol pumps. These agreements also contain provisions for non-disclosure of details in the form of confidentiality clauses. This has affectively gagged Aboriginal communities, they are unable to speak out about provisions that they don't agree with, or raise criticisms about the Government or the agreement. Shared Responsibility Agreements now take the place of the Aboriginal and Torres Strait Islander Commission (ATSIC) where the former ATSIC regional councils filled these roles (the council members were all elected by their community). Today, the Indigenous Co-ordination Councils (ICCs) who are bureaucrats from the Federal Office of Indigenous Affairs manage Shared Responsibility Agreements. Basically, these public servants who have little or no links to the community were simply employed too oversee the formation of Shared Responsibility Agreements, implementation and funding for the agreements.

Many current commentators have labelled Practical Reconciliation a complete failure and a move back to past paternalistic policy of Australian Governments. The Coalition however has promoted it in a positive language. For example, Senator Amanda Vanstone Minister for Federal Aboriginal Affairs defended Practical Reconciliation by stating that,

It's very paternalistic to say these people can't speak for themselves and tell us what they want... They may not speak bureaucratic language but they do know what the problems are, they do know what their solutions are.

These agreements are a form of practical reconciliation. (Vanstone, 2005, www.reconciliation.org.au)

However, the detractors such as Aboriginal Senator Aden Ridgeway from the Democrats in the upper house (the Senate) has labelled these Shared Responsibility Agreements as,

The biggest disaster of them all. They are completely ad hoc, there are no benchmarks, there are no targets. How will these agreements- which are different every time you talk about them- result in improvements to the lives of Indigenous people across the country? (Ridgeway, 2005, www. democrats.org.au)

William (Bill) Jonas the Aboriginal and Torres Strait Islander Social Justice Commissioner went further when delivering a paper at the Moving Forward Conference at the University of New South Wales Sydney 15–16 August 2001.

The Government's failure to recognise the links between the past and the present is testament to the limitations of its 'practical reconciliation' approach. This is demonstrated by its response to the recommendations of the report relating to reparations. (Jonas, 2001, p. 3)

Shared Responsibility Agreements are being compared to past Queensland Protection Acts for Aboriginal people for example, "the agreements are reminiscent of the infamous Queensland Acts, which required that Aborigines on reserves kept the gates closed and love their children" (McCausland, 2005, http://www.jumbunna.uts.edu.au).

Michael Mansell has even gone further in saying that these agreements are in breech of *Racial Discrimination Act 1975* simply because these agreements are imposing a level of conditions that the rest of the Australian community are not subjected to. He even asserts that because of this racism the Shared Responsibility Agreements where consent has been given by Aboriginal communities are still unlawful. "Consent cannot make lawful that which is unlawful" (Pennells, 2004, page 1).

These Shared Responsibility Agreements are a social contract where by the Coalition Government of John Howard has procedural rights over Aboriginal communities and their regulations and control. These agreements provide governments with financial control and conditions dictated by Government over Aboriginal communities. With no regard for jurisprudential consequences. They are designed with one purpose in mind and that is to take away the rights of Aboriginal communities with no procedural fairness.

Finally the Australian Government has a duty of care to provide the same provision and level of services and entitlements to all Australians irrespective of where they live, what their religious background is, or what their skin colour is. It is a right all Australians citizens enjoy and expect. There is a minimal level of services that all Australians take for granted, such as clean water, a petrol pump, a swimming pool or air conditioning in their work place, or a high school in their community. Shared Responsibility Agreements are paternalistic and racist.

These agreements are about division when they are only directed towards Aboriginal people. It is a fiduciary duty that all Australians expect of their Government so why are Aboriginal people treated differently within Australian law and society.

SELF DETERMINATION

At the moment the Australian Commonwealth Government is leading a forthright public debate against Aboriginal management of Aboriginal communities. With the highly controversial sacking of the Mutitjulu Council Northern Territory mid 2006 and placing it under administration appointed by the Federal Office of Aboriginal Policy Coordination. The Mutitjulu Council and the Australian community were told that this was "the Australian government's new approach to Aboriginal communities" (Graham, 2006, www.nit.com.au/news/story). The reason as we have been told but unsubstantiated is because of the rampant abuse of family violence, sexual abuse, alcoholism, drug addiction, and crime. The appointment of an administrator by Government is meant to have the effect of improving conditions by taking control of financial management, and the administration of the Mutitjulu community to invest and direct resources. Further an ultimatum by the Federal Office of Aboriginal Policy Coordination demanding that the Mutitjulu Aboriginal community is to provide accommodation to Government workers (Graham, 2006). The Mutitjulu community has only "43 community houses with the approximately population of 400 people" and with most of these people either on welfare or work for the dole (Graham, 2006, www.nit.com.au/news/story). The Aboriginal people of this community live in extreme poverty and do not receive services that the rest of the Australian community take for granted. The community has also been threatened that if they speak out they will lose funding (Graham, 2006).

Since the election of the Howard Government in 1996 the coalition has publicised its self-management philosophy. The Government has been playing politics with public opinion with its numerous attacks on Aboriginal council's accountability and authenticity of claims to cultural heritage (Neill, 2002, pp. 17–18). The authenticity of cultural heritage can be exemplified by the many struggles for protection of sacred places against development. These struggles often have contradictory consequences and are crucial questions in the context of contemporary struggles to reassert Aboriginal rights to ownership. In South Australia in 1993 a case was brought to the Federal court to stop the destruction of significant cultural heritage, it became known as the Hindmarsh Island case.

THE INTEGRITY OF ABORIGINAL KNOWLEDGES

The major problem for Aboriginal peoples around the country is the inability of the political machinery to accept Aboriginal knowledges and beliefs. In Australian society Aboriginal people are demonised as drug abusers, as alcoholics, as perpetrators of domestic violence and welfare dependent. The very public nature of the debates also question authenticity and Aboriginal spiritual beliefs these debates attack at the very integrity of Aboriginal society and knowledges for cultural heritage.

Between, 1993–1996 public and Government debate raged unabated, in regard to the authenticity of Aboriginal claims to the cultural heritage of Hindmarsh Island in South Australia. "There were several Federal and High court challenges, a royal commission' and a 25-year ban on development which was overturned, in favour of the development of a bridge linking Adelaide to Hindmarsh Island. It was reported widely that Aboriginal women fabricated the story in order to 'stymie a proposed development of the bridge" (Neill, 2002, pp. 20–21). However, in 1998 earth works for the construction of the bridge unearthed human remains at the location that the women indicated adding weight to their claims. The debacle also saw the new government of Howard dictate to State governments that they must amend their Aboriginal Heritage Laws to meet new Federal standards. Aboriginal cultural heritage laws changed around the country to meet the new standards as prescribed by the Federal Government. Aboriginal Australians see these new cultural heritage laws as development legislation rather than Cultural Heritage Protection laws. These new laws have very few heritage provisions and are mainly concerned with development procedures and administration by public servants.

In 1998 the Federal Government approved the development of an open cut mine for extraction of Zinc against the express wishes of the Gurdanji people (Traditional owners) of the Northern Territory. The owners of the mine want to divert the "McArthur River, to further exploit zinc deposits" at the mine (Bowling, 2003, http://www.abc.net.au). The Gurdanji people are concerned about loss of sacred sites and the impact on the environment with the diversion of the river. They are also concerned about contamination of hazard matter when flooding occurs flowing into the environment from the bond wall around the pit when the monsoons rains come. The owners of the mine have completed an environmental impact study and have delivered this to the Federal government and are now waiting final approval. The politics of development and jobs over Aboriginal cultural heritage, environment and social dislocation of Aboriginal people will win out. "The coalition Governments claims its role is to support and strengthen the central institutions and values of Australian" is ideologically and fundamentally opposed to any self-government or justice (Dodson, 1997, p. 11).

Across Australian no matter where Aboriginal people live Aboriginal disadvantage can be measured by life expectancy, poor socio-economics, lack of material prosperity, poor standards of health and incarceration rates. When viewing the statistics, it is fair to say that Aboriginal Australia is a community in crisis. However, one Aboriginal community has reversed this trend. The Aboriginal community of Utopia north east of Alice Springs has blended western frameworks with traditional frameworks to provide a better standard of living for the 1000 Aboriginal people living in several outstations. Most people live in traditional style houses, augment their diets with traditional foods, and use traditional medicines to meet their health care requirements. The community is self-managed and combines modern management styles with traditional methods based on Aboriginal law. The people of Utopia speak their language and still hold ceremonies to manage country and culture crime is low and substance abuse is very minimal. The "locals are about 70 per cent less likely to be hospitalised for heart problems and, unlike other Aboriginal communities, there has been no increase in obesity over the last 30 years.... has a mortality rate almost 40 per cent lower than the Northern Territory's Indigenous average" (Richard, 2006, www. news.ninemsn.com.au).

Aboriginal Australia has long bemoaned that when true self-determination and positive outcomes are being achieved the Australian government de-funds services to the community. Utopia is one example that on all social indicators they are performing as a well-balanced community but the federal Government in its neo conservative economic rationalist approach has threatened to cut funding to key projects. The Howard Government threatened to take control of all service provisions to Utopia because the Utopian community is isolated and is a collective of '16 outstations'. The Howard Government also reasoned that Aboriginal communities were not economically viable and not sustainable. Howard questioned the economic viability of all Aboriginal outstations and Aboriginal self-management of Aboriginal communities. To justify de-funding programs to these communities the Howard Federal government openly in public forums demonised these communities by stating that "abuse and disease are rife in some communities" (Richard, 2006, www.news.ninemsn.com.au).

CONCLUSION

In Australia today neo conservative politics and ideology are stifling debate by using negative politics in the public domain. The coalition government of John Howard believes the Australian people gave him a mandate to change the social fabric of Aboriginal Australia by creating idealistic policies. These are viewed by Aboriginal people as similar to past paternalistic policies of assimilation and integration into a White Australia based on a single mindedness of suppression. The bipartisan politics of Australian political parties can be marked by bullying and stand over tactics by withdrawing economic assistance from Aboriginal communities and people for acceptance of public policies aimed at destroying Aboriginal aspiration for sovereignty.

The policies are designed to attack the very fabric of the cultural patterning of Aboriginal people today. It is a tide that is orchestrated to wash away knowledge of traditional law and observance of traditional customs and practice that is ignominious in the normalising of Aboriginal people as criminals, welfare dependant, drunks and corrupt. Finally the democratically elected governments of Australia at the state and federal level are morally bankrupt with their media savvy projection of Aboriginality. This political savvy limits public scrutiny of half-truths told and unable to be interrogated by the realities of disadvantageous, and the prostitution of all things Aboriginal by political progressivist ideloguery.

D. KERWIN

REFERENCES

ABC Radio. Vanstone Snubbed at Reconciliation Talks. *The World Today.* Retrieved May 31, 2005, from http://www.abc.net.au/worldtoday/content/2005/s1381072.htm accessed on 15 November 2006.

ABC Radio. Mulan Deal a Return to Native Welfare Days: Dodson, PM. Retrieved December 9, 2004, from http://www.abc.net.au/pm/content/2004/s1261745.htm at 1 August 2005.

Altman, J. C. (1987). *Hunter-Gatherers today: An Aboriginal economy in North Australia.* Canberra, ACT: Australian Institute of Aboriginal Studies.

Australian Government, *Shared Responsibility Agreements.* (2005). Retrieved November 20, 2006, from www.indigenous.gov.au/sra/nsw/fact_sheets/nsw06.html at 1 August 2005.

Berndt, R. M. (Ed.). (1970). *Australian Aboriginal anthropology: Modern studies in the social anthropology of the Australian Aborigines.* AIAS, University of Western Australia Press.

Bowling, M. (2003). *Traditional owners oppose NT mine plan.* LATELINE. Retrieved November 20, 2006, from URL: http://www.abc.net.au/lateline/s801785.htm

Dodson, M. (1997). Law and justice in grave jeopardy. *The Age 'News Extra',* Saturday 1 November, 1997, p. 11.

Duffy, H. M., MP. (1992). Attorney General, Speech to the House of Representatives Hansard 3, November 1992. In *Aboriginal and Torres Strait Islander Social Justice Commission: First Report 1993.* Canberra, ACT: Australian Government Publishing Service.

Graham, C. (2006). The new rules of engagement. *National Indigenous Times,* p. 112, 25 August 2006. www.nit.com.au/news/story.aspx?id=7647

Howard, H. J., MP. (2006). Prime Minister, Speech. *Address to the Quadrant Magazine 50th Anniversary,* Sydney, NSW. Retrieved November 12, 2006, from www.pm.gov.au

Human Rights and Equal Opportunity Commission Act (1986). Human Rights and Equal Opportunity Commission Website Media Releases 2005.htm

Indigenous Employment Policy for Queensland Government Building and Civil Construction Projects. Retrieved November 20, 2006, from http://www.trainandemploy.qld.gov.au

International Covenant on Civil and Political Rights, Article 1. Retrieved November 20, 2006, from www.unhchr.ch/html/menu3/b/a_ccpr.htm

Jonas, W. (2001). A conference paper. *Moving Forward Conference.* University of New South Wales, Sydney 15–16 August 2001.

Karvelas, P. (2005). Blacks teens told: leave lands for work. *The Weekend Australian,* 23–24, April 2005.

Keating, H. P. J., MP. (1992). *The Redfern Park Statement, Australia Launch of the International Year of Indigenous People,* Redfern, 10 December 1992.

King, M. L. (1963). *Our Struggle.* Retrieved November 20, 2006, from BGGS-A13\JB\T:HEN\ 10HIST\I-HAVEADRM

Kristiansen Kari, M. S., & Cox, K. (2006). Shared responsibility agreements: Legally or morally binding? *Indigenous Law Bulletin, 6*(11), 8. 2005.

Mansell, M. (1989). Treaty Proposal. *Aboriginal Law Bulletin, 2,* 37, April 1989.

McCaustand, R. (2005). *Shared Responsibility Agreements between governments and Indigenous communities: practical reconciliation or paternalistic rhetoric.* Jumbunna Research Unit University of Technology, Sydney. http://www.jumbunna.uts.edu.au

Neill, R. (2002). *White Out: How politics is killing black Australian.* Crows Nest Sydney, NSW: Allen and Unwin.

Pearson, N. (1993). Reconciliation: To be or not to be- separate Aboriginal nationhood or Aboriginal self-determination and self-government within Australia? *Aboriginal Law Bulletin, 3*(61), April 1993.

Pearson, N. (2000). *Our Right to Take Responsibility.* Cairns Queensland: Noel Person and Associates.

Perkins, C. (1995). *Recognition rights and reform, A report to Government on Native Title social justice measures.* Woden ACT: Aboriginal and Torres Strait Islander Commission, Commonwealth of Australia.

Response by Government to the Royal Commission. (1992). Aboriginal Deaths In Custody, 1. Australian Government Publishing Service Canberra, ACT.

Reynolds, H. (1975). Problems in Australian History. *Aborigines and settlers: The Australian Experience 1788–1939.* Cassell Australia, Victoria.

Reynolds, H. (1996). *Aboriginal Sovereignty: Three Nations One Australia?* Sydney, NSW: Allen and Unwin Pty Ltd.

Richard, P. (2006). *People live longer in Aboriginal Utopia.* Retrieved October 16, 2006, from http://www.news.ninemsn.com.au/article

Sawer, G. (1988). *The Australian Constitution.* Canberra, ACT: Australian Government Publishing Service.

Social Justice Report. (2002). Aboriginal and Torres Strait Islander Social Justice Commissioner. Human Rights and Equal Opportunity Commission Sydney, NSW.

Stokes, G. (1994). Australian Political Thought: Editorial Introduction. In S. Geoff (Ed.), *Australian Political Ideas.* Kensington, NSW: UNSW Press.

Stanner, W. E. H. (1968). *The Boyer Lectures: After the Dreaming.* Sydney, NSW: Australian Broadcasting Commission.

Sutton, P. (2001). *The Politics of Suffering: Indigenous Policy in Australia Since the Seventies.* Conference paper Australian Anthropological Society, University of Western Australia, 23 September 2000.

Williams, C., & McMahon, A. (2005). Back to the future: Deserving and undeserving in the welfare state. In A. McMahon, J. Thomson, & C. Williams (Eds.), *Understanding the Australian Welfare State: key documents and themes* (pp. 163–172). Croydon, Victoria: Tertiary Press.

Newspaper articles

Dodson, P., & Pearson, N. The Dangers of Mutual Obligation. *The Age* (Melbourne), 15 December 2004, p. 17.

Pennells, S. Rules Unfair, Say Proud Mulan People. *The Age* (Melbourne), 10 December 2004, p. 1.

Wenham, M. *Nothing but a monumental racist rip-off.* http://www.news.ninemsn.com.au/article. Date accessed 16/10/200613/09/05

Speeches

John Howard Prime Minister of Australia. (2000). address to *Corroboree:* Towards Reconciliation. Retrieved October 16, 2006, from http://australianpolitics.com/news/2000/00-05-27.shtml

Amanda Vanstone Senator Federal Minister for Aboriginal Affairs May. (2005). *National Reconciliation Planning Workshop.* Retrieved October 4, 2006, from www.reconciliation.org.au

Speech by Senator Aden Ridgeway (2005, March). *Indigenous Policy: no care, no responsibility.* Retrieved October 4, 2006, from http://www.democrats.org.au/news/index.

ANNETTE WOODS AND GREGORY MARTIN

9. FABRICATING RECONCILIATION: HOWARD'S FORGETTABLE SPEECH

We live in an inherently unstable and disabling post-ideological and post-historical period. Since the collapse of communism, any rival ideology that poses a serious challenge to the hegemony of the market is either discredited or held to be dangerous. Perhaps even more ominously, since the 9/11 terrorist attacks in the United States the global security landscape has been radically transformed and there is little room left for widespread resistance, opposition or subversion (McLaren and Martin, 2004). Capitalism, particularly in its neoliberal form, is heralded as able to solve the problems of state failure and social inequality. Yet, it should be clear now that there has been no triumph of capitalism. At the end of a prolonged period of economic upswing, it is now possible to discern that the contemporary model of neoliberal capitalism has produced geographies of uneven development and spacialised disadvantage. Indeed, the unfolding global financial meltdown has brought renewed attention to the inherent failures of capitalism. Today, there is a growing sense of unease and anxiety around the world that has led to vigorous debates about economic ideas and policy agendas. Despite the optimism of true believers, as the bolt is slid against the door of social mobility, the everyday reality of uneven development and inequality is reflected in Australian society.

Averting its eyes from such collateral damage (suffered unevenly in the lead up to the financial crisis now sweeping the world), the Howard Conservative Coalition government followed the neoliberal template to create the conditions for prosperity. But as successive generations are sucked into the propellers of the economy, there is always the danger of discontent and conflict. Leaving nothing to chance, the role of the capitalist state is to reconcile these inherent contradictions, tensions and antagonisms across both ideological discursive and geographical space in order to promote the health and well being of the accumulation process. Confronted with new global realities, it seeks to promote a sense of belonging and attachment that is compatible with desired ideas, values and beliefs. Rolling back the historic gains of social struggle that underlay the post-war consensus and the Keynesian era of social democracy, the emphasis is on production of ideal citizen-subjects who are self-calculating, self-regulating and self-sufficient. Subjected to an intensive and continual neoliberal expectation, this is the form of self-governance, empowerment and democratisation that is valorized as a virtue or public good in itself. It is at that point that the present plight of Indigenous Australians and the wider inequities rife in the landscape challenge the meritocratic myth of the Australian Dream.

G. Martin, D. Houston, P. McLaren and J. Suoranta (eds.), The Havoc of Capitalism:
Publics, Pedagogies and Environmental Crisis, 131–156.
© *2010 Sense Publishers. All rights reserved.*

In this chapter, John Howard's policy speech to The Sydney Institute, a conservative think tank, on October 11, 2007 as the Australian Prime Minister of the day, is analysed within the frame of discourse analysis to make visible how the speech works in old ways to dress up neoliberal policy as new and reformist. Taking centre stage, Howard pointed to concrete steps undertaken to achieve what he called a "new reconciliation." This cynical manoeuvre, which put reconciliation back onto the election agenda (after it was earlier derided for its divisive and muddle headed symbolism), constituted a "neoliberal quickstep" (Reiger, 2006) or quickfix of sorts. The speech was also used as a place to reintroduce the Northern Territory Intervention, which at the time was purported to be a response to child abuse and Indigenous community dysfunction.

On June 21, 2007, the former Prime Minister John Howard and his Minister for Indigenous Affairs Mal Brough, announced at a press conference that the government had decided to put "boots on the ground" with a police-military style intervention in the Northern Territory (NT)[1]. The justification for the intervention was the *Ampe Akelyernemane Meke Mekarle*, or 'Little Children are Sacred' report (Northern Territory Board of Inquiry into the Protection of Aboriginal children from Sexual Abuse, 2007) which documented the appalling living conditions Aboriginal children suffer in the Northern Territory. Using the report as a political tool in an election year, Howard declared a "national emergency" and announced that he wanted the army, police and business managers to take control of NT Aboriginal communities (Pilger, 2008; Robson, 2007)[2]. Exposing this heavy-handed charade and its overarching paternalism, Behrendt (2008) notes that "As details of the intervention plan emerged, one of the first things that became apparent was that the intervention strategy made no reference to the *Ampe Akelyernemane Meke Mekarle*, 'Little Children are Sacred' report on which it purported to rely. It has followed none of its recommendations" (p. 15).

In a speech to The Sydney Institute on June 25, Howard (2007) even justified the NT Intervention by comparing the situation in Aboriginal communities to the Hurricane Katrina disaster in the United States. Despite the small government ideology of his Liberal conservative party, Howard said,

> Many Australians, myself included, looked aghast at the failure of the American federal system of government to cope adequately with Hurricane Katrina and the human misery and lawlessness that engulfed New Orleans in 2005. We should have been more humble. We have our Katrina, here and now. That it has unfolded more slowly and absent the hand of God should make us humbler still. It's largely been hidden from the public - in part by a permit system in the Northern Territory that keeps communities out of view and out of mind.

Clearly, the Howard government was not entirely to blame. Australia has a long history of racist policy and public and political disregard that can also step up to take some responsibility. However, no matter what had been done in the past, the status of a "national emergency" gave Howard just cause, in the name of innocent children, to suspend the Racial Discrimination Act and implement "special measures" including taking control of Aboriginal lands (Behrendt, 2008).[3] What matters here, as Hinkson (2007) argues, is that "the discourse of a national emergency also works very effectively to ground the crisis firmly in the present, severing the issue of child abuse from any consideration of the quagmire of past governmental neglect" (p. 7).

Spurred on by the *Ampe Akelyernemane Meke Mekarle*, 'Little Children are Sacred' report, Howard's speech at the Sydney Institute on October 11, 2007 details a new approach to Indigenous affairs in Australia, a looking forward and no longer to the past (Hinkson, 2007).[4] Here, an analysis of how the language of Howard's policy speech develops binary divisions and calls on rhetorical devices of political talk identified by Wetherell and Potter (1992) in their seminal work on racism talk within the speeches of New Zealand politicians, demonstrates that little has changed in the content and approach. It was indeed a neoliberal dressing up of the old as new. Without appearing visible within a regime of Whiteness (McLaren, 1995), Howard's speech offers a contemporary example of how the new racism of the liberal state is performed through discourses of denial and moral panic. In this chapter, then, we explore the discursive fabrication of Howard's 'new reconciliation' and its policy implications in Australia.

DISCOURSE ANALYSIS

The linguistic turn evident as an influence in the social sciences for more than four decades, has resulted not just in an increased interest in the significance of language and discourse in social life, but also in the development of a collection of analytic 'techniques' focussed on discourse and text. In this chapter we call on techniques of analysis from the family of discourse analysis to unpack the framing of traditional neoliberal responses to policy – in this case that policy specifically related to Indigenous affairs in Australia – as 'new' and different.

Defining discourse is difficult with the term being used very differently within different disciplines. We take discourses to be forms of representation. Discourses construct and define individuals as they interact within them. This notion of discourse moves away from definitions that take account of discourse as language only and toward a broader notion that encompasses much more than language or text (Foucault, 1972). So for us discourses become actualised as social practices. Texts and language are only elements of discourse. Discourse is somehow more than language. And it is this 'more' that governs who will speak, and about what, with what authority, within which social contexts (Foucault, 2000). Discourses support statements of truth that "found, justify, and provide reasons and principles" (Foucault, 2000, p. 231). Individuals have access to certain discourses to make sense of the social realities in which they engage. Miller (1997) describes an individual's balance sheet of discourses as "conditions of possibility" which enable certain actualities and deny access to others (p. 33).

So discourses do much more than represent reality, they also constitute reality (Foucault, 1972). As individuals we are not free to express any thought, our ideas and thus ways of thinking about and knowing things are constrained within discourses. A discourse excludes ideas which are outside its boundaries, and in this way allows us to represent objects, events and concepts only in particular ways – according to particular regulated ways of doing things and talking about things.

Based on this definition of discourse, discourse analysis then is about representing language use as social practice. The task of such an analysis must be "to see how broader formations of discourse and power are manifest in the everyday quotidian aspects of texts in use" (Luke, 1995, p. 8). In describing the task of analysis of discourse, Foucault states:

> A task that consists of not - of no longer - treating discourses as groups of signs (signifying elements referring to contents or representations) but as practices that systematically form the objects of which they speak. Of course, discourses are composed of signs; but what they do is more than use these signs to designate things. It is this more that renders them irreducible to the language (langue) and to speech. It is this 'more' that we must reveal and describe. (1972, p. 49)

Critical discourse analysis, as presented by Fairclough (2001b) consists of three interrelated processes of analysis allied to three dimensions of discourse. This model, and subsequent versions of it, (Chouliaraki & Fairclough, 1999; Fairclough, 2001a) has become popular within education research, and is used extensively within the field. Such a model "attempts to bring together linguistic detail with social theory" (Rogers, 2002, p. 253), so in this way allows for the analysis to move beyond language or text. According to this model of analysis the three dimensions of discourse are:

1. the text
2. the processes of production and interpretation of that text (interaction)
3. the social conditions of the text's production and interpretation (context)

Each of these dimensions of discourse requires a particular dimension or stage of analysis, and these are:

1. description - which is the stage interested with the properties of the text
2. interpretation - which is concerned with the relationship between text and interaction
3. explanation - which is concerned with revealing the relationship between interaction and social context. This relates to the social determination of processes of production and interpretation and the social effects of this. (Fairclough, 2001b)

As analysts we are committing to the project of analysing more than just text - rather we commit to analysing "the relationship between texts, processes, and their social conditions, both the immediate conditions of the situational context and the more remote conditions of institutional and social structures" (Fairclough, 2001b, p. 21). This form of analysis aims to denaturalise the universal truths and the ideological assumptions within the text being analysed by focussing on the discursive and its links to other material effects.

In this chapter we utilise Fairclough's model as a foundation to build a discourse analytic for analysis (for a more detailed explanation of this analytic see Woods, 2004). We also call on what is represented as a précis of method (Florence, 2000) where Foucault sets out several fundamentals for analysis of discourse. These include first, a distrust of universal truths. This distrust does not require outright rejection necessarily but does require that the validity of such universal truths be tested (Florence, 2000, p. 461). This requires more than noting that the universal truths are possibilities only because of their social and cultural context. The essentialist notions underpinning a neoliberal globalised understanding of our current context require deeper unpacking.

The second analytic move in the framework that we are working within for this paper is to proceed to the level of concrete practices for analysis. This analytic point enables us to interpret relations between the speech, the literacy event of presenting the speech, and the social practices that embed the act of presenting a political speech. This allows a broader focus and makes visible patterns and themes within the data. The representations evident in texts "only become real, socially operative, if they are embedded in social interaction, where texts are produced and interpreted" (Fairclough, 2001b, p. 117) as part of the social practices and contexts of institutions. Once we had selected the Howard text as data, we proceeded to interrogate the text for the representations – of people, events, and objects - that become viable and legitimate within it and its context of delivery. This incorporates what Fairclough (2001b) discusses as the descriptive phase of analysis with its textual focus, but also what is labelled as interpretation in his model. Interpretation deals with discourse as interaction with a productive and interpretive focus. Moving between analysing the text and interpreting the text's production context allows for an understanding of what happened behind the text to begin to emerge.

At this level it is important to attempt to capture a notion of discourse as a "practice that we impose on things" (Foucault, 1971, p. 22). The principle of specificity of discourse "is the located practice which produces the regularity of discourse, the functions for a subject, the positions for a subject, the possible technologies, the objects and the behaviours that the term discourse encompasses" (Threadgold, 2000, pp. 48–49). A particular text cannot be understood in its entirety according to any one discourse and additionally no one prior system of signs or semiotics will unpack the dimensions of any discourse. So it is important to move to and from textual analysis to the analysis of interaction or context and also to broader social formations throughout the analysis process. Moving forward and back between 'stages' or dimensions of analysis allows for some of the complexity of language as social practice to be unpacked. In this paper for example, we pay particular attention to the narrative structure of the speech and the different phases of the narrative structure as they play out to present 'newness' within tradition. We focus attention on Howard's use of binary opposition to unpack the way in which the new is set in opposition to the old while at the same time remaining embedded in this tradition – what we have labelled as a "neoliberal quickstep" (Reiger, 2006) or quick fix.

Finally the analytic framework that we use to frame this analysis works to allow us to "address practices as a domain of analysis" (Florence, 2000, p. 262). This analytic focus requires that the textual and interpretive analysis be related back to relevant social and institutional formations. In this way, the purpose of analysis moves well beyond a simple text analysis. Instead it unpacks the "external conditions of its (the text's) existence" (Foucault, 1971, p. 22). So the focus of the analysis can be what subjects become legitimate, and are able to be known as particular versions of subjects within particular contexts. We are able to ask what gets done to the agenda of an apology and formal recognition to the Indigenous people of Australia within the context of this speech and others like it? What work gets done by another non-apology? How does everything old become new again? In this way it is possible to see how broader formations of discourse and power are manifest in the everyday literacy practices and uses of texts within current neoliberal politics in capitalist society.

ANALYSING DISCOURSE WITHIN A POLITICAL 'NON-APOLOGY'... AGAIN

So within a public speech, or public presentation of policy, which purports to present a 'new' perspective for framing Reconciliation - within a country which had yet to acknowledge its 'old' heritage of institutional racism and exploitation - how is it possible for Aboriginal and Torres Islander peoples, the elected officials, and Australian society generally, to be talked about? What subjectivies are attributed to these groups of people within the political talk of a leader, who in retrospect we know was preparing for the launch of a federal election after being comfortably in power for more than ten years? The analysis that follows will endeavour to unpack how John Howard, as a leader, sets the initiative he introduces as being a new direction, while hedging his bets and embedding this 'newness' in conservative traditional approaches.

The immediate concern for the analysis presented here is Australian Prime Minister John Howard's[5] address to The Sydney Institute on 11th October, 2007. The speech was delivered just three days before the PM announced what would prove to be his hardest fought election campaign, leading to a subsequent defeat after more than ten years in office. It is legitimate to assume then that this speech was not delivered just to the primarily supportive audience at The Sydney Institute – although it is probably no coincidence that its delivery was to such a supportive conservative physical audience. Instead this speech was being delivered to the boarder Australian electorate, an electorate that Howard knew he would soon be facing in a bid to form a conservative government for a record fifth term, and one to whom he must already be aware he was increasingly having difficulty sounding legitimate. Howard had made an art of identifying with his beloved 'middle Australia' and yet after more than 10 years his relationship with this sector of the constituency was strained – he was tying himself in knots in an attempt to identify the position that this group wanted him to take. This goes some way to explaining his attempts to walk the boundary between 'new' approaches and 'old' consistent and traditional ways.

The speech also needs to be contextualised in the announcement 100 days earlier of the Government's emergency Intervention into Northern Territory Indigenous communities, an intervention that purported to be a response to the *Ampe Akelyernemane Meke Mekarle*, 'Little Children are Sacred' report (Northern Territory Board of Inquiry into the Protection of Aboriginal Children from Sexual Abuse, 2007). The Intervention was in fact at best a political attempt to capitalise on the homogenised social conscience of broader Australian society, and at worst an innovative renewal of colonisation for the year 2007. So while Howard on several occasions called the Intervention a 'watershed' (including in lines 40-43 of this speech transcript, see Appendix 1), public opinion was mixed and generally lukewarm. Consequently the Intervention quickly became the property of the Minster for Families, Community Services and Indigenous Affairs of the time, Mal Brough[6]. One hundred days later and just prior to announcing the election, Prime Minister Howard had a second attempt at rewriting his history, to claim a socially conscious politician identity, one aware of Indigenous issues and hardships, by addressing The Sydney Institute on the issue of incorporating a new Statement of Reconciliation into the Preamble of Australia's Constitution. This speech is analysed here as a text representative of others within the neo-conservative tradition, where it has become fashionable to present incarnations of the same policy directions as new policy.

However while this speech is representative of others in the conservative tradition in this regard, as a non-apology it resists the trend evident in the acts of political leaders throughout the past 10 years. The political apology has become "a form of political speech with increasing significance and power" (Luke, 1997, p. 344) and popular amongst western leaders such as Clinton, and Blair (Augoustinos Lecouteur & Soyland 2002). Howard made the non-apology his own over a ten-year period, and while this example proved to be his last as the Prime Minister of Australia it is significant. A chance missed to commit to reform and regeneration of Indigenous communities and Indigenous policy and practice, instead this speech wraps an old non-apology and policy in new robes and announced nothing that would work to change the circumstances of the Indigenous poor and marginalised in Australian society. This is not the first analysis of a Howard speech on issues related to Indigenous affairs or reconciliation. The analyses of such political events are almost as prolific as the events themselves (see as examples Luke, 1997; Augoustinos, Lecouteur & Soyland, 2002). However what this archive of analyses allows us to recognise is the politically motivated and strategic practice involved in 'becoming' a particular identity as a political leader. Through these analyses, we see similar discursive practices and indeed content, across the ten years of Howard's reign, aimed at similar outcomes and focused on letting the public come to believe the rhetoric through familiarity. This in itself is a significant finding.

Following one of the foundational purposes of discourse analysis - that is to make contradictions apparent (Wodak, 1999, p. 186) - the initial phase of this analysis involved looking for "instances of paradox" (Woods, 2004, p. 182) within the speech. One such contradiction that emerged in the transcript was the shunting between prolific references to 'newness' and a continual representation of this supposed new approach as no more than "an affirmation of well-worn liberal conservative views" (lines 194–195 Appendix 1). To unpack this juxtaposition further, our analysis will first present an analysis of the speech as a narrative account. Luke (1997) discusses the fashion in which political texts "locate agency and power with individual political, parties, policies and institutions" and we would add the routines and practices of politics. Luke (1997) discusses the fashion in which "the texts of government locate agency and power with individual political leaders, parties, policies and institutions" and goes on to claim that such texts can be "viewed as narratives that construct governments as heroic protagonists" (p. 359). In this case, the narrative structure seems to work to embed the 'new' policy in 'tradition', as a way to represent stability. We move to suggest that this phenomenon works along side Howard's use of binary division throughout the speech to imply 'newness' and thus difference from past policies. Finally several issues related to rhetorical device and language choice are unpacked as we consider how these discursive practices work within the speech.

THE 'NEW' NARRATIVE OF RECONCILIATION: WHERE EVERYTHING OLD IS NEW AGAIN

We begin our analysis of this speech by unpacking the narrative structure of the speech as a whole before focussing on several key sections so that a specific focus on the use of binary division and rhetorical device can be taken. In 1997, Luke called on the work of Lyotard to frame up a technique of parsing the "story grammar" of a similar speech made by Howard also in 1997 (p. 359). Luke was investigating the place of the 'non-apology', taken eventually as Howard's trademark, within a context where other like politicians were embracing the apology as a politically productive act. Based in the narrative deconstruction suggested by Luke (1997, p.360), we represent the narrative structure of the speech used as data for this paper here:

Howard's 'New' Reconciliation Narrative

Setting: Contextualisation of this latest policy suggestion in Australian History Summit and the NT Emergency Intervention

Key Protagonist: 'New' Reconciliation

Goal: Aboriginal Australia to join the mainstream economy as the foundation of economic and social progress

Condition of support: The sense of balance that Australia has found in 2007

Threat: Not getting a 'better balance' – as has occurred in the past because "the dominant paradigm for Indigenous policy" would not allow this to be achieved and because "this whole area has been one that I (Howard) have struggled with during the entire time that I (he) has been Prime Minister"

Resolution: Formally recognise the special status of Aboriginal and Torres Strait Islanders as the first peoples of our nation by putting to the Australian people a referendum to make a change to the Preamble of the Australian Constitution

Outcome: Recognition that Indigenous struggle is the struggle of all Australians and that while ever Indigenous citizens are marginalised that 'we' are all diminished

Consequence: New settlement for Indigenous policy in Australia – which stands at the intersection between rights and responsibilities

Narratives generally set the scene by describing the context or setting in which the narrative will unfold (Luke, 1997). This is not the case in Howard's speech. Instead he contextualises the announcement of 'new' reconciliation within a context of the History Summit announced and initiated some twelve months earlier and the more recent Emergency Intervention into Northern Territory Indigenous Communities announced 100 days earlier (for an analysis of how the elimination of the standard narrative 'setting of the scene' is indicative of Howard's style see Luke, 1997). After a short acknowledgement and welcome (lines 1–2 Appendix 1) Howard moves to reiterate the purpose and successful outcomes of the History Summit (lines 3–36 Appendix 1) with only a brief and general introduction to the actual topic of this speech (lines 18–24 Appendix 1). This short topic introduction itself is the first instance of the speech working to place the 'new' within an historical archive through the use of figurative language such as: "one that transcends the past, the present and the future" (line 19 Appendix 1); and "unfolding story" (line 24 Appendix 1); and the use of temporal markers such as "generation", "1950s and 1960s" and "business of our time" (lines 21 & 23 Appendix 1). The setting is then expanded further to take in a contextualisation of the Emergency Intervention (lines 36–46 Appendix 1) which is described as a 'watershed' in Australian Indigenous affairs and the foundation of aims to complete unfinished business through decisive steps that "go further and aim higher" (line 36 Appendix 1).

This relatively long description of the setting ensures that the protagonist of this narrative – the 'new' Reconciliation – is firmly embedded in a history of conservative Indigenous affairs policy in Australia. Howard manages to hedge his bets as such by providing consistent policy embedded in this history, while at the same time naming it as a 'new' "more positive and unifying approach to Reconciliation" (line 46 Appendix 1). It is at this point that the first shunt from old to new is evident. In the sections that follow, we use Howard's own narrative divides – indicated in the transcript (Appendix 1) by bolded headings, to organise the analysis.

As Howard moves to actually introduce and define 'new Reconciliation' as the protagonist of the narrative (lines 47–86 Appendix 1) 'newness' is fore grounded. The word new (acting as adjectival to paradigm, Reconciliation, alignment and generation) appears 6 times and works together with phrases such as "a coming together of forces I have not witnessed in 32 years of public life" (line 59 Appendix 1) to recontextualise the policy initiative from being embedded in the old and stayed, to being a new initiative for new times.

Supporting these lexical choices in this work, are the binary oppositions set up within this section of the text. Table 1 demonstrates the binaries set up throughout this section of the speech.

In this way the text sets up those who support group rights as individuals who lack the ethic to take responsibility. As such these same individuals are represented as supporting the rights of all Indigenous people to passive welfare and communal

Table 1. Binary opposites within section A new paradigm, lines 47 to 86 (Appendix 1)

Line	Entity	Link	Entity
49	individual rights and national sovereignty	prevail over	group rights
50	group rights	are and ought to be subordinate to	both the citizenship rights of the individual and the sovereignty of the nation
53	a balance of rights	and	responsibilities
53	a balance of practical	and	symbolic
76	a new generation of Indigenous leaders	(implied opposition to)	(implied) current and past Indigenous leaders who do not have intellectual firepower
82	the cancer of passive welfare	(implied which will be replaced by)	opportunity provided through education, employment and home ownership
84	partnerships that respect communal land rights	(implied opposition to)	partnerships that that encourage wider economic opportunity (based on those rights)

land rights. The text frames them as being opposite to those who support individual rights and national sovereignty. These we are told are individuals who take responsibility and who want wider economic opportunity provided through Western education systems, mainstream employment and home ownership. In this section then the 'new' reconciliation is clearly set as being about new directions and a shedding of a more traditional 'welfare' approach.

As the speech shifts to discuss moving "toward a better balance" (lines 87–144 Appendix 1), Howard also shifts from this focus on 'newness' and returns to a fastidious embedding of this 'new' policy into his own history of leadership. In a classic "neoliberal quick step" (Reiger, 2006), he presents his 'new' approach as that which was indeed his old approach, that which he had always been aiming toward achieving. Again he calls upon a pattern of language to set up his approach as binary opposite of the "dominant paradigm for Indigenous policy". By setting up this protagonist which works – or indeed has worked – as a threat to Howard's now ten year old 'new' approach, Howard again is able to hedge his bets. He is able to achieve a 'new' policy initiative to launch for his election campaign and a traditional, conservative approach that has passed the test of time, having been integral to his approach throughout his ten-year term. Howard begins this section with the following statement:

> I'm the first to admit that this whole area is one I have struggled with during the entire time that I have been Prime Minister. (Lines 87–88 Appendix 1)

In this self-representation Howard achieves a construction of himself as an honest man, one who can admit his faults and limitations, but at the same time as one who takes Indigenous affairs seriously and who has worked hard in this policy area "during the entire time" (line 87 Appendix 1) of his office. Howard, we are told has "struggled", and this lexical choice implicates hard work and toil, perhaps emotional turmoil and trial for not having succeeded to make change. In this way Howard's self-representation here, and again later in the speech (lines 113–124), works as a 'stake inoculation'. This concept is described by Potter (1999 as cited in Augoustinos, Lecouteur & Soyland 2002) as a discursive practice that works to minimise the likelihood or validity of criticisms. Howard uses this device to protect himself from criticisms for his lack of success in the area of Indigenous policy over a 10 year period by stating the obvious – he has failed – but by putting forward the confession as an inoculation against any attack for this failure by others. He then moves to explain why it has been necessary for him to challenge the "dominant agenda" (line 92 Appendix 1) of reconciliation, one that he claims is based on shame and guilt of non-Indigenous Australians. This naming of one section of our society works to set Indigenous and non-Indigenous peoples as opposites, reminding the listener that the collective of 'ordinary Australians' of the "Australia I (the Prime Minister) grew up in" (lines 93–94 Appendix 1) does not include Indigenous Australians. This section of Howard's narrative is an imperialist narrative, marking out Australia's colonial past as one of "shared destiny" (lines 95–96 Appendix 1) where exclusion is conducted on the basis of problems with the excluded group themselves and their inability to 'fit' with – and perhaps even work hard enough to be part of - the superior culture who generously offer this shared destiny for all.

This part of the speech is where Howard sets up the threat to his resolution. With a rhetorical device known as 'ontological gerrymandering' (Woolga and Pawluch, 1985 cited in Augoustinos, Lecouteur & Soyland, 2002, p. 117), he sets boundaries around what will be seen as an appropriate response or representation of 'reconciliation', and what will be discarded as outside the bounds of appropriate – indeed what will be represented as the threat within this unfolding narrative. What Howard defines as "old reconciliation" (lines 104-105 Appendix 1) is constructed as relating to:

shame and guilt of non-Indigenous Australians; a repudiation of the Australia I (Howard) grew up in; a rights agenda that led ultimately and inexorably towards welfare dependency; a philosophy of separateness rather than a shared destiny (lines 92–96 Appendix 1).

In a demonstration of the predictability of concepts and patterns presented by Howard in speeches on this topic over a long period of time, a similar description of 'reconciliation that will not work' in a 1997 speech by Howard at the Reconciliation Council, is analysed by Augoustinos, Lecouteur & Soyland (2002). A decade later these risky characteristics of reconciliation are still being described by Howard, used as they are here to set the old reconciliation as problematic, and contrasted to his 'new' reconciliation as a "fundamental correction to the previously unbalanced approach to rights and responsibility" (lines 110–111 Appendix 1). By mapping the boundaries around 'what we are talking about today', Howard sets himself up as legitimately able to produce yet another non-apology, all the while presenting opinions and perspectives that are a decade old as 'new'.

He begins this latest non-apology by first presenting a second self-representation (lines 113–124 Appendix 1). Again he produces an image of an honest man who "acknowledges" his limitations, and who "fully accepts my (his) share of the blame" for the lack of success so far (line 116 Appendix 1), who was "emotionally committed" but "mistaken in believing" (lines119–120 Appendix 1). He reminds listeners of his traditions and history, as a man he can be no more than "an artefact of who I am and the time in which I grew up" (lines 123–124 Appendix 1). After this reminder of his traditional and conservative approach, based in a history of goodwill – another example of a stake inoculation, Howard delivers his non-apology.

I have always acknowledged the past mistreatment of Aboriginal people and have frequently said that the treatment of Indigenous Australians represents the most blemished chapter in the history of this country. Yet I have felt – and still feel – that the overwhelming balance sheet of Australian history in a positive one. In the end I could not accept that reconciliation required the condemnation of the Australian heritage I had always owned. At the same time I recognise that the parlous position of Indigenous Australians does have its roots in history and that past injustices have a real legacy in the present. (lines 125–133 Appendix 1)

This non-apology is based within the propositions investigated by Wetherell and Potter (1992) as the foundations of racist talk by politicians in New Zealand. They describe 10 such propositions which are listed here:
1. Resources should be used productively and in a cost-effective manner.
2. Nobody should be compelled.
3. Everybody should be treated equally.
4. You cannot turn the clock backwards.
5. Present generations cannot be blamed for the mistakes of past generations.
6. Injustices should be righted.
7. Everybody can succeed if they try hard enough.
8. Minority opinion should not carry more weight than majority opinion.
9. We have to live in the twentieth century.
10. You have to be practical. (Wetherell & Potter 1992, p. 177)

Augustinos, Lecouteur, & Soyland (2002) discuss how these propositions provide a basic legitimacy or accountability to racist ways of knowing and doing because they fit well with some common sense assumptions about how the world works as held within western liberal nations. Howard calls on these propositions as liberal statements of truth – common sense and without question - and by doing so presents his argument against a reconciliation founded on recognition and (symbolic) visibility of past injustices as outside the bounds of productive reconciliation. After all the opinions and needs of the minority can not be given more value than majority opinion – 'we' should not feel the need to be ashamed, as while we might acknowledge the past, we can not be required to field the blame for what those in the past have done – "you have to be practical" and just get on with it (Wetherell & Potter, 1992, p. 177).

So by self-representing himself as an honest man who acknowledges but should not be required to apologise for his shortcomings, setting the ontological boundaries around what productive reconciliation cannot be, and producing yet another non-apology, Howard uses this section of his speech entitled as it is "getting a better balance" to provide the space for him to present and define his approach to reconciliation as a resolution to the threats and complications that have challenged reconciliation in the past. He introduces this resolution next:

> I believe we must find room in our national life to formally recognise the special status of Aboriginal and Torres Strait Islanders as the first peoples of our nation. (lines 134–136 Appendix 1)

Then despite previously claiming that symbolic representation will not change the pragmatic every day experience of Indigenous Australians – their misery in fact (lines 107–109 Appendix 1), Howard constructs this Australian 'other' as configured within the symbolic representations of art and dance. He praises the "blossoming of Indigenous art and dance and the way it gives unique expression to Australian culture" (lines 141–143 Appendix 1) as being part of the strong "affirmation of Indigenous identity and culture" (lines 139–140 Appendix 1) required to solve the crisis of social and cultural disintegration. He advocates a level of respect of difference, but only on the grounds of 'cultural' activities such as dance. In this way he is able to marginalise the very real issues of disadvantage and uneven or spacialised development that is the day to day experience of many Indigenous Australians, to smooth over or make less visible the messiness of racialised inequality by presenting a respectful representation of this 'other' based on somewhat tokenised dimensions.

As Howard's speech narrative moves to finally announce the 'new' initiative (A rare convergence lines 144–207 Appendix 1), he takes the time to configure Australian society as united and on a track toward convergence. Wetherell and Potter (1992) describe a 'togetherness repertoire' as a rhetorical device that works to present the proposition or resolution as having the support of all. This rhetoric represents the resolution to the Indigenous policy issue - as a universally received truth. Here it is not possible to discern the exclusion of Indigenous Australians, nor the setting of Indigenous and non-Indigenous peoples as binary opposites. Instead by calling on the collective term of *Australian people* Howard resists a representation of a divided nation of haves and have-nots, of the majority and the marginalised other. Instead, all Australians are represented as wanting to "move toward a new settlement of this issue" (lines 145–146 Appendix 1). As Howard then frames himself as part of this collective he announces that:

> If re-elected, I will put to the Australian people within 18 months a referendum to formally recognise Indigenous Australians in our Constitution...and their special (though not separate) place within a reconciled, indivisible nation. (lines 146–151 Appendix 1)

The language choices within this section of the speech work to represent Howard as the "heroic protagonist' (Luke, 1997, p. 359) of this narrative. He is presented as both decisive and strong, but also as at one with the people. The speech in lines 144–169 for example places Howard, identified as I, as the most often used participant. In table 2 we set out the processes and circumstances attributed to Howard (I) as participant. As an example of how these language choices work to attribute Howard the central status within the resolution to this 'old' problem, note how the participant I is matched with many mental and relational processes such as *share, commit, aim, hope, seek, believe*. This works to construct Howard as both leading the push toward the 'new' reconciliation but also grounds this work in a shared approach with 'the Australian people'.

Table 2. Processes and circumstances that work with the participant I (Howard) in lines 144–169.

Process	*Circumstance*	*Process type*
share	that (the Australian people's) destiny	mental
am	here tonight	relational
announce	that if elected	verbal
(will) put	to the Australian people…	material
(would) commit	immediately to working in consultation…	relational
(would) aim	to introduce the bill…	mental
(would) seek	to enlist wide community support…	mental
(would) hope	to secure the sort of overwhelming vote …	mental
(would) aim	to secure the sort of overwhelming vote…	mental
believe	this is both realistic and achievable.	mental
see	this as a dignified and respectful reconciliation…	mental

To remind the listeners that this work is grounded in the needs and desires of the Australian people, Howard frames this presentation of the 'new' initiative once more by calling on a togetherness repertoire (Wetherall and Potter 1992):

It rests on my unshakeable believe that what unites us as Australians is far greater than what divides us. (lines 167–168 Appendix 1)

The announcement of Howard's 'new' reconciliation then is grounded in history and self-representations of Howard as traditional and conservative, but claimed as 'new' through the continual setting of this 'new' approach as a binary opposite to 'old' approaches. What is missed in this representation is that Howard has led the country for more than ten years prior to delivering this speech, and to his own admission this 'new' reconciliation is "little more than an affirmation of well-worn liberal conservative ideas" (lines 194–195 Appendix 1). And yet in what we have called the well-worn and classic "neoliberal quickstep" (Reiger, 2006), Howard represents his 'new reconciliation' as innovative at the same time as embedding the approach in the old, all the while without taking responsibility for past failures under his previous ten years of leadership.

In this short analysis we have demonstrated the language choices that have set up the binary divisions required to produce the chimera of 'newness', and the rhetorical devices called upon to place this newness in traditional and conservative neoliberal political approaches to Indigenous issues.

CONCLUSION

Washing his hands of the past, Howard's "new statement of reconciliation" which is analysed here, was a cynical manoeuvre, announced three days before declaring the date of the Federal election[7]. Without adequate consultation, Howard claimed he wanted to forge a "national consensus" for reconciliation. Yet, he refused to issue a formal apology because it would "only reinforce a culture of victimhood," and because "I have felt – and still feel – that the overwhelming balance sheet of Australian history is a positive one. In the end I could not accept that reconciliation required the condemnation of the Australian heritage I had always owned." (Appendix 1) What emerged, then, was a classic case of old philosophical wine in new discursive bottles. Looking at Howard's "new reconciliation" as a discursive or "racialized regime of representation" (Hall, 1997, p. 245), allows us to uncover the ideological assumptions that underpin the making of race and nation in Australia. It is at this stage of the analysis that it again became possible to see how broader formations of discourse and power are manifest in literacy acts such as political speech making within current neoliberal politics in capitalist society. In effect, how narrative performs the settler state in order to create a shared geography and sense of belonging.

Whilst refusing to say sorry on behalf of the Federal Government and Australia generally for past injustices or to offer a separate Treaty, Howard's "new reconciliation" was a discursive ploy that enabled him to undercut the legitimacy of claims for redress— of unfinished business. Like Dorothy clicking her heels three times, Howard believed that he had the power to put the past behind him by simply announcing his destination of choice. The official discourse that claims that the past is over and that it is time now for practical reconciliation constituted a state-sanctioned discourse of remembering and forgetting. Wetherall and Potter (1992) discuss the language of politicians in relation to their use of "rhetorically self sufficient arguments" (p. 177) which once said, and by calling on the common sense assumptions and ideological beliefs of the broader public, look natural and beyond doubt – in other words they stand as universal truths. Augoustinos Lecouteur, & Soyland (2006) matched Wetherell and Potter's findings of politician talk in New Zealand, when they identified the use of these same rhetorical devices in the language used by Howard in his address to the Reconciliation Convention in May 1997. The propositions that: *you cannot turn the clock backwards, present generations cannot be blamed for the mistakes of past generations, and we have to live in the twentieth century* are three of the ten rhetorical propositions put forward as common in the talk of politicians by both Wetherell & Potter (1992) and Augoustinos, Lecouteur, & Soyland (2006), and work to support the state-sanctioned discourse of remembering and forgetting that we discuss here.

Against the historical backdrop of a racist and antipodean imaginary, the Commonwealth government's construction of Aboriginal Australians as deviant "other" demonstrates the resilience of colonial hegemony. Moving between the past and present, the establishment of "colonial relationships of a racist, exploitative and coercive nature" must be understood within the historical context of settler states such as Australia that have a possessory interest in the Aboriginal land base (Green, 1995; Lipsitz, 1998). And because the fabrication of discourse through the use of rhetorical devices and language choices has become so refined, it was easy to get swept up in Howard's narrative. However, it also worked to perform the white colonial settler state, with significant discursive and material effects.

Traditional colonial discourses have positioned Aboriginal peoples as lazy and indulgent, as a people who needed to be controlled and "civilized." Likewise, the current NT intervention is being conducted under the guise of "protection." The new neoliberal mantra of "good governance" echoes that ethnocentric and racist sentiment. In the aftermath of the NT Intervention, Brown and Brown (2007) argue:

> In many respects, a new (or rekindled) language emerged, the language of "Aboriginal deficit". The media were awash with claims of "paedophile rings", of a culture that "accepted and protected" the raping of children, of "customary law being used as a shield to protect abusers". The inference was that all Aboriginal men are "perpetrators", all Aboriginal children are abused, and that these abuses — fuelled by alcohol, petrol and kava — are compounded by social dysfunction that is largely the consequence of a "primitive" and "barbaric" culture." Public commentary allowed the seeds of change to be sown, change that "required" a "new paternalism", "normalisation" or "mainstreaming"; that called for the closure of "unviable remote communities"; that touted the "failure of self-determination"; that required an end to "political correctness gone mad" and the "pouring billions of dollars down the toilet."

Despite most money for the so-called "Aboriginal problem" disappearing into an unwieldy white bureaucracy, it is easy for politicians to take umbrage at such so-called funding "black holes" and discursively construct Aboriginal community governance as costly, wasteful and inefficient. Against this racist backdrop, Dodson writes, "Public policy that celebrates Indigenous culture has been shunned. We are left with a vague sense that the problems of the present-day crisis have no history and that the way forward is for Indigenous people to abandon their identity and be absorbed into European settler society" (p. 22). Designed to de-emphasize group conflict with an emphasis on individual rights under a rational liberal policy framework, the patronising and stereotypical discourses of neoliberalism promise to remedy the deficiencies of the Keynesian welfare state with a focus on market driven forms of governance.

Having tied himself up in knots trying to win the approval of the white electorate, Howard's "new statement of reconciliation" pointed to the dominant position of the white majority as well as the structural benefits of Whiteness and institutionalised racism. As the outcome of a specific history of struggle, that includes the shaping and reshaping of the multiple discourses of reconciliation, Howard's speech provides a classic case study of processes of colonial restructuring in Australia. This includes reworking and transforming an influential and powerful political discourse into a "new" shape, and tying it more closely to discourses of development, nation building and neoliberalism.

Set against this backdrop, the newly elected Labor government led by Kevin Rudd announced that part of its motivation for supporting the NT intervention is to "assimilate" Aboriginal people "as workers, home owners and consumers" (Eatock, 2008; see also Clancy, 2008). To foster entrepreneurship and economic development in Aboriginal communities, the current Minister for Families, Housing, Community Services and Indigenous Affairs, Jenny Macklin, said it was imperative to "encourage private home ownership" and give potential investors "incentive to invest", e.g., creating opportunities for leases for mining on Aboriginal land (Head, 2008). Such punitive and draconian measures as the NT Intervention demonstrate that the making of neoliberal policy in Australia does not represent the end of colonisation or territorial struggles, but rather the intensification of a pernicious form of "internal colonisation". Establishing the legitimacy for state intervention, the official policy discourse of Aboriginal peoples as "add-ons", peripheral only within the larger discourse of the meritocratic Australian Dream, has justified the colonial denigration and devaluing of traditional cultural bonds and social roles including community ownership of land under customary law. In the aftermath of the Rudd apology[8], it remains to be seen whether a systemic policy that works to move the present toward the future is possible when anchored within the past.

APPENDIX 1: (NUMBERS ADDED, BOLD AND HEADINGS IN
ORIGINAL RELEASE)

11 October 2007
TRANSCRIPT OF THE PRIME MINISTER
THE HON JOHN HOWARD MP
ADDRESS TO THE SYDNEY INSTITUTE
SOFITEL WENTWORTH HOTEL, SYDNEY

The Right Time:
Constitutional Recognition for Indigenous Australians

1. Gerard and Anne Henderson, members of The Sydney Institute,
2. my fellow Australians.
3. Earlier today I released a small document on a big topic – Australian History.
4. It's a road map for the teaching of Australian History in Years 9 and 10.
5. It takes forward a project I launched some 21 months ago, on Australia Day
6. eve 2006. I called then for a root and branch renewal of the teaching of
7. Australian History in our schools.
8. My sense – confirmed by work done for last year's Australian History Summit
9. – was that Australian History in our schools had, to a worrying degree, fallen
10. victim to neglect and complacency. In some cases, it had simply gone
11. missing. Vast numbers of students had no exposure to a coherent and
12. sequential understanding of our national story.
13. I believed then, and I believe now, that if this country is to live up to its full
14. potential and its highest ideals we must turn this around. We're not there yet.
15. But I think we'll get there. I want to thank Gerard Henderson and many others
16. too numerous to name who have devoted their time and intellectual energy to
17. this task.
18. Tonight my focus is another topic of utmost national importance; one that
19. transcends the past, the present and the future of Australia and that goes to the
20. heart of our national identity and shared destiny.
21. For my generation – Australians who came of age in the 1950s and 1960s – it
22. has been ever present; a subject of deep sorrow and of great hope. The
23. challenge, and unfinished business, of *our* time. It is the place of Indigenous
24. people in the profound, compelling and unfolding story of Australia. In the
25. speech where I launched the Australian History project last year I spoke at
26. length on the secret of the modern Australian Achievement – our national
27. sense of balance. I said then that: 'Balance is as crucial to a well-ordered
28. society as it is to a full human life. It should not be mistaken for taking the
29. middle road or splitting the difference. Nor does it imply a state that is static
or
30. a nation at rest. 'Quite the opposite. A sense of balance is the handmaiden of
31. national growth and renewal. It helps us to respond creatively to an uncertain

32. world with a sense of proportion. 'Keeping our balance means we reform and
33. evolve so as to remain a prosperous, secure and united nation. It also means
34. we retain those cherished values, beliefs and customs that have served us so
35. well in the past.'
36. The sense of balance Australia has found in 2007 allows us now to go further
37. and to aim higher. The time is right to take a permanent, decisive step towards
38. completing some unfinished business of this nation. A little more than 100
39. days ago I spoke at The Sydney Institute on the topic of the Government's
40. emergency intervention in Northern Territory Indigenous communities. This
41. intervention – and in particular the public's reaction to it – has been a
42. watershed in Indigenous affairs in Australia. It has overturned 30 years of
43. attitudes and thinking on Indigenous policy. The response from people around
44. Australia has again highlighted to me the anguish so many Australians feel
45. about the state of Indigenous Australia and the deep yearning in the national
46. psyche for a more positive and unifying approach to Reconciliation.

A new paradigm
47. This new Reconciliation I'm talking about starts from the premise that
48. individual rights and national sovereignty prevail over group rights. That
49. group rights are, and ought to be, subordinate to both the citizenship rights of
50. the individual and the sovereignty of the nation. This is Reconciliation based
51. on a new paradigm of positive affirmation, of unified Australian citizenship,
52. and of balance – a balance of rights and responsibilities; a balance of practical
53. and symbolic progress. It is this balance which holds the key to unlocking
54. overwhelming support among the Australian people for meaningful
55. Reconciliation.
56. Some will say: Surely we've been here before. What's different now? Good
57. question. I'm convinced we are dealing today with a new alignment of ideas
58. and individuals; a coming together of forces I have not witnessed in 32 years
59. of public life. As always, the Australian people themselves are the best guide.
60. Let me quote from just one of the many letters I have received since the
61. Government announced the Northern Territory intervention. It is from Mrs
62. Terry Meehan, now living in Melbourne. Her late husband, Dr Ken Meehan,
63. was the sole doctor of Yarrabah Aboriginal Community in Queensland for
64. many years, looking after some 2,000 indigenous people. She writes that: 'His
65. whole life was dedicated to the welfare of mankind but especially indigenous
66. peoples both in New Guinea and Australia. … During my time as his wife in
67. Yarrabah I watched with frustration and anguish at the devastation alcohol
68. abuse caused. 'The local canteen only served full strength beer and of course
69. was run by the local council. The number of alcohol related deaths was great –
70. but we weren't allowed to speak about it publicly at that time. 'You have
71. taken a much needed step in order to make a difference to help these
72. wonderful people become a proud people.'
73. A major catalyst for the new alignment I spoke about is the rise of the
74. Indigenous responsibility agenda and the intellectual firepower which a new

75. generation of Indigenous leaders has brought to Australian politics. I've been
76. reminded that, in fact, the Indigenous responsibility agenda is an old agenda;
77. the agenda of Faith Bandler and Neville Bonner among others.
78. At its core is the need for Aboriginal Australia to join the mainstream
79. economy as the foundation of economic and social progress. This is at the
80. heart of the work the Australian Government is pursuing under the Federal
81. Minister Mal Brough's leadership. The central goal is to address the cancer of
82. passive welfare and to create opportunity through education, employment and
83. home ownership. We seek partnerships which respect communal land rights of
84. Indigenous Australians, but with a view to encouraging wider economic
85. opportunity based on those rights.

Towards a better balance

86. I'm the first to admit that this whole area is one I have struggled with during
87. the entire time that I have been Prime Minister. My instinct has been to try and
88. improve the conditions for indigenous people within the framework of a
89. united nation and unified Australian citizenship. I have never felt comfortable
90. with the dominant paradigm for Indigenous policy – one based on the shame
91. and guilt of non-indigenous Australians, on a repudiation of the Australia I
92. grew up in, on a rights agenda that led ultimately and inexorably towards
93. welfare dependency and on a philosophy of separateness rather than shared
94. destiny. This nation spent (and wasted) a lot of time in the last 30 years toying
95. with the idea of a treaty implying that in some way we are dealing with two
96. separate nations. To me, this goal was always fundamentally flawed and
97. something I could never support. We are not a federation of tribes. We are one
98. great tribe; one Australia. I still believe that a collective national
99. apology for past injustice fails to provide the necessary basis to move forward.
100. Just as the responsibility agenda is gaining ground it would, I believe, only
101. reinforce a culture of victimhood and take us backwards.
102. I said a couple of years ago that part of my problem with the old
103. Reconciliation agenda was that it let too many people – particularly in white
104. Australia – off the hook.
105. It let them imagine they could achieve something lasting and profound
106. through symbolic gesture alone, without grappling in a serious, sustained way
107. with the real practical dimensions of indigenous misery. There had to be a
108. fundamental correction to the unbalanced approach to rights and
109. responsibilities. This in no way diminishes the importance of government
110. responsibility in providing resources and services.
111. I acknowledge that my own journey in arriving at this point has not been
112. without sidetracks and dry gullies. There have been low points when dialogue
113. between me as Prime Minister and many Indigenous leaders dwindled almost
114. to the point of non-existence. I fully accept my share of the blame for that.
115. On the night of the 1998 election I publicly committed myself to endeavouring
116. to achieve Reconciliation by the year 2001. In the end, that did not happen.

117. I recognise now that, though emotionally committed to the goal, I was
118. mistaken in believing that it could be achieved in a form I truly believed in.
119. The old paradigm's emphasis on shame, guilt and apologies made it
120. impossible to reconcile the goal with the path I was required to tread. The
121. challenge I have faced around Indigenous identity politics is in part an artefact
122. of who I am and the time in which I grew up.
123. I have always acknowledged the past mistreatment of Aboriginal people and
124. have frequently said that the treatment of Indigenous Australians represents
125. the most blemished chapter in the history of this country.
126. Yet I have felt – and I still feel – that the overwhelming balance sheet of
127. Australian history is a positive one. In the end, I could not accept that
128. Reconciliation required a condemnation of the Australian heritage I had
129. always owned. At the same time, I recognise that the parlous position of
130. Indigenous Australians docs have its roots in history and that past injustices
131. have a real legacy in the present.
132. I believe we must find room in our national life to formally recognise the
133. special status of Aboriginal and Torres Strait Islanders as the first peoples of
134. our nation.
135. We must recognise the distinctiveness of Indigenous identity and culture and
136. the right of Indigenous people to preserve that heritage. The crisis of
137. indigenous social and cultural disintegration requires a stronger affirmation of
138. Indigenous identity and culture as a source of dignity, self-esteem and pride.
139. This is all the more so at a time when the blossoming of Indigenous art and
140. dance – and the way it gives unique expression to Australian culture – is
141. something we all celebrate and share.

A rare convergence

142. The Australian people want to move. They want to move towards a new
143. settlement of this issue. I share that desire which is why I am here tonight. I
144. announce that, if re- elected, I will put to the Australian people within 18
145. months a referendum to formally recognise Indigenous Australians in our
146. Constitution – their history as the first inhabitants of our country, their unique
147. heritage of culture and languages, and their special (though not separate) place
148. within a reconciled, indivisible nation.
149. My goal is to see a new Statement of Reconciliation incorporated into the
150. Preamble of the Australian Constitution. If elected, I would commit
151. immediately to working in consultation with Indigenous leaders and others on
152. this task. It would reflect my profound sentiment that Indigenous Australians
153. should enjoy the full bounty that this country has to offer; that their economic,
154. social and cultural well-being should be comparable to that of other
155. Australians. I would aim to introduce a bill that would include the Preamble
156. Statement into Parliament within the first 100 days of a new government. A
157. future referendum question would stand alone. It would not be blurred or
158. cluttered by other constitutional considerations. I would seek to enlist wide
159. community support for a 'Yes' vote. I would hope and aim to secure the sort
160. of overwhelming vote achieved 40 years ago at the 1967 referendum.

161. If approached in the right spirit, I believe this is both realistic and achievable.
162. I see this as a dignified and respectful Reconciliation process. It is founded on
163. the notion that we are all Australians together; bound by a common set of laws
164. which we must all obey and from which we are entitled to equal justice. It
165. rests on my unshakeable belief that what unites us as Australians is far greater
166. than what divides us.
167. A positive affirmation in our Constitution of the unique place of Indigenous
168. Australians can, I believe, be the cornerstone of a new settlement. I sense in
169. the community a rare and unexpected convergence of opinion on this issue
170. between the more conservative approach which I clearly identify with and
171. those who traditionally have favoured more of a group rights approach. It is a
172. moment in time which should be seized, lest it be lost. Reconciliation can't be
173. a 51–49 project; or even a 7–30 project. We need as a nation to lock-in behind
174. a path we can all agree on. I hope the steps on Australian History that I
175. announced today can also make a practical contribution. As I said at the time
176. of the Australian History Summit, you can't have a proper comprehension of
177. Australian history without an understanding of indigenous history and its
178. contribution to the Australian story. Summit participant Jackie Huggins has
179. written that an Australia where all our young are taught the continuing story of
180. indigenous Australians as part of our nation's history 'may not seem like such
181. a remarkable outcome but it is'. Indeed, she argues, 'the teaching of our
182. shared story is the key to reconciliation because it allows us to understand
183. each other and to build healthy, respectful relationships'.
184. There is a window to convert this moment of opportunity into something real
185. and lasting in a way that gets the balance right. But I suspect it is small. Noel
186. Pearson has made the point to me that Australia seems to go through 30 to 40
187. year cycles on indigenous affairs: periods of reorientation and attempts to find
188. new solutions (assimilation in the 1930s; equality and self-determination in the
189. 1960s and '70s) followed by decades of denial of the lack of progress in
190. between. Some will no doubt want to portray my remarks tonight as a form of
191. Damascus Road conversion. In reality, they are little more than an affirmation
192. of well-worn liberal conservative ideas.
193. Their roots lie in a Burkean respect for custom and cultural tradition and the
194. hidden chain of obligations that binds a community together. In the world of
195. practical politics they owe much to the desire for national cohesion Disraeli
196. spoke to in 19th Century Britain – another time of great economic and social
197. change. And in a literary sense they find echoes in Michael Oakeshott's
198. conservatism and the sense of loss should precious things disappear. In the
199. end, my appeal to the broader Australian community on this is simpler, and far
200. less eloquent. It goes to love of country and a fair go. It's about understanding

201. the destiny we share as Australians – that we are all in this together. It's about
202. recognising that while ever our Indigenous citizens are left out or
   marginalised
203. or feel their identity is challenged we are all diminished. It's about
204. appreciating that their long struggle for a fair place in the country is our
205. struggle too.

Conclusion

206. I am a realist. True Reconciliation will become a reality only when it delivers
207. better lives for Aboriginal and Torres Strait Islander people. That, quite
208. frankly, will be the work of generations. I'm also an incurable optimist about
209. this country. I always have been. And I always will be. I'm in no doubt that if
210. we continue to get the big things right Australia's best years are still ahead of
211. us. My optimism has always found its greatest nourishment in the character of
212. the Australian people. Reconciliation – at its best – is, and must be, a people's
213. movement. Now, for the first time in a long time, we can see the outline of a
214. new settlement for Indigenous policy in Australia.
215. It stands at a point of intersection between rights and responsibilities; between
216. the symbolic and the practical. It is, to be sure, less an end point than a point
217. of light that can guide us to a better future. We're not there yet. But if we keep
218. our balance, we can get there soon.

NOTES

[1] Australia has six states and two mainland territories.

[2] Despite some prominent dissenting voices in the wider community, the Intervention had bi-partisan support from the federal Labor Party, even if it was critical of some of the measures such as the abolishment of the CDEP scheme and removing the permit system.

[3] Cheering the market as a remedy for the failure of the Keynesian welfare state and Aboriginal governance systems, the intervention could be framed as a land grab that constitutes the "unfinished business" of the liberal democratic settler state (Pilger, 2008; Sharp, 2007/2008).[3] Under the NT Intervention, the take over of townships, currently held under the Native Title Act 1993, through the imposition of five-year leases, removed community ownership of land. [3] Using its power of compulsory acquisition to administer townships, the government also suspended the permit system that required permission from traditional owners to enter their land. These measures were justified as part of Howard's (2007) promise in his speech on June 27th "…to ensure property and public housing can be improved."[3] At the time, he claimed, "If that involves the payment of compensation on just terms as required by the Commonwealth Constitution, then that compensation will be readily paid" (Howard, 2007). Contrary to this, the direct intervention into pre-existing Aboriginal property rights raised questions about "just-compensation provisions" including for those communities that "rely on the income earned from issuing permits" (Hunter, 2007). Many Aboriginal leaders, with grassroots support in the wider community, were convinced that the government used alleged sexual abuse as "a Trojan horse to resume total control of our lands" (Turner cited in Robertson, 2007). For example, the NT Intervention was seen to encourage the break up of remote communities and townships making mining and the transport of toxic waste including nuclear material close to Aboriginal communities less controversial and more difficult to be resisted (Nixon, 2007; Robson, 2007).[3]

[4] The authors of the report, such as Pat Anderson, have been highly critical of the NT Intervention (Hunter, 2007).

[5]   John Howard lost the Australian Federal election to the now Prime Minister Kevin Rudd and his Labour party on 24th November after 10 years and four terms in office. Howard also lost his seat of Bennalong – only the second time in history that an Australian Prime Minister has not retained his own seat at an election.

[6]   Mal Brough was one of the key Howard Ministers who also lost his seat at the 2007 Federal election.

[7]   Following Rudd's landslide electoral victory on 25 November 2007, Alexander Downer revealed that the aim of the intervention into Northern Territory communities was to generate 'electoral bounce' (Altman, 2007/2008, p. 5).

[8]   Since the election, the Rudd Labor government has made some important symbolic gestures, including a formal apology to the Stolen Generations at the first sitting of the new Parliament on February 13th 2008 and making a commitment to "close the gap" in indigenous life expectancy through a range of health and education initiatives. However, the NT intervention has created a new wave of dispossession and social problems. As Lyle Cooper, Acting President of Bagot Community has said "I thank you Prime Minister Rudd for your apology (but) it's an invasion all over again. We are being told where to shop, what to eat, how to act and how to live" (Darwin Aboriginal Rights Coalition cited in Pariah, 2008). Following a promising start, the PM Kevin Rudd and Aboriginal Affairs Minister Jenny Macklin are now officially the face of the continuing intervention. Despite repeated calls to scrap the intervention, the Rudd government recently committed (after a review) to providing ongoing support for it (Karvelas, 2009).

REFERENCES

Altman, J. (2007/2008, December–January). Will the NT intervention now unravel. *Arena Magazine, 92*, 5–6.

Augoustinos, M., Lecouteur, A., & Soyland, J. (2002). Self-sufficient arguments in political rhetoric: Constructing reconciliation and apologising to the stolen generations. *Discourse and Society, 13*(1), 105–149.

Behrendt, L. (2008, April 17). The pointed view: Act like you mean it Kevin. *National Indigenous Times, 151*. Retrieved July 27, 2008, from http://www.nit.com.au/opinion/story.aspx?id=14663

Brown, A., & Brown, N. (2007). The Northern Territory Intervention: Voices from the centre of the fringe. *The Medical Journal of Australia*. Retrieved September 12, 2008, from http://mja.com.au/public/issues/187_11_031207/bro11318_fm.html

Chouliaraki, L., & Fairclough, N. (1999). *Discourse in late modernity. Rethinking critical discourse analysis*. Edinburgh, UK: Edinburgh University Press.

Clancy, E. (2008, July 24). *Justice-where the bloody hell are ya? An Phoblacht*. Retrieved July 29, 2008, from http://www.anphoblacht.com/news/detail/33307

Dodson, P. (2007). Whatever happened to reconciliation? In J. Altman & M. Hinkson (Eds.), *Coercive reconciliation: Stabilise, normalise, exit Aboriginal Australia* (pp. 21–29). North Carlton, Vic: Arena Publications.

Eatock, P. (2008, June 14). Aboriginal control of Aboriginal Affairs. *Green Left Weekly*. Retrieved July 30, 2008, from http://www.greenleft.org.au/2008/755/39008

Fairclough, N. (2001a). Critical discourse analysis. In A. McHoul & M. Rapley (Eds.), *How to analyse talk in institutional settings*. London, UK: Continuum.

Fairclough, N. (2001b). *Language and power* (2nd ed.). London, UK: Longman.

Florence, M. (2000). Foucault (Robert Hurley and others, Trans.). In M. Fabian (Ed.), *Aesthetics, method and epistemology* (Vol. 2, pp. 459–463). London, UK: Penguin.

Foucault, M. (1971). Orders of discourse. *Social Science Information, 10*(2), 7–30.

Foucault, M. (1972). *The archaeology of knowledge*. New York, USA: Pantheon Books.

Foucault, M. (2000). Questions of method. In J. Faubion (Ed.), *Power. Essential works of Foucault 1954–1984* (pp. 298–325). New York, USA: The New Press.

Gee, J. (1991) *An introduction to discourse analysis. Theory and method.* London, UK: Routledge.

Green, J. (1995, Fall). Towards a détente with history: Confronting Canada's colonial legacy. *International Journal of Canadian Studies, 12.* Retrieved July 27, 2008, from http://sisis.nativeweb.org/clark/detente.html.

Hall, S. (Ed.). (1997). *Representation: Cultural Representations and Signifying Practices.* London, Thousand Oaks: Sage Publications.

Head, M. (2008, March 4). After Rudd's "apology" to indigenous people: Australian government extends welfare "quarantining" and land grab. *World Socialist Web Site.* Retrieved June 7, 2008, from http://www.wsws.org/articles/2008/mar2008/abor-m04.shtml

Hinkson, M. (2007). Introduction: In the name of the child. In J. Altman & M. Hinkson (Eds.), *Coercive reconciliation: Stabilise, normalise, exit Aboriginal Australia* (pp. 1–12). North Carlton, Vic: Arena Publications.

Howard, J. (2007, June 25). John Howard's address to The Sydney Institute. *Australians for Native Title and Reconciliation.* Retrieved September 17, 2008, from http://www.antar.org.au/content/view/444/1/

Hunter, B. (2007). Conspicuous compassion and wicked problems: The Howard government's National Emergency in Indigenous Affairs. *Agenda, 14*(3). Retrieved September 17, 2008, from http://epress.anu.edu.au/agenda/014/03/mobile_devices/ch07.html

Karvelas, P. (2009, March 6). Macklin extends intervention. *The Australian.* Retrieved March 6, 2009, from http://www.theaustralian.news.com.au/story/0,25197,25145772-601,00.html

Lipsitz, G. (1998). *The Possessive Investment in Whiteness: How White People Profit from Identity Politics.* Philadelphia: Temple University Press.

Luke, A. (1995). Text and discourse in education: An introduction to critical discourse analysis. *Review of Research in Education, 21,* 3–48.

Luke, A. (1997). The material effects of the word: Apologies, Stolen Children and pubic discourse. *Discourse: Studies in the Cultural Politics of Education, 18*(3), 343–368.

McLaren, P. (1995). White terror and oppositional agency: Towards a critical multiculturalism. In C. Sleeter & P. McLaren (Eds.), *Multicultural education, critical pedagogy, and the politics of difference* (pp. 33–70). Albany, NY: State University of New York Press.

Northern Territory Board of Inquiry into the Protection of Aboriginal children from Sexual Abuse. (2007). *Ampe Akelyernemane Meke Mekarle "Little Children are Sacred" Report.* Northern Territory, Australia: Northern Territory Government.

McLaren, P., & Martin, G. (2004). The legend of the Bush Gang: Imperialism, war and propaganda. *Cultural Studies/Critical Methodologies, 4*(3), 281–303.

Miller, G. (1997). Building bridges: The possibility of analytic dialogue between ethnography, conversation analysis and Foucault. In D. Silverman (Ed.), *Qualitative research theory, method and practice.* London, UK: Sage Publications.

Nixon, S. (2007, October 27). Aboriginal group fights Canberra's 'land grab'. *The Age.* Retrieved September 17, 2008, from http://www.theage.com.au/news/national/aboriginal-group-fights-canberras-land-grab/2007/10/26/1192941340620.html

Pariah – People Against Racism in Aboriginal Homelands. (2008). National Statement & Call-out for Endorsement – National Day of Protest on June 21. Retrieved June 7, 2008, from http://www.pariahnt.org/news/

Pilger, J. (2008, March 29). Australia's hidden empire. *Green Left Weekly.* Retrieved July 27, 2008, from http://www.greenleft.org.au/2008/745/38551

Reiger, K. (2006). A neoliberal quickstep: Contradictions in Australian maternity policy. *Health Sociology Review, 15*(4), 330–340.

Robson, P. (2007). The corporate interests behind Howard's land grab. *Green Left Weekly.* Retrieved September 17, 2008, from http://www.greenleft.org.au/2007/731/37864

Robson, P., & Windisch, M. (2008, March 1). Indigenous women: Welfare quaretine a disaster. *Green Left Weekly.* Retrieved July 27, 2008, from http://www.greenleft.org.au/2008/742/38411.

Robertson, D. (2007, July 26). Govt orchestrating a land grab: Aboriginal leaders. *Lateline.* Retrieved September 17, 2008, from http://www.abc.net.au/lateline/content/2007/s1962845.htm

Rogers, R. (2002). Between contexts: A critical discourse analysis of family literacy, discursive practices, and literate subjectivities. *Reading Research Quarterly, 37*(3), 248–270.

Sharp, N. (2007/2008, December–January). Between fear and hope: Invasion by stealth 2007. *Arena Magazine, 92*, 31–34.

Threadgold, T. (2000). Poststructuralism and discourse analysis. In A. Lee & C. Poynton (Eds.), *Culture and text. Discourse and methodology in social research and cultural studies* (pp. 40–58). Lanham, MD: Rowmn & Littlefield Publishers Inc.

Wetherell, M., & Potter, J. (1992). *Mapping the language of racism: Discourse and the legitimation of exploitation.* Hemel Hempstead: Harvester Wheatsheaf.

Wodak, R. (1999). Critical discourse analysis at the end of the 20th century. *Research in Language and Social Interaction, 32*(1–2), 185–193.

Woods, A. (2004). *The contexts and purposes of school literacy pedagogy: 'Failing' in the early years.* Unpublished Doctoral Thesis, The University of Queensland.

ALISON SAMMEL AND SHAUNEEN PETE

10. RE(A)D AND WHITE: DISCUSSING ETHNICITIES AND THE TEACHING OF WHITENESS

Ali: Dialogue can be the midwife of inspiration, reflection and understanding. Yet, in our very busy practices of formal learning and teaching less time is dedicated to moments of deliberate, casual, cheerful or heated academic dialogue with our peers. I find that much of our daily conversations tend to focus on administration or logistic functions, or a deconstruction of said tasks, but rarely do we focus on emerging ideas of our chosen disciplines or explore their underlying neoliberal agendas. This is unfortunate, as I know from experience that many of my own pedagogic insights came from the rich, dynamic interplay started over a coffee, or the red scribbles on a dissertation, or a random comment in a hallway, or more playfully, a jest muttered in a pub. This chapter seeks to capture this dynamic by documenting a conversation between two colleagues reflecting on the ongoing presence and pressure of colonialism in education and what it means at a practical level for their pedagogy.

We start this conversation with the assumption that colonialism is alive and well in the formal education systems in which we teach – Canada and Australia. We maintain that the inherent racism currently occurring in Western classrooms is neither a natural phenomenon, a 'neutral' way of things, nor is it unanticipated or unpredictable. Similar to hurricane Katrina, institutional racism in education is a consequence of political disposability (Giroux, 2006) and governments at all levels are continuing to either ignore, or inadequately respond to these chronic cases of everyday inequity. Indeed, fundamentally, the capitalistic machine is benefiting from it. We are colleagues who strongly disagree with this oppression and engage in the pedagogy journey of resisting this inequity. Our teaching and research explores the complexity of why the education system is under-prepared for, or feels little sense of responsibility towards those who are marginalised. Similar questions are still being asked about the US government and those most marginalised in New Orleans. However, in education, the answers are now coming in the form of 'Standards' that speak to the 'Valuing of Diversity' (Sammel and Martin, 2008) but these liberal understandings of diversity do not acknowledge the politics of oppression and give the same status to 'gifted and talented' students as they do to 'class, gender, and race' (see Gore, 2001; Mills, 2006; Villegas & Lucas, 2002 for more on this).

With the agenda to challenge the current dysfunctional and unjust education system, and with the intention of seeing our pedagogy as a political activity for embracing social change, we come together to engage in developing more

G. Martin, D. Houston, P. McLaren and J. Suoranta (eds.), The Havoc of Capitalism: Publics, Pedagogies and Environmental Crisis, 157–168.

meaningful ways to talk about teaching White privilege to our students and to explore our own learning. To do this, we like Gadamer's (1989) concept of the fusing of "Horizons", and the importance he places on dialogue. When Gadamer (1989) writes of horizons he is referring to conscious and subconscious perceptions, beliefs and biases that are brought into any discussion. These horizons are two fold: a historical horizon (defined by the past and the traditions that have resulted from it) and a present horizon (that encompasses all that is believed and understood by a person at this moment in their current situation). They are interconnected as the historical horizon influences the present horizon and as such, must be acknowledged and examined so that the present horizon can be better understood. The explorations of these horizons results in what Gadamer (1989) refers to as their fusing. In this fusion, the historical horizon remains fixed, while the present horizon "is continually in the process of being formed because we are continually having to test all our prejudices" (Gadamer, 1989, p. 306). It is through dialogue between the two horizons that understanding can grow. Gadamer (1989) proposes that developing a rich understanding is not something that can be achieved individually, but through dialogue when people lay open their experiences and horizons, and entertain the possibility of change and growth.

This chapter will attempt to capture our discussions about the social construction of education for diversity. Shauneen, what has been your goal in teaching about diversity?

Shauneen: I am a First Nations woman from Saskatchewan. My original goal was always to work for the empowerment of Indigenous peoples in my province. I ended up working in mainstream institutions teaching white middle class predominantly Christian (referred to from herein as WMCC) students. The great dilemma for me was that I ended up empowering WMCC students to take up the charge of diversity education – and have not worked all that directly with Indigenous undergraduate students. I expected to teach Indigenous peoples in a way that critiqued normative constructions (curriculum, instruction, etc) and at the same time provided space for us to Indigenize the curriculum in new ways. However, the students in my classes needed an introduction into the constructions of difference (race, class, gender, sexual orientation). They needed a vocabulary for speaking about norm and otherness. For many of them, this first glance at difference was very uncomfortable. Denial, dismissal, and minimization (Henry & Tator, 2006) of other people's experiences were common expressions of my students. In many ways teaching this particular group of students took me very far away from my original goals of emancipating Canadian First Nations and Métis students.

To begin with, I need to state that I did not come to the work of teaching about whiteness in a direct way. After my teacher training, I taught, and became a district consultant specializing in Aboriginal Education. During that time, I worked on a Master's degree in Educational Administration and later also completed a Ph.D. in Higher Education administration. Both fields were (white) male – dominated. This construction was one that I ended up identifying in my thesis; and speaking against in my dissertation. My awareness of whiteness grew during the years in which I was a graduate student. At that point, I became overwhelmed by the dominance of whiteness. To be sure, I had grown up brown in urban Saskatchewan, and was aware that I was different. As a young person I understood that my status as a First Nations girl/woman meant I was not treated the same as those around me. However, I did not see white as the problem. It was not until I started teaching, and later while studying in graduate school did I begin to question every aspect of curriculum, every assumption about teaching, and every idea about leadership: only then did I more fully understand the connections between dominance and whiteness. What about you Ali, how did you come to know whiteness?

Ali: My story is reflective of the white middle class girl growing up in urban Australia. For me, there was nothing but 'white' in my early life, and if there had been anything slightly 'off white' it went unnoticed. So, like most white Australians, I did not see white. I did not 'see' any ethnic complexity except for the strange 'pigeon English' that the Boarders of the private girls' school I went to, used to speak. Most of us 'local' daygirls could never quite understand what these students, who had lived in Papa New Guinea, were saying. The racial beings of those around me, (let alone the implications of my own colour), remained unexamined and unnamed well into my twenties. My first two university degrees came and went without 'seeing' another ethnic group. The only recollection I have is noticing the growing numbers of Asian tourists, and hearing how 'they' where buying all 'our' land for golf courses. There were always mutterings of Australian Aboriginals, but for me they were confined to the black velvet pictures with spears and kangaroos on my Aunty Mirrie's wall. In hindsight I lived with the daily implications of the White Australia Policy[1].

This changed when I moved to Canada. I was 23 and I remember the first time I met a woman who was black. It became wonderfully clear that Toronto was very different from Australia: it was the epitome of the exciting, exotic 'other' that you travelled the world to see when you are young and ready to explore. Even though I appreciated that I had a different 'culture' (as I was the 'Australian other' with my accent and stories), what I didn't appreciate was that I too had a 'colour'. For many years I believed that I (or anybody who was visibly 'white') had no racial presence: that was what my Black friends had. They had the Canadian and/or Jamaican culture but they also had a racial identity. This seemed true for my First Nations friends as well: they seemed to have both culture and colour. Racial identity or ethnicity, in this way of thinking was more a determinate of skin pigment or biology. I did not yet appreciate that race was not about science, but rather related to the cultural, social, values, beliefs, and lifestyle differences of people that are shaped by complex interaction between themselves, others and their place, space and time. Over the years through my friends, students, and activist work, I began to understand how wars around race and power were building, defusing, engaging, won, lost, acknowledged and made invisible at individual levels nearly daily for people. My mind began to be alert to forms of infrastructural racism. I came to understand how the polite etiquette I had been taught perpetuated racism. However, it was not until I understood the social construction of 'race' that I appreciated that I had an 'ethnicity' and this 'race' had a past, present, and possible futures. It was not until I started working with the First Nations people in Canada that I began learning and teaching about the social construction of whiteness. However, I had been a teacher at high schools and universities for many years at this point and had never even heard of this concept, even though I lived its benefits daily. What was your experience?

Shauneen: When I accepted a term faculty position in the Faculty of Education, I continued to learn about the social construction of whiteness (McIntosh, 1988; McIntyre, 1997). As a neophyte instructor, my department provided me with course outlines developed by other professors. I learned about whiteness and White privilege because it was a required chapter of the anti-oppressive curriculum that I was asked to teach. I, like you, both as a teacher and educational consultant, did not have an awareness of the social construction of whiteness, nor an understanding of racial dominance. I learned in the practice of teaching WMCC students that white students a) don't know/admit that they are white; b) think that admitting that they are white is somehow racist; c) don't know/admit that race is socially constructed; d) don't believe that white is the norm. They prefer to buy into the ideas that being colour-blind is good; and that meritocracy is possible. Once again, reflecting back on the question, and on the topic of this book I would have to say that like my students examination of their own whiteness; my understanding of the social construction of dominant education came late in life, and I observed that it was often denied, dismissed and minimized by those in my classroom. The great myth is that schooling is somehow culturally neutral – when in fact it very much reflects the dominant norms of the context in which we find ourselves. Very clearly the readings in the course showed that schooling, school curriculum, teaching, and instructional norms are raced, classed and gendered (Briskin, 1994; Overall, 1995; Anyon, 1994; McMullan, 2004; Sleeter, 1993; Harper & Cavanagh, 1994). After the first year of teaching these courses, I came to realize that I would have to actively expose white racial identity construction, and privilege to my students if I ever expected to be involved in the process of change in education. This realization reminded me once again how far away from my goal of empowering Indigenous peoples my professional work was taking me. I wondered if structurally, by teaching my WMCC students the language of anti-oppression, whether I was once again privileging them in their formal schooling. Did I provide them with new and powerful language and understandings that would re-assert their positioning in regard to educational change? I wondered if our First Nations and Métis undergraduate students were gaining similar access to this powerful language?

Ali: There is a lot in what you have said here. My students react along fairly similar and predictable lines when learning about White privilege. There are many emotions: anger, guilt, resentment, joy. For the majority, initially, there is mainly anger. I found the reasons the students give for these emotions are complex, but at the root is the idea of injustice: injustice they perceive committed towards themselves and to others. Like your students, I found that many of my students didn't want to believe that they were in any way associated with a discursive practice (Whiteness) that sustains Eurocentric worldviews through inherited laws, ideologies, infrastructures, policies, beliefs and actions (Shome, 1999). I believe some students thought that, as their professor, I was using my position and bias to indoctrinate them about White privilege (which could be an interesting point to discuss, as I am. Not many of my colleagues promote a critique of hegemonic forces that include White privilege and capitalism. Nor do they ask students to examine who they are and where they stand relative to these positionings). But for most, the realisation that racism is an everyday occurrence and is embodied within the dominant institutional order and inscribed within the social relations of everyday life, offered an understanding of how White privilege and racism can be render unacknowledged and invisible to some groups within society.

The students are also communicating anger or guilt at their own ignorance for not knowing. For many it is the first time they have been invited to think about how infrastructures, ideologies, policies, beliefs, and values are laden towards the dominant microcultures of the Australian society and how they have been socialized into a society where inequities based on race are inherently justified. They communicated beginning to see how the structures around them, as well as their own words and practices were influenced by racism. At first, many questioned the validity of White privilege, suggesting if it were 'true' they would have been told about it before now. However, there were others in the class who attested to its legitimacy through their own, or their family's, experiences. This was usually when many students wanted to become less-white, or find ways of connecting with some long-lost ancestral linage that made them more marginalised than their current status afforded them. This was always an interesting part of the course, for at this stage, the majority of students are in discomfort with the content; most are clumsy with language and thoughts, although a few are soaring high with their new wings, confidence and voice. These few students, now given the space, are choosing to speak loudly against racism. Some are just naming it, whereas others are re-imagining new pedagogic futures. For me, this re-imagining is the aim of the course, however, as much as I attempt to provide safe spaces within the classroom, I worry about the emotional safety etc., of these brave students in their choosing to speak out and educate others. In saying this, I would love for you to expand on how you believe you might be privileging your WMC students by asking them to engage with the language of anti-oppression.

Shauneen: As a racial minority I carry with me my experiences with race, racism, and other forms of oppression. This story when told, is often dismissed, denied, and minimized by those closer to the norm, which many question - "it all happened a long time ago, why can't you (they) let go?" For my First Nations and Métis students, our visibility often leads those closer to the norm to ask us to share our story, regardless of whether the environment is safe for us to share this story in the first place. Once told, my racial minority students often experience the very same denial, dismissal and minimization to their stories as well. As marginalized bodies, we, my racial minority students and I, share in a common experience of at once being placed in the spotlight as "ethnic specialists" with an important story to share, and the contrary experience of having that story not respected: For us the Norm's responses say loudly to us: You Lie! We wonder as to why we should share at all. In turn, when I learned the language of oppression, I found the words made good tools to offset the power imbalance. I felt better armed to confront whiteness, as the power of the language gave me confidence. I learned quickly that I could disarm some individuals with a carefully placed "institutional forms of oppression" or "structural racisms". On the other hand, in some circles I was labelled not only a liar for telling our truth, but now I was named as an angry racist bitch for speaking about the truth of White racial privilege! In any case, having lived the story, and carrying the language of anti-oppression was not enough to sway the power. When my neophyte WMCC students began to speak of systems of oppression in their circles of influence (family, church, work, school, and friends) knowing the language of anti-oppression gave them more credibility within those circles. They were often unchallenged; in fact, many of them were escalated for their newfound proficiency in anti-oppressive knowledge ways. Not surprisingly, many now provide leadership in the area of "diversity training" throughout mainstream organizations in the Prairie Provinces. The irony is not lost on me. I am aware in this moment that these words in print once again raise up my vulnerability; I await the name-calling even as I type. I've learned that the discomfort is common in this work.

Ali: Yes, Shauneen, I agree, this is White privilege playing out. I know that as a white, middle class woman, especially in many circles within Australia, I would most likely be asked to conduct a workshop on 'diversity' than one of my Aboriginal counterparts. This reflects peoples 'comfort' zones for many people even today would be more 'comfortable' working with a white woman than an Aboriginal one. We still have a long way to go towards equity. Interestingly, I recently turned down conducting such a workshop within my university and instead advocated for infrastructural change, most importantly employing an Aboriginal person as a PVC for Diversity and Academic Affairs to lead a team to conduct a systemic review of policies and practices relating to programs, teaching and learning and staffing in relation to diversity. This action was not looked upon favourably.

The aggressive labels such as the angry racist bitch, or even just being called 'an angry woman' were titles that took me a while to get used to. They are said to keep me in my socially constructed acceptable, place: and sometimes they still work. Often I replay the conversations in which I have spoken up, wondering if I could have said something differently, and each time, I feel physically drained. Sometimes I worry about the consequences of speaking out in these unsafe, unsupported spaces. These situations are still not easy to deal with. But more and more I feel the need to speak up when things are said, even when people who have seniority say them. I find I have a style in speaking up now. I deliberately speak calmly, and gently, and pose my thoughts in the form of a question; however, more often than not I am angrily attacked. I have found this is more apparent in Australia than Canada.

Shauneen: Ali, do you mean as a white women speaking out in Australia? As a white woman teaching in both locations, I am curious about the geographic/ socially constructed differences that you've experienced.

Ali: To speak to my experiences in returning to my place of birth, Australia, after living and teaching in Canada for sixteen years, I think I need to provide some context about Australia. To do this, I thought I would seek the help of a wonderful article by Robert Hattam and Stephen Atkinson. The authors searched Australian education department websites for the term 'antiracism' and found policies that adopted simplistic views that generally ignored structural, historical, political or institutional forms of racism (Hattam & Atkinson, 2007). My own analysis of educational standards in Queensland (Sammel & Martin, in press) support this and warn of the consequence of the current liberal versions of multiculturalism via governmental educational choices. We suggest that Australians are not formally educated about the complex historical, political, and social constructions of the 'norm' and of the 'other' (where 'race' predominately holds court). Therefore, speaking out against the daily embodiment of racism, especially when it is so integrated within our everyday lives (yet for some so invisible), sparks debates. Now, I would not be so bold as to say that Canada's educational policies are outstanding in their antiracist offerings, although I would say that there is a difference, but I can't say that this alone speaks to the differences that I have experienced between the two cultures. I will say that the lived experience of pedagogy in a classroom is more complex than the ideological positioning of government policy and this discussion is unfortunately outside of the scope of this chapter. I do believe that it is our responsibly as teacher educators to ensure that pre-service students understand the complex structural, historical, political, institutional and individual dimensions of racism as a first step towards becoming agents able to negotiate change within their daily curricula. Without this, those who speak out will continue to be resisted due to ignorance.

Shauneen: You teach a course that addresses issues in education, and you include a section about White privilege and its impacts in education. Tell me more about what you do and what you have found?

Ali: To provide you with some background, in my course for the one-year graduate education program, I had over one hundred students and I wanted to find out a bit about who they were. So I conducted a survey and found that a large majority of these students chose to identify as middle class and white, and only a small percentage suggested they have ever personally experienced racism. I would suggest these students are demographically reflective of the usual cohort of students I teach. In the past I have found that the vast majority have commented that they were not told about concepts of White privilege. Therefore, in the lectures, tutorials and through readings, we explore how the entire process of formal education, indeed the Western processes of creating and sustaining knowledge, is intimately connected to structures of power that value certain voices, beliefs and actions and, consciously or unconsciously, marginalise or completely silence others. I also require the students to raise critical questions about what they have understood diversity to encompass and to start to explore how teaching and Western cultural ideals are not 'natural' but are historically constructed. We start to investigate what this knowledge means for our future pedagogic actions.

Many authors (Aveling, 2006; Frankenberg, 1993; Hattam & Atkinson, 2006) have lamented on how 'race/ethnicity' and 'diversity' have been constructed in terms of some unspoken (usually homogenised and essentialised) 'other'. Instead of promoting the premise that diversity and inclusive pedagogy is about learning about the other, or helping the 'other' learn, I wanted to work with my students so we could explore the complexities of what Peggy McIntosh calls our "invisible weightless knapsack of special provisions, maps, passports, codebooks, visas, clothes, tools, and blank checks" (McIntosh, 1988). In this course the students were asked to reflect on their own backpacks/knapsacks. However, in their assignments many focused on the other rather than unpacking their own cultural assumptions. My students found it easier to name, explore, and generate strategies to 'fix' the other rather than to reflect on their own experiences or beliefs that normalised the social construction of the other. This should be no surprise really, as this is how White privilege functions. It shimmers everywhere: in colonised countries it's the infrastructure of how we think and process the world around us and yet it makes us feel very uncomfortable to acknowledge this. The consequences of hegemony and White privilege are indeed a cerebral labyrinth! How have you addressed this in your classes?

Shauneen: I wonder how these reflect your own white experience in teaching the course - I find that I am a bit more blunt with my students asserting, "this is your work as a white educator". Like yourself I follow a pattern of exploration: we examine the manner in which knowledge is socially constructed; we insert diverse voices feminist, working class, black, Indigenous, gay/lesbian; then examine the colonial past and the social constructions of race, ethnicity, and identities; then we examine the historical constructions of whiteness as exposed in the readings on our colonial past. Students learn to layer broad statements such as "knowledge is socially constructed"; the politics of identity are informed by the dynamics of power relationships and context; and more importantly, that while those closer to the norm see and name the other, what often goes unexplored is how whiteness has also been created and how White privilege is affirmed structurally". The exercise of stepping back from their feelings about this curriculum and moving to crafting statements informed by the literature assists some of them to embrace the curriculum and pedagogy of the class. Again I am explicit: good teachers are those who understand their own identities and the implications that their worldviews have on their instructional beliefs and pedagogical practices.

I also don't like to let them off the hook – this is their work. I put the responsibility of reflective practice back on them in a realistic way. "Carry this around for a while - see how it operationalises in your life, notice your responses to whiteness, and white racial constructions in your world". Some of the students do so. But I am realistic, this stuff is too new for many of them, some outright refuse, they assert "this is just one class - I can set aside what I find discomforting and just do the bare minimum to get me through the class"; other students are outright hostile, and respond "you can't make me do this" or "I won't change everything I know for the likes of you" and my simply calm response usually is "how is this stance a privilege as well?" I don't expect immediate responses, and say so. I then tell them how their discomfort is an example of the manner in which their normative schooling has oppressed them as well. I tell them I don't blame them as individuals, but see how the whole system of schooling has denied them the opportunity to learn in any other way. They have been rewarded for not seeing difference, not believing the other and being unable to see for themselves other options. As they process this view of social oppression, I step back and just notice their responses, and remind myself "this is just one class, I am not out to transform the world, but only maybe one or two minds at a time". At that point we begin to look at how conformity in the WMCC is a requirement. As those students who actively engage in the critique of whiteness begin to have their own experiences in responding or noticing whiteness...they share those stories with their classmates. And in that way, they begin to unpack what it means to be white and not feel guilty only. They find a healthier middle ground for themselves.

Ali: The idea of comfort and discomfort is an important one to explore, as these are powerful motivators. I am aware that by engaging with this content I am structuring my pedagogy to create spaces of discomfort for my students. Therefore, I use the pedagogy of discomfort as a tool. I force, through the use of assessments, my students into reflective places where they often communicate discomfort. This is also seen throughout the course in the highly charged conversations and the intense emotions around the lectures, reading and activities. As a teacher, it has taken me a long time to learn not to 'save' the students in their moments of discomfort, and try to make it all calm and smooth and 'nice' again. It has taken me a long time to deal with my own discomfort of witnessing my students in discomfort.

Shauneen: Once again the language we use can be elitist...we speak of discourses, discursives, oppressions etc I wonder if we chose the common sense ways of speaking about these issues whether students would engage in new ways with the curriculum.

Ali: I agree. What I have been curious about this year is how my students took up the concepts associated with White privilege, but rejected this term. In groups, we discussed why they did not like the term 'White privilege'. For some it was the word 'white'. Upon understanding the concept they argued that in other geographic places, the same oppressive infrastructures are in place, and yet 'white' is not the dominant hegemonic ethnicity. Therefore, would it not be better to have a more consistent term? They expressed many views about the term 'white'. However, for the majority of students it was the term 'privilege' they resisted. These students did not feel particularly privileged, even though they did appreciate they were indeed benefiting from White privilege. The semantics for these students, many low socio-economic, were so adversarial that they almost disengaged upon hearing these words. They spoke to the multiple levels of oppression that the term White privilege itself silences. For this reason, I might try to teach the same concepts, and use the same processes but start with a different language, one that does not disengage the students at the beginning. I might introduce these concepts as *the social construction of norm and other* and speak to its complexity. I will see if the students enter into the dialogue differently. Then, I will introduce the term and explore with them why it might be called this. Shauneen, has this been your experience?

Shauneen: When I teach this topic I have the students push the tables back, and ask them to stand around the walls of the room. I ask them to play a game with me – take a step forward/backward for each comment that applies to you. If you are racially white take a step forward. If you grew up in a two-parent home take a step forward. If your one parent attended university take a step forward, if both did take two steps. If your first language is English take a step forward. If you attend French Immersion schooling take a step forward. Even just on these few questions – White privilege becomes exposed as being differently available to students. They begin to see how class indicators within whiteness re-create otherness. Alternatively, I do the activity with myself: I grew up with heterosexual, married parents – two steps forward; my parents both attended university – two steps forward; my parents both worked – two steps forward for me; both my parents spoke English – two steps; my dad spoke Cree – I step back; I grew up urban – 1 step forward...etc. I also demonstrate the disadvantage as it plays out in my other contexts – for example at my reserve – I don't speak Cree...1 step back; I grew up urban – 1 step back etc; or at the grocery store where my credentials are not visible – I am brown 1 step back; etc. By doing so I assist my students in understanding the fluidity of oppression and privilege depending on the context and the cultural capital (skills, knowledge, contacts, language etc) valued within that specific context. They/we begin to articulate a set of Norms/norms: the Capital Letter Norm used here refers to those of the white, male, middle-class etc which dominants in Western cultures; alternatively norm - with lower case letters - refers to the norms of the diverse social groups in which we operate. As such they are resigned to the complexity and politics that the language poses in the class. Their next task is to practice speaking about what they have learned with those in their social networks in a manner that is reflective of the commonsense way of speaking within those networks. Perhaps I will end here with a story.

In my second year working with you Ali, I had the privilege of speaking with the mother of one of my former students. When we introduced ourselves she asked, "Are you *the* Dr. Pete?" To which I blushed. She continued, "I want to thank you for teaching our daughter last year. Yours was the most challenging course for her, and she would often engage us with stories of the challenges of working through the discussions and content". She paused, and then continued "It wasn't easy for her father and I, and as we tried to understand and offer her some support she began to share with us her readings, and we would begin to discuss the content". I listened, intrigued. She said, "I want to thank you for this very difficult reading package that you placed not only in front of our daughter and her classmates, but also for ourselves, her father and I. The readings and discussions took us to places that challenged how we looked at ourselves. We could not wait to hear from our daughter how the class discussions went each day, and were not surprised that they reflected our own conversations held around the dinner table the night before". I found the exchange to be a pivotal moment for me, I realized that perhaps I hadn't been empowering Indigenous people in a direct way, but perhaps I was helping to clear a path for our/their forthcoming successes, by assisting their future teachers, colleagues, and neighbours to challenge their own perceptions of social change.

The power of sharing our teaching stories here is that in our commonsense language, in the method of conversational reflection, we gift our audience with some insights on our collective knowing. In this manner, we provide a glimpse into the nexus of our shared horizons. As in all good conversations, some lessons are taught, some are learned and some are yet to be understood. Thank you Ali, I've always enjoyed the energy of our exchanges and in this medium we have explored a new level of story sharing.

NOTES

[1] The White Australia policy is the term used to describe Australia's approach to immigration (the historical legislation and policies) from 1901 to 1973. The first of the formal policies was The Immigration Restriction Act 1901 and was effective in ensuring only people from 'certain' countries could immigrate to Australia. The Act was 'to place certain restrictions on immigration and to provide for the removal from the Commonwealth of prohibited immigrants'. It was only in 1975 that the Australian government passed the Racial Discrimination Act that made racially-based selection criteria illegal (http://www.foundingdocs.gov.au/scan.asp?sID=144).

REFERENCES

Anyon, J. (1996). Social class and the hidden curriculum of work. In J. Kretovics & E. J. Nussel (Eds.), *Transforming Urban Education*. Boston: Allyn and Bacon.

Aveling, N. (2006). 'Hacking at our very roots': rearticulating White racial identity within the context of teacher education. *Race, Ethnicity and Education, 9*(3), 261–274.

Briskin, L. (1994). Feminist pedagogy: Teaching and learning liberation. In L. Erwin & D. MacLennan (Eds.), *Sociology of Education in Canada: Critical Perspectives on Theory, Research, and Practice*. Mississauga, ON: Copp Clark Longman.

Frankenberg, R. (1993). *The social construction of Whiteness: White women, race matters*. Minneapolis, MN: University of Minnesota.

Gadamer, H. (1989). *Truth and Method* (J. Weinsheimer & D. G. Marshall, Trans.). New York, NY: The Crossroad Publishing Company.

Giroux, H. (2006). *Stormy weather: Katrina and the politics of disposability*. Bolder: Paradigm Press.

Gore, J. M. (2001). Beyond our differences: A reassembling of what matters in teacher education. *Journal of Teacher Education, 52*(2), 124–135.

Harper, H., & Cavanagh, S. (1994). Lady bountiful: The white woman teacher in multicultural education. *Women's Education, 11*(2), 27–33.

Hattam, R., & Atkinson, S. (2007). Reconciliation as a frame for rethinking racism in Australia. *Social Identities, 12*(6), 683–700.

Henry, F., & Tator, C. (2006). *The colour of democracy: Racism in Canadian society* (3rd ed.). Toronto, ON: Nelson.

McIntosh, P. (1988). *White privilege and male privilege: A personal account of coming to see correspondences through work in women's studies*. Retrieved October 25, 2007, from http://seamonkey.ed.asu.edu/~mcisaac/emc598ge/Unpacking.html.

McIntyre, A. (1997). Constructing an image of a white teacher. *Teachers College Record, 98*(4), 653–681.

McMullan, J. (2004). Race, ethnicity and inequality. *Understanding social inequality: Intersections of class, age, gender, ethnicity and race in Canada*. Don Mills: Oxford University Press.

Mills, C. (2006). *Pre-service teacher education and the development of socially just dispositions: A review of the literature.* Paper presented at the Australian Association for Research in Education (AARE) Conference, Adelaide, 27–30 November.

Overall, C. (1995). Nowhere at home: Toward a phenomenology of working-class consciousness. In C. L. Carney Dews & C. Leslie Law (Eds.), *This Fine Place So Far From Home: Voices of Academics from the Working Class* (pp. 209–220). Philadelphia: Temple University Press.

Sammel, A., & Martin, G. (2008). "Othered" pedagogy: The praxis of critical democratic education. In D. E. Lund & P. R. Carr (Eds.), *Doing Democracy and Social Justice Education.* New York: Peter Lang.

Sleeter, C. (1993). How white teachers construct race. In C. McCarthy & W. Crichlow (Eds.), *Race Identity and Representation in Education* (pp. 157–171). New York: Routledge.

Shome, R. (1999). Whiteness and the politics of location. In T. K. Nakayama & J. N. Martin (Eds.), *Whiteness: the communication of social identity* (pp. 107–128). California: Sage Publications.

Villegas, A. M., & Lucas, T. (2002). Preparing culturally responsive teachers: Rethinking the curriculum. *Journal of Teacher Education, 53*(1), 20–32.

PART III: TRANSFORMATIONS: PEDAGOGY, ACTIVISM AND THE ENVIRONMENT OF JUSTICE

OLLI-PEKKA MOISIO, ROBERT FITZSIMMONS AND
JUHA SUORANTA

11. DON'T YOU SEE HOW THE WIND BLOWS?

The process of revolutionary social transformation must begin in the hearts,
minds and social relations of people, and in that sense it has already begun.
Individuals and groups, in various locations throughout the world, have
begun to challenge capitalism. (Allman, 2001a, p. 2)

The matrix of hope is the same as that of education – becoming conscious of
themselves as unfinished beings. It would be a flagrant contradiction if
human beings, while unfinished beings and ones conscious of their
unfinished nature, did not insert themselves into a permanent process of
hope-filled search. Education is that process. (Freire, 2004, p. 100)

We have affluence, but we do not have amenity. We are wealthier, but we
have less freedom. We consume more, but we are emptier. We have more
atomic weapons, but we are more defenseless. We have more education, but
we have less critical judgment and convictions. (Fromm, 1981, p. 61)

Watchman, what of the night?
The watchman says:
Morning comes and also the night
If you will inquire, inquire:
Return, come back again. (Isaiah 21:11–12)

INTRODUCTION

Part of the legacy of critical revolutionary pedagogy goes back to the upheavals of
the 1960s, although the meaning of the legacy is by no means clear. Mark
Kurlansky (2005) belongs to those, who have tried to search the meaning of that
era by pointing out that there were four distinctive historic factors creating the
overall atmosphere and the special mood of the 1960s. First there was the civil
rights movement which gave a general idea of what political dissent can be; then
there was a generation of young people who, at least partly through that idea, tried
to get rid of all possible and impossible authorities; thirdly there was a war in
Vietnam that was hated all over the world; and finally there was television which,
as a rather new technological invention, was coming of age. With it came a special

G. Martin, D. Houston, P. McLaren and J. Suoranta (eds.), The Havoc of Capitalism:
Publics, Pedagogies and Environmental Crisis, 171–194.
© 2010 Sense Publishers. All rights reserved.

feature of same-day broadcasting which made a world as a global village. All these elements brought people together in an unprecedented way for a short moment; as Kurlansky puts it:

> 1968 was a time of shocking modernism, and modernism always fascinates the young and perplexes the old, yet in retrospect it was a time of an almost quaint innocence. Imagine Columbia students in New York and University of Paris students discovering from a distance that their experiences were similar and then meeting, gingerly approaching one another to find out what, if anything, they had in common. With amazement and excitement, people learned that they were using the same tactics in Prague, in Paris, in Rome, in Mexico, in New York. With new tools such as communication satellites and inexpensive erasable videotape, television was making everyone very aware of what everyone else was doing, and it was thrilling because for the first time in human experience the important, distant events of the day were immediate. (2005, p. xvii)

In this article we want to argue that the revolutionary spirit of 1960 lasted only few moments, and was over after the heydays of 1968. Its victories were turned into postmodern politics of difference, and its critical, and revolutionary praxis into postmodern "speaking of tongues," and a retreat into local narratives (Sanboumatsu, 2004, p. 49). We want to point out that the spirit of 1960's is needed now more than ever, although it is hard to imagine that a common language of radical politics could be developed. As Kurlansky reminds us, the common experience of "the world found as new," as it was in the 1960s, might not happen ever again, for in some deep sense of the word, the whole idea of "new" has become more or less banal (p. xvii). This is partly due to the fact that the experience of the present has been saturated by the media industry, and its commercial messages, and by the uses of the new information technologies. As Kurlansky writes: "We now live in a world in which we wait a new breakthrough every day" (p. xvii) – and we might add: we are living in a world which is ever more hungry for new catastrophes every minute – whether they are new tsunamis, hurricanes, wars, terrorist attacks or yet another sniper or a school shooting. These kinds of events have been changed from the catastrophes involving individual human beings into the raw material of the production apparatus.

The problem of the new is acute in the context of radical pedagogy as we want to promote new ways of seeing and acting in the world. But we must ask, in what sense is critical pedagogy producing or helping to promote the emergence of the new in the overall context of any given society? How can teachers recognize that something new has emerged as this recognition is obviously based on the tradition, concepts and ways of doing things in some specific culture? Theodor W. Adorno (1997) wrote in his *Aesthetic Theory* that "the relation to the new is modeled on a child at the piano searching for a chord never previously heard. This chord, however, was always there; the possible combinations are limited and actually everything that can be played on it is implicitly given in the keyboard. The new is longing for the new, not the new itself: that is what everything new suffers from" (p. 32).

Ernst Bloch (1986, pp. 195–222) wrote in his *Principle of Hope* how the new can be articulated as the horizon of the real possibilities. These real possibilities are not invented longings or abstract constructions of ideal worlds but products of shared culture created thorough knowledge that is focused on the historically given and re-reading it as the cipher that is pointing the way beyond. In these concrete utopias, as Bloch named these programs based on real possibilities, hope is the driving force of knowledge. Hope whispers to us the new contained in the given and our hunger drives us to fill the emptiness of the current situation. In this sense the new is a dynamical interaction of different dimensions of the now. It is not a view from somewhere but the view within the given. If we think of the role of critical emancipatory pedagogy in this process, it is obvious that serious enactments should be made to pedagogical theory be it critical or conventional.

One possible way is to articulate teaching as a constant critical analysis of the given time. With this the idea of teaching material becomes challenged and it looses it usual inertness and becomes fluid -- but not fluid in the sense of relativism. The process of production of knowledge becomes dynamic in the historical sense. Karl Marx wrote in his Theses on Feuerbach, that "the question whether objective truth can be attributed to human thinking is not a question of theory but is a *practical* question. Man must prove the truth, i.e., the reality and power, the this-sidedness [Diesseitigkeit] of his thinking, in practice. The dispute over the reality or non-reality of thinking which is isolated from practice is a purely scholastic question" (p. 3).

If critical pedagogy is to help foster the emergence of autonomous thinking and acting its idea of teaching material should become practical in the sense Marx outlined above. This practical activity is critical collaborative production of knowledge in a sense that it teaches to re-read the given situation critically. This practical critical activity means both internal and external criticism. "Internal critique involves the critical evaluation of the principles and guidelines of the production of knowledge. External critique aims at critical analysis of the connections of the knowledge produced in social processes and its interpretations and exploitations in other social processes" (Suoranta & Moisio, 2006, p. 10).

In this article we will see how the student movement and the civil rights movement in the United States can be read as a pedagogical activity in a sense articulated above. Critique is to be seen as a fundamentally pedagogical enterprise. At the same time we will articulate, as a side project, how this idea can be connected to certain ideas of the Frankfurt School of critical theory as a view from below. In this sense critical theory can be seen as an educational project. We will argue that critical theory can be seen as a critical analysis of time and theoretical activity which has a practical content. As Max Horkheimer (1937) once wrote that critical theory is an "intellectual side of the historical process of proletarian emancipation" (p. 215). And, as we want to think, critical pedagogy driven by critical theory can be an ethico-intellectual side of human liberation.

THE SUMMER OF 69

It was summer of 1969 when a group of young US citizens came together to write an essay entitled 'You Don't Need A Weatherman To Know Which Way The Wind Blows'. In that essay young people from different classes, sexes, groups and ethnic backgrounds showed that they did not want guidance in knowing where the political wind was blowing. For them it was a radical wind raging across the soil of the United States, and other countries; and it was blowing toward revolutionary change. In the wind, there was a genuine struggle underway against capitalism, racism, imperialism, and monopolistic media power. Among others, writer and filmmaker Tariq Ali (2005) has captured in vivid detail the mood and energy of those formative years as he tracks the growing significance of the nascent protest movement.

One of the central focuses for these young revolutionaries was the violence perpetrated by the Vietnam War – not just in Vietnam but also in "the mother countries" – like the US, and France. The guiding impulse was placed on social justice, and the various national liberation struggles throughout Latin America, Africa, and Asia. Radical educational voices, especially Brazilian educator Paulo Freire, had their firm places in these struggles for people's autonomy, and political transformation.

The boundaries set by these young people were rather plain in context. Taking their cue from Mao, for example, they defined quite naively who their friends were and who their enemies were based on the relationship that one had with United States imperialism. There was no middle ground in the political choices made. The ultimate goal of this oppositional setting was quite simple: to build a mass socialist political consciousness among the population, and to get people to understand the necessity of political revolution in which all working people would be involved (Ashley et al. 1970, p. 73). Even if there was an obvious ideological distortion that we now know, this is actually a true Gramscian theme, and an idea of humanist socialism in general. All efforts in challenging capitalism or other coercive social settings and structures, and their repressive conditions have to be educational in nature, and very social relation formed in the struggle against capitalism needs to be an educative relation (Allman, 2001a).

Erich Fromm discussed humanist socialism at length which he saw primarily as an educational project. In fact in his eyes the basis of this educational praxis was the self-education of individuals which was produced via the idea of life long learning as an adult education. For example it was "especially important to give each person the possibility of changing his occupation or profession at any time of life" (Fromm, 1981, p. 83). It is obvious from the previous quote that Fromm (1997, p. 6) was critical towards the collectivized discussion of the emancipatory critique of the established socialist movements as he saw that they (i.e. the Russian communist party etc.) had contempt for individual dignity and humanistic values. Fromm (1981) understood that the principle that underlines socialist humanism is that "every social and economic system is not only a specific system of relations *between things and institutions,* but a system of *human relations*" (p. 75). This he saw was the fundamental departure point of Marx's critique of bourgeoisie society not the goal of leveling down of individual differences.

He also criticized the usual rhetoric of the leaders of communist and capitalist regimes. He saw that in both sides of the cold-war front people and governments showed in their reasoning what he called pathology on normalcy. The idea is that what is to be seen as normal is the statistically normal way of being, acting and judging in the world (Fromm 1951, pp. 12–21). How this pathology could have been cured is obviously educational in nature as what was needed was a fundamental change in individual capacities of judgment and also in her overall emotional attitude towards the world and other human beings. This change called for an education that did not educate only some part of the human being but the human being as a whole; education whose aim was not only to produce new laborers for the production apparatus or new consumers for consumer society but education that changed the situation, Fromm (1981) diagnosed:

> Education, from primary to higher education, has reached a peak. Yet, while people get more education, they have less reason, judgment, and conviction. At best their intelligence is improved, but their reason – that is, their capacity to penetrate through the surface and to understand the underlying forces in individual and social life – is impoverished more and more. Thinking is increasingly split from feeling, and [...] modern man has come to a point where his sanity must be questioned. (pp. 66–67)

If we look at the situation of radical movements in the 1960's it is quite easy to say *post festum* that socialism was a distant dream for youth participating in the movements, perhaps even an abstract utopia. But it was important for them to actively enlist the support of the "masses" for the socialist agenda. The endeavor for mass support was to be one of education—an education of the street, where social ills would be actively discussed, where such ills would turn into a people's struggle, and where this struggle would build not just a "political consciousness" but a "revolutionary consciousness", which would be both "active" and "conscious" in opposing imperialist aims (See Ashley et al., 1970, p. 74). This idea connects critical pedagogy to certain basic ideas in Frankfurt School critical theory and also to Marx's ideas about how to arrange education promoting political change. We will come to these issues in the later parts of this article.

The very same questions these young people asked in 1969 are still very much pertinent, and need to be answered: How do we reach the people, what kinds of struggles do we build, and how do we make a revolution of mind? But now we can include one more critical question: How to reach the mainstream, and majority of societies, those working men and women who are in the struggle for survival, a survival for their daily life, and a survival for a less killing work life? How is it possible to turn their struggle for survival into a struggle for a more humane way of life where each person's conditions are humanly formed not by capitalistic market but by the values of critical humanism? This is one of the core issues which needs to be incorporated into the lexicon of critical pedagogies.

For the revolutionary youth of the 1960s, such phrases as 'critical humanism' and 'socialism in practice' referred to the actual seizure of power. The process entailed local engagement, commitment, and struggle in people to people initiatives in their communities. The bigger wind behind these initiatives was to create a base for a mass revolutionary movement to challenge the capitalist ruling class. It was a movement that put a lot of faith "in the masses of people", but also recognized their role as vanguards (Ashley et al., 1970, p. 90). More importantly, it was to be a movement engaged in educating people toward a transformative consciousness. The critical mind was to be focused on "revolution as power struggle" between the masses, and the capitalist state. To quote these youth:

> On the one hand, if we, as revolutionaries, are capable of understanding the necessity to smash imperialism and build socialism, then the masses of people who we want to fight along with us are capable of that understanding. On the other hand, people are brainwashed and at present don't understand it; if revolution is not raised at every opportunity, then how can we expect people to see it in their interest, or to undertake the burdens of revolution? We need to make it clear from the beginning that we are about revolution. ... We have to develop some sense of how to relate each particular issue to the revolution. (Ashley et al., 1970, p. 75)

It has become evident that during the present stage of capitalism—one that is mean and lean cut as well as blatantly focused on profit for profit's sake with total disregard to human well being—we do need weathermen to tell us which way the wind blows. This being said, we are most certain that violence is not the answer in any form. Rather we must remind ourselves of the fact that capitalism itself represents a brutal form of structural violence, and needs to be resisted by critical praxis focused in popular education, and anti-capitalist education against the ruling class ideology (see Crowther, Galloway & Martin 2005). In this critical pedagogy is following the basic tenets of humanist socialism envisioned by Fromm. As he wrote, "humanistic socialism is radically opposed to war and violence in all and any forms. [...] It considers peace to be not only the absence of war, but a positive principle of human relations based on free cooperation of all men for the common good" (Fromm, 1981, p. 76).

Writing from the perspective of the Black community, and the Black Power movement, Stokely Carmichael and Charles V. Hamilton (1967) once wrote: We "must raise hard questions, questions which challenge the very nature of the society itself: its long standing values, beliefs and institutions" (p. 34). In the same way, in critical pedagogy we need educators, teachers, academics, and otherwise revolutionary minded individuals who are willing, and able to problematize the world, that is to raise difficult, and silenced questions that are directly linked to and challenge the very foundations of capitalist society, and before all, and make these questions as public issues. To be able to actualize this educational system a fundamental re-orientation is required. For example the idea of expertise in academic education needs to be redefined as a collective social expertise (see Suoranta & Moisio, 2006). As Carmichael and Hamilton (1967) stated, this demands that radical educators themselves become self-critical and -reflexive: "To do this, we must first redefine ourselves. Our basic need is to reclaim our history, and our identity ... We shall have to struggle for the right to create our own terms through which to define ourselves, and our relationship to society, and to have these terms recognized" (34–35). In order for a critical strategy to succeed, it must focus on transforming the basic assumptions of what it means to be human. And we also need to change the definition of the capitalist social formation, and our role in its "psychological control" over the daily life (see Carmichael & Hamilton, 1967, p. 35).

CRITICAL PEDAGOGY AS A THEORY-PRAXIS PROBLEM

What becomes perfectly clear in this state of events is the central role of critical pedagogy: to confront the psychological control at its root, and to allow human beings to bring forth alternative definitions, and descriptions for an alternative way of living. For this to happen, we will need to confront our idea of capitalism as a pro-active ideology inside our own life-worlds and in fact our psychological structure. This will entail a process of dissection – a breaking apart of illusion, and myth that are pivotally centered in the experience of capitalism.

In the sphere of education, the main aims are those of helping to develop the critical powers of the individual and to provide a basis for the creative expression of his personality – in other words, to nurture free men who will be immune to manipulation and to the exploitation of their suggestibility for the pleasure and profit of others. Knowledge should not be a mere mass of information, but the rational means of understanding the underlying forces that determine material and human processes. Education should embrace not only reason but the arts. Capitalism, as it has produced alienation, has divorced and debased both man's scientific understanding and his aesthetic perception. The aim of socialist education is to restore man to the full and free exercise of both. It seeks to make man not only an intelligent spectator but a well-equipped participant, not only in the production of material goods, but in the enjoyment of life. (Fromm, 1981, p. 82.)

How this can be accomplished is one of the core issues in the theory and practice of critical pedagogy. Let us make some preliminary suggestions. Firstly, one of the most essential ingredients for a capitalist free, conscious and critical life is the ability to dream. It is crucial in realizing fundamental change towards humanly formed conditions. Abolishing the predatory rule of capital would be impossible without the ability to dream of a concretely better life, and an alternative social existence. In fact even this demolition might produce a new barbarism if it did not contain the self critical movement and the possibility to envision the sights beyond the given power settings. Even Marx did not believe in abstract negation but only in an *aufhebung* of the given processes; i.e. in changing these processes into qualitatively new, more fulfilling processes.

Ernst Bloch (1986) argued that history is the container full of living options and possibilities for the action that can be carried out in the future. That is why Bloch speaks about the tendency-latency of the now. All the unrealized potentialities that are sediment and latent in the present and the signs and foreshadows that indicate the tendency of the direction and movement of the present into the future must be grasped and activated by an anticipatory consciousness that at once perceives the unrealized emancipatory potential in the past, the latencies and tendencies of the present, and the realizable hopes of the future. To bring these ideas into pedagogical settings we want to argue that adult educators, and other cultural workers need to ask students to recollect the past, to situate the present socially, politically and economically, and to strive toward a future built upon a utopian universality that creates the conditions for groups to liberate themselves in their own contextually specific ways from all forms of oppression, domination, alienation and degradation.

The ability to dream is a necessary component in any circumstance. When people have the ability to dream they may begin to mentally project the necessary course of action in conceiving a more humane reality for all. But we must ask is there place for critical dreaming anymore? In this respect the following words by the Nobel-prize winner Günter Grass (2005) are to be taken seriously, for those who still want to dream, hope, and criticize are "ridiculed by slick young journalists as 'social romantics', but usually vilified as 'Do-gooders'. Questions asked as to the reasons for the growing gap between rich and poor are dismissed as 'the politics of envy'. The desire for justice is ridiculed as utopian. The concept of 'solidarity' is relegated to the dictionary's list of 'foreign words'" (p. 5).

Secondly, critical pedagogy needs to address – within the educational framework – people's ecological, material and cultural poverty. With the term "poverty" we are not referring to the lack of all sorts of goods, but to material abundance and ecological devastation epitomized in consumer culture. In a sense if we look at the amount of goods produced in the consumer culture we are wealthier than ever but at the same time our life outside the productive activity is in many senses poorer than ever before. If we look into the history of capitalism, we easily see the drastic change that has happened in the ownership ideology of the past. In *Liquid Life* Zygmunt Bauman (2005) argues that the logic of continuously accelerating consumption places an increasing emphasis on disposal even more than on acquisition. This emphasis is obviously in contradiction to long-term ownership of previous capitalisms. Indeed, Bauman sees long-term ownership as having become a burden rather than a mark of success. It is obvious that this logic is devastating to the environment and human beings in the countries that form the production basis for the global capitalism.

We might also want to argue that this logic of continuously accelerating consumption has changed important factors that once produced so called social capitalism that Richard Sennett (2006) portrays in his *Culture of the New Capitalism.* In the beginning of 1970 the Bretton Woods-contracts expired and the massive cultural change in the workings of capitalism started to happen. In this process the long term ownership ideology of the previous capitalism was gradually displaced and its place was taken by "the forces of impatient capital" that worked for short term profits. Sennett argues that when early capitalism and its modern versions of social capitalism still depended on the face-to-face owner ship and strict bureaucratic line of command this new capitalism is much more like a MP3-player. Even though there is a central gore that handles all the processes the linear system of information is displaced with the jumping around. In this sense we need to be careful when using the word capitalist as there are no capitalists in a sense Marx used the term or at least not many of them anymore. The real problem is that most of the well to do western people are connected to the global productive system via different retirement allowance funds that roam freely across the globe trying to find best places to breed more money.

Thirdly, critical pedagogy needs to bridge the gap between the objectives of the pedagogy, and the cultural, material and ecological poverty of the population. This bridge will need to be strong, firm, and built on a good theoretical and practical foundation if it is to succeed as a transforming pedagogical force. What needs to be considered is the ability of people to problematize the current capitalist-consumer culture in its totality, and not just parts of a whole. We need to show connection and not fragmentation. This will be an extremely difficult yet not impossible task to accomplish for critical educators within the capitalist entity. Rather than erasing students' cultural formations, critical pedagogy unearths the debris of the dialectically fashioned self of capital from the oppressive strongholds of the empire of capital and re-articulates what it means to be the subject rather than the object of history. All this needs the development of critical perception; in Paula Allman's words,

> It enables people to know what needs changing, but it has also two other very essential functions. This critical, dialectical, perception together with an engagement in creating our conditions of existence is what it means to be fully human, and it is the right of every person, not of some privileged few. Furthermore, it is this perception of reality that creates the will or the motivation in people to risk themselves in revolutionary struggle (Allman, 2001, p. 93).

To develop such a critical perception of our lived reality is a prime task for critical pedagogy but at the same time it forms a fundamental problem for all activity that is focused on such a task. One easy way is to put the task on the shoulders of teachers and start to develop certain ideas about what kind of personality structure or way of living human beings should have if they want to make change happen. But this answer is far too easy compared with the task we are facing. It is obvious that a strong conviction is needed from teachers but this conviction is not enough by itself. World history has shown to us in too much detail what might emerge from our naive individual acts of good will, if we forget this fact. But at the same time without such a stand and life perception, the process of social change will be extremely difficult to implement both in school practice and also in life practice.

Fourthly, the critical educator needs the ability to bring people out of their material and cultural poverty, and into an action-mode in which they, as a collective force, can take charge in creating their own "conditions of existence". To move people away from doing capitalism, they will need to possess the skills not just to comprehend lived reality but also to tackle that reality and to change that reality. Those skills are seen in one's pedagogical practices, as one art teacher has noticed so aptly:

> A major aspect of my teaching is awakening and fostering some kind of analytical process among students. Calling into question certain ways of doing things is a process that every art students have to go through for themselves. It does not necessarily come from art theory. But in any case, it is very closely linked with being aware of your relationship with the surrounding world, both the world at large and the art world. And also what you yourself do in relation to the history of contemporary art and the making of contemporary art. (Rastenberger, 2002, 27)

Although she focuses on her own subject-related practice, her teaching philosophy can also be incorporated into other disciplines. We need to begin to call into question the way we are doing things and also to question the way and in whose interest this life process is being conducted. Human beings will need to know what needs to be changed in their own life-world through their own experience in that life-world. In other words, we need a critical pedagogy which touches our souls, and senses. But how to do exactly this is quite a difficult question to answer. What is the starting point of radical learning where human beings begin to understand that there is a need to change the way they have previously done things. It is quite obvious that the starting point should contain something else other than only cognitive material (i.e. knowledge) as we have in our world enough of it but too little change (see Moisio, 2008).

If there is to be found a valid point of departure to radical learning the critical education formed around it can create "weather persons." They have the skills to dissect and to explain the direction in which the wind is actually blowing. They also have the skills to make people understand and comprehend the wind in all its strength, force and tranquility. They predict the direction of the wind, and create the atmosphere for seeing specific possibilities from the inner movements of the wind. A pedagogy built upon these perspectives and practices seeks to understand the underlying motives, interests, desires and fears of draconian shifts in education policy and it contests ascribed methods of producing knowledge.

The aim of weather persons is to raise new productive ideas through conscientious, creative thinking toward a more conscious way of doing life. A major focus needs to be located in ideological work as educative praxis. But this movement is paradoxical as the point is not to debase the individual but quite the opposite. Critical pedagogy must put as its key component the goal of promoting the individual, autonomous thinking and her knowledge of the ethical implication of her thought and action. As this is the main point that capitalism is trying to abolish from every aspect of our life world. In this sense the concept of *real education* cannot be separated from *real life and political struggles*. Through political struggle, humankind can begin to dig deep into practical human activity.

WHERE THE STORM FRONT IS FORMING?

Today we need a new offensive as we need to be on the attack against capitalist tyranny in all aspects of our collective and individual lives. This struggle is about human bonding against a capitalist ideology that has a pit bull mentality that people are experiencing across the globe. Pit bull capitalism attacks labor, seeks cuts in social expenditure, hurts the working people through draconian practices of wage reductions, longer working hours, pension reforms, and forces greater productivity and worker compliance in numerous work place practices. It throws aside workers and places the workers into the dustbin of life without conscience or guilt; it has a psychopathic disposition in its attempt to delete the human from her own being.

Regardless of capitalist ferocity, we need to discuss a new educational strategy that not only puts hope and dreams on the active agenda, but also has the hurricane wind force to usurp the rabid saliva of capitalist accumulation spreading across the globe. We want to claim that we need our own educational pit bulls. But we also know that critical pedagogy is no traditional pit bull. It has teeth but they are in the heartbeat of humanity. And if the pit bull of critical pedagogy is ferocious, it's ferocious is in the defense of humanity, and not in destroying the human essence located in the flesh and bone of the human species, and in the human spirit. Thus it is necessary for radical thinkers and teachers to boldly declare that by coming closer together they can discover and know who they are, and what is wrong, and ugly in the world. They must hold the belief that only by working together people can read the world in a dialectical manner. This is one of the starting points of all genuine critical pedagogy.

Toward this end, teachers in critical pedagogy will need to reflect how children are educated in a corporate sponsored society. But this thinking will need to go beyond reinterpreting interpretations that may reinvent the role of capital in our life-world. Rather, a genuine critical pedagogy creates a new vision for education – a vision that embraces more holistic learning possibilities focusing on the human potentiality for creating more life affirming communities. This requires active movements away from capital, and into a movement of social and economic transformation that recognizes human being's innate ability for collective aspirations that maximizes the ethics of caring, commitment and social responsibility. It will also require a thorough analysis of the role of education in the support of corporate interests. It is not enough to naively suppose that knowledge or enlightenment would do the trick. It is obvious that there are vast amounts of knowledge in the world but not enough perspectives and will to see and act differently. This is obviously the question of the political aspects of education known as reproduction, and students' possibilities to raise above their circumstances and earlier forms of consciousness.

Marx's answer to the problem of new ways of schooling that would promote the emergence of knowledge about the possibilities of individual persons acquiring the needed abilities to act responsibly was a polytechnic principle of education (see Small, 2005). In this he followed his basic ideas that theory and praxis should not be separated from each other. This separation was a product of the division of labor between mental and physical work. In his theory of education he focused on the education of the working class in capitalist society. Marx's (CW6) point was not that there was no education for this class but that there actually was "elements of political and general education" by the middle class but only to their own special interests (p. 493). What was lacking was education that was focused on the needs of proletarian class.

It is obvious who the targets were. Adam Smith wrote in his magisterial book *The Wealth of Nations* about the need for general education. Previously in his book he had diagnosed the problem that was introduced by the division of labor. The division of labor produced one dimensional human beings who were obviously needed in terms of the overall specialization of people in their own field of expertise. The dilemma which he confronted was that he had found that his great discovery – the division of labor – was now inducing a state of torpor in the minds of workers which was stupefying their intellects. Smith (1776) wrote that "in the progress of the division of labor [...] the great body of the people, comes to be confined to a few very simple operations, frequently to one or two. [...] [People] naturally loses, therefore, the habit of such exertion [i.e. understanding, invention], and generally becomes as stupid and ignorant as it is possible for a human creature to become" (p. 987). To prevent this from happening Smith argued that the government should take pains for it by producing general education of the common people. In his mind "the education of the common people requires attention from the state more than that of people of rank and fortune, whose parents can look after their interests, and who spend their lives in varied occupation chiefly intellectual" (Smith, 1776, p. 989).

Smith argued that common people cannot educate themselves as they do not have the required time for this. Since common people are engaged in simple and uniform tasks in order to maintain their lives, it is necessary to provoke their minds with mental stimuli which would encourage them to speculate about their own otherwise dull occupations. Latin, Smith (1776, p. 991) thought, was useless for this purpose but geometry and mechanics would be an ideal addition to reading, writing and arithmetic.

It was an obvious fact for Smith that poor parents could not afford to buy their education so the state should intervene to help them. State sponsorship in his eyes, as in the eyes of most classical economists, should not cover everything because teachers would start to duck out from their occupation (West, 1964). This idea is distinctive to Adam Smith's views on public education. While he believed in achieving education for all, his solution did not lie in abolishing school fees and making education free at the point of use. Instead fees should be subsidized "so that even a common laborer can afford it", and the teachers should only partly be paid from public funds, "because if he was wholly or even principally paid by it, he would soon learn to neglect his business" (Smith, 1776, p. 991).

But this was not Smiths main argument in support for state intervention in education. As E. G. West writes in a unpublished[1] article: "even when parents had become rich enough through their productivity increases associated with the division of labor, they would be so stupid as to spend their money unwisely and neglect the education of their children". Public education was for Smith (1776) the necessary part of a well ordered and productive society as it provided the means to promote peoples "martial spirit", of keeping people "more decent and orderly" and "less apt to be misled into any wanton or unnecessary opposition to the measures of government" (p. 994). Education would be in this sense a measure against alienation produced by the division of labor.

Marx saw thorough Smith's fatalistic vision, the main goal of which was the protection of private property via the protection of the state. He argued, that "Smith recommends education of the people by the state, but prudently, and in homeopathic doses" (CW 35: p. 368). Marx saw that the government was a reactionary force itself but for Smith it or the law was a key of removing the basic imperfections that result from social-economic life. In this sense Smith might be connected with Rousseau as they both saw that the basic alienation of human beings was a result of social interaction (see Rousseau 1754). In Smith's system the socialist revolution that was the aim of Marx would have been "the dreadful disorder." According to Smith avoiding "enthusiasm" was among the main goals of education.

In *Critique of Gotha Program* Marx (CW 24) writes skeptically: "Equal elementary education"? What idea lies behind these words? Is it believed that in present-day society (and it is only with this one has to deal) education can be equal for all classes? Or is it demanded that the upper classes also shall be compulsorily reduced to the modicum of education — the elementary school — that alone is compatible with the economic conditions not only of the wage-workers but of the peasants as well?" (p. 94). Behind these questions lies a fundamental disbelief that Marx had towards the re-organization of education in his own times as a way of emancipatory activity. Education was already free in some parts of Europe and the United States at the time, but "if in some states of the latter country higher education institutions are also 'free', that only means in fact defraying the cost of education of the upper classes from the general tax receipts" (CW 24, p. 94). In the Gotha program the heavy thrust was put upon the role of the State in the education of individuals. This Marx found out absolutely objectionable.

> Defining by a general law the expenditures on the elementary schools, the qualifications of the teaching staff, the branches of instruction, etc., and, as is done in the United States, supervising the fulfilment of these legal specifications by state inspectors, is a very different thing from appointing the state as the educator of the people! Government and church should rather be equally excluded from any influence on the school. Particularly, indeed, in the Prusso-German Empire (and one should not take refuge in the rotten subterfuge that one is speaking of a "state of the future"; we have seen how matters stand in this respect) the state has need, on the contrary, of a very stern education by the people. (CW 24, p. 95.)

It was obvious for Marx that Smith articulated the fundamental dilemma of the dominant class. In the course of history it had become aware of the fact that the more it gives to the education of the laboring poor the more it gives them the tools to stand against their own social status and power. Like he wrote in *The Eighteenth*

Brumaire of Louis Napoleon "The bourgeoisie had a true insight into the fact that all the weapons it had forged against feudalism turned their points against itself, that all the means of education it had produced rebelled against its own civilization, that all the gods it had created had fallen away from it" (CW 11, p. 142); or the quote in *Capital*: "As far as I can see, the greater amount of education which a part of the working-class has enjoyed for some years past is an evil. It is dangerous, because it makes them independent" (CW 35, p. 405 note 59).

In Marx's (CW 20) eyes public education would as the combination "of paid productive labour, mental education bodily exercise and polytechnic training, [...] raise the working class far above the level of the higher and middle classes (p. 189)." Marx (CW 20) is not interested in the problematic of other classes in society as he documents it quite forthrightly: "If the middle and higher classes neglect their duties toward their offspring, it is their own fault. Sharing the privileges of these classes, the child is condemned to suffer from their prejudices" (pp. 18–189). It is quite clear that this is something that needs to be kept in mind as Marx is not talking about general education but the general education of a specific class in a specific historical and social-economical situation.

There are also obvious discrepancies in the arguments concerning "industry education". In the earliest formulation of this topic Marx (CW 6, pp. 427–428) uses quite pessimistic and ironic rhetoric and argues for the provision of a measure of education by the workers if looked from the viewpoint of their own possible advantages. This is what he means by the purely economic view to education. From this angle the productive system has always used industry education as a means to improve the possibilities of production. This is the point of the division of labour as seen from the development of different expertise in the various fields of industry. This does not mean that this kind of education would not be beneficial for the workers, quite on the contrary, but what is relevant here is the fundamental warning that Marx gives for the naïve overestimation of what can be achieved with reformed education in the overall context of the given society.

The previous negative and pessimistic tone changes to a much more positive tone in *Capital*. Here Marx points to the positive effects resulting from the education of the working people in their work life. Education within modern industry encourages the universal mobility of the labourers and in this way benefits workers by developing their various capacities in a way which overcomes the harm done by the division of labour. Marx's argument from *Capital* is worth quoting at this point in length:

> But if Modern Industry, by its very nature, therefore necessitates variation of labour, fluency of function, universal mobility of the labourer, on the other hand, in its capitalistic form, it reproduces the old division of labour with its ossified particularisations. We have seen how this absolute contradiction between the technical necessities of Modern Industry, and the social character inherent in its capitalistic form, dispels all fixity and security in the situation of the labourer; how it constantly threatens, by taking away the instruments of labour, to snatch from his hands his means of subsistence, and, by suppressing his detail-function, to make him superfluous, We have seen, too,

how this antagonism vents its rage in the creation of that monstrosity, an industrial reserve army, kept in misery in order to be always at the disposal of capital; in the incessant human sacrifices from among the working-class, in the most reckless squandering of labour-power and in the devastation caused by a social anarchy which turns every economic progress into a social calamity. This is the negative side. But if, on the one hand, variation of work at present imposes itself after the manner of an overpowering natural law, and with the blindly destructive action of a natural law that meets with resistance at all points, Modern Industry, on the other hand, through its catastrophes imposes the necessity of recognising, as a fundamental law of production, variation of work, consequently fitness of the labourer for varied work, consequently the greatest possible development of his varied aptitudes. It becomes a question of life and death for society to adapt the mode of production to the normal functioning of this law. Modern Industry, indeed, compels society, under penalty of death, to replace the detail-worker of to-day, grappled by life-long repetition of one and the same trivial operation, and thus reduced to the mere fragment of a man, by the fully developed individual, fit for a variety of labours, ready to face any change of production, and to whom the different social functions he performs, are but so many modes of giving free scope to his own natural and acquired powers. (CW 35, p. 489.)

With these two arguments made by Marx we should bear in mind that we should not attach too much significance to the possibility of reforming the educational system in the established society. To change circumstances in the present society is too complex a task and needs other perspectives than the educator can provide by herself. It is a collaborative task where educators are invited to interact with other perspectives to our life world. It is obvious that within educational settings this broadening of perspectives can be reached most easily by interacting with the perspectives of students and inviting them to contribute to the elaboration of the education practices.

STUDENTS MOVING FROM RE-ACTION TO ACTION

Radical pedagogy starts from the premise that the goal of education is not to achieve the highest productivity in the form of economic productivity. The goal is that as a group of individuals we would promote the highest human productivity. This means in the context of practical education that students spend *most* of their energy doing things that are meaningful and interesting to them. This does not mean that the general goals of different fields of study are forgotten or thrown away, but that simply, that students are allowed to reach this content from the view point of their own experiences. As Fromm (1981) writes "it must stimulate and help to develop *all* his human powers – his intellectual as well as his emotional and artistic ones" (p. 77). This is the point where the movement from re-action to action could start. This movement forms a knot where the different aspects of learning come together as a constellation of thought, emotion and action.

In this connection it might be useful to introduce a concept of "the activating stimuli" that Fromm develops in his *Anatomy of Human Destructiveness*. The activating stimuli incites the student to strive towards something. This striving is something more than a mere being-driven-towards something that simple stimulus produces. In a sense we might see the teacher as an activating stimuli. But the teacher needs some intervention or mediation to do just this. In Fromm's (1973) eyes activating stimuli "requires a 'touchable' stimulee in order to have an effect – touchable not in the sense of being educated, but of being humanly responsive. On the other hand, the person who is fully alive does not necessarily need any particular outside stimulus to be activated; in fact, he creates his own stimuli" (p. 270).

To be able to promote this kind of individual human productivity, educational practices and settings need to become centers *committed* to the elaboration of radical pedagogy. If we argue for example that there is a deep need for school curricula that place emphasis on the relationship between ecological awareness and human existence it is obvious that we need much more than only paper to do just this. We need practical settings that promote this goal. Michael Albert tries to elaborate a new kind of concept of activism in the following long quote. It tells us something valuable if we want to promote the role of students in re-reading educational practices.

Imagine students asking why their curriculum produce ignorance about international relations, ignorance about market competition's violations of solidarity, sagacity, and sustainability.

Imagine students deciding enough is enough. Maybe one particular student who wears a funny hat and has a history of being aloof, or perhaps one who looks straight as a commercial and was high school class most likely to have a million friends, will write a song about masters of the universe - and unseating them. Maybe another student will write about floods drowning people's hopes, and about a rising tide of our own compassionate creation lifting people's prospects. Maybe another student will write about resurgent racism and sullying sexism, and then about combative communalism and feminism and their time finally coming. And maybe students will hum the new tunes and sing the new lyrics - and rally, march, sit in, occupy, all while waving a big, solid fist.

Imagine students not just sending out emails to their friends and allies, but entering dorms and knocking on every door, initiating long talks, communicating carefully-collected information and debating patiently-constructed arguments that address not only war and poverty, but also positive prospects we prefer.

Imagine students earmarking fraternity and sorority members, athletes, and scholars, for conversation, debate, incitement, and recruitment. Imagine students come to see their campuses as places that should be churning out activists and dissent and come to see themselves as having no higher calling than making that campus-wide dissent happen.

Imagine students schooling themselves outside the narrow bounds of their colleges, learning that there is an alternative to cutthroat competition and teaching themselves to describe that alternative and to inspire others with it, to refine it, and especially to formulate and implement paths by which to attain it.

Imagine students, now sharing many views and much spirit, angry and also hopeful, sober and also laughing, sitting in dorms and dining areas forming campus organizations, or even campus chapters of a larger encompassing national community of organizations – perhaps something called students for a participatory society this time around – or even students for a participatory world – and maybe even having each chapter choose its own local name. Dave Dellinger SPS. Emma Goldman SPS. Malcolm X SPS. And for that matter, Rosa Luxembourg SPS, Emiliano Zapata SPS, Che Guevara SPS. And so on.

Imagine, in short, students rising up with information, relentless focus, and some abandon too, becoming angry, militant, and aggressive, but keeping foremost mutual concern and outreaching compassion.

Imagine all this pumping into the already nationally growing U.S. dissent against war and injustice, pumping into the neighborhood associations and union gatherings and church cells and GI resistance, a youth branch willing to break the laws of the land and to push thoughts and deeds even into revolutionary zones. Imagine students singing, dancing, marching, and law breaking up a storm.

That is something the antiwar movement, the anti corporate globalization movement, the movement for civil rights and against racism and sexism, the movements for local rights against environmental degradation, the movements for consumer rights against corporate commercialism, and the labor movement too, all need.

Radical educators may have a role in promoting such an action. To be one step closer to achieving this role they need to set forth curricula for new possibilities, and actions that actively involve people in transforming their social and ecological environments with a firm belief in the possibility to effect change by their own direct intervention in social and economic settings and practices. This being said, a critical pedagogy that is an alternative pedagogy tries to help students to articulate new possibilities that would unleash a differing way of living life. The result would hopefully allow human beings to lead a new way of life by increasing the level of passion against injustice, oppression, and exploitation found not just in human resources but also within the confines of the capitalist socio-economic formation.

The most important form of struggle is through practical experience. The role that education will play in generating the experience through practical struggle is formed inside pedagogy. The focus needs to be clear. Since we are dealing with pedagogy, the main thrust is on the next generation.

Critical pedagogy needs to be generational if it is to be successful in building new ethics through educational practice. But this is not all. The future orientation of critical pedagogy is self-evident. It is not a one-off pedagogy in educating the "masses." The process is continuous and relentless in stressing not just a new ethical outlook but also in emphasizing a new morality in building a new social formation with and by the hands of the human beings. In other words, radical pedagogy is predicated upon uplifting human beings so that they can discover their own power and develop the ethical criteria to achieve a critical humanist morality to replace the moral degeneracy of the capitalist ideology of continuous economical growth.

One way to interpret this idea is to understand it from the perspective of common people. Education is always an ideological act in that it can either co-opt the populace into a social structure that is in contradiction to peoples' own interests or it can give the population the necessary moral fiber and skills necessary to combat a capitalist social order. For the end result is not only to create a new social practice but also a new ideological framework for this social practice to succeed.

Today the message that emanates from the capitalist superstructure is that of flexibility and adaptability to the society's status quo that in turn becomes an avenue for corporate oppression. Right-wing protocol demands more and more from ordinary workers in all branches of production. People sacrifice their flesh and blood to the business enterprise, which reaps the reward in value-added profit. The overall socio-political ethos is directed away from critical social awareness and into a "community" of greed, self-interest and blind competition. What the right-wing protocol demands is total subservience to the dominant mode of production. There is no debate outside the boundaries set by the economic and political elite of the capitalist state. The message is ideological brute force from the standpoint of corporate interests. Opposition to these corporate interests is usurped and placed into one of contradiction, conflict and antagonism on behalf of a hegemonic corporate state.

Nowhere is the maxim of adaptability more clear than in the manner empire states are treating their youth. Dreams are sold by any means necessary. A U.S. Army Special Forces advertisement asks: "Are you tough enough for Special Forces?" Toughness sells among low-income kids, especially those on the edge. Along with other good citizens they want to reach for the "American dream." Besides the dream (not coming true), "there is no higher calling than service in the US armed forces," proclaims President Bush.

The military's recruiting strategies are copious. Earlier recruiters had open access to college campuses, and high school corridors. Now they are knocking on the doors of public schools, wanting to get student's names, and addresses straight from the school office, selling their after school military programs to 10–12 year old "cadets" drilling with wooden riffles and chanting time-honored marching cadences. "New Junior ROTC (Reserve Officer Training Corps) programs are being introduced in high schools across the country, and lately kids as young as 11 are being invited to join pre-ROTC at their elementary and middle schools" (Houppert, 2005, p. 17).

The youth of the world who were supposed to be the future and promise of humanity – 'apples of our eyes' – are foot soldiers of raging state terror, "the prolific father of all terrorisms" (Galeano, 2005). State terror, says Eduardo Galeano, "finds the perfect alibi in the terrorisms that it generates. It sheds crocodile tears each time the shit hits the fan, then feigns innocence of the consequences of its actions." And it pays to cry and lie for a good cause like democracy. "The world spends $2.2 billion per day – yes, per day – on the military industry of death" (...) There is no more lucrative business on the face of the earth than this practice of industrial-scale assassination" (Ibid.).

In addition to military-economic wars across the globe, the corporate class has declared a class war against the working class. The political ideology of the capitalist state has been strategically tied to instituting drastic change inside the life-world of the working class. This has had a detrimental effect on the human being's physical and spiritual well-being. No longer can people feel secure in their work (if they have a job), or their daily life practices. The corporate state juggernaut strangles the welfare state through "made for destruction" initiatives that create the core idea of risk invention into the social community. As Alan Freeman (2004) has stated: "Every apparently economic choice is, in reality, social. We can choose a society of basic rights – education, health, housing, child support and a dignified pension – or greed, pandemic inequality, ecological vandalism, civic chaos, and social despair" (p. 2). It would not be an understatement to declare that the corporate beast has chosen the latter. What we are now witnessing is a declaration of war against the social. It is not uncommon to experience the intensification of life as corporate spin masters call for longer working days, slashes in social spending, tax cuts for the rich, wage reductions, increasing the pension age, and a slash and burn attempt to transform the planet into a made for profit ball of wax (see McLaren, 2004). The plan of attack is fierce in its aim of derailing working class gains forged in struggle for social and economic emancipation.

TRAGEDY OF OUR TIMES

We live in tragic times and no country is immune to this tragedy. Our planet is now overflowing with many personal tragedies and although these tragedies seem to be both visible and invisible, these tragedies certainly exist. To list the misfortunes that are now infesting our plant like a swarm of locusts would be a momentous undertaking. We would need to list country after country, continent after continent. Nothing has been untouched – AIDS, HIV, poverty, human displacement, human hopelessness and malaise, social alienation, injustice and exploitation have all taken the life giving blood from people's veins. We have become victims of privatization and deprivation. These and other current ills that infect our societies have had a direct impact on the human condition, and on the human species.

In March 2004, during a discussion at the New York Society for Ethical Culture, Cornel West asked Toni Morrison, an African-American writer the following question: "How would you characterize our historical moment?" Morrison gave two traits for our current epoch: fear and melancholy. She fears for her own country – the United States of America. Millions share her fear but they also fear for their own personal lives. Her melancholy springs from what the US has become. Fear and melancholy are very much a part of everyone's lives, if not consciously, then at least subconsciously. But we can also claim that there are three other characteristics to describe our historical moment: risk, uncertainly and human invisibility.

To be invisible is when people refuse to recognize that you are a human being. To be invisible is when you lose your sense of human dignity. As Ralph Ellison (1995) wrote in the opening page of his novel *Invisible Man*: "I am invisible, understand, simply because people refuse to see me" (p. 3). To be invisible is to realize that people no longer recognize your existence and your struggle to live in harmony inside the social world. And this invisibility has become a sad fact of life for millions of inhabitants across the globe. This invisibility does not concern only the social honour of individual human beings but also an individual's sense of her own intrinsic value. Human dignity is a part and parcel of the *decent society* that Avishai Margalit (1996) sees as a countermovement against what he calls *shame* and *guilt societies*. In these kinds of societies social life is based on constant humiliation of individual human beings; their hopes, needs, longings and moral demands stay unheard. Their human dignity is systematically violated. In this respect a decent society would be a non-humiliating society. One of the main questions in Margalit's book *The Decent Society* is why should institutions respect humans as humans? According to Margalit there are at least three possible grounds on which we can base our possible answer to the previous question. First, a Kantian oriented "positive justification" according to which respect can be justified by identifying some specific human traits. Secondly, a "skeptical solution" based either on a factual practice of respect or wide acceptance of an "idea of respect." As a third possibility, Margalit introduces his own preference, a "negative justification" of respect. This mode of justifying respect is grounded on the avoidance of physical and symbolic cruelty that social institutions can impose on people (Margalit 1996, pp. 62–84).

When we look at the global situation, we can argue that today families are invisible, children are invisible, women are invisible and men are invisible. As we awake each morning to a consumer ideology, what is not invisible is the commodity itself. We have become a commodity of flesh and bone – a commodity to be bought and sold on the open market. But what is even more alarming is that in the western world we have grown into this self-sacrifice. Capitalists, whoever they may be, do not have to force us to do what is against our better understanding. We are ready and willing to sell our selves to whatever and whoever may give us the promise of the stability and improvement of livelihood.

We want to propose the following draft hypothesis. Transformations in economic conditions that have been going on for the past 30 or so decades have generated a breakdown in the existential viability of the previous social character based on industrial society. This has produced a kind of existential vacuum. Like Victor Frankl (1959) once argued in his *From Death-Camp to Existentialism*, the will to meaning is the most basic factor if we want to understand human motivation. When this will is not met there emerges an existential vacuum that is filled up in Frankl's observations by the will to power or the will to pleasure. Because in our new form of social and economical practices there was yet no viable social character the deeper level needs of the individual were addressed by the system imperatives operating on the level of power and pleasure.

German psychoanalyst Rainer Funk (2006) has proposed that this new orientation that answer to our deep psychic needs can be called post-modern I-am-me orientation (pp. 52–61). This new orientation fits best in the total scheme of corporate life.

the psychoanalytic understanding of the post-modern I-am-me orientation unquestionably shows that what is good for an economy and a society, namely, the offering and selling of "fabricated" ability, is not good for human being and his mental health. Like all nonproductive social character orientations the postmodern I-am-me orientation also supplies each individual with the "medications" enabling him or her to avoid perceiving his or her socially produced illness. The medication for the I-am-me oriented person is called "made" ability. As long as he or she has this at his or her disposal, he or she can function relatively symptomless and without distress in daily life. He or she only suffers from a "pathology of normalcy." Neither he nor she must sense his or her existential dependence on the medication of "fabricated" ability as long as everyone else lives the same way and does not feel "addicted" to the medication. (Funk, 2006, p. 60)

In a similar sense Lauren Langman (2001) has proposed a new character type which she calls "carnival character." This character type brings to the foreground the fundamental principles of selfhood in global capitalistic settings which are "underpinned by narcissistic pathologies." Langman (2001) argues that "the most typical expressions of the carnival character as the "social character of our age" are an intertwining of self esteem based on ambition/accomplishment expressed in work and self indulgent privatized hedonism in the realms of leisure as a means to glean recognition and/or establish relationships." In these relationships other human beings, and the self among them, are seen as a "self objects." These flexible objects are easily replaced and this all happened in the change taking place in capitalism.

Whereas repression among the bourgeois traders was a critical moment in the transition from feudalism to modernity, once industrialization and mass production reached a certain point in which there were likely to produce a crisis of overproduction, capital needed to invent or colonize new realms. It was in this context that capitalism began to move from the production and transportation of basic goods and raw materials to the mass production of consumer goods ranging from home appliances and cars to prepared foods, fashions, cosmetics and entertainment. It is at this point that the "captains of consciousness" begin to insinuate the desire to spend (on consumer goods) into the psyche and colonize desire (Ewen, 1976). But the critical thrust of advertizing and public relations was to "buy now"-meaning to erode the internalized restraints on savings and thrift. While this process began in the 1920, perhaps the emblematic shift in consciousness took place in the 60's when Playboy magazine heralded the sexual revolution-as another moment of the consumer society. While it encouraged occupational success, the sign of that success was consumer sophistication. Knowing which wine went best with Ramsey Lewis and Oysters Rockefeller got the aspiring young (male) executive laid (Langman 2001).

Within this objectified commodity fetish, there is uncertainty and life risk. When the human being becomes an objectified form, she becomes a disembodied commodity and as such, becomes a 'person' without substance. No longer possessing a human body we become unseen and unfelt not only in the workplace but also inside the social. And here lies the risk and uncertainty. Every commodity relationship runs the risk of being discarded or being placed in a pile of garbage. A commodity has an uncertain future. Its value is determined by its usefulness. When a human being is reduced to the commodity form, her usefulness always comes into question and hence, the uncertainty of life and risk.

In order to see this condition, we will need to confront the world and help students to do so also. No longer can we tolerate the human being becoming a disembodied object to be abused at will by global corporate capitalism. The reaction of the corporate state to a person's humanity is one of appropriation and humiliation. In its worst form, our humanity is appropriated into a 'junk' commodity in a throw away society. At its best, we are a mere appendage to a machine that strips our mind away from a collective existence and a collective resistance. As a community, we are numbed and dumped into an acting role on reality television where the aim is the planned obsolescence of a human life.

Within this context, a critical pedagogy can, in its best forms, confront the narrow, selfish and covetous ideology of the neo-liberal order as represented by the capitalist social formation. This it can achieve by venturing to the generative themes of the students and see them as active participants in the communal life of their surrounding social settings. As neo-liberal ideology confronts its own inner beast, the radical pedagogical task will need to become more confrontational with corporate reality. There can be no gray zone here. When human suffering produced by social settings becomes the norm, the response to such suffering needs to be strong and fierce not only in its condemnation but also in its confrontation. The pedagogical task is to bring to the forefront the concept of social non-humiliating humanity as a way of life. This need to create a social presence in the life-world becomes a prime mover toward a more humane formation to inhabit. Our problem, however, is how to attack the neo-liberal ideology of exploitation and capital accumulation with out surrendering ourselves to the same logic that we are accusing it in the first place.

To confront it, we need a pedagogy that helps people to defend themselves against an enemy that is backed by a political, economic, and military machine. It is obvious that the viewpoint starts from below, from the eyes of the one individual and her needs, longings and moral demands. Corporate capitalism treats us as a mass by promising to us the fulfillment of our individuality. What is the real problematic is that the mass is needed to stand against the current global settings but at the same time the real problem is the lack of individuality. We already are the mass as our inner life has been standardized quite thoroughly as global capitalism is based on that. What becomes imperative is to form pedagogical settings that enable individuals to articulate their own needs, and their own experiences in a social and collective plane without the need to fit these experiences in to a seamless totality. What is furthermore needed is not an action for the sake of action, but action that is promoted by a strong theoretical point of view that starts from the non-synchronous elements in our societies.

When we speak of oppression we refer to the daily practice of our everyday lives. Hundreds of thousands of workers are in fear of losing their livelihoods throughout the world while others are struggling through the garbage to feed themselves. We are also witnessing skyrocketing drug addiction and a general sense of malaise as we confront our worst realities of mental exhaustion and illness. The level of illicit drug intake is also spiraling upward as is the level of alcohol consumption. But what needs to be stressed is the importance to have a pedagogy that emphasizes moral outrage about the state of our social commons and our planet. We need to be passionate about people and the state of our world. We need to feel with our hearts the grief, the fear and the hope that is a part of our life-world. Critical pedagogy is not just academic research; it is much more than as pedagogy of the heart and senses. It attempts to humanize the world through struggle and hope as an educational part of the political aim to change repressive economical and social as well as cultural and spiritual conditions. Hope must include the understanding of the inner soul of capitalism as an economic and political formation in its entirety, and yet it also means the following: "Thinking, speaking, feeling, apprehending, giving a destiny to liberated hands different from just supporting body movement, creating intelligence and communicating it, comparing, valuating, opting, breaking away, deciding, ideating, living socially" (Freire, 2004, p. 98).

NOTES

[1] Article can be found from the web: http://www.ncl.ac.uk/egwest/pdfs/Adam%20Smith's%20 Proposals %20on%20Public%20Education.pdf

REFERENCES

Adorno, T. W. (1997). *Aesthetic theory* (H-K. Robert, Trans.). Minneapolis, MN: University of Minnesota Press.
Albert, M. (2005). *Embark now*. Retrieved September 4, 2005, from www.zmag.org/content/showarticle. cfm?SectionID=1&ItemID=8631
Allman, P. (2001). *Revolutionary social transformation*. Westport, CT: Bergin & Garvey.
Allman, P. (2001a). *Critical education against global capitalism*. Westport, CT: Bergin & Garvey.
Ali, T. (2005). *Street-fighting years*. London & New York: Verso.
Ashley, K., Avers, B., Dohrn, B., Jacobs, J., Jones, J., Long, G., et al. (1970). *You don't need a weatherman to know which way the wind blows*. In H. Jacobs (Ed.), *Weatherman*. Berkeley, CA: Ramparts Press.
Bauman, Z. (2005). *Liquid life*. Oxford, UK: Oxford University Press.
Bloch, E. (1986). *The principle of hope* (Vol. 1). Cambridge, MA: MIT.
Carmichael, S., & Hamilton, C. V. (1967). *Black power: The politics of liberation in America*. New York: Vintage Books.
Crowther, J., Galloway, V., & Martin, I. (2005). *Popular education: Engaging the academy*. Leicester, UK: NIACE.
Ellison, R. (1995). *Invisible man*. International Vintage Publishers.
Evans, L. (1970). Letter to the movement. In H. Jacobs (Ed.), *Weatherman*. Berkeley, CA: Ramparts Press.
Foster, J. B. (2004). Empire of barbarism. *Monthly Review, 56*(7), 1–15.
Frankl, V. (1959). *From death-camp to existentialism. A psychiatrist's path to a new therapy*. Boston: Beacon Press.
Freire, P. (2004). *Pedagogy of indignation*. Boulder and London: Paradigm.
Freeman, A. (2004, October 12). Why not eat children. *The Guardian*. Retrieved September 3, 2005, from www.guardian.co.uk/comment/story/0,3604,1324934,00.html (3. 9. 2005)

Fromm, E. (1955). *The sane society*. New York: Holt, Rinehart and Winston.

Fromm, E. (1973). *The anatomy of human destructiveness*. New York: Owl Books.

Fromm, E. (1981). *On disobidience and other essays*. New York: Seabury Press.

Fromm, E. (1997). *Marx's concept of man*. New York: Continuum.

Funk, R. (2006). The psychodynamics of the postmodern "I-am-me" orientation. *Fromm Forum*, 52–61.

Galeano, E. (2005). When Maxims mislead. *The Progressive*, *69*(9), 22–23. Retrieved September 3, 2005, from progressive.org/?q=mag_galeano0905

Houppert, K. (2005). Who's next? *The Nation*, *281*(7), 15–20. Retrieved September 3, 2005, from www.thenation.com/doc/20050912/houppert

Grass, G. (2005). The high prize of freedom. *The Guardian*, 4–5.

Guevara, E. (1968). Ideology of the Cuban Revolution. In *Che Speaks* (pp. 18–23). New York: Grove Press.

Kurlansky, M. (2004). *1968: The year that rocked the world*. New York: Random House.

Langman, L. (2001). *The "Carnival Character" of the present age*. Paper originally presented at the 2000 Socialist Scholars Conference, March 31 – April 2, 2000. Retrieved September 3, 2005, from http://www.angelfire.com/or/sociologyshop/langfr1.html

McLaren, P. (2004). Discussing hope and strategy through education: The opening of the fundacion Peter McLaren de pedagogia critica at the Universidad Tijuana. Retrieved September 22, 2004, from www.dissidentvoice.org

Marx, K. (CW 5a). Theses on Feuerbach. *Collected works* (Vol. 5). New York: International Publishers.

Marx, K. (CW 5b). The german ideology. *Collected works* (Vol. 5). New York: International Publishers.

Marx, K. (CW 6). Wages. *Collected works* (Vol. 6). New York: International Publishers.

Marx, K. (CW 11). The Eighteenth Brumaire of Louis Napoleon. *Collected Works* (Vol. 11). New York: International Publishers.

Marx, K. (CW 20). The International Workingmen's Association, 1866. Instructions for the Delegates of the Provisional General Council The Different Questions. *Collected Works* (Vol. 20). New York: International Publishers.

Marx, K. (CW 24). Critique of Gotha Program. *Collected Works* (Vol. 24). New York: International Publishers.

Marx, K. (CW 35). The Capital Vol. 1. *Collected Works* (Vol. 35). New York: International Publishers.

Moisio, O-P. (2008). What it means to be stranger to oneself. *Journal of Educational Philosophy and Theory*. (forthcoming)

Rastenberger, A-K. (2002). Making thinking. *Frame News*, *2*, 27–28.

Rousseau, J. J. (1754). A discourse on a subject proposed by the academy of Dijon: What is the origin of inequality among men, and is it authorised by natural law? Retrieved January 25, 2008, from http://www.constitution.org/jjr/ineq.htm

Sanbonmatsu, J. (2004). *The postmodern prince: Critical theory, left strategy, and the making of a new political subject*. New York: Monthly Review Press.

Sennett, R. (2006). *The culture of the new capitalism*. London: Yale University Press.

Smith, A. (1904). *The wealth of nations*. New York: Bantam Books.

West, C. (2004). Cornell West & Toni Morrison converse on race and politics in America at the New York Society for Ethical Culture. Interview video. Retrieved September 3, 2005, from www.freespeech.org March 24, 2004.

OLLI TAMMILEHTO

12. MAJOR INTENTIONAL SOCIAL CHANGES AS A POLITICAL PERSPECTIVE

INTRODUCTION

This essay is an attempt to think anew one of the traditional key issues in political thought: should we change the political system or reform it. I am not trying to prove that one of the parties in the historical dispute was right after all. Instead, I endeavour to reflect what we should think of the issue in the light of our present situation and perspectives opened up by some contemporary social theories.

The paper at hand is a preliminary text for a larger work. Therefore, it contains many tentative thoughts and probably unfounded thinking experiments. That is also why my references to the relevant literature are very limited. Accordingly, I am more than grateful for any hints, comments and criticisms.

My starting point is the observation that there is a conspicuous mismatch between the state of the world and the prevalent political praxis: we live in the world of actual and potential major social changes but the mainstream non-clandestine politics is totally concentrated to minuscule reforms.

Major, in many ways revolutionary social changes are not a strange thing for an inhabitant of today's world. So-called globalization means unprecedented concentration of wealth, information resources and power to a few persons and organizations in a few countries. In less than two decades a substantial part of human communication has been made dependent on mobile phones and the Internet. The majority of the still living women and men have witnessed how a whole socio-political system, expected to persist for centuries, collapsed in 1989–1991.

On top of this, it seems that some forces connected to humanity are pulling the rug from under the feet of the present – and wide variety of other conceivable – social systems: the global climate is changing rapidly along with the whole chemical, electromagnetic and biological composition of our daily environment.

To avert a climatic catastrophe, it is necessary to reduce the emissions of CO_2 and other greenhouse gases radically. According to Integovernmental Panel on Climate Change a cut of 50–85% is needed by the year 2050 if we are to keep carbon concentration in the atmosphere below 400 parts per million[1]. Above that level it may be not possible to prevent some potentially catastrophic processes as the death of Amazon rainforest and sea level rise of several meters. To attain such a

G. Martin, D. Houston, P. McLaren and J. Suoranta (eds.), The Havoc of Capitalism:
Publics, Pedagogies and Environmental Crisis, 195–205.

global target, the Global North should reduce its emissions even much more. Fairness demands that, because old industrial countries are responsible for most of the historical emissions threatening the climate. However, IPCC's emission cut target is probably too moderate. Many leading climate scientists say that the global climate is much more sensitive to greenhouse gas emissions and other radiation forcings than IPCC's models estimate[2]. Accordingly, emission reductions should be even more drastic and rapid. But even IPCC's target is difficult to achieve by techinical fix. Anyway more radical cuts are clearly only possible by a a major change in our lifestyle. Such change entails a great change in the structures and processes of out society.

DESIRED MAJOR CHANGES

In this situation it is natural that many people wish that all these rapid changes would stop and they would be allowed to live in their old ways. However, they do not always realize that this halt would constitute a major social change in itself. Yet probably the majority of people have wishes which go even further: they yearn for a decisively more ecological, just, democratic and equal world. Many opinion polls all over the world tell about these wishes, e.g., in the Gallup International's millennium survey conducted in 1999 – probably the world's largest opinion poll – a clear majority of respondents thought that environmental protection is more important than economic growth[3]. This is a radical preference in the era when the environment is systemically sacrificed at the altar of the economy. In the same vein, the great majority of Finns have repeatedly over a couple of decades been of the opinion that "striving to continuous economic growth man will gradually destroy the Nature and ultimately himself"[4].

The same applies to global justice. The rise of the global justice movement, which is erroneously called the "anti-globalization movement", is an indication of deep dissatisfaction with the present situation. Of course, those active in movements are nowadays always a tiny minority, but according to global opinion polls, half of the people support the movement and the majority its goals[5]. In the Gallup International's recent global poll conducted in 68 countries, poverty or the gap between rich and poor is considered the main problem facing the world[6].

There is also a widespread perception that political systems are not at all as democratic as they are desired and proclaimed to be. Two thirds of the respondents in Gallup's global opinion poll say that "my country is not governed by the will of the people." This even though most of the 60 participating countries were formal democracies. This dissatisfaction was not concentrated in the poor countries: the majorities of the populations of Western Europa and North America feel also that their "country is not ruled by the will of the people" even though generally they do endorse "the election process as being free and fair"[7]. In a more recent global poll, about half of the people did not trust parliaments. The same proportion of people had lost their trust in governments, legal systems, media and companies[8].

REFORMIST MAINSTREAM

However, these ongoing or desired big changes are not reflected in the work at political arenas. The activity of parties, representatives, NGOs and even most movement activists is totally concentrated on achieving small social reforms. This is understandable in the case of those politicians who accept all the ongoing major social changes and who do not endorse people's wishes for change. But the strange thing is that also the great majority of those politicians and activists who are not at all satisfied with the state of the world do the same: make enormous effort to bring about minuscule changes in legislation, state and municipal budgets, administration or individual decisions. This happens even though many of the politicians themselves perceive that most reforms are watered down and the overall situation is worsening.

On the other hand, even the discussion on major intentional social changes is pushed out of the scope of political rationality. Even the term that is historically used to signify these changes, 'revolution', is so much loaded with negative connotations that it is difficult to speak about political revolution in the Global North in neutral or positive terms without being ashamed. Revolutions are conceived as necessarily violent and counterproductive, and therefore dangerous. However, after Thomas Kuhn's well-known book9 it has been quite normal to speak of revolutions in other fields: politicians and activist cannot make revolutions but surely scientists, philosophers, artists and software engineers.

We end up in a paradoxical situation: major intentional social changes are wished for but at the same time and often by the same people they are flatly opposed. This happens in the world that is changing rapidly anyway and the trend of the change seems to be very negative from the standpoint of humanistic-ecological values.

Our condition appears to be hopeless. Is there any way out? Why is there such a paradoxical attitude to change?

PETRIFIED CONCEPTS

Of course this disjunction of desire and action is very useful for powers that be. But apart from functional explanations, one might look at the prevalent concepts of reform and major social change. It seems that they became petrified sometimes during the last century. These notions enter into discussions as fixed starting points and do not allow any elaborations.

Reformism is associated with progress. The present order is perceived as at least reasonably good and no major structural changes are needed. Problems are not related to the main structures or processes in society. Parliamentary process or formal democracy is the method of solving our problems for which a prospering market economy provides the needed resources. Accumulation of small improvements will ultimately constitute a big change but we must wait at least a century or so for that to come true.

On the other hand, major social changes are either conceived as spontaneous or unintentional cataclysms like those caused by natural catastrophes and wars, or else they are wicked attempts made by some fanatics. These attempts are necessarily accompanied with undemocratic means and great violence because a large majority of people don't really want big changes – those desires referred above are mere thoughtless wishes. But even by these brutal means revolutions ultimately fail because common consent for the new rule is absent. The paradigmatic case of revolution is of course the popular interpretation of the Russian Revolution of 1917 and its aftermath.

However, on a closer look it is obvious that both of these mainstream conceptions of intentional social change are inadequate.

FAILING REFORMS

The mainstream concept of reformism is based on a number of hidden assumptions that hardly hold true in today's world. For instance, its idea of progress is founded on the premise that the flow of reforms is somehow faster than the flow of new problems. With the earth experiencing rapid social, technological and ecological changes this is difficult to believe.

The economy is conceptualised as a continuous source of utility. In fact, it is also a continuous source of disutility because profits are generated by externalizing a large part of the production, marketing and distribution costs to the society and the environment[10]. Therefore, when you are using the economy as a resource base for reforms, you are – to use a Finnish idiom – like a magpie on a tarred roof: when he gets the beak off, the tail gets stuck and so on.

One of the pillars of mainstream thought is that the economy is a kind of machine: its utility maximizing entities are bound to similar laws as physical particles in the space – laws governed with almost the same differential equations as used in physics[11]. Therefore the market discourse used when speaking about the economy is about a natural beast which must be harnessed but the harness must not be too tight to cause the beast to bolt.

However, even a temporal step out of this discourse, a short reflection on one's own experiences and casual reading of economic news, reveals that the economy is a big, criss-crossing power structure. Because of their position on the top of a hierarchal company organization or the income and wealth pyramid, some men and a few women have enormous power over other people's fate. They can consume the energy and wellbeing of hundreds of thousands people just to satisfy the trivial needs of their own or their projects. All this they can do like tyrants without any democratic control.[12]

The political conception of economy deconstructs yet another central assumption in reformist thought: the idea that the legislative and executive powers of states are broadly speaking independent of the economy. They are assumed to be dependent only in the same way as the master is dependent on his horse[13]. But when it appears that there is no horse pulling the plough but a group of people getting their commands from somewhere else or commanding many people including the master, the situation gets very complicated.

In fact there exists masses of research literature that shows how even in "established democracies" the powerful economic circles influence and even infiltrate state legislatures and bureaucracies[14]. They make crucial decisions that are often completely the opposite what the great majority of the population wants[15]. Furthermore, the main policy of the states is to get the economy to grow, i.e., get more powerful. On top of this, the states almost in unison promote "liberalisation" which often means facilitating corporations bigger than a state to operate and wield power within its borders[16]. It is of little wonder that people think: "my country is not governed by the will of the people".

All this means that the probability of successful humanistic-ecological reforms accumulating and constituting a major positive change is very low. A much more probable outcome is that in spite of occasional successes the situation will keep getting worse.

UNKNOWN REVOLUTIONS

On the other hand, the idea that the only alternative to reformism is a violent, undemocratic and counterproductive revolution rests also on several questionable premises. One of those is that all historical revolutions have been especially violent and that the violence was due to small fanatic minority imposing the revolution on the rest of the population.

This is, however, only one of the possible readings of the historical record. Another reading is that revolutions as people's uprisings and starting points for the process of building new social structures have often been rather nonviolent. Violence association with revolutions is caused most often by those forces within and outside the country that want to stop the revolution and from the fact that they have happened during a war[17]. For example relatively little fighting was needed to overthrow the Batista regime in Cuba because of the widespread dissatisfaction and the massive uprising of the people[18].

Also in Russia to topple the tsarist and the following provisional regime and to start to organize the economy democratically, only modest violence was required. But the Bolsheviks needed massive violence to stop revolutionary people to hollow the basis of centralized power in the country[19]. Workers and peasants all over Russia practiced grassroots democracy establishing factory and village committees. Economic self-management would, however, in the words of Grigory Zinoviev, chairman of Petrograd's Workers' Council, "interfere with the carrying out of the main political policies, concentration of all power in the hands of the proletarian avant-garde, the avant-garde of the Revolution, which is the Communist Party."[20]

The collapse of the Soviet Bloc was almost totally nonviolent: Both the grassroots movement that was the immediate cause for the collapse and the counter-movement from above which established the new centralized order did not use violence in the conventional sense. Indirectly the counter-movement's death toll is huge also in this case because it imposed economic austerity measures causing severe impoverishment of the great majority of the population[21].

The most crucial hidden assumption in the dominant political thinking is that people and society really are what you see in the official institutions. Society is the state plus the official economy. People are citizens, voters, schoolchildren, students, patients, workers, employees, craftsmen, professionals, entrepreneurs, employers, owners, investors, debtors and consumers. Or if they cannot be characterized by a positive relation to these institutions, they are defined negatively: people are minors, disabled, retired, unemployed, poor, misfits, delinquents, criminals and foreigners. What they are or do additionally is of marginal importance. From this perspective society is, by-and-large, a well-functioning whole that can only be changed modestly.

REALLY EXISTING ALTERNATIVES

But underneath and parallel to the official structures and roles, there is another world of thought, activity and social relations.

This consumer may curse the market-chain because she must buy again poisonous tomatoes from Spain and bread full of additives. That well-payed employee may hate his socially irresponsible employer and plans how he could use his inside knowledge to sabotage the company. This unemployed engineer may organize an exchange circle in her neighbourhood and feels that for once she is doing something important. That investor may read histories of revolutions and dreams about a new social upheaval. This retired teacher may be an active member of a social justice group and learns to appreciate the views of young and radical fellow-activists.

However, most important is that the majority of these and those dutiful citizens, workers and consumers are also mothers and fathers. When their children are small, they produce an enormous amount of food, cleaning, care and other essential services unpaid at their home. Usually the only thing preventing them from breaking down under the workload is the help given by informal circles of friends, relatives, neighbours and peers.

The informal work by parents, unemployed, retired and other people as well as social relations supporting it, are so extensive that one can speak about an alternative economy existing in the middle of any modern society. It is not based on the logic of markets or capitalism, even less it is a planned economy. It resembles the gift economy recorded in many anthropological studies[22]. But because barter and informal, socially embedded market relations occur in it also, it is not pure gift economy. Maria Mies and some other German anthropologists have started to call it the subsistence economy[23].

In addition to the subsistence economy and partly overlapping with it, there is another already existing alternative economy: that is based on common wealth created by Nature and cultures. Concrete manifestations of material common wealth are, for instance, the air that we breathe, the sun that warms us, the winds that cool us, the ability of most women to give birth, wild animals and plants, rivers and most lakes, oceans, deserts and a large part of the forested areas, cities and villages, public libraries, schools, hospitals and cheap public transportation systems. Nonmaterial examples are most of the genetic information and scientific knowledge, open-source software like Linux, local knowledge, folk wisdom and common sense, folklore and a large part of popular and high culture.[24]

Accordingly, the informal sphere of the society is not at all of marginal importance: its proper functioning and continuing existence are often a matter of life and death. Therefore people are often ready to fight if this economy is threatened. These conflicts are widespread because from the official perspective the informal sector contains only poorly utilized resources that must be brought into productive use. In the fight to defend the informal economy, alternative forms of political organizing and democratic decision-making develop[25].

Thus both in politics and in economy there is all the time going on a wide variety of such important activities, social interactions, group formations and other processes which are not integrated into the official institutions. The institutionalisation process of society is incomplete and open. The society is not so rigid and fixed as it seems to be. In a way there exists 'social surplus' that makes society more flexible and explains many phenomena which cannot be accounted for if one looks only at the institutional structures.

The same applies on the individual level to subject formation. The personality of a woman or a man acting both in official and informal roles has many fractures. This inconsistency is increased by the fact that official institutions are full of internal contradictions and often the dominant ideology is insufficient to contain them.[26] For instance, the official doctrines of states and companies are full of noble principles, the emptiness of which is obvious for many insiders. This "subjective surplus" is partly channelled to unofficial activities, partly it exists only as dreams and as potentiality for a future society. Thus even under the polished face of a most loyal and diligent worker and citizen there may be a surprise waiting.

On the other hand, the official social institutions like states and companies are not static formations but social processes that must be created anew all the time. They are full of internal cleavages and struggles. Workers and employees, on the one hand, and owners and employers, on the other hand, are often pulling the strings in opposite directions and want to get rid of each other.[27]

This all means that when a major social change is happening, its motor is the social and subjective surplus which comes more and more from the background to the fore. The primary front-line between the old order and the new horizon is not the one between them and us. Instead it will divide almost everyone from inside. In this perspective the question of violence in major social changes takes a new light: You have no reason to kill a person if a half of him is already on your side and the other half may follow. There is no need to impose violently a revolution on others if most of these are already partly in the social change movement or on the threshold of entering it.

The collapse of the Soviet Bloc is a case of the phenomenon. At least decades before the big change the society and people were riddled with cleavages between the official and the unofficial. Anyone travelling in these countries usually came across these fractures. Officially a person was a dutiful cleric in a state institution, but in practice he used his time to organize food and other necessities for his relatives or did voluntary work in a cultural heritage association. He was a master in double-thinking. The cleavages found its expression in political jokes circulating everywhere. People worked half-heartedly and in practice sabotage was widespread. Accordingly, the economy and political apparatus functioned poorly. When things started to change, one and the other found their oppositional side even among the party elite. Soon the hollowed-out society collapsed.[28]

RATIONAL PRAXIS

One of the background assumptions of this paper is non-determinism: history is open and human action can change its course. Neither the present order is determined to persist nor an oppositional movement to win. But the odds of winning can increase a lot by our actions. When people see no chance for their humanistic, ecological and democratic values to come true in this order, they should try to change it. And surely a huge number of people are already doing it in hundreds of different ways. They protest, march, demonstrate, block and boycott. They build concrete alternatives materially, socially or spiritually and engage in prefigurative action which models a future society. They withdraw their allegiance to the system and hollow it from inside.

Sometimes a confrontational attitude will work but not always. Sometimes activities not visible to the rulers are rational choices. Sometimes even a perverted adoration of the rulers will yield results. For example the Sakalava of Madagascar are loyal mainly to the dead members of the dynasty. In Kongo people made their kings so sacred that they could not rule any more. Kings could move only inside a small building or they had to be castrated.[29]

When a major global social change stirred by millions of actions and non-actions really gets going, most people probably do not realize that it is happening. It may be that a political revolution has already started.

But most probably the global society is in a bifurcation state: It is at the crossroad being able to move to two opposite directions. The society can as well move to a kind of fascist totalitarianism as change structurally to be able to heed humanistic and ecological values. To further the latter we need myriads of different kinds of actions – but actions imbued with a perspective of a major change. If you invest your whole energy to make the present order a little bit less evil, the lesser level you accept tomorrow will be monstrous. Or to paraphrase Wittgenstein: Wovon man nicht sprechen wagt, darüber muss man verzweifeln – Whereof one dare not speak, thereof one must be hopeless.

NOTES

[1] Barker et al 2007, 39
[2] See e.g. Hansen et al. 2007, Kerr 2007, Oppenheimer et al. 2007
[3] 50,000 people in 60 countries were interviewed. This represents a total global population of 1.25 billion. http://www.peace.ca/gallupmillenniumsurvey.htm .
[4] For example in the winter 2004-2005 75% of Finns were of this opinion, Torvi and Kiljunen 2005

[5] see e.g. New Perspectives Quarterly 2/7/02 http://www.digitalnpq.org/global_services/global_ec_
viewpoint/02-07-02.html and http://www.yachana.org/reports/wsf3/

[6] Voice of the People Survey 2005, Gallup International, October 2005,http://extranet.gallup-
international.com/uploads/internet/Hunger%20&%20Poverty%20VoP%202005.pdf

[7] http://www.peace.ca/gallupmillenniumsurvey.htm

[8] Voice of the People Survey 2002, Gallup International, http://www.voice-of-the-people.net/ContentFiles/
files/VoP2004/Presentation%20given%20to%20the%20media%20in%20Davos%2021st%20January%
202004.doc

[9] Kuhn 1962

[10] The idea of externalized costs was first brought up by William Kapp in 1950: Kapp 1950

[11] See e.g. Mirowski 1988

[12] See e,g, Korten 1995, Chomsky 1999, Lummis 1996

[13] This assumption is made even by such a critical thinker as Jürgen Habermas, see e.g. Habermas
1998, p. 122–124

[14] Concerning the concrete situation in Germany see Jänicke 1990, in Finland Ruostetsaari 1992, in the
EU Balanyá, et al. 2000

[15] See e.g. Chomsky 1999

[16] See e.g. McMurtry 1998, Chossudovsky 1997

[17] See e.g. Foran 2002, Bookchin 1996, Graeber 2004

[18] Paige 2002

[19] See e.g. Brinton 1975[1970], Voline 1990[1947], Goldman 1970

[20] Goldman 1970, chapter 52

[21] See e.g. Chossudovsky 1997

[22] On gift economy see e.g. Mauss 1970, Temple 1988

[23] Bennholdt-Thomsen and Mies 1999, Bennholdt-Thomsen, et al. 2001. Alfredo L. de Romaña calls it
"autonomous economy", Romaña 1989

[24] See Tammilehto 2003, Lummis 1996, McMurtry 1999, Berkes 1989, Bollier 2002

[25] See e.g. Solnit 2004, Abramsky 2001, Graeber 2004

[26] On fractured subject see e.g. Henriques, et al. 1984, Fairclough 1989, Foucault 1972

[27] See Holloway, 2002

[28] This is partly based on my own observations. I made about 20 trips to the Soviet Union, Poland,
GDR and their successor states in the years 1986-1996.

[29] Graeber 2004 p. 59–60

REFERENCES

Abramsky, K. (Ed.). (2001). *Restructuring and resistance: Diverse voices of struggle in Western Europe.* London: Resres Books.

Balanyá, B., Doherty, A., Hoedeman, O., Máanit, A., & Wesselius, E. (2000). *Europe Inc.: Regional & global restructuring and the rise of corporate power.* London: Pluto.

Barker, T., Bashmakov, I., Bernstein, L., Bogner, J. E., Bosch, P. R., Dave, R., et al. (2007). Technical Summary. In B. Metz, O. R. Davidson, P. R. Bosch, R. Dave, & L. A. Meyer (Eds.), *Climate Change 2007: Mitigation. Contribution of Working Group III to the Fourth Assessment Report of the Intergovernmental Panel on Climate Change.* Cambridge: Cambridge University Press

Bennholdt-Thomsen, V., Faraclas, N., & Werlhof, C. V. (Eds.). (2001). *There is an alternative: Subsistence and world-wide resistance to corporate globalization.* London: Zed Books.

Bennholdt-Thomsen, V., & Mies, M. (1999). *The subsistence perspective.* London: Zed Books. (Original work: Eine Kuh für Hilary, Die Subsistenzperspektive, 1997)

Berkes, F. (Ed.). (1989). *Common property resources: Ecology and community-based sustainable development.* London: Belhaven.

Bollier, D. (2002). *Silent theft: The private plunder of our common wealth.* New York: Routledge.

Bookchin, M. (1996). *The third revolution: Popular movements in the revolutionary era.* London and New York: Cassell.

Brinton, M. (1975[1970]). *The Bolsheviks & Workers' Control 1917 to 1921: The State and Counter-Revolution.* London and Detroit: Solidarity ja Black & Red. Retrieved January 26, 2008, from http://www.spunk.org/texts/places/russia/sp001861/bolintro.html.

Chomsky, N. (1999). *Profit over people: Neoliberalism and global order.* New York: Seven Stories Press.

Chossudovsky, M. (1997). *The globalisation of poverty: Impacts of IMF and World Bank Reforms.* London; Atlantic Highlands, NJ and Penang, Malaysia: Zed Books & TWN.

Fairclough, N. (1989). *Language and power.* London: Longman.

Foran, J. (Ed.). (2002). *The future of revolutions: Rethinking radical change in the age of globalization.* London: Zed.

Foucault, M. (1972). *The archaeology of knowledge and the discourse on language.* New York: Pantheon.

Goldman, E. (1970). *Living My Life* (Vol. II). New York: Dover. Retrieved January 26, 2007, from http://dwardmac.pitzer.edu/Anarchist_Archives/goldman/living/livingtoc.html

Graeber, D. (2004). *Fragments of an anarchist anthropology.* Chicago: Prickly Paradigm Press. Retrieved January 9, 2007, from http://www.prickly-paradigm.com/paradigm14.pdf

Habermas, J. Z. (1998). *The inclusion of the Other: Studies in political theory.* Cambridge, UK: Polity Press.

Hansen, J., Sato, M., Kharecha, P., Lea, D., & Siddall, M. (2007). Climate change and trace gases. *Philosophical Transactions of The Royal Society A, 365,* 1925–1954. Available online: http://pubs.giss.nasa.gov/abstracts/2007/Hansen_etal_2.html

Henriques, J., Hollway, W., Urwin, C., Venn, C., & Walkerdine, V. (1984). *Changing the subject: Psychology, social regulation and subjectivity.* London: Methuen.

Holloway, J. (2002). *Change the world without taking power: The meaning of revolution today.* London: Pluto Press.

Jänicke, M. (1990). *State failure, the impotence of politics in industrial society.* Cambridge, UK: Polity.

Kapp, K. W. (1950). *The social costs of private enterprise.* Cambridge, MA: Harvard University Press.

Kerr, R. A. (2007). Pushing the Scary Side of Global Warming. *Science, 316*(5830), 1412–1415.

Korten, D. C. (1995). *When corporations rule the world.* London: Earthscan.

Kuhn, T. S. (1962). *The structure of scientific revolutions.* Chicago: University of Chicago Press.

Lummis, C. D. (1996). *Radical democracy.* Ithaca, NY: Cornell University Press.

Mauss, M. (1970). *The gift: Forms and functions of exchange in archaic societies.* London: Routledge & Kegan Paul.

McMurtry, J. (1998). *Unequal freedoms: The global market as an ethical system.* Toronto, ON: Gramond Press.

McMurtry, J. (1999). *The cancer stage of capitalism.* London: Pluto.

Mirowski, P. (1988). *Against mechanism: Protecting economics from science.* Totowa, NJ: Rowman & Littlefield.

Oppenheimer, M., O'Neill, B. C., Webster, M., & Agrawala, S. (2007). The Limits of Consensus. *Science, 317*(5844), 1505–1506.

Paige, J. M. (2002). Finding the revolutionary in the revolution: Social science concepts and the future of revolution. In J. Foran (Ed.), *The future of revolutions: Rethinking radical change in the age of globalization* (pp. 19–29). London: Zed.

de Romaña, A. L. (1989). An emerging alternative to industrial society, the autonomous economy, Part 1: The vernacular/informal sphere vis-à-vis the formal/industrial sector. *Interculture, XXII*(3), 79–169.

Ruostetsaari, I. (1992). *Vallan ytimessä, Tutkimus suomalaisesta valtaeliitistä.* Helsinki, Finaland: Gaudeamus.

Solnit, D. (Ed.). (2004). *Globalize liberation: How to uproot the system and build a better world.* San Francisco, CA: City Lights Books.

Tammilehto, O. (2003). *Globalisation and dimensions of poverty.* Helsinki: Ministry for Foreign Affairs, Department for International Development Cooperation. Retrieved January 9, 2007, from http:/www.tammilehto.info/globpov.htm;
  http://global.finland.fi/english/publications/pdf/tammilehto_globalisation.pdf.
Temple, D. (1988). The Policy of the 'Severed Flower', a Letter to the Kanak. *Interculture, 98,* 10–35.
Torvi, K., & Kiljunen, P. (2005). *Onnellisuuden vaikea yhtälö.* Helsinki, Finland: EVA.
Voline. (1990[1947]). *The unknown revolution.* Montréal, QC: Black Rose Books.

ALEXANDER LAUTENSACH AND SABINA LAUTENSACH

13. A CURRICULUM FOR A SECURE FUTURE: AGENDA FOR REFORM

THE FAILURE OF HIGHER EDUCATION

At the turn of the millennium, humanity finds itself in a global environmental crisis. The rates of resource depletion are increasing; the global human population continues to grow out of control; pollution continues with its consequences on climate, habitat quality and public health; we see unprecedented rates of species extinctions caused by the worldwide modification of ecosystems through habitat depletion, modification of landscapes and climate, and through species displacement. The two most pressing problems among those are human overpopulation *cum* overconsumption and global warming. Human security in its comprehensive sense, which includes sociopolitical, health-related, economic and environmental dimensions (Lautensach, 2006), is threatened by those developments on many fronts (Union of Concerned Scientists, 1992; McMichael, 2001; UNEP-MAB, 2005).

There is overwhelming evidence that the crisis is anthropogenic. Specifically, the five causative and self-reinforcing processes include economic growth, population growth, technological expansion, arms races, and growing income inequality (McMichael, 1993; Furkiss, 1974; Coates, 1991). Humanity is most likely now in a situation of overshoot, where unsustainable environmental impacts are eroding the source and sink capacities of ecological support structures (Catton, 1980; McMichael, 2001; Wackernagel et al., 2002). Overshoot results if the signals that the system communicates back to the population are delayed, distorted, ignored or denied, which in turn causes detrimental behaviour to continue unchecked.

In this crisis, the greatest amount of harm is done by people with higher degrees (Orr, 1999a; Priesnitz, 2000). This realisation arises from the observation that the vast majority of people in crucial decision-making positions have tertiary qualifications (Lautensach, 2003, p. 196). The five self-reinforcing processes mentioned above are to a large part propelled by the ill-advised, short-sighted and self-serving decisions of this minority who holds a considerable amount of political power. Another major contribution to the crisis obviously comes from larger parts of the population whose behaviour, through omission and commission, fuels those processes causative to the crisis (Cosgrove, Evans, & Yencken, 1994). But even those people tend to be citizens of OECD countries, and many of them have received some tertiary education. An empirical correlation appears evident between higher education and inadequate decision-making.

G. Martin, D. Houston, P. McLaren and J. Suoranta (eds.), The Havoc of Capitalism:
Publics, Pedagogies and Environmental Crisis, 207–227.

The fact that a large number of well-educated people continue to make decisions that are blatantly counterproductive in the present situation indicates that somehow all that education has failed. This failure of higher education manifests itself in two ways. Education results in the transmission of harmful or counterproductive values, beliefs and attitudes, or at least it fails to prevent their transmission through other avenues (Postman & Weingartner, 1969). This includes the teaching of a large amount of material that is factually wrong (Orr, 1992, 1999a). Education also fails to widely elicit alternative, more productive learning outcomes, namely ecological concepts and the values, beliefs and attitudes that would provide the basis for sustainable living (Postman, 1997; Smith & Reynolds, 1990; Laney, 1990). Summarising a substantial number of published analyses (Lautensach, 2003), the deficiencies of the current educational outcomes include a lack of the life skills required for a sustainable society of the future, few skills for moral reasoning, and inadequate analytical skills. Underlying these results is a general inattention to affective learning outcomes (Van Matre, 1990; Werdell, 1974). Value-related outcomes, wherever they are specified in prescriptive documents, are often not translated from ill-defined goal statements to specific instructional objectives and teaching methodology (Lautensach, 2003).

If we accept the correlation between higher education and bad decisions - how conclusive is the evidence for causation? The answer to this question depends on what particular manifestation of the crisis we focus on, and at what scale. For example, the answer to the question whether inadequate education is causing global warming is arguably affirmative. Without being taught to hold unrealistic confidence in misleading conceptions of progress most of humanity would never have ended up in this insane rut of fossil fuel dependence. But is education also to blame for the loss of rainforests in Borneo? Here the causative connection seems more tenuous. Two important variables in this causation are the extent of power wielded by educated individuals in a particular context and the contribution made by formal (tertiary) education to the relevant attitudes and values of those individuals (Raths, Harmin, & Simon, 1978). What seems undisputable is that education systems worldwide could perform far better towards preventing and mitigating the crisis.

Some people might concede that false education causes the crisis, and they might even acknowledge the mitigative potential of educational reform, but they would still object to the idea of a moral duty for educators to make such attempts. Two considerations suggest that such a duty exists. The first is based on the principles of non-maleficence and beneficence in medical ethics. The principles of medical ethics are applicable to education because the relationship between the learner and the teacher bears a fair resemblance to that between the patient and the doctor. The second consideration rests on intergenerational justice which posits a moral duty on every individual not to jeopardise the security of future generations. Because of the amount of influence that educators wield over the moral basis of behaviour in their graduates, this duty is greater with educators than with many others. Through omission and commission, present educational practices violate this duty to an extent that contravenes the spirit (if not the letter) of institutional mission statements worldwide.

EDUCATIONAL SOLUTIONS

Given that the *status quo* of educational practice carries considerable potential for improvement, and given the moral duty for educators and institutions to reform education, the question arises how this educational shortfall could best be addressed. We will now outline the agenda of a program for curriculum reform. Even though our arguments are largely based on observations from secondary and tertiary education, this plan is applicable in principle to all levels. We shall restrict our suggestions to formal education and leave the educational roles of the media, the entertainment industry and general cultural influences for another occasion.

One overarching goal of the proposed curriculum is to lay the moral groundwork for a globally sustainable society. Tam (1998) eloquently pointed to the social justice dimension of this goal: "Unless a society wishes to deny the opportunity of a specified class of people to deal competently with certain types of issue in life, it must view education as the overall development of citizens, and not narrowly as the granting of occupation-specific passports" (pp. 58–59). Additional urgency is contributed by the growing volatility of the job market and the accelerating technological advancement in many fields (Tarrant, 1989; Entwistle, 1996). Elsewhere (Lautensach, 2003) one of us argued that a transition towards sustainable living can be managed under the ideals of efficiency, restraint, adaptation and structural reform. In behavioural terms, those ideals set the direction of the proposed curriculum. A second overarching goal is to create motivation in the individual towards paying restitution to ecosystems and threatened species in compensation for past wrongdoings. This goal is informed by the realisation that at this advanced stage of the crisis, aiming merely for sustainability[1] will no longer suffice. In accordance with the significant role played by the normative concept of progress (Lautensach & Lautensach, 2004), those two goals are pursued by emphasising the development of alternative values, attitudes and beliefs, to form a new substantive concept of progress. This proposition accords with widely held opinions among environmental educators (Nicholson-Lord, 2001).

In order to pursue those goals effectively, the reform of education has to address the causes for its current failure as outlined above. As pointed out, this means to stop teaching counterproductive beliefs and values, and to teach appropriate concepts and values more effectively. A third agendum arises out of considerations of tactical expediency and distributive justice, namely to implement a pedagogy of liberation. We shall now explain what reforms are necessary under these tripartite agenda. Detailed learning outcomes of this new curriculum were outlined elsewhere (Lautensach, 2004).

STOP TEACHING COUNTERPRODUCTIVE BELIEFS AND VALUES

As we stated above and argued more fully elsewhere (Lautensach & Lautensach, 2004), an educational program in pursuit of the goals of sustainability will need to effectively counteract the dominant concept of progress. The dominant ideology of progress draws its power from beliefs and values that are partly reproduced through enculturation at large, but to a large part they are specifically transmitted through formal education. One important set of agenda for reform, then, will be designed to interfere with those systemic mechanisms of ideological reproduction. This can be accomplished in two ways. Firstly, educational reform must counteract the hegemonic influence of ideologies that serve to perpetuate the dominant concept of progress. Those ideologies include the following beliefs, values and attitudes: Economic growth as a good in itself; cornucopianism[2]; complacent optimism; omnipotence of science & technology (Orr, 1998); moral nihilism & materialism (Allsop, 1972; Margulis, 1997); consumerism (Ekins, 1998); freedom from nature and dominion over it (Fien, 1993). Another target is represented by the neoliberal concept of individualism since "the problem with individualist ideologies ... is that they in fact leave prevailing power relations, however unjust, firmly in place" (Tam, 1998, pp. 78–79).

A second objective is to prevent the perpetuation of anthropocentric values. This argument is presented in more detail elsewhere (Lautensach, 2003). In brief, anthropocentric ethics represents the major conceptual and moral obstacle on the way towards implementing the four goals of sustainability, by lending support to the moral claims of the dominant concept of progress (Bateson, 1972). Furthermore, anthropocentrism as a concept suffers from internal inconsistencies. The anthropocentric vision of human flourishing is conceptually incoherent, ill-defined and shallow. The conceptual constraints of anthropocentrism itself preclude a more concise definition which would take into account the utter dependence of the flourishing of humanity on the health of ecological support structures. Also, pursuing the anthropocentric concept of human flourishing is ultimately counterproductive, even from the view of the anthropocentrist herself, because anthropocentrists tend to discard undiscovered potential benefits of nature. The required shift towards more ecocentric ethics relies on to a large extent value education. It amounts to a moral paradigm shift that extends beyond environmental values into how we conceptualise the moral position of humanity in the world. Among the moral concepts that have to be unlearned here are human-nature dualism and the ideals of freedom from nature and human dominion.

A number of strategies can be enlisted towards the goal to counteract those ideologies. Existing curriculum must be re-assessed and re-interpreted. As the bulk of the counterproductive learning outcomes appear to result from implicit value messages and omissions from the curriculum (Roszak, 2000), the focus of analysis should be directed at the null curriculum and the hidden curriculum. Much of the burden of this analytical task must fall on the educator until such time as more helpful guidelines and resources become available. Some of this analysis should also be carried out by the learner, as will be argued more fully below. Educational practice must also help to diminish the influence of counterproductive propaganda messages from outside of the educational institutions. An essential requirement towards all of those strategies is the educational objective of getting the learner to unlearn counterproductive concepts as a prior condition to learning, an objective that has been largely ignored since Postman and Weingartner (1969, p. 208) first called attention to it.

TEACH APPROPRIATE BELIEFS AND VALUES IN MORE EFFECTIVE WAYS

Foremost among the positive goals for reform must be the teaching of an environmental ethic that is consistently ecocentric. This encompasses several values and attitudes that will be described further below. Another group of desirable learning outcomes consists of beliefs and attitudes of the new ecological paradigm which is to replace the dominant social paradigm (Fien, 1993). They include dependence on nature, integration within the natural environment, the recognition of natural limits to consumption and to technological development, concern for future generations and respect for nature (Taylor, 1986). A third group of outcomes are defined by certain skill gaps and by the cognitive reasons ('mental habits') for human behaviour that resulted in overshoot. They translate into cognitive as well as affective learning outcomes (de Silva, 1997).

Curricula will have to be re-focussed in order to enlist more academic disciplines in the efforts of finding sustainable solutions to the human predicament. For example, the gradual inclusion of ecological principles into curricula of economics during the 1980s has led to the development of the new field of ecological economics and an international society and journal by that name. Ehrlich and Ehrlich (1990) argued that, because economics carries considerable political weight and economists hold considerable influence over politicians, this development should be augmented by enriching primary and secondary curricula with the basics of ecology (Margulis, 1997, p. 311). "From here forward, a university education that is not environmental education is no education at all" (Rolston, 1996, p. 189).

The obsession with the present and past has to be mitigated by a more forward-looking stance. This includes learning about the crisis (Madsden, 1996) and about current trends and probable future scenarios (Delcourt & Delcourt, 2000; Stern, Dieltz, & Kaloff, 1993; Werdell, 1974). It also includes several attitude changes as will be explained below. Parochialism of form and content (Perelman, 1976) has to be addressed at all levels of education. The goal here is contingent with Perelman's (1976) 'ecological education' towards a 'softworld perspective', educating learners to be competent in finding solutions rather than selling a particular position on limits to growth. New solutions can be found with the help of new values and new assumptions. However, none of this guarantees that the learner will actually act on such insights. This requires a pedagogy of liberation.

IMPLEMENT A PEDAGOGY OF LIBERATION

Why is it important that the learner takes action on his/her insights and convictions? Achieving a sustainable society requires a transformative effort, unlike the more passive transition to post-industrial society (Perelman, 1976, p. 196). Social transformation will be necessary in order for the required changes in human behaviour to be adopted by the wider population and to take root in our culture. Such a process depends on a sufficient contingent of competent graduate transformers. The abovementioned two reform agenda of ceasing the reproduction of counterproductive ideologies and of teaching appropriate objectives in more effective ways do not go far enough here. A change of course in value education would doubtlessly have an effect on the ways in which the learners evaluate their actions and those of others. But such a strategy leaves it more or less up to chance to what extent the change in ethics will result in a change in behaviour. This concern is addressed under our third agenda point of reform, to implement a pedagogy of liberation. It is designed specifically to help empower and motivate the learner towards taking action. Unless the learner is prepared to think and act for him/ herself on the basis of recent learning, neither can the reasons for overshoot be entirely eliminated, nor can we expect to win the race against time. We argue here from a humanistic perspective of learning by developing the concept of self, based on the work of Abraham Maslow (1968) and Carl Rogers (Rogers & Freiberg, 1993).

Liberation from what? Exploitative dependencies acting from within the learner and structural constraints acting from without tend to hinder any deliberate change to more sustainable living. The former are an inevitable outcome of enculturation and constitute a web of habits, institutional relationships and ideologies that govern the learner's interactions with society – such as consumerism, the work ethic and misguided theories of progress. For most people this web of dependencies makes it virtually impossible to adopt a sustainable way of life, through commission or omission, unless they free themselves of at least some of those conceptual constraints and replace them with more helpful relationships (Ekins, 1998). Without receiving some directed help through education, the learner may not be able to accomplish this. From without, the existing power imbalances are ill-suited to mitigate the situation and they often constitute part of the problem. The global economic system has placed severe limitations on the consumer in terms of real choices, without any political mandate to do so, and to the detriment of the public good. The liberalisation of trade, the privatisation of state assets and the commodification of nature under the dominant concept of progress have led to intensified destruction of ecosystems and resource depletion worldwide. This imposition of socio-political and socio-economic contexts on humans by other humans with the effect that short-sighted exploitative behaviour becomes their only possible course of action constitutes an act of oppression (Barber, 1998). The educational reforms we propose are designed to liberate the learner from the influences of the dominant paradigms and structures that perpetuate those internal dependencies and external constraints.

The objective of this liberation is not only to enable the individual learner to change his or her ways of living, it is the destabilisation in the long term of those oppressive structures and relationships to prevent backlashes. In this counter-hegemonic mission our proposed pedagogy resembles the liberation pedagogies advocated by the Freirian school of critical theorists. As with the political oppression targeted by the Freirians, the mechanism of the oppression relies on a rigidly hierarchical system where almost everybody acts as the oppressor as well as the oppressed (Young, 1992).[3] The oppression operates through and results in alienation (from the environment as well as from each other) and fragmentation rather than solidarity. It invades the culture of the oppressed (as seen, for instance, in the 'branding' of teenagers and the encouragement of indifference towards animals) and silences their personal voices. It can manifest itself in exploitation, marginalisation, powerlessness, cultural imperialism, and violence (Young, 1992). It forces individuals to follow prescriptions (those of consumers) and to become spectators instead of actors. It replaces the freedom to act with "the illusion of acting through the action of the oppressors" (Freire, 1986, p. 33). Public education at this stage plays an essential part in habituating the young learner to this situation and in achieving compliance (Galbraith, 1984; Beder, 2000; McLaren, 1986; Connell, 1977; Bowles & Gintis, 1976; Lautensach, 2003). Counter-hegemonic education aims to accomplish the opposite, to relieve the learner from this habituation to oppression.

How is this liberation expected to come about? As Paolo Freire (1986) noted decades ago, education systems are largely ill-equipped to tackle oppressive political situations. In the absence of effective political support from the authorities, educator and learner have to transcend this oppressive situation by working together through a process referred to by the Freirians as *conscientisation*. It involves a set of educational strategies resulting in the empowerment of the learner and in the achievement of a critical consciousness. This critical consciousness will permit and ensure the unmasking of oppressive structures, and it is relevant wherever such oppressive structures exist. Through the process of conscientisation the learner becomes empowered to take action and to engage in attempts to convince others of her newfound views. The empowerment of the learner represents an important aim of educational reform towards sustainability. Empowerment is one of six general aims in the proposed curriculum and I will elaborate on it below; but the agenda of liberation reach into all the other aims, as effective progress towards them depends to a large extent on the learner's ability to re-examine her own values and beliefs, and to take action.

SIX GENERAL AIMS

The curriculum that we propose is organised into six general aims that form groups of learning outcomes. They include the adoption of a concept of progress that is informed by sustainability; the replacement of anthropocentrism with an ecocentrist environmental ethic; the acquisition of requisite skills; a vision for and awareness of the future that includes change and sustainable solutions; a non-parochialist view of environmental values and academic inquiry; and the liberation from exploitative dependencies. The proposed curriculum follows Perelman's (1976) recommendation for a curriculum for ecological education to be multilevel, interdisciplinary, problem-centred, future-oriented, global, and humanistic.

Across those six general aims extend as common threads the three above-mentioned agenda of counteracting undesirable educational outcomes, encouraging such outcomes as are conducive to the general aims, and empowering the learner to take action. The appended table shows an overview of those negative and positive outcomes for each of the six general aims. It also contains lists of proximate instructional objectives that were either proposed in the literature or are obviously and directly conducive to those aims. Lastly, a sample of the specific methodology towards those objectives is presented at the bottom of the table. Besides the three agenda, other obvious common features among those six general aims include the emphasis on ideological change, the prevalence of values and attitudes among educational outcomes, and a propensity for action informed by those values. A detailed description and explanation of those six general aims and their respective learning outcomes was given elsewhere (Lautensach, 2004). We shall summarise them here only briefly.

Re-define progress as achieving sustainability- The proposed curriculum is to address both the impediments to feedback that have led to overshoot and the root causes for unsustainable behaviour. This first general aim is concerned with changing the dominant concept of progress in the learners towards a concept that incorporates effective feedback and that informs more sustainable behaviour. We propose that this aim be pursued through two strategies: enabling the learner to critically analyse the dominant concept of progress for contradictions (McPeck, 1981), and encouraging the development of a personal ethic of sustainability by extending existing values of justice towards future generations and ecosystems.

Replace anthropocentric values with ecocentric values- The majority of technical recommendations on how to deal with the crisis are of little worth inasmuch as they fail to transcend the culturally imposed conceptual and moral constraints of anthropocentrism (Merchant, 1980; Shepard, 1998). Since anthropocentrism constitutes part of the problem only a critical appraisal of its shortcomings and its eventual replacement by alternative ethics can deliver effective solutions (Eggert, 1999). Our proposed ecocentric curriculum combines an ecosocialist pedagogy of liberation with a deep green vision of transforming personal values, in order to counteract the dominant anti-environmental ethic with which traditional education systems promote cornucopian and consumerist ideals (Cohen & Lazerson, 1973, p. 319). The general aim of value transformation is pursued in four stages: developing a critical attitude to question anthropocentrism, acquiring the requisite cognitive skills to do so, adopting the new ecocentric values, and developing an attitude to act on one's values (Knapp, 1983; Raths et al., 1978).

Remedy skill gaps- The condition of overshoot in the global crisis results primarily from certain peculiarities in the human psyche that enable people to deny the signs of crisis. Cognitive reasons for denial include the inability to perceive one's environment in a holistic way, the inability to extrapolate to global dimensions, the inability to extrapolate to the long term; and difficulties with sifting significant information from nonsense. A second group of deficiencies consists of the negation of moral responsibility and a lack of moral scruples. They are best described as moral ineptitudes, rather than as the absence of specific cognitive skills. A third group of reasons for denial, sometimes referred to as 'mental habits', are wishful thinking, self-deception, groundless optimism, and *akrasia* (weakness of will)[4]. These deficiencies can be remediated in three consecutive stages. First, the learner has to perceive the gaps in him/herself and in others and realise their significance. Secondly, he or she has to become aware of and understand the causes of those gaps as well as remedial opportunities. Thirdly, the learner has to make the effort to mitigate them. Different skills and attitudes are required at each stage.

Re-orient education towards the future- Closely connected with the remediation of skill gaps is the general aim of providing the learner with a vision for the future that takes into account the rapid environmental changes and the resulting socio-political upheavals we can predict from current trends. Only with sufficient vision of this kind will the learner be able to proactively cope with the rapid and widespread change the world is beginning to experience now (Fullan, 2001). The changes in attitudes and values proposed above are both necessary and sufficient for this change in vision.

Eliminate parochialism from education systems- The existence of intransigent barriers between disciplines and academic departments has been referred to as parochialism of content and form, respectively (Perelman, 1976). Both have been implicated in the failure of higher education (Orr, 1999b, p. 232; Wren-Lewis, 1974, pp., 163–164). They inhibit all those really radical advances that depend on the development of fundamentally new ways of thinking because they confine the learner to the present. It seems that the learner can only develop a vision focused on the future by asking questions about the conceptual and administrative boundaries of academic endeavour. Such questions inevitably refer to norms and concepts outside of the discipline, which makes their discussion difficult and controversial in the traditional academy (Brennan, 1996, p. 95). This situation has had particularly detrimental consequences when multi-faceted problems are reframed as technical and are addressed by technologists through technical means (Sosa, 1996, p. 49). What Whitehead (1967, p. 6) called "the fatal disconnection of subjects" has reduced academia to a cacophony of mutually unintelligible professional jargons ill equipped to facilitate the kind of transdisciplinary work required to cope with the crisis. An example is the lack of engagement and dismissive contempt with which James Lovelock's Gaia model (Lovelock, 1995) was received by those who should have known better (Abram, 1985).

We can identify four problems caused by parochialism. It reinforces the curricular compartmentalisation of environmental education; it tends to cloud people's vision for the future, as pointed out above; within a discipline, it hinders the asking of important questions about ends, means and norms, which leads to inadequacies in professional ethics; and it disposes people towards a misleading assessment of risks and novel concepts, diverting our attention from the crisis. The latter two effects arise particularly from an inattention to transdisciplinary aspects of investigation both by teacher and learner. What distinguishes the more competent among professional practitioners is how they deal with those problems. But individual efforts need to be reinforced by educational reform. The reform of content focuses on new curriculum elements on ethics, factual beliefs, attitudes and skills. The reform of form is directed at institutional structures and practices such as administration, constitution, research funding, physical structuring of the learning environment and the organisation of teaching and learning. Each aspect affects the others, but our general focus on curriculum predicates a certain bias towards the parochialism of content.

As a first strategy, the learner needs to recognise that in the light of the crisis ecological considerations belong into every human endeavour, and this recognition needs to be reflected both in the curriculum and in the organization of the institution (Catton, 1980). A second strategy to counteract parochialism of content is to use a multidisciplinary introduction to Gaia theory to help induce an attitude of respect, humility and wonder in close connection with factual information. The third strategy to counteract parochialism consists of a multidisciplinary examination of the manifestations of the crisis.

Empower the learner to take action- A recurring theme across these general aims is the liberation of the learner from exploitative dependencies acting from within the learner and from structural constraints acting from without. This liberation is necessary to enable the learner to take action on newly found insights and convictions. The learner becomes liberated as a result of empowerment, which in turn is a result of conscientisation. Empowerment in this context means that the learners acquire the critical skills (McPeck, 1981) necessary to reassess their way of life and to selectively unlearn what was wrongly taught, as well as the requisite moral norms and ideals to encourage action. This will allow the learners to overcome the subversion of information and to accept moral responsibility for their environment and for the future of their fellow humans (Pybus & McLaughlin, 1995).

Conscientisation refers to educational strategies designed to achieve empowerment of the learner, which draws together most of the learning outcomes under the six general aims. True to Freire's (1986, p. 36) original idea, conscientisation enables the learners to progress from a state of 'submerged consciousness' to a state of critical consciousness where they become aware of oppressive and exploitative dependencies, and where they become motivated and informed to counteract those dependencies in solidarity with others (Findlay, 1994). During this process the learner becomes alert to his mental habits and develops a disposition towards counter-hegemonic critique. True to its semantic origin, conscientisation in this context also includes as a significant moral component the development of an ecological *conscience* in the learner, functioning as the moral component of the learner's new substantive concept of progress. While consciousness governs thought and sentiment, conscience channels action – which is, after all, what empowerment and liberation is all about. However, our pedagogy of liberation derives its immediate legitimacy from the imperatives of the global crisis, not exclusively from considerations of interhuman justice as in the case of other liberation pedagogies. Its goals are informed by ecocentrism rather than by anthropocentric communitarian or libertarian ideals. The kind of moral conscience called for in this context, therefore, is quite different from the one Freire might have intended.

Despite those differences between the Freirian interpretation of conscientisation and our own, its pursuit in the classroom can benefit significantly from the insights provided by Freirian liberation theory. One of those insights states that no educational process can be neutral or disinterested with respect to existing power relationships (Grant & Zeichner, 1984, p. 15), as some liberal educationists (such as

Peters, 1966) claimed. Once the learner has realised that education remains inevitably partial, she is more likely to develop a reasoned stance that may differ from that of her pro-hegemonic teachers. Much of her success depends of course on the minority of teachers who practice resistance in support of the learner (Carlson, 1988). In turn, the success of such a critical theory of curriculum depends to a crucial extent on its application to teacher education, because it is the new teachers that are more likely to innovate (Robottom, 1987). The liberation and empowerment of the learner must be informed by communitarian ideals to prevent atomistic individualism (Haste, 1996; Suzuki & Dressel, 2002), and the teacher's support plays a valuable role in establishing communitarian thinking.

The chances of success of any educational reform can be increased if it anticipates and pre-empts political opposition. Revolutionary changes are frequently compromised by backlash effects, and contemporary movements such as environmentalism and feminism are no exception. Our proposed pedagogy seeks to develop a critical consciousness that will put into question the 'business as usual' approach to 'development' and that will fundamentally challenge the social values, structures, authorities and conventions that support that approach. Specifically, it is set to destabilise the conceptual straitjacket imposed on the education sector by the globally dominant ideology of progress. This is likely to result in political difficulties that a successful pedagogy must weather (Fien, 1993).[5]

It is important for this program of critical pedagogy to prepare the learner for her inevitable encounter with backlash in order to minimise its impact. With regard to the environmental movement, backlash manifests itself primarily in the two ways in which information is being subverted, commonly referred to as 'greenwash' and 'brownlash'. Both greenwash and brownlash rely extensively on the near monopoly exercised by a minority of corporate entities over the mainstream media (Beder, 1997; Edwards, 1998, 1999; Suzuki & Dressel, 2002). The ability of the learner to recognise and accurately assess tactics of greenwash and brownlash and to interpret media reports correctly represents an important component in her empowerment. The learner must become able to recognise the inadequacies, half-truths and untruths contained in such reporting (Ehrlich & Ehrlich, 1996), and to attempt her own, deeper analysis, relying on cognitive skills and affective dispositions.

SUMMARY

Several common themes emerge that shape the general focus of this pedagogy for sustainability. Firstly, it takes a holistic approach across all the dimensions of human development: the intellectual, emotional, spiritual, moral and physical. It extends over all academic disciplines. It also takes a global focus, despite the national idiosyncrasies of public education systems and the ultimately local or national character of educational reform, because only a global vision can inform appropriate local measures. The overarching aim of our efforts for reform is to facilitate a sustainable existence of acceptable quality for the species *Homo sapiens* on the planet Earth and to balance that priority against its impact on non-human nature. The fact that specific regional ecological, cultural, political and individual conditions may differ in their conduciveness towards that aim does not take away from its global applicability. That is to say, no region, community, culture or individual should be entirely exempt from the obligation to help. But beyond that global obligation we recognise differences in degrees of obligations, in potentials for improvement, and in potentials for making a difference. Those differences may be geographical, national, cultural and individual in nature.

Secondly, this pedagogy clearly emphasises values. Many analyses of the crisis and its causation (reviewed in Lautensach, 2003) indicated that without a change in prevailing values the crisis could not be effectively addressed.[6] We also argued (Lautensach, 2003) that value education is possible, desirable and practical. As far as educational solutions are concerned, affective learning outcomes thus must take priority over cognitive ones. Others have come to similar conclusions (Giroux, 1981; Sylvan & Bennett, 1994; Toffler, 1974; Bosselmann, 1995). In many respects, affective learning outcomes can be considered the most important results of the educational process because they render other outcomes more achievable (Caduto, 1983; Raths et al., 1978). It also can culminate in exomotivation[7] which would make the educator's task easier. Another reason why this pedagogy is focused on values is because most curriculum reforms have tended to neglect the essential role played by education in determining values (Lautensach, 2003). Not surprisingly, few of those reforms lived up to the expectations of their protagonists. Our proposed curriculum is supposed to address that gap which is essentially political; methodologies for value education have long been available (Caduto, 1983; Ryan, 1981; Silver, 1976; Van Matre, 1990).

This emphasis on values has to be explicit and selective. Much of the currently taught values are contained in the hidden curriculum and the null curriculum, which have tended to remain conservative even in the face of some progressive reforms in explicit curriculum and teaching methodologies. The issues presented to students for resolution are posed within a pluralistic, consensus view of society, which implies the equality of all values and opinions and ignores the role of conflict and the use of various forms of power in environmental decision making (Maher, 1988). This lack of direction necessitates that, as the foremost agendum in the new curriculum, values must be presented explicitly and as *unequal*. Efforts at increasing social justice must be reconceptualised with the ecological crisis as the highest priority. The adoption of an 'ecological morality' (Allsop, 1972, p. 38) is analogous to the mitigation through human rights theory of the ignorance, self-righteousness and greed had informed the 'progress' of colonialism in past centuries, and it can be justified to the learner with similar moral arguments, based on justice and on virtue (Durkheim, 1961; Etzioni, 1995).

A third recurrent theme in this pedagogy is its critical orientation with respect to dominant ideologies. The current widespread emphasis in tertiary education on discipline mastery has served to reinforce the dominant ideologies of progress and anthropocentrism through habituation via the hidden curriculum. The curriculum we advocate here is oriented towards ecological validity and sufficiency, focussing on destabilising the dominant anthropocentric ideology of progress. This destabilisation of a hegemonic ethic and its replacement with an ecocentric alternative becomes possible when a sufficient number of learners develop a critical consciousness, which empowers them to take action.

The critical pedagogy for sustainability shares with the liberal model of education as proposed by John Dewey and others a certain atomist bias towards the learner as a thinking, feeling individual who can be empowered through self-realisation. An important prerequisite for the learners to be able to take action on their convictions and aspirations is that they feel confident, safe and competent to do so. This feeling is predicated on a certain degree of liberation from dependencies of habit, ideology and institutional context. The most significant element in those agenda of liberation is the subversion of consumerism and the mitigation of the conceptual and moral constraints it imposes on communities and individuals. In that sense, our proposed pedagogy calls for certain strategies and methods adopted from Freirian liberation pedagogy. Critical pedagogy contributes a significant body of theory on empowerment of the learner; and it provides a modicum of counterbalance to the influence of technocratic educators who now dominate the professional development and training especially of new teachers (Pike & Selby, 1988; Bowers, 1993).

Lastly, our proposed curriculum emphasises action. For the educator this means that once a clear consensus on several ethical issues exists, one should act on these rather than suspend all attempts at moral education just because one cannot reach agreement in some remaining areas (Dewey, 1966; Etzioni, 1995) – or, as Bowers (1993) put it, "we do not need a master plan, only a clear sense of the direction in which we must move, and a full sense of awareness of the consequences if we fail" (p. 217).

NOTES

[1] We use the term sustainability as defined by Lemons (1996), "the continued satisfaction of basic human physical needs, such as food, water, shelter, and of higher-level social and cultural needs, such as security, freedom, education, employment, and recreation", along with "continued productivity and functioning of ecosystems" (p. 198). We regard the popular 'Brundtland' definition of sustainability (WCED 1987) to be quite useless because of its lack of conciseness, inattention to metaethical considerations and its neglect of fundamental ecological limitations.

[2] The term cornucopianism refers to the curious belief that there are no hard limits to the growth of economies, human populations, and rates of resource use (Ehrlich & Holdren, 1971). It has inspired generations of orthodox economists and those who trust in their conceptual models (Lutzenberger, 1996). A minority of less prejudiced experts has begun to challenge them (Daly & Cobb, 1994; Henderson, 1999).

[3] As Foucault has observed in another context, only a very small minority, situated at the top of the societal pyramid, engages in oppressive behaviour out of a conscious choice they made free from duress. By his or her own habitual (and at times compulsive) patterns of consumption, a consumer at once contributes toward the oppression of others and is being oppressed. At the same time, the consumer is continuously assured by advertising that the road toward maximising their personal freedom (another unquestioned ideal) is built on maximum consumption, and, worse, that failure to follow this course will result in loss of face. In this way, most members of consumer societies have

become both oppressed and oppressors. An analogous effect, where some members of a disadvantaged gender oppressing their fellow victims, has been recognised in the feminist literature.

[4] *Akrasia* or 'weakness of will' or 'moral incontinence' was described by Aristotle as the phenomenon of people not behaving in noble, rational, reflective and virtuous ways even when they have been amply instructed in what those characteristics entail and they feel quite motivated to adhere to them. The word stems from the Greek verb for 'to coddle', 'to pander to'. Much of seemingly 'stupid' behaviour is probably caused by *akrasia*, such as the consumption of environmentally harmful products or engaging in self-abusive behaviour, while being fully aware of the consequences. *Akrasia* is strengthened by the 'Cry Wolf' effect of erroneous warnings.

[5] Postman (1997) asserted that in the U.S. the opposition to a true pedagogy of liberation is powerful and relies on the continuing irrelevance of most school curricula. That is not to say that those opponents are against educational innovation *per se* (p. 57). On the contrary - Postman noted that they can be usually relied upon to give unflagging support to instructional television, computer-aided instruction, team teaching, whiteboards, movable chairs, more textbooks, the use of audiovisual technology, and other innovations that "play no role in effecting significant learning" (p. 57). He argued that "the enthusiasm that community leaders display for an educational innovation is in inverse proportion to its significance to the learning process" (p. 57). In New Zealand as well, the vibrant and agonised concerns of educational reformists of the 1970s have been almost entirely subsumed under a deluge of narrow-focussed technicism as part of the neo-liberal economic revolution (Armstrong, 1999). Our own professional experience confirms this assessment.

[6] "The history of cultures and social formations is unintelligible except in relation to a history of value orientations, value ideals, goods values, value responses, and value judgements, and their objectivisations, interplay and transformations." (Fekete, 1988:p. i)

[7] Exomotivation refers to the motivation of the learner to pass on to others his/her newfound insights and to convince them of their significance (Ornell, 1980).

REFERENCES

Abram, D. (1985). The perceptual implications of Gaia. *The Ecologist, 15*, 21–28.

Allsop, B. (1972). *Ecological morality*. London: Frederick Muller.

Armstrong, G. A. W. (1999). After 25 years: Paolo Freire in New Zealand 1974. In P. Roberts (Ed.), *Paolo Freire, politics and pedagogy: Reflections from Aotearoa-New Zealand* (pp. 23–33). Palmerston North: Dunmore Press.

Barber, B. R. (1998). *A place for us*. New York: Hill and Wang.

Bateson, G. (1972). *Steps to an ecology of mind*. New York: Ballantine.

Beder, S. (1997). *Global spin: The corporate assault on environmentalism*. Carlton North, Victoria: Scribe Publications Pty Ltd.

Beder, S. (2000). *Selling the work ethic: From Puritan pulpit to corporate PR*. Sydney and London: Scribe Publications and Zed Books.

Bosselmann, K. (1995). *When two worlds collide - Society and ecology*. Auckland: RSVP Publ. Co.

Bowers, C. A. (1993). *Education, cultural myths, and the ecological crisis: Toward deep changes*. Albany, NY: State University of New York Press.

Bowles, S., & Gintis H. (1976). *Schooling in capitalist America: Educational reform and the contradictions of economic life*. New York: Basic Books.

Brennan, A. (1996). Incontinence, self-deception, shallow analysis, myth-making, and economic rationality. In J. Callicott & F. J. R. da Rocha (Eds.), *Earth summit ethics: Toward a reconstructive postmodern philosophy of environmental education* (pp. 93–114). Albany, NY: State University of New York Press.

Caduto, M. (1983). A review of environmental values education. *Journal of Environmental Education, 14*(3), 12–18.

Carlson, D. (1988). Beyond the reproductive theory of teaching. In M. Cole (Ed.), *Bowles and Gintis revisited: Correspondence and contradiction in educational theory* (pp. 158–174). Lewes, UK: The Falmer Press.

Catton, W. R., Jr. (1980). *Overshoot: The ecological basis of revolutionary change*. Urbana, IL: University of Illinois Press.

Coates, J. F. (1991). The sixteen sources of environmental problems in the 21st century. *Technological Forecasting and Social Change, 40*, 87–91.

Cohen, D. K., & Lazerson, M. (1973). Education and the corporate order. In M. B. Katz (Ed.), *Education in American history: Readings on the social issues*. New York: Praeger.

Connell, R. W. (1977). *Ruling class ruling culture: Studies of conflict, power and hegemony in Australian life*. Cambridge: Cambridge University Press.

Cosgrove, L., Evans, D., & Yencken, D. (Eds.). (1994). *Restoring the land: Environmental values, knowledge and action*. Melbourne University Press.

Daly, H. E., & Cobb, J. B. (1994). *For the common good: Redirecting the economy toward community, the environment, and a sustainable future* (2nd ed.). Boston: Beacon Press.

Delcourt, P., & Delcourt, H. (2000). *Ten personal strategies for living well in an age of global warming*. White River Junction, VT: Chelsea Green Publishing.

de Silva, P. (1997, October 1–3). *Linking nature, ethics and culture through effective environmental discourse*. Paper presented at the International Conference on Environmental Justice, University of Melbourne.

Dewey, J. (1966). *Democracy and education*. New York: Free Press.

Durkheim, E. (1961). *Moral education* (E. Wilson & H. Schnurer, Trans.). New York: Free Press of Glencoe.

Edwards, D. (1999, May/June). Greenwash - Co-opting dissent. *The Ecologist, 29*(3), 172–174.

Edwards, D. (1998, January/February). Can we learn the truth about the environment from the media? *The Ecologist, 28*(1), 18–22.

Eggert, J. (1999). *Song of the Meadowlark: Exploring values for a sustainable future*. Berkeley, CA: Ten Speed Press.

Ehrlich, P. R., & Ehrlich, A. H. (1990). *The population explosion*. New York: Simon and Schuster.

Ehrlich, P. R., & Ehrlich, A. H. (1996). *Betrayal of science and reason: How anti-environmental rhetoric threatens our future*. Washington, DC: Island Press.

Ehrlich, P. R., & Holdren, J. (1971). The impact of population growth. *Science, 171*, 1212–1217.

Ekins, P. (1998, November/December). From consumption to satisfaction. *Resurgence, 191*, 16–19.

Entwistle, H. (1996). Knowledge of most worth to citizens. In J. Demaine & H. Entwistle (Eds.), *Beyond communitarianism: Citizenship, politics and education* (pp. 193–220). London: Macmillan.

Etzioni, A. (1995). *The spirit of community*. London: Fontana.

Fekete, J. (1988). Introductory notes for a postmodern value agenda. In J. Fekete (Ed.), *Life after postmodernism: Essays on value and culture*. London: Macmillan.

Fien, J. (1993). *Education for the environment: Curriculum theorising and environmental education*. Geelong, Victoria, Australia: Deakin University Press.

Findlay, P. (1994). Conscientisation and social movements in Canada: The relevance of Paolo Freire's ideas in contemporary politics. In P. McLaren & C. Lankshear (Eds.), *Politics of liberation: Paths from Freire* (Chap. 6). London: Routledge.

Freire, P. (1986). *Pedagogy of the oppressed*. New York: Continuum Pub. Co.

Furkiss, V. (1974). *The future of technological civilisation*. New York: Braziller.

Fullan, M. (2001). *Leading in a culture of change*. San Francisco: Jossey-Bass.

Galbraith, J. K. (1984). *The anatomy of power*. London: Hamish Hamilton.

Giroux, H. A. (1981). *Ideology, culture and the process of schooling*. Lewes, UK: The Falmer Press.

Grant, C. A., & Zeichner, K. M. (1984). On becoming a reflective teacher. In C. A. Grant (Ed.), *Preparing for reflective teaching* (pp. 1–18). Boston: Allyn & Bacon Inc.

Haste, H. (1996). Communitarianism and the social construction of morality. *Journal of Moral Education, 25*, 47–55.

Henderson, H. (1999). *Beyond globalisation: Shaping a sustainable global economy*. New York: Kumarian Press.

Knapp, C. E. (1983). A curriculum model for environmental values education. *Journal of Environmental Education, 14*(3), 23–26.

Laney, J. T. (1990). Through thick and thin: Two ways of talking about the academy and moral responsibility. In W. May (Ed.), *Ethics and higher education* (pp. 49–68). New York: Macmillan Publishing Co.

Lautensach, A. (2003). *Environmental ethics for the future.* Unpublished doctoral dissertation, University of Otago.

Lautensach, A. K., & Lautensach, S. W. (2004, Winter/Spring). The challenge of global sustainability. *New Thinking, 2*(1). Retrieved February 7, 2008, from http://www.new-thinking.org/journal/globalsustainability.html

Lautensach, A. (2004, November 30). A tertiary curriculum for sustainability. In *Proceedings of the annual conference of the Australian Association for Research in Education,* The University of Melbourne. Retrieved February 7, 2008, from http://www.aare.edu.au/04pap/lau04260.pdf

Lautensach, A. (2005, May). The values of ecologists. *Environmental Values, 14*(2), 1447–1456.

Lautensach, A. (2006). Expanding human security. *Australasian Journal of Human Security, 2*(3), 5–14.

Lemons, J. (1996). Afterword: University education in sustainable development and environmental protection. In J. B. Callicott & F. J. R. da Rocha (Eds.), *Earth summit ethics: Toward a reconstructive postmodern philosophy of environmental education* (pp. 193–217). Albany, NY: State University of New York Press.

Lovelock, J. (1995). *The ages of Gaia - A biography of our living Earth* (2nd ed.). Oxford University Press.

Lutzenberger, J. (1996). Science, technology, economics, ethics, and environment. In J. B. Callicott & F. J. R. da Rocha (Eds.), *Earth summit ethics: Toward a reconstructive postmodern philosophy of environmental education* (pp. 23–45). Albany, NY: State University of New York Press.

Madsden, P. (1996). What can universities and professional schools do to save the environment? In J. B. Callicott & F. J. R. da Rocha (Eds.), *Earth summit ethics: Toward a reconstructive postmodern philosophy of environmental education* (pp. 71–91). Albany, NY: State University of New York Press.

Maher, M. (1988). The powers that be: Political education through an environmental study. *Australian Journal of Environmental Education, 4*(3), 1–8.

Margulis, L. (1997). Science education, USA: Not science, not yet education - the ecology example. In L. Margulis & D. Sagan (Eds.), *Slanted truths. Essays on Gaia, symbiosis and evolution* (pp. 307–316). New York: Springer Verlag.

Maslow, A. (1968). *Toward a psychology of being.* New York: Van Nostrand.

McLaren, P. (1986). *Schooling as a ritual performance.* London: Routledge & Kegan Paul.

McMichael, A. J. (1993). *Planetary overload: Global environmental change and the health of the human species.* Cambridge, UK: Cambridge University Press.

McMichael, A. J. (2001). *Human frontiers, environments and disease: Past patterns, uncertain futures.* Cambridge: Cambridge University Press.

McPeck, J. E. (1981). *Critical thinking and education.* New York: St. Martin's Press.

Merchant, C. (1980). *The death of nature - women, ecology and the scientific revolution.* San Francisco: Harper & Row.

Nicholson-Lord, D. (2001, July/August). Green scene. *Resurgence, 201,* 10–16.

Ormell, C. (1980). Values in education. In R. Straughan & J. Wrigley (Eds.), *Values and evaluation in education* (pp. 71–95). London: Harper and Row.

Orr, D. R. (1992). *Ecological literacy: Education and the transition to a postmodern world.* Albany, NY: State University of New York Press.

Orr, D. R. (1998, November/December). Technological fundamentalism. *The Ecologist, 28*(6), 329–332.

Orr, D. R. (1999a, May). Education for globalisation. *The Ecologist, 29*(2), 166–168.

Orr, D. R. (1999b, June). Rethinking education. *The Ecologist, 29*(3), 232–234.

Perelman, L. J. (1976). *The global mind: Beyond the limits to growth.* New York: Mason Charter.

Peters, R. S. (1966). *Ethics and education.* London: Allen & Unwin.

Pike, G., & Selby, D. (1988). *Global teacher, global learner.* London: Hodder & Stoughton Educational.

Postman, N. (1997). *The end of education: Redefining the value of school.* New York: Alfred Knopf.

Postman, N., & Weingartner, C. (1969). *Teaching as a subversive activity.* Harmondsworth: Penguin.

Priesnitz, W. (2000). *Challenging assumptions in education – From institutionalised education to a learning society.* Toronto: The Alternate Press.

Pybus, E., & McLaughlin, T. H. (1995). *Values, education and responsibility.* St. Andrews: Centre for Ethics, Philosophy and Public Affairs.

Raths, L. E., Harmin, M., & Simon, S. B. (1978). *Values and teaching: Working with values in the classroom* (2nd ed.). London: Charles E Merrill.

Rogers, C., & Freiberg, H. J. (1993). *Freedom to learn* (3rd ed.). New York: Merrill.

Robottom, I. (Ed.). (1987). *Environmental education: Practice and possibility.* Geelong, Victoria, Australia: Deakin University, ECT339 Environmental Education.

Rolston, H., III. (1996). Earth ethics. In J. B. Callicott & F. J. R. da Rocha (Eds.), *Earth summit ethics: Toward a reconstructive postmodern philosophy of environmental education* (pp. 161–192). Albany, NY: State University of New York Press.

Roszak, T. (2000). *The gendered atom: Reflecting on the sexual psychology of science.* London: Green Books.

Ryan, S. K. (1981). *Questions and answers in moral education.* Bloomington, IN: Phi Delta Kappan Educational Foundation.

Shepard, P. (1998). *Nature and madness.* Atlanta, GA: University of Georgia Press.

Silver, M. (1976). *Values education.* Washington, DC: National Education Association.

Smith, D., & Reynolds, C. (1990). Institutional culture and ethics. In W. May (Ed.), *Ethics and higher education* (pp. 21–31). New York: Macmillan Publishing Co.

Sosa, N. M. (1996). The ethics of dialogue and the environment. In J. B. Callicott & F. J. R. da Rocha (Eds.), *Earth summit ethics: Toward a reconstructive postmodern philosophy of environmental education* (pp. 47–70). Albany, NY: State University of New York Press.

Stern, P. C., Dieltz, T., & Kalof, L. (1993). Value orientations, gender and environmental concern. *Environment and Behaviour, 25*(3), 322–348.

Suzuki, D., & Dressel, H. (2002). *Good news for a change: Hope for a troubled planet.* St. Leonards, NSW: Allen & Unwin.

Sylvan, R., & Bennett, D. (1994). *The greening of ethics.* Cambridge, UK: The White Horse Press.

Tam, H. (1998). *Communitarianism: A new agenda for politics and citizenship.* New York: New York University Press.

Tarrant, J. M. (1989). *Democracy and education.* Aldershot, UK: Avebury.

Taylor, P. (1986). *Respect for nature: A theory of environmental ethics.* Princeton, NJ: Princeton University Press.

Toffler, A. (Ed.). (1974). *Learning for tomorrow: The role of the future in education.* New York: Random House.

Torbert, W. (1972). *Learning from experience: Toward consciousness.* New York: Columbia University Press.

UNEP-MAB (Millennium Assessment Board). (2005). *Living beyond our means: Natural assets and human well-being.* London: UNEP-WCMC. Retrieved from http://www.millenniumassessment.org/en/products.aspx

Union of Concerned Scientists. (1996). *World scientists' warning to humanity.* Cambridge, MA: Union of Concerned Scientists (18 November 1992). Reprinted in Ehrlich, P. R., & Ehrlich, A. H. *Betrayal of science and reason: How anti-environmental rhetoric threatens our future* (pp. 233–250). Washington, DC: Island Press.

Van Matre, S. (1990). *Earth education...A new beginning.* Greenville, W.VA: The Institute for Earth Education.

Wackernagel, M., Schulz, N. B., Deumling, D., Linares, A. C., Jenkins, M., Kapos, V., et al. (2002). Tracking the ecological overshoot of the human economy. *Proceedings of the National Academy of Sciences (USA), 99*(14), 9266–9271. Retrieved February 8, 2008, from http://www.pnas.org/cgi/reprint/99/14/9266.pdf

WCED (World Commission on Environment and Development). (1987). *Our common future: The brundtland report.* Oxford: Oxford University Press.

Werdell, P. (1974). Futurism and the reform of higher education. In A. Toffler (Ed.), *Learning for tomorrow: The role of the future in education* (pp. 272–311). New York: Random House.
Whitehead, A. N. (1967). *The aims of education* (1st ed.). New York: The Free Press (1929).
Wren-Lewis, J. (1974). Educating scientists for tomorrow. In A. Toffler (Ed.), *Learning for tomorrow: The role of the future in education* (pp. 157–172). New York: Random House.
Young, I. M. (1992). Five faces of oppression. In T. E. Wertenberg (Ed.), *Rethinking power*. Albany, NY: State University of New York Press.

GENERAL AIMS	1. Re-define Progress	2. Replace Anthropocentrism with Ecocentrism	3. Remedy Skill Gaps	4. Re-orient Education Towards the Future	5. Eliminate Parochialism	6. Empower the Learner to Take Action
Negative outcomes (to be counteracted)	Consumerism and its driving forces; Materialism; Scientism and technologism; Technological interpretations of sustainability; Neo-liberal concept of personal liberty; Moral nihilism and materialism; Cornucopianism; Defining progress as economic growth; False potential of laissez-faire policies; Colonialist progress and its driving forces;	Anthropocentrism in all forms; Human-nature dualism; Freedom from nature/dominion over nature; Anthropocentric interpretations of property.	Cognitive reasons for denial, including the inability to extrapolate; wishful thinking, self-deception, groundless optimism, *akrasia*; Negation of moral responsibility and lack of moral scruples;	Fatalistic attitude towards the future; Nostalgic yearning for the past; Groundless optimism: Scholastic dogmatism in science education;	Moral relativism, Liberal pluralism, *Laissez-faire* attitude to academic inquiry and anthropocentric influences in it; Blind spots for the limits of one's academic discipline;	Dependencies on habits (e.g. urban lifestyle, consumerism), institutions (e.g. the services and products of multinational corporations), ideologies (e.g. the 'work ethic');
Positive outcomes (to be encouraged)	Personal property interpreted as responsibility to care; sufficiency; Adopt a way of life in reflecting efficiency.	A critical attitude towards anthropocentric practices; Extend communitarian values (justice, love, wisdom, fulfillment) to the	Holistic view of one's environment, extrapolation to global and to the long term ('ecological literacy'); Analysis of values	A vision of the future that accommodates environmental change and ecological constraints; Empathy with other people and future generations;	Moral universalism with respect to sustainability and ecocentrism; extrapolative skills as in no.3; Cross-disciplinary environmental	Motivation for action; Striving for equity in access to resources, consumption levels, reproductive obligations while respecting ecological limits;

	restraint, adaptation, structural change (*); respect for limits to growth; recognise the interdependence of species and obligations to future generations;	non-human realm; humility; wonder and awe of nature; Value sapience & sentience, quality of experience in non-humans; Adopt Gaian ethics; Ecocentric spirituality; Recognise intrinsic value and evolutionary continuity;	(including one's own); acceptance of personal moral responsibility for the environment, and personal accountability in speech and action; attitude to act on one's values; Learning II and III (Torbert 1972);	A positive attitude towards change; thinking in post-industrial and zero-growth scenarios; apply scientific and ecological analysis to other fields; Precautionary attitudes to environmental risk-taking; Awareness of historical continuity;	awareness;	'counter-hegemonic' attitude to question dominant ideologies, authority and conventions; Conscientisation of teacher and learner; Personal growth without atomistic paralysis;
SPECIFIC EDUCATIONAL OBJECTIVES	Develop a sense of self-worth; Critically challenge pro-natalist attitudes and policies; Question the 'work ethic';	Adopt meta-values (survival of civilisation, extended communitarianism); immersion in values as opposed to distancing; make it socially acceptable to show affection; recognise the counterproductive nature of anthropocentric assumptions;	Develop life skills; Capacity for learning (esp. Learning II) and for flexible response; Evaluate hidden assumptions (e.g. in the technological imperative); Develop affections and show emotions;	Apply analytical skills to evaluate traditions and habits; apply skills required for adaptation to change (as in no.3); "Become acquainted with the means of your survival". Recognise the connection between cultural adaptation and sustainability; show an openness to ideas about the future but recognising uncertainty; develop a personal value base for one's future lives;	Use Earth systems science as an object of study and as a tool for study; Analyse curriculum for counterproductive contents; Structural reform within educational institutions Recognise values in science;	Critical analysis of the curriculum by the learner; Deconstruct the values and processes behind decisions about the environment; Detect and oppose greenwash (analytical skills); Effectively counteract brownlash; Learn not to be moved by crowds;

METHODS					
Extend the four principles of bioethics to future generations; strengthen the values of liberty and autonomy; examine the reasons for the global environmental crisis; teach ecology in transdisciplinary ways; conceptualise the Earth as a quasi-closed system.	Education in and for the environment; make values explicit; critical examination of value statements; cross-disciplinary earth systems approach;	Establish connections with concepts the learner feels strongly about; Exercises involving the solving of environmental problems relying less on reductionism;	Explore future scenarios; associate with environmentalist NGOs; Use utopian scenarios as a teaching tool to identify priorities;	Include ecological models, Earth systems science and ecocentric values into all disciplines; Institutional reform to penetrate academic barriers and to facilitate local self-sufficiency; targets of this reform are teacher education, continuing education, granting policies and management.	Analyse media reports for motivations and implicit messages; Critical dialogue and 'critical praxis';

(*) This item applies to more than one general aim.

TAPIO LITMANEN

14. DECONSTRUCTED TOURAINE: THE RADICAL SOCIOLOGIST FOR THE SAKE OF SOCIAL ACTORS AND SOCIETY[1]

The academic and political significance of Professor Alain Touraine is such that he can be regarded as an important intellectual not only in France, but also in Europe. Quite recently he has expressed his views about liberalism and the welfare state. He has said that there is no such thing as a liberal state, but that liberalism is a shock treatment which we use when society is shifting from one system of control of the economy to another. The problem is that there is no model for the new system. He stresses the importance of renewing the welfare state through major political reforms. For him these reforms will have to be as big as the social democratic project was in the early years of industrialization. Rescue of the European welfare state is important for him, because the welfare state and social security are symbols of our civilization. The pressure for change is being generated through the citizen's fear of insecurity, not by any single political force.

This short description of Touraine's recent political statements embodies Alain Touraine's thinking. First, he is not afraid of expressing his political views. Second, for him the role of social science is closely linked to politics and policy-making. Third, he does not trust classical objectivism, where the researcher seeks to distance him/herself from the subject of his/her investigation and tries to avoid personal involvement. Fourth, his background in history can be seen not only in his statements, where he emphasises the importance of historical actors, but also in his theory. Fifth, as Matti Hyvärinen (1985) has expressed it, Touraine is militant like his fellow countryman, Pierre Bourdieu (d. January 2002). Both are militant in two ways: they perceive themselves as critics of society without (any longer) being marxists; both are committed sociologists and swear by sociological knowledge, which is, if not always a way to a better society, at least an instrument for the emancipation of individuals or actors. Sixth, as Crozier (1996) has characterized Touraine, he is a maverick despite his prestigious training at the Ecole Normale Supérieure. A maverick and "normalien" means in this case a person who is self-assertive, independent, a free-thinker, a wanderer and courageous. For instance, Touraine left the Ecole Normale to work in the mines to experience first-hand the plight of the miners. He spent time in Hungary to learn not only from the outside but also from the inside the transition to socialism. His wanderings also include a year in Chile (1956–57) as an advisor to the Institute of Industrial Sociology and fieldwork in Poland while studying the Solidarity movement.

G. Martin, D. Houston, P. McLaren and J. Suoranta (eds.), The Havoc of Capitalism: Publics, Pedagogies and Environmental Crisis, 229–252.

Although authors have described Touraine as a scholar of politics, strategy and figuration of the political will (e.g., Hyvärinen, 1985), for instance, Daniel Pécaut (1998) has argued that despite these obvious interests, essentially he asserts the primacy of social actors and the system of social action, relegating (transferring) politics to a secondary and subordinate role. Therefore the aim of this article is to explore Alain Touraine' thinking: as an influential contemporary sociologist, whose work has been devoted to understanding and analysing the role of social movements in societal transformation processes, as well as in developing theoretical tools and systems of interpretation on the complex interplay between the societal structures and social action. The emphasis of the article is on social movements and theory of social action. Thus this article is grounded mainly on Touraine's writings of the 1970 and 1980s and so omits most of his important recent contributions (e.g., Touraine, 1995, 1997, 2000, 2001) to the general sociological debate.

TOURAINE AS A CONTROVERSIAL INTERNATIONAL SOCIOLOGIST

Touraine's work is internationally recognized in both the disciplines of sociology and politics, although until recently more in continental Europe and Latin America than in the Anglo-Saxon world. The editors of the book *Alain Touraine*, Jon Clark and Marco Diani (1996), write that his work is highly relevant to key debates in the social sciences in the 1990s, most notably his writings on social action, social movements, democracy and modernity. Bauman (1983) sheds light on Touraine's role in sociology by explaining Touraine's pioneering role in the study of how history is made by people. He further elaborates on the revolutionary character of Touraine's ideas bringing up three important aspects of Touraine's work. First, Bauman pays tribute to the fact that Touraine's ideas regarding the intrinsic pliability of social reality alongside the undetermined and creative nature of collective action were formulated as long ago as 1974 (*Production de la société*) and mature already in 1978 (*Le Voix et le regard*). Second, he praises the radical and uncompromising nature of his ideas, which challenged the 'deterministic' tradition of sociology. Third, Bauman states that perhaps Touraine's most enduring heritage is to have gone beyond the stage of ideology-critique and translated his theoretical framework into a boldly designed and indefatigably executed programme of research.

In his research Touraine has managed to combine developing theoretical entities with empirical research programmes. For instance, Oommen (1996, p. 111), characterises Touraine as an acute theorist and astute researcher. At the theoretical level his achievements are both on what might be called 'meta-theoretical', meaning his theory of social action, and on the more middle-range level, in his developing of the theory on how societies transform themselves from one type to another, e.g., from industrial to post-industrial (Scott, 1996, p. 77). The more empirically oriented Touraine has analysed social movements in at least three types of societies. The first of these are the post-industrial (or programmed) democratic capitalist societies to which Touraine refers as our type of society. Although

Touraine refers to the programmed society as a whole, the reference is to France or Western Europe. His empirical studies, such as on the student movement of 1968 and anti-nuclear protest, were done in France. The second type is the industrial, socialist totalitarian societies. Here Oommen refers to the study of the Solidarity movement in Poland. The third type is the industrializing, non-democratic, dependent societies which are economically controlled by a foreign bourgeoisie. Here Oommen refers to Touraine's analysis of the revolution in Chile. In contrast Scott (1991) focuses our attention on an ambitious project Touraine has had already for decades. Touraine has constructed a unique theoretical and methodological system, which consists of both a comprehensive analysis of contemporary society and a method which can broadly be called 'critical'. This he has done by also bringing to bear the theories of many major figures in the sociological tradition, not merely the 'classics,' but also more contemporary figures such as Parsons and Merton. Scott (1991, p. 29) compares Touraine's project to the corresponding project by Habermas, where the concern is in developing a theory which promises a research program. The difference is that Touraine has developed a method of research which accords with his theoretical and historical speculations.

Alexander (1999) perceives Touraine as having a unique position among the leading theorists in the world, not only because of his desire to understand, analyse and explain a changing world, but also because of his ambition to follow Marx's dictum that the reason for understanding the world is to change it. This deeply historical and political intellectual was the only important theoretical sociologist who took the conflicts of the 1960s and 1970s seriously and systematically. Among the three most important predecessors or influential scholars[2] to Touraine, Marx is the one to whom Touraine can best be compared as, according to Alexander (ibid.), he identified with these new social movements just as strongly as Marx had identified with the old ones, and with the same intellectual ambivalence. The sociological significance of Touraine lies both at the level of general theory, e.g., social action theory or the theory of post-industrial society, but also at level of one particular field in sociology, namely social movement research. To quote Alexander on Touraine, one may say that in the spirit of Marx's theory:

> Touraine tried to develop a grounded theory of the contradictory, anti-human forces and dynamics of post-industrial society, and to identify, on the basis of structural strains, social groups that were bound to overturn them. Like many people in those times, Touraine was convinced that it was possible to carry out this revolutionary change. What made him different from others was that he had developed a highly original theory of why. (Alexander, 1999, p. 100)

To evaluate further Touraine's contribution to sociology and particularly to the field of social movement studies, we can ask what is so enduring in Touraine's studies on social movements. Scott (1996) stresses that the reason why Touraine's analysis of social movements has been so influential in social movement research within both sociology and political science is that he has "recognized earlier than perhaps anyone else the significance of social movements not merely as objects of empirical investigation, but also as stimuli to the development of social science itself' (p. 77). Fuchs' (2000, p. 70) answer is that Touraine indicated the constructive side of social movements during an age when they were perceived either as symptoms of disturbed, alienated and hysterical masses or reactions to structural changes in society. Touraine's novel idea was to give movements a central role in the working of society[3], that is to say that social movements are important actors at the heart of the social fabric itself. Brincker and Gundlach (2005, p. 366) conclude that in sharp contrast to the tendency within the mainstream of sociology to analyse how processes and structures determine action, Touraine's main contribution to contemporary sociology is in drawing attention to the impact of collectives on social change.

Aronowitz (1988) argues that Touraine may be the leading social theorist to continue the tradition of seeking to discover the conditions that can produce social relations in which freedom and not repression prevails, but he is also widely regarded as one of the world's major students of contemporary social movements. What marks Touraine from his sociological contemporaries, according to Aronowitz (ibid., p. xii) is his intrepid efforts to comprehend the new without regard to the possible consequences for the truth status of received wisdom. Touraine was an exception among the scholars in trying to understand the student movement of the 1960s, because of his disposition to understand students sympathetically as historically significant actors. Aronowitz describes how Parsons interpreted the demonstration by thousands of students for Free Speech against the repression of the "technoversity" from a Freudian perspective and ascribed the causes of disruption to a displaced Oedipal conflict. Another example is Daniel Bell, who perceived such indications of change as confirmation of his thesis that contemporary democratic countries have found mechanisms to overcome the need for ideology, whereas Touraine viewed the student movement as the coming into power of new social agents, who arm themselves with path breaking ideologies (Aronowitz, 1998, pp. xi–xii).

Although Touraine is highly esteemed, the perception of Touraine's work and theories has varied from enthusiasm to strong criticism. For instance at the beginning of his career he founded a special journal, *Sociologie du Travail*, in 1959 together with Michel Crozier, Jean-Daniel Reynaud and Jean-René Tréanton. Michel Crozier (1996) says that during those days Touraine was the most enterprising and successful guru in their group of young sociologists and that he had the gift of inspiring young people and obtaining grants from government agencies. Crozier's sceptical assessment of the importance of Touraine as a leading sociologist of their generation is that his brilliance was due to his personality and not his academic credentials. Clark & Diani (1996) point out that Touraine's major publications, and the elaboration and application of the method of sociological intervention, have excited controversy for more than forty years, starting with his empirical study of shop floor work at Renault, published in 1955 and continuing into the late 1990s with the publication of his *Critique de la modernité* (1992, English translation *Critique of Modernity* 1995) and his extended essay on democracy (1994).

THEORY OF SOCIAL ACTION

The body of Alain Touraine's work constitutes a "sociology of action", as the title of his doctoral thesis published as *Sociologie de l'action* (1965) proclaims. For him society is a product of collective endeavour, conscious decision-making and organization, not one of immovable social structures, petrified and autonomous social systems or determinist social forces. Society is not a stable structure, which is held together by meta-social forces. For him "society is the result of its decisions, which themselves refer back to the interests, arguments, conflicts, and transactions by means of which [...] there occur the changes that point in the direction of a greater diversification, a growing flexibility, a relaxation of social norms, symbolic systems, and constraints" (Touraine, 1977, p. 3). The term relaxation refers to a state of affairs which is the opposite of that in Durkheimian sociology, according to which modern societies are characterized not so much by common or collective or even universal social norms or values, but by greater diversification, growing flexibility, and relaxation of norms, symbolic systems and constraints. Although a feeling of unity is felt inside a social movement, in general Touraine does not perceive so much space for the feeling of unity, because decision making is bound up with the interests of different parties, and conflicts, e.g., about appropriate means to achieve goals, and multiple transactions. Thus society is a product of "a conflict or at least constant negotiation in which the aim is to bring together the actors involved and broaden the field of acceptable reforms" (Touraine, 1996, p. 294). Social evolution is not seen as continuous or linear, and it cannot be reduced merely to a general tendency of social systems towards growing differentiation, complexity, and flexibility, as more emphasis is given to these kinds of historical actors. Touraine wants also to differentiate between various systems of historical action. These systems of historical action correspond to a particular mode of knowledge, type of accumulation, and cultural model. At the end of the 1970s Touraine saw the beginning of a post-industrial society, one which is characterized by self-production of itself.

Touraine shares some of the tenets of rational action theory, namely an emphasis on social action rather than on social structures, but he does not believe that the theory of action can be methodologically individualistic. The rejection of individualism is seen in his ideas of a sociological actor. In the first place, subjects are social, not isolated egos and second, they are embedded in historical projects in which the stakes are not merely goods but also identities. Third, sociological actors can also be collectives with fluid identities, in other words, social movements (Scott, 1996, pp. 78–79).

Combining functionalism and conflict theory in a theory of social action is an indication of Touraine's creativity or even perhaps of an obsession to challenge conventional ways of thinking (see e.g., Arnason, 1986, p. 138). Touraine adopts the functionalistic idea that shared norms and values lie behind the behaviour of actors, but at the same time emphasises that the actors are aware of those norms and values. For him actors compete for control over the system of norms which govern the rules of the game (meta-theory of action). He shares the idea of conflict theory that there is always struggle and divergence of interest.

The ultimate aim of conflictual collective action and social struggle is control over historicity. As Touraine has stated, the historicity of a society is the set of cultural models through which it gave meaning to its experience (Touraine, 1996, p. 330). Crystallisation of this aspect of the relationship between society and history is given by Arnason (1986, p. 148). He interprets Touraine's idea on historicity by saying that historicity represents "history in society", i.e., the ability of society to initiate and shape its own history, whereas on the contrary social change involves "society in history" as it is impossible to separate the internal field of historicity from the broader horizons and the more far-reaching dynamics of inter-societal configurations. Another slogan provided by Touraine himself is that historicity is society's "capacity to act upon itself" (Touraine, 1977, p. 379) or, simply, the self-production of society (ibid.). The components of historicity are: 1) the cognitive model, e.g., the emergence of modern science and scientific thinking and its impact on societal development; 2) form of accumulation, by which Touraine refers to the idea of productive investment and economic capability to transform productive activity, not to the surplus withdrawn from consumption or not used in a directly productive way; 3) the cultural model, i.e., an image of creativity which translates the self-determinative and self-transformative capacity of society into a more concrete project and channels it in a specific direction (Touraine, 1977, p. 18 and p. 66; Arnason, 1986, pp. 142–143).

SOCIAL MOVEMENTS AS SOCIAL ACTORS

The advice Touraine (1981, p. 29) gives to a scholar who is interested in studying social movements is not to get stuck on the idea of exceptional and dramatic events arranged by social actors. Although social movements may in the form of massive mobilizations and impressive mass appearances indeed express the collective will of the people, and may have an effect on public policy or political decision making, the picture is biased if no thought is given to social theory. When conceptualized from the perspective of conflict theory, social movements are not only "moments of omnipotence", but they lie permanently at the heart of social life. From the perspective of consensus theory order comes first and anything that tilts the balance is interpreted as an exception. For Touraine it is the work society performs on itself which comes first. Here Touraine refers to the idea that in the societal fabric norms, institutions and practices are invented. Although his emphasis is on this societal innovation process, he has to admit that these "products" do not evolve randomly out of nowhere, but are guided by cultural orientations. These cultural orientations, which he calls historicity, consist of patterns of knowledge, types of investment, and cultural models. It is important to notice that for Touraine this idea of cultural determination is present only because within society there is continuous struggle over the social control of historicity, which Touraine interprets as a class struggle. His idea is that the sociology of social movements cannot be separated from the representation of society as a system of social forces competing for control over the cultural field. Therefore social movements are not a marginal rejection of order; instead they are central forces fighting one against the other to control the production of society by itself and the action of classes seeking the shape historicity. Thus his definition of a social movement:

> A social movement is the collective organized action through which a class actor battles for the social control of historicity in a given and identifiable historical context. (Touraine, 1981, pp. 31–32)

In order to indicate how permanent such a definition of a social movement is in Touraine's sociology of action, we can compare it to his recent work (e.g., Touraine, 2004). Before revealing his recent definition of a social movement, let me clarify the controversial message of his article "On the frontier of a social movement". Touraine suggests that we should all but abandon the concept for two reasons. First, he points out that it is related to a certain type of society (for example, industrial society), which, following the logic of the definition, seems to lock the scholar into a type of society that belongs mainly to the past. Therefore we no longer need to use the notion of social movements unless we are dealing with really important social movements. Second, the recent societal development to which we refer to by the term globalization has, according to Touraine, shifted the sites of and issues in conflicts considerably. Touraine is interested in real social movements, where the struggle is over control of the mode of cultural development. Such movements like the anti-globalization movement have to have real importance for the development of conglomerates of societies, not singular societies. In his list of priorities the only movements which are worth studying are those that challenge the mechanisms of globalization. He is no longer interested in social movements which operate within a well-defined political or territorial field ruled by an elite or ruling class and which also set social categories in opposition. In other words, he rejects the idea that the concept of social movement should be applied to just any kind of collective action, conflict or political initiative. He suggests that it would be wise to reserve use of the category 'social movements' to refer to the group of phenomena that have in fact received this name over the course of a long historical tradition.

> The essential thing here is to reserve the idea of social movement for a collective action that challenges a mode of generalized social domination. I mean by this that a social relationship of domination cannot provoke an action that deserves to be called a social movement unless it bears upon all of the main aspects of social life, thus extending far beyond the conditions of production in one sector, or of commerce or trade in another, or even of the influence exerted on information and education systems. (Touraine, 2004, p. 718)

Earlier his goal was to seek the social movement which could replace the workers' movement in industrial society and the bourgeoisie movement in mercantile society (Touraine, 1971), while admitting that social movements have much cultural capacity. The search for a collective agent comparable to the working class can be seen in his definition of a social movement. He writes that social movements are, in essence, "... *the conflict action of agents of the social classes struggling for control of the system of historical action*" (Touraine, 1977, p. 298; italics in original text). An indication of this capacity is cultural innovation, which, according to him, is not truly linked to a social movement unless it is polemical (Touraine, 1977, p. 330). Here, for Touraine, cultural innovation is only valid in cases where it challenges the mechanisms of cultural reproduction maintained by the dominant class. Touraine makes use of a fairly mechanical distinction between the ruling or dominant class and popular class. His ambitions are in understanding how profound the consequences of the transformation of society from manufacturing-based to information-based production have been for the nature of social relations throughout the social field, in particular on class power. For Touraine the principal opposition between the classes results from the fact that the dominant class disposes of knowledge and control information, not only wealth and property (Touraine, 1971, p. 61). Older conflicts have become instutionalized (workers' movement) and new social movements come in being to resist the new forms of domination (Scott, 1996, p. 81). Therefore not merely the source, but also the focus of conflict has shifted away from relations of production and the state towards civil society and culture.

Scott (1996, p. 82) argues that Touraine is a pioneer of culturalist interpretations of the new social movements. This is because Touraine emphasises that 1) the aims of movements are cultural rather than political; 2) they operate in civil society rather than the state; and 3) they are concerned with life-style and quality of life issues rather than political and economic issues of distributive justice and rights. Also Tucker (2005, p. 53) praises the cultural elements of Touraine's theory, where the creativity of social actors is the central ingredient of any good society. In contrast, Knöbl (1999) argues that Touraine was very late in thinking about the heterogenization of living conditions, individualization of life designs, and the process of cultural pluralization. It became increasingly apparent in the 1970s and 1980s that hopes for a unified dynamic of social conflict were not going to be fulfilled. The field of collective actors was too fragmented. A uniform social arena in which a few collective actors struggle for a cultural model of society lost gradually theoretical and empirical relevance. The idea of "unity of historical action and historical meaning" and a unified historical dynamic contain the same kinds of assumptions as the functionalism Touraine was criticizing. Touraine's main interest was the cultural orientation of movements.

There is also a lack of institutional analysis in Touraine's work. Institutions and structures were viewed at most as the less important, marginal conditions of endlessly continuing processes. Thus the mobilization of a social movement was assumed to be more or less given, quite unlike the resource mobilization approach (Knöbl, 1999, p. 412). Because Touraine neglected the institutional arrangements in the political system and in civil society, he overestimated the dynamics of new social movements. Brincker and Gundelach (2005) point that one reason for this lack of institutional analysis lies at the heart of Touraine's theory of social change. In the line with the Marxist tradition Touraine sought to identify "the real social force" behind the social changes in question. To understand the nature of societal reality and transformation processes we must seek the central social conflict of our time. This conflict embodies the struggle over 'historicity', i.e., control of direction of social change. Problems emerge when this kind of "pure" theory of social action is interpreted in the context of a more realistic theory of social development. The shift from industrial to post-industrial society also means a structural change in the settings of the main social struggles. Previously, in the industrial society, the central social conflict took place within the economic sphere where workers and capitalists were in opposition whereas in the post-industrial society the relationship between the economic processes of capital accumulation and key social struggles are more difficult to analyse. According to Touraine, the central social struggle has shifted from the sphere of production to the cultural arena as social actors struggle over knowledge, information and control of historicity. Brincker and Gundelach (ibid., p. 367) argue that Touraine has forgotten to integrate the economic structure of society into the theory of collective action and social change. They state that present-day civil society does not have the same kind of structural force as accumulation with respect to social change. They ask whether social forces and the structural foundations of social change belong to completely different spheres, civil society and the market, or is it more correct to assume that the fundamental driving force in society is the state.

Despite Touraine's extensive work on contemporary social movements his earlier formulations received at least two sorts of caveats. Arnason (1986, p. 151) refers to these criticisms by emphasising that we have to bear in mind that even in industrial society the co-existence of several important social movements is a fact, whereas Touraine has argued on behalf of single important movements in the scene of historical action and has neglected to analyse the importance of the increased reflectivity that he ascribes to social movements. Alan Scott (1996) has stated that there is a contradiction between Touraine's theory of social action and his theory of post-industrial society. Scott concludes his analysis by stressing that the theory of social action is context-specific, historical and restricted and the theory of post-industrial society[4] is general, teleological (periodization of society) and historicist (meaning that social changes can be traced back to changes in production techniques).

But we shall not bear false witness against Touraine, as in one of his recent articles he has tried to overcome some of the criticism. First, he proposes a more general and also ahistorical definition of a social movement, one where a social movement is seen as a combination of a conflict between organized social adversaries and a shared reference by both adversaries to a cultural 'stake' without which they would not confront each other (Touraine, 2004, pp. 718–719). Here the emphasis is on the shared battlefield or areas of debate on which both parties agree. Second, he takes into account the possibility that seemingly innocent conflicts may not only bear a resemblance to a social movement, but also that small conflicts may have rather general symbolic importance (ibid., p. 719). Third, the method of sociological intervention includes the idea that social actors may not themselves be aware of their ultimate objectives. Sociologists have to intervene in the social reality and try to help the actors deeply involved in a conflict to raise the level of understanding of their situation and the real aims of their action. Fourth, he concludes his intellectual experiment by stating that there is a need to maintain the concept of social movement in the study of contemporary societies, of whatever type, even if they seem at first glance not to require the use of such concepts. For him the continuity of sociological analysis is more important than is the observation of the profound differences that exist from one societal type to another.

SOCIAL ACTOR AS A PRIMARY CAUSE

Touraine is intellectually engaged by the very basic question of how to understand the complex interplay between social actor, social relations and social order. The configuration of a social system is a very fundamental question in sociology. His ambition is to study the actor as an autonomous being, as an agent of transformation of his environment and of his situation, as a creator of imaginary worlds, and as capable of referring to absolute values or of being involved in love relations (Touraine, 2000, p. 900).

This seemingly naïve definition in no way means that Touraine perceives the actor as disconnected from the material world or from different social, economic, or cultural circumstances. This can be seen from his definition of sociology[5]. He employs a classical definition of sociology, where the emphasis is on the study of social relations. These relations are meaningful and take place within a social framework defined either as a social order, as a process of social change, or as both at once. Interestingly enough, Touraine understands social circumstances as both affecting social actors and modified by social actors, but he does not focus on the intermediate levels between social relations and the social order. There we might find those more concrete societal structures, such as, the social, economic and cultural structures "around the actor". His purpose is to remain on a very high level of abstraction. He admits, of course, the need for socio-economic, socio-historical or socio-anthropological studies, but for him it is more important to operate on another level of abstraction. He sees the social actor in the context of the social system: i.e., more important than analysing the actor in varying contexts is to understand the social actor in the framework of a general social theory.

The domain of sociological exercises is study of the relations between social determinism and freedom, between the application of social norms and reference to human values, and between institutional order and practices that voluntarily deviate from such norms. Touraine never tires reiterating his basic axiom that social actors are capable of acting and producing even irrevocable changes, when interpreted from the point of view of history.

> Actors … are not defined by their conformity to rules and norms, but by a relation to themselves, by their capacity to constitute themselves as actors, capable of changing their environment and of reinforcing their autonomy. (Touraine, 2000, p. 902)

Touraine is not interested in routine or every-day dimensions of social action. It is rather difficult to imagine Touraine as a family researcher or a researcher of education or on the upbringing of a child, where routine, repetition, socialization of norms occupy a major role. For him the fascinating element in social action is nonconformity, innovative disobedience, creative discordance and the ability to overcome social norms and institutions. If, by accident, Touraine were to become interested in, e.g., family research his interest would fall into the study of disharmonious family life or children's attempts to escape omnipresent socialization. In emphasising the autonomy and independence of individuals over social norms and institutions Touraine operates with the concept of the Subject[6]. This is because the idea of the Subject contains the idea of opposition to the classical conception of socialization as the internalization of institutionalized norms, and in particular education, as a means inhabiting social roles. Therefore Touraine (1996, p. 307) emphasises the German word Bildung, which refers in particular to increasing of individual's capacity to act freely and responsibly, to be an actor and an innovator and to be able to resist forces and pressure.

Touraine explains that the idea of the Subject is founded on the premises of his theory of society, which allows no room for transcendental principles such as the existence of God or the perfect society. The most elementary action of all is resistance to society, which should be interpreted "...as the search for a self-created human being who is also a creator of his social environment to the extent that he is involved in conflicts, negotiations and the struggle for freedom" (Touraine, 2000, p. 909). Here he refers to the idea of the Subject, i.e., to individual and collective claims to the right to become free actors.

In a recent article Touraine acknowledges at least two reasons for developing an actor- and subject-oriented society. First, he refers to societal development, which has eroded the ability of social systems to produce norms. Capitalism and industrialization as modernizing forces have produced conditions where legal and political institutions have lost their control over social life. Second, his analysis indicates that we have to acknowledge that there is a tendency for political and economic domination of the Subject, and also manipulation and cultural alienation (Touraine, 2000, p. 909). The obligation of sociologists is to intervene in these kinds of processes and to bring forth demands for reforms.

PROGRAMMATIC SOCIOLOGY

A crucial question for the self-understanding of sociologists is "Why do we need sociology as a discipline?" The answer to the question also provides instruments for legitimizing the discipline's role in society. For Touraine there is a danger in these kinds of questions, because sociology can easily be made a prisoner of societal institutions and it may face difficulties in freeing itself from the dominant class in order to function as a creative force. The history of the discipline during the 20th century shows that sociology has been an important instrument in the modernization of societies, and that before that pre-sociological ideas were associated with the triumph of industrialization, of industrial capitalism and the colonial empires. In some of his writings (e.g., Touraine, 1985) his basic interest has been criticism of the dominant image of society in sociology or the idea of how sociology is dominated by the ideology of modernization. The aim of these types of generalisations has been to offer a stepping stone toward his alternative, namely the sociology of social action. The one-sidedness of Touraine's image of sociology has been elaborated by Arnason (1986). His analysis suggests that Touraine should not neglect the legacy of theorists whose relationship to modernity is more problematic, e.g., Max Weber's analysis of the paradoxes of modernity (ibid., p. 140).

Touraine has given an answer to this question about the role of the discipline not only from the point of view of a single practitioner but from the point of view of systems theory. Already at the end of the 1960s he perceived that sphere of sociological analysis was growing, because societies as social systems were increasing their capacity to act on themselves (Touraine, 1971, p. 232). At the end of his book he proposed a question for himself: Why sociologists? His answer was that a new type of society, the post-industrial or programmed society, was gradually being organized and that the progress of sociological analysis has to be combined both with society's will to react to its own changes, and with the social and cultural conflicts through which the direction of those changes and the form of the new society may be debated. He strongly questioned the need for an analysis of behaviour, because an analysis of the society as a whole was urgently needed. A society is then understood as a system of action, a network of cultural orientations and power relationships. (ibid., pp. 228–229).

For Touraine societies learn to know themselves sociologically when they recognize themselves as the products of their labour and their social relations and when what at first seems to be a set of social data is recognized as being the result of a social action, of decisions or transactions, of domination or conflicts (Touraine, 2000). The self-reflection, self-evaluation and increasing self-control of societies has produced a situation where societies are coming to recognize themselves as a network of actions and relations. For him the social self-reflection of societies (with the help of the social philosophy of progress) has reached a level of solid certainty about their ability to have total control over themselves.

Touraine views sociology as being concerned with the study of actors and communication. The sociology of the actor is seen as a specific domain of sociology, where the interest is in the study of the relations between social determinism and freedom, between the application of social norms and the reference to human values, and between institutional order and practices that voluntarily deviate from such norms. "The study of social movements constitutes the heart of a sociology of the actor" (Touraine, 2000, p. 907). Despite his devotion to social movements we should not forget that his analysis also functions on the macro level. Thus beside social movements the other actors in his social theory are society itself and social classes. He reduced social classes to two opposing camps, the ruling class and popular class, which struggle over historicity.

Touraine's answer to the question "Why do we need sociology?" is that actors, particularly subordinated groups, need sociology to enable them to act on the stage of historical action and to discover the highest possible meaning of their action. The sociologist must create a social situation where an entire group is forced to interact with their real opponents who hold positive or negative positions in relation to itself (Touraine, 2000, p. 906). Therefore the role of the sociologist has to be active, not passive.

> sociologists must create an adequate context, not only by choosing the time and space for the observation, but by directly intervening. (Touraine, 2000, pp. 903–904)

The aim of the sociologist is to reveal claims, conflicts and debates which are often overshadowed by the authority of social norms and by repression, which is imposed for the sake of institutions or of those who hold positions of power. The critical stance adopted by Touraine can be seen in his definition of the social norm.

> social norms have not [...] been created for the common good, but rather [...] they are the expression of a power which endangers the freedom, responsibility and the dignity of people. (Touraine, 2000, p. 904)

POLITICALLY ORIENTED SOCIOLOGY

An important epistemological question every sociologist has to ponder over and over again is the political function of knowledge produced in her/his studies. In Touraine's vision of the political function of sociology in contemporary societies there is a strange ambiguity, because he only partially rejects objectivism, and smuggles the objectivism-subjectivism dispute into his method of studying social movements. Clearly he neglects the idea that sociologists have to find universal laws of social action or laws of history and society. This is something many sociologists agree and is nothing new in the sense that varying social and cultural contexts increase the difficulty of developing an all-embracing explanation for social action or societal development. It is more difficult to agree with him that sociologists have to intervene in social struggles, as scholars are not observers who remain outside the field, but they should be regarded as interlocutors and even activists. Here we see Touraine siding with the aims of the social movement under study.

With these considerations in mind we may lean to the view that Touraine is subjectivist or that his sociology is politically oriented, but this does not mean that we should hesitate in judging Touraine. Two observations can be made on this issue. Firstly, the key to understanding phrases like, "sociologists do not lay outside the field", is Alain Touraine's moral commitment to the role of sociologist as a catalyst accelerating societal development without full participation in the process. In order to serve societal development (or the struggle over the control of historicity) sociology must produce knowledge for the social actors instead of, as in the conventional way of thinking, producing knowledge of social actors. Or to be more precise, the aim is to engage activists in a prolonged series of discussions aimed at making subjects reflect upon the meaning of their action, and ultimately raising that action to "a higher level of struggle".

Secondly, his manoeuvre of importing the objectivist-subjectivist distinction into the method of sociological intervention deserves comment. For Touraine the sociologist must be close to the action, but must also keep at a distance from it, i.e., the researcher should not identify with the group she/he is studying. The aim of the sociological intervention is to enable the group to undertake self-analysis and the sociologist to do analysis of their self-analysis. Together, researchers and actors seek to develop hypotheses for bringing to light the hierarchy of meanings that shape collective action.

An intriguing question concerns how Touraine perceives the object of sociological research. His methodological advice is that sociologists have to delve deeply enough within subjectivity to reach what constitutes the individual, or the group, as an actor. One has to go beyond subjectivity to discover subjectivation[7], meaning that sociologists have to search for how an individual or a group represents itself as an actor seeking to impose their own ends on their environment (Touraine, 2000, p. 911; see also, Tucker, 2005, p. 49).

Thus from the point of view of the researcher the starting of a process of self-analysis of a social movement means being simultaneously an objective investigator of self-analysis and the actor of an intervention emphasising the subjective meanings the actors in the movement attach to their action. More complexity attached to the role of a scholar leads to Touraine's claim that in the actual intervention phase at least two sociologists are needed. One has the role of agitator who organizes the group, prepares the confrontations, conducts the sessions, and helps the group "agitate" - pushing it to the limit. The other scholar is more in the service of science in the sense that she/he must work as a secretary taking minutes, recording discussions, preparing the reports of the session, providing documents etc. Both during and after the intervention the agitator has to interpret the subjective meanings of actors and produce a hypothesis, which the groups can discuss and finally accept as the real or objective meaning of their action. During the intervention process the secretary can also become a counsellor or even analyst participating actively in the self-analysis of the group.

Moreover obscurity in the objectivism-subjectivism dilemma generates the idea of permanent sociology. The final outcome of the process of sociological intervention is to produce something permanent or lasting. To understand what it means, we need to take a look at the intervention process. The intervention consists of four phases, the first of which the group bears testimony to the collective action, as in a group interview organized by an interlocutor. During the second phase activists take distance from their role as activists rejecting their natural language as a frame of reference. The third phase is when the group adopts an analytical viewpoint as a result of conversion negotiated jointly with the analyst. Finally, sociology takes a back seat as the action moves forward into the phase of permanent sociology, now that it has enabled analysis to progress continuously and the movement to act on the basis of an increasingly clear image of itself, its opponents and their field of conflict (see, e.g., Touraine, 1981, p. 183). In addition to the logic of social action, Touraine has an axis of social change, which refers to the functioning of the society, changes in the society or even changes of type of society.

In the phase of permanent sociology, the discipline has made its contribution both to the actors and to society in general, and the knowledge produced in co-operation with the actors is not - as mentioned earlier - knowledge of the actors but knowledge for the actors to continue their collective action at a more conscious level. As a result sociologists may have speeded up societal development, because actors have a more comprehensive understanding of their "real" aims in society. We should emphasise that the acceleration of societal development is conditional, because the reaching of the aims depends on the political action the actors are taken after the process.

SOCIOLOGICAL INTERVENTION AS AN EPISTEMOLOGICAL INNOVATION

The life and the writings of Touraine tell to us that there are benefits in getting involved. Pécaut (1996, p. 159) stresses that nothing would be more false than to attribute to Touraine a lack of interest in political themes. His personal stance, as well as his numerous works which constitute interventions in particular political circumstances, are more than sufficient to demonstrate this. It is interesting that he locates the political dimension within the context of the social. Touraine clearly is not in agreement with the idea of conservative sociology, where one important rule is that the sociologist should not meddle with things that are none of his/her business in questions of society and societal development. To clarify this rejection of naive objectivism, we should look at his most influential methodological innovation, namely sociological intervention.

Touraine's early writings show that his methods were drawn from stock in the sociological trade (Dubet & Wieviorka, 1996, p. 55). Early writings about social movements (*Le Mouvement de Mai, ou le communisme utopique* 1968 or *Vie et mort du populaire* 1974) relied heavily on a historical method (owing to his initial education) that combined document analysis, interviews and observation. With *La voix et le regard* (1978) Touraine proposed a method he called sociological intervention.

Sociological intervention as a methodology marked a radical break with the then stake of play of the subjectivism-objectivism debate. For Touraine it was important to make a distinction between social scientific knowledge and knowledge produced through natural scientific procedures. The reason why Touraine regards social scientific knowledge as a special type of knowledge in opposition to the natural scientific kind is because of Touraine's commitment to ideas that sociology and social action have to be in relations of interaction and that the object of the study must be included as an active subject in production of knowledge. The sociologist can give feedback from scholarship to social action and thus aid the social actors in their struggle to achieve their aims on the stage of historical action. The other side of the epistemological distinction is that a sociologist cannot construct external descriptions of actions or ideologies, because these do not bring us close enough to an understanding of social phenomena. The crucial point is to be involved in social action and to let the actors participate in the production of knowledge.

> the purpose of this research work is to contribute to the development of social movements. ... Our real objective is to enable a society to live at the highest possible level of historical action instead of blindly passing through crises and conflicts. (Touraine, 1981, p. 148)

Touraine had both theoretical and historical motives for developing a new method for studying society, societal development and social actors. For him it was theoretically important to develop an analytical method for the sociology of action, formalized as a theoretical system in *The Self-Production of Society* (1977) (original *Production de la société* 1973). For a sociologist living through the turbulence of that decade it was a duty to interpret the ongoing historical changes in industrial society; however in addition to this, the sociologist had the heroic mission of intervening in contemporary societal developments.

As the aim was to test hypotheses about post-industrial society with new social movements in the leading role, the method had to enable both the direct observation and analysis of these relations. A precondition for this methodological development work was the refinement of theory. He rejected the idea that society should be conceptualized by thinking only about its institutions[8]. Instead, Touraine saw that society should be defined in terms of social relations: organizations and their relations to authority, political decisions and the influences leading to them, and class relations and systems of order considered in their role of exclusion and elimination. Sociology's chief task was to bring these kinds of invisible social relations to the surface. This has to be done through active intervention: "We must come face to face with the social movement" (Touraine, 1981, p. 142). Thus the most important actors are collective actors: social classes and social movements. They enter into the centre of Tourainian analyses. These actors fight for the realization and institutionalization of values and they question and overstep given social structures again and again.

In focussing on the social actor Touraine saw that, e.g., in any social struggle social relations have to be understood as organized or ranked in a hierarchy, each level having its own rationale or logic. A social actor's identity cannot be separated from the social relations wherein it is formed nor from the meaning given to these relations. By defining their identity, social actors also identify their opponents and delimit the field in which common issues bring actors together and set them at odds, i.e., define the conflicting elements. This is the system of IOT - interplay between the principles of identity, opposition and totality.

In *The Self-Production of Society* Touraine (1977) emphasises that interpreting social action from the perspective of historicity is not only a means to understanding singular events or past actions in the context of a long process which leads up to the present but also, and at least equally if not more importantly allows events, particularly actions, to be viewed from the perspective of the non-determinate future, which is an ongoing process. For instance collective action can be defined as a social movement insofar as it challenges other social actors who are contending for control over the cultural model of a particular phase of societal development. For Touraine collective action is a social movement only at this level.

UNDERSTANDING TOURAINE AS A SOCIOLOGIST

Touraine arrived on the scene of French intellectual life in the late 1940s. Despite its honourable history, French sociology was then in a shabby-genteel condition. This poor state of affairs was the direct and indirect result of the two world wars.

The First World War created a generation gap. For instance, most of Durkheim's students were killed in the war and the master himself died in grieving. The few survivors were drafted into positions of academic power and almost forgot sociology. Crozier (1996, p. 9) describes their generation in sociology as a generation without fathers: no elder figure was there to help them or provide a feeling of security. The Second World War also increased the gap between the French academic world and the international trends of the period. By the time of Liberation the discipline's past had been wiped out and for France, a country with a great respect for history and the world of ideas, this was something unique. Aronowitz (1988), analysing for the context of Touraine's appearance in the field of sociology, argues that during the first two decades after the Second World War three paradigms held sway. The general theorist, structuralist theorist and middle range theorists were more interested, respectively, in issues like the survival and recovery of European societies, social processes as articulations of transhistorical social forms, and the study of social problems in specific institutional conxtexts than the classical preoccupations of sociology, namely sources of change, the place of ideology and politics in history and the fundamental character of social relations. Within this context, where almost all social scientists except Marxists had turned away from questions of historical agency, such as class and power, Touraine occupied a unique position. Although his interests were also in issues like the problem of historicity (i.e., how society is like cybernetic system functioning towards itself but also self-monitoring, self-correcting and self-modifying itself) and the cultural model by which we represent ourselves and also act, the categories of class relations and accumulation were crucial for his work.

Crozier (1996) emphasises that French sociology was stuck in the rationalist philosophy of the 1900s. This provided an opportunity for the younger generation of sociologists, who reached intellectual maturity in the 1950s and ultimately obtained recognition in the early 1960s. Sociology was to be reconstructed anew. Crozier, Touraine and their fellows experienced a great sense of freedom from the past, which was attractive for young people who had a pioneering spirit. Lack of empirical work was obvious and there was hardly any fieldwork being done on French society. Young pioneers and their research assistants and students started a counter movement against the rationalist philosophy of their pre-war elders. This counter movement was to last till the end of 1968. They had a passion for fieldwork, their methodological orientation was that through empirical knowledge they would rebuild the world; they were Marxists in their orientation, but believed more in fieldwork, which would or would not confirm the theory; they were fascinated by new methods, like interviewing, surveys, qualitative methods, research design, but above all about meanings instead of simple counting. This research movement gave rise to the special journal, *Sociologie du Travail*, which was founded in 1959 by Touraine, Reynaud, Tréanton and Crozier.

Crozier's (1996) analysis of their movement indicates that there were contradictions within it. First of all there was a tension between empiricism, which held centre stage, and the new revolutionary philosophy. It was probably difficult to effect a compromise on the priorities within sociology, because, as Crozier has pointed out, empirical analysis destroyed the simplicity of the theory that modern social problems were rooted in working conditions and work relationships. Secondly it was difficult to combine the romantic spirit of revolution with the technocracy of Gaullist government (independent-mindedness versus utilitarian answers). Finally, because sociology was recognized by the authorities as a leading modernizing discipline, it became a popular field and the sociology of work its most popular sub-field in the 1960s.

America was seen as the Mecca of the social sciences and many believed that the social scientific know-how originated there. However, a number of young French sociologists fiercely opposed American policy and were inclined to side with the USSR. Touraine had spent time in America and he valued the training he had received. In the mid 1960s they experienced the "Golden Age" of French sociology. The student revolution brought it to an end. The events of May 1968 in Paris were both difficult and challenging for Touraine. He was deeply involved as he was close to the CFDT (Confédération française démocratique du travail), a labour union, which was dominated by socialists, and it was imbued with a new kind of thinking about society. In the eyes of his own generation he had been too involved, but in the eyes of the younger generation not enough. He was already then a bridge-builder between empirical work and social theory, between the revolutionary left and Gaullist technocrats, between university students and university authorities, between political commitment (to the left) and fierce independence of mind and spirit. This seemingly chaotic situation matured his sociological thinking. Bauman (1983) describes this period thus:

> Touraine's sociological revolution had been triggered off by shock waves sent through the intellectual Paris by the spectacular failure of the abortive political revolution of May 1968. Everyone emerged from the experience with his/her pen-holding fingers singed. (p. 596)

Unlike, e.g., Althusser and others of the obdurate left who found the "safe haven of 'theoretical praxis' which no prospective street riots could penetrate", Touraine went in the opposite direction (Bauman, 1983, p. 596) In his colourful account of the consequences of these events to Touraine, Bauman explains how "[T]he streets of Paris had not been yet swept clean of the student graffiti and the broken glass, when in *La Société post-industrielle* Touraine proclaimed the approaching 'class struggle without classes', the impotence of the institutionally entrenched old conflicts and the task of sociology as the midwife of confrontations and the struggles to come" (ibid., p. 596). After that he distanced himself from Paris and went first to Chile and then to Los Angeles (Freiberg, 1977).

CONCLUDING REMARKS: UNDERSTANDING TOURAINE'S SOCIAL THEORY

What characterizes Touraine's works are a particular kind of radicalism and the avoidance of conventional sociological thinking (see, e.g., Knöbl, 1999, p. 404). In addition to this we can say that Touraine's social theory is also characterized by a kind of dualism, the use of dialectical method in developing relevant conceptualizations, and in some cases this appears to consist of contradictions. His social theory is an idiosyncratic combination of the creative power of individualism and collectivism over social structures; he balances between complete voluntarism while recognizing the existence of determining social forces; he perceives societal evolution from the perspective of societal cybernetics but puts faith in the capability of the social actor on the stage of historical action; and he rejects the idea of ahistorical rational action in favour of more contextual rational action, in which the interventions of social sciences can be included.

Freiberg (1977, p. xi–xvi) has compared the American sociology of the 1960s and 1970s to its European counterpart, and sees Touraine as a representative of the latter. Freiberg notes that already during his American years Touraine was philosophical and full of theoretical thinking. For him the most exciting thing was to know a sociologist working with a unified, theoretically sophisticated perspective. When compared to American sociologists of those times Touraine's students were surprised by how different was the "European" way of interpreting, e.g., the events surrounding the student movement. Whereas, according to Freiburg, for American sociologists the social world was "a haphazard collection of independent events", Europeans "searched for the unity hidden beneath the surface of everyday phenomena" (ibid., p. xii). Touraine symbolized the European way of thinking sociologically (broad societal issues) and conducting research (contextualize singular events philosophically and historically).

The above distinction drawn between European and American sociology may not be the whole truth, because Touraine, despite his criticism of Talcott Parson's functionalist theory, owes a debt to the American sociologist. The other theoretical issue concerns his critique of economically determined Marxism. According to Knöbl (1999) in both cases Touraine's criticism is based on Sartrean ideas of radically free individuals and the freedom of the subject. Arnason (1986, p. 138) agrees with Knöbl about the dual nature of Touraine's project, but stresses that one has to bear in mind Touraine's affinity with Marx. Arnason states that before the second half of the 1980s Touraine's sociological project was characterised by interconnections between a radical critique of functionalism, a rejection of the Marxist tradition while sharing a fundamental affinity with Marx and a professedly post-socialist analysis of post-revolutionary societies.

Touraine's sociology exists in a special relation to Talcott Parson's structural functionalism, which continued to dominate sociology in the 1960s. Touraine's theory of social action is partly a critique of the Parsonian consensus model, because Parson was far too much of a consensus theoretician to comprehend the collective conflicts of modern industrial societies. Despite his fierce criticism Touraine adopted some functionalist ideas about social systems, cultural values and norms, but stressed the importance of conflict in societal development.

Knöbl (1999) has drawn our attention to Touraine's passion for freedom and actors with free will. Touraine rejects ideas about social order and a unified society, and stresses the freedom and possibilities of human action. Touraine's critique of structuralist functionalism was harsh because functionalism left no room for actors to shape their own lives and, in particular, direct the development of their societies. Touraine was influenced by Sartrean Philosophy, although he had difficulties in applying Sartre's ideas to sociology. One problem was that the concept of freedom inherent in Sartre's thinking was highly individualistic. Sartre's idea of isolated individuals with a radically free choice of values was not a suitable basis for his theory of social action. Touraine developed this idea of freedom sociologically and was far more interested in collective actors than individuals. He emphasised that individual and collective behaviour is never absolutely free and unconnected. They are bound together.

The importances of traditions are diminishing and are being replaced by the kinds of knowledge needed for the self-steering of society (decisions and debates or conflicts produced by decisions). Societies are free to choose and make decisions and they have become disengaged from the constraints of traditions. The emphasis is more on voluntarism than determinism, because the determining forces are few and there is a multitude of options, decisions and choices. Touraine rejects both liberalism and Marxism, because they "converge toward the economically oriented analysis of social behaviour, which cannot be but marginal to the sociologist" (Touraine, 2000, p. 908).

Arnason (1986, p. 147) has revealed how Touraine's sociological project has been influenced both by theoretical and real world societal developments. On the level of his own culture the backdrop (the New Left debate of the 1950s and 1960s) to Touraine's thoughts is political critique of the petrified structures of the left-wing parties (particularly the French Communist Party) as their theory was a biassed towards economically oriented Marxism and towards the determinism which ruled out any creative dimension to individual or collective behaviour; however it is more important to note how he has sought to understand contemporary societal developments during the post-war period both in the West and in the East. Arnason (1986, p. 148) suggests that Touraine's approach to post-revolutionary societies is more distinctive than his specific version of the idea of post-industrial society. His argument is that although *The Self-Production of Society* does not contain any detailed discussion of Soviet-type societies, its conceptual apparatus is clearly designed to serve this purpose among others.

> In particular, the class structure of industrial society is defined in such a way that a recurrent pattern of conflict can be identified without obscuring the differences between capitalist and non-capitalist variants, and the Marxist-Leninist doctrine can be understood as a particularly rigid version of a cultural model that centres on the idea of progress. (Arnason, 1986, p. 148)

Aronowitz (1988, p. xiii) argues that Touraine is not a historical or epistemological essentialist, because of his devotion to three issues: 1) class relations as the proper object of knowledge, not social class itself, 2) social agency and social action without predeterminating the course of the action and 3) the struggle over the cultural model which determines the agenda of action itself. This rejection of essentialism can be seen in the idea of social relations, which implies a system of mutual determination in which action has consequences for changing power relations and the shape of the system itself. Therefore, class relations are both a determinate and an indeterminate category. It is determinate, because it specifies both a system of action and the actors that constitute it. It is indeterminate insofar as the struggle entails a contest over who will set the agenda of action itself, and who determines the cultural model. Touraine's theoretical scheme is that history is made up of social actors, not merely constructed by the conjunction of elements of structured totality. Moreover, Touraine (1981) perceives that scholars can hasten the process of historical transformation:

> In analysing the nature of a struggle, intervention reveals to the actors their utmost capacity for historical action, thus helping them to raise the project level of their movement. Such is its function: knowledge and action associated. (p. 216)

NOTES

[1] The author wishes to thank, first and foremost, professor Alain Touraine for encouraging and inspiring young students in their studies. While visiting at the University of Jyväskylä on 18 November 2002 professor Touraine participated in our seminar and actively engaged in an interview by the students. The Department of Social Sciences and Philosophy held a seminar on Social Movements, where the aim was to familiarise the students with social movement theories and particularly Touraine's theories and his social movement theory. The course included introductory lectures about Alain Touraine as a sociologist, about his social theory and about his methodological thoughts, given by senior assistant Tapio Litmanen, and particularly Touraine's own lecture, "The Breakdown of European Social Movements". Touraine's lecture was part of an annual lecture series dedicated to Professor Emeritus Martti Takala. The aim of Prof. Touraine's visit was to contribute to the long-standing research that Professors Martti Siisiäinen and Kaj Ilmonen and senior lecturer Esa Konttinen have advanced. One outcome of Professor Touraine's visit was that he became an Honorary Doctor of the University of Jyväskylä in May 2004. Special thanks goes also to the students of this sociological course, who came from various backgrounds, such as sociology, political science, cultural policy, philosophy and language studies, and from different universities, as the institute has eight Erasmus exchange agreements based on an international network of researchers in social movements. Leena Aholainen, Minttu Helin, Elina Hirsjärvi, Njeri Kiguru, Päivi Kivelä, Hannele Kosonen, Tomi Oinas, Tytti Ollila and Antti Sadinmaa were the students from the University of Jyväskylä. Marcin Mlynczak and Bartlomiej Wozniak were exchange students from Adam Mickiewicz University, Poznan. Jana Safrova came from Charles University, Prague and Judit Zotter from Eotvos Lorand University, Budapest. Together with the senior lecturer, the students worked during the autumn term, participated in lectures, read Touraine's production (especially the book "The Voice and The Eye"), wrote essays and engaged in debate. The efforts of the seminar were aimed at being able to discuss with professor Alain Touraine about his theories and studies during the meeting. An earlier version of this paper was presented at the Annual Sociological Conference of the Westermarck Society, Joensuu 1.-2.4.2005. Acknowledgement also to lecturer Michael Freeman, who checked the language. Research funding for this study was provided by the Academy of Finland (project no. 106322) and is gratefully acknowledged.

[2] Other theoretical influences have come from the developer of functionalism Talcott Parsons and existentialist philosopher Jean-Paul Sartre. Needless to say, this conception of Touraine's theoretical roots is an artificial one as he is famous for his wide reading, but it serves the purpose of this introductory article. The influence of Parsons and Sartre will be explored later in this article.

[3] In The Voice and the Eye (1981) Touraine gives a definition of both society and social movement. "A society is a hierarchized system of systems of action. *Action is the behaviour of an actor guided by cultural orientations and set within social relations defined by an unequal connection with the*

social control of these orientations" (ibid., 61, italics in original text) "... I hold that the cultural field, the historicity of a society, represents the stakes in the most important conflicts. Society is conflictual production of itself. The idea of social movement should therefore be preferred to that of conflict. The field of historicity is the ensemble formed by the class actors and by that which is at stake in their struggles, i.e. historicity itself. *The social movement is the organized collective behaviour of a class actor struggling against his class adversary for the social control of historicity in a concrete community.* (ibid., 77, italics in original text)

[4] Touraine's 1969 "*La Société post industrielle*" (English translation 1971) was immediately translated into several languages and became, next to Daniel Bell's equally successful "*The Coming of Post-Industrial Society*" (1973) four years later, a standard work for the early sociological debate on processes of change within European-American modernity (Knöbler, 1999, p. 410).

[5] He needs a definition when looking for the "right" method to employ in studying social actors, specific methods for use in sociological research and, finally, when redefining the object of sociology.

[6] Tucker (2005, p. 55) points out that the subject is for Touraine 1) an attempt to combine instrumental rationality and cultural meanings into a coherent unity, 2) a process, not a person, 3) historically developed as it was earlier associated with nation-state and working class and nowadays operates on a more personal level, 4) attempt to create and sustain a coherent personal narrative in a social context defined by choices and change, 5) takes place in a social context as both the individual's integrity and others right to individuation must be recognized, 6) constituted in intercultural communication, 7) reflects the rise of a desire for authenticity and the right to define one's experience.

[7] Put briefly, subjectivation refers to the idea that the collective actor realizes its potential for social change (Brincker & Gundelach, 2005, p. 372) or to the process where a critical subject realizes its distance from social roles and generates liberating visions of social life (Tucker, 2005, p. 49). In trying to construct a more sophisticated understanding of subjectivation we can refer to how Warnier (2001) describes Foucault's idea of subjectivation. Warnier (2001, pp. 10-11) has stated that, as a matter of fact, Foucault never really gives strict and unequivocal definitions of it, but writes that subjectivation brings two dimensions of the subject to the fore. First, the subject is the acting and desiring subject in his/her relations to the other and to the ethical law. As such he/she is also the self-knowing subject. Second, the subject is the acting subject insofar as he/she is subjected to sovereignty. The two aspects are closely linked because acting means acting by oneself and on the actions of other subjects. Action on other people's actions defines the space of power, and, when organized, assumes the shape of historically construed 'governmentalities'. The process of subjectivation is, according to Warnier, confrontation with other subjects mediated by moving in a material world. In such a confrontation, the subject finds a number of givens that are required for him/ her to structure his/ her own desire. Such givens are his/her own sexed body, whatever his/her own sexual preferences, the social setting in which he/she was born, with its language, material culture, social and political organization, and significant others such as parents or siblings that he/she did not choose. In other words: being a subject is not primarily being what one chooses to be.

[8] Interpreting a society from the point of view of a system of action, Touraine emphasises that society is a hierarchy of systems of action whereas, in contrast, action is the behaviour of an actor guided by cultural orientations and located within social relations. The social relations within the system of action are defined by unequal connection with the social control of these cultural orientations (Touraine, 1981, p. 61).

REFERENCES

Alexander, J. C. (1999). Why we might all be able to live together. An immanent critique of Alain Touraine's pourrons-nous vivre ensemble? Review Essay. *Thesis Eleven, 58*(1), 99–105.

Arnason, J. (1986). Culture, historicity and power: Reflections on some themes in the work of Alain Touraine. *Theory, Culture & Society, 3*(3), 137–152.

Aronowitz, S. (1988). [Foreword]. In A. Touraine (Ed.), *Return of the actor: Social theory in postindustrial society* (pp. vii–xx). Minneapolis, MN: University of Minnesota Press.

Bauman, Z. (1983). Book reviews: Alain Touraine, Zsuzsa Hegedus François Dubet and Michel Wieviorka. Anti-nuclear protest. The opposition to nuclear energy in France. Cambridge University Press 1983 and Alain Touraine, François Dubet and Jan Strzelecki. Solidarity. Poland 1980-81. Cambridge University Press 1983. *Sociology, 17*(4), 596–598.

Brincker, B., & Gundelach, P. (2005). Sociologists in action: A critical exploration of the intervention method. *Acta Sociologica, 48*(4), 365–375.

Clark, J., & Diani, M. (Eds.). [Introduction]. *Alain Touraine* (pp. 1–8). London: Falmer Press.

Crozier, M. (1996). [Alain Touraine: A pioneer in the New French Sociology]. In J. Clark & M. Diani (Eds.), *Alain Touraine* (pp. 9–32). London: Falmer Press.

Dubet, F., & Wieviorka, M. (1996). [Touraine and the Method of Sociological Intervention]. In J. Clark & M. Diani (Eds.), *Alain Touraine* (pp. 55–76). London: Falmer Press.

Fine, R. (1998). The fetishism of the subject? Some comments on Alain Touraine. *European Journal of Social Theory, 1*(2), 179–184.

Fuchs, M. (2000). Articulating the world. social movements: The self-transcendence of society and the question of culture. *Thesis Eleven, 61*(1), 65–85.

Freiberg, J. W. (1977). [Foreword]. In A. Touraine (Ed.), *The self-production of society* (pp. xi–xvi). Chicago: University of Chicago Press.

Girling, J. (1998). *France: political and social change*. Florence, KY, USA: Routledge.

Hamel, J. (2001). The focus group method and contemporary French sociology. *Journal of Sociology, 37*(4), 341–353.

Hyvärinen, M. (1985). Alain Touraine: visio, teoria ja praksis. [Alain Touraine: Vision, Theory, and Praxis]. *Politiikka, 27*(4), 277–289.

Knöbl, W. (1999). Social Theory from a Sartrean point of view: Alain Touraine's theory of modernity. *European Journal of Social Theory, 2*(4), 403–428.

Pécaut, D. (1998). [Politics, the political and the theory of social movements]. In J. Clark & M. Diani (Eds.), *Alain Touraine* (pp. 159–172). London: Falmer Press.

Scott, A. (1991). Action, movement, and intervention: Reflections on the sociology of Alain Touraine. *Canadian Review of Sociology and Anthropology, 28*(1), 29–46.

Scott, A. (1996). [Movements of modernity: Some questions of theory, method and interpretation]. In J. Clark & M. Diani (Eds.), *Alain Touraine* (pp. 77–92). London: Falmer Press.

Touraine, A. (1971). *The post-industrial society: Tomorrow's social history: classes, conflicts and culture in the programmed society*. New York: Random House.

Touraine, A. (1977). *The Self-Production of Society*. Chicago: University of Chicago Press.

Touraine, A. (1979). *The may movement: Revolt and reform*. New York: Irvington.

Touraine, A. (1981). *The voice and the eye: An analysis of social movements*. Cambridge: Cambridge University Press.

Touraine, A. (1985). An Introduction to the Study of Social Movements. *Social Research, 52*(5), 749–787.

Touraine, A. (1995). *Critique of Modernity*. Cambridge, MA: Blackwell Publishers.

Touraine, A. (1996). [A sociology of the subject]. In J. Clark & M. Diani (Eds.), *Alain Touraine* (pp. 291–342). London: Falmer Press.

Touraine, A. (1997). *What is democracy?* Boulder: Westview Press.

Touraine, A. (2000). *Can we live together? Equality and difference*. Cambridge, UK: Polity Press.

Touraine, A. (2000). A method for studying social actors. *Journal of World-Systems Research. Special Issue: Festschrift for Immanuel Wallerstein - Part II, 6*(3), 900–918.

Touraine, A. (2001). *Beyond neoliberalism*. Cambridge, UK: Polity Press.

Touraine, A. (2004). On the frontier of social movements. *Current Sociology, 52*(4), 717–725.

Touraine, A., Hegedus, Z., Dubet, F., & Wieviorka, M. (1983). *Anti-nuclear protest: The opposition to nuclear energy in France*. Cambridge: Cambridge University Press.

Touraine, A., Wieviorka, M., & Dubet, F. (1987). *The workers' movement*. Cambridge: Cambridge University Press.

Tucker, K. H., Jr. (2005). From the imaginary to subjectivation: Castoriadis and Touraine on the performative public sphere. *Thesis Eleven, 83*(1), 42–60.

Turner, C. (1998). Touraine's concept of modernity. *European Journal of Social Theory, 1*(2), 185–193.

Warnier, J-P. (2001). A praxeological approach to subjectivation in a material world. *Journal of Material Culture, 6*(1), 5–24.

BIOGRAPHY

Ms Tamar Cohen is a final year undergraduate student in Environmental and Human Geography at the University of Queensland.

Ms Janine Dunleavy is a coordinator and senior tutor in the Indigenous Knowledge and Education course at the School of Education, University of Queensland and is currently completing a Masters of Environmental Education program at Griffith University.

Robert FitzSimmons is currently teaching at the University of Lapland, Finland. His research interests are associated primarily with Critical revolutionary pedagogy and Marxism.

Henry A. Giroux currently holds the Global TV Network Chair Professorship at McMaster University in the English and Cultural Studies Department. His most recent books include The University in Chains: Confronting the Military-Industrial-Academic Complex, 2007) Against the Terror of Neoliberalism (2008), and Youth in a Suspect Society: Democracy or Disposability? (2009). His primary research areas are: cultural studies, youth studies, critical pedagogy, popular culture, media studies, social theory, and the politics of higher and public education.

Sandy Grande is an Associate professor in the Education Department at Connecticut College and also works as a research consultant for the Ford Foundation. Currently she is serving as a Visiting Professor and Director of the Education Department at Barnard College. Her research and teaching are profoundly inter- and cross-disciplinary, and interfaces critical, feminist, Indigenous and Marxist theories of education with the concerns of Indigenous education. Her book, Red Pedagogy: Native American Social and Political Thought (Rowman and Littlefield, 2004) has been met with critical acclaim. She has also published several articles including "Critical Theory and American Indian Identity and Intellectualism," The International Journal of Qualitative Studies in Education, and "American Indian Geographies of Identity and Power: At the Crossroads of Indigena and Mestizaje," Harvard Educational Review.

Donna Houston is a Lecturer in the department of Environment and Geography at Macquarie University, Sydney. Her research interests focus on the interconnections between place, cultural memory, pedagogy and social and environmental trans-formation.

Nathalia Jaramillo is an Assistant Professor, College of Education, Purdue University. She is also affiliated faculty with the department of American Studies.

Douglas Kellner is George Kneller Chair in the Philosophy of Education at UCLA and is author of many books on social theory, politics, history, and culture, including Camera Politica: The Politics and Ideology of Contemporary Hollywood Film, co-authored with Michael Ryan; Critical Theory, Marxism, and Modernity; Jean Baudrillard: From Marxism to Postmodernism and Beyond; works in cultural studies such as Media Culture and Media Spectacle; a trilogy of books on postmodern theory with Steve Best; and a trilogy of books on the media and the Bush administration, encompassing Grand Theft 2000, From 9/11 to Terror War, and Media Spectacle and the Crisis of Democracy. Author of Herbert Marcuse and the Crisis of Marxism, Kellner is editing collected papers of Herbert Marcuse, four volumes of which have appeared with Routledge. Kellner's latest book is Guys and Guns Amok: Domestic Terrorism and School Shootings from the Oklahoma City Bombings to the Virginia Tech Massacre. His website is at http://www.gseis.ucla.edu/faculty/kellner/kellner.html

Dale Kerwin is a proud Goorie (Aboriginal) man from the Worimi Nation, New South Wales. He is passionate about Aboriginal rights to ownership and management for cultural heritage resources. When Aboriginal people were liberated in the late 1960's and educational institutions were opened to Aboriginal people he went and enrolled in tertiary studies. He has since achieved over a 20 year period Diploma of Primary Teaching, Graduate Diploma of Museum Studies and Cultural Heritage Management, Masters of Philosophy, thesis- *Whose Rights: Aboriginal Rights for Tangible and Intangible Property*. He has also just recently been awarded a PhD for his study of Aboriginal trading paths, thesis- Aboriginal *Dreaming Tracks or Trading Paths: The Common Ways*. He remains committed to furthering knowledges about Aboriginal cultural heritage and taking Aboriginal people from the foot note of Australian history to being inscribed on the body of Australian history.

Ville Lähde, born 1972, is a researcher specializing in environmental philosophy. For well over a decade, he has been publishing and lecturing on environmental and related issues in academic circles, public sphere and political events. He has also been active in various political movements which focused on environmental issues, animal rights and developmental issues. During 1995–2002 he was the chief editor of the environmentalist journal 'Muutoksen kevät'. The journal published 30 issues and acted as a common forum for a host of political movements in Finland. Currently Ville Lähde is the article review editor and occasional essayist of the Finnish philosophical journal 'niin & näin'. In his academic life, he has studied especially Critical Theory and Rousseau's philosophy. His MA thesis was on Herbert Marcuse's philosophy. He is currently finishing his PhD in philosophy in the University of Tampere, on the meanings of the word 'nature' in Rousseau's philosophy.

Alexander Lautensach, PhD. is assistant professor in the education program of the University of Northern British Columbia, Canada. His research expertise includes environmental ethics and human behavior, determinants of human security in the areas of health and environmental support structures, science education and values, and teaching for sustainability. He is associate editor of the *Journal of Human Security*. He has twenty years of teaching experience at the secondary, tertiary, graduate and continuing education levels in life sciences, education and philosophy at eight universities in New Zealand and across Canada. He has published over thirty research articles in molecular biology, ethics and education. He can be reached at alexl@unbc.ca.

Sabina W. Lautensach, Ph.D. is the Director of the independent Human Security Institute in British Columbia, Canada and a member of the academic staff of the European University Centre for Peace Studies (EPU). Dr Lautensach has lectured at the Royal NZ Navy Officer School in International Relations and at the Mahatma Ghandi University in Kerala, India. She is also the editor-in-chief of the *Journal of Human Security* and serves on several editorial boards. Dr. Lautensach currently lectures on a variety of topics within the field of international relations/Human Security. In addition to her consulting work as a political anthropologist, she is also a specialist in international environmental negotiations and has participated in numerous fora on environmental issues within an international context. She can be reached at salaut@gmail.com.

Ph.D. Tapio Litmanen is senior assistant in sociology at the University of Jyväskylä. He has conducted several research projects on social movements, environmental conflicts and nuclear technology issues. His doctoral thesis "The struggle over risk" dealt with nuclear power disputes and anti-nuclear movements. Quite recently he has studied and published also about peace and anti-war movement.

Peter McLaren is Professor of Urban Education at the Graduate School of Education and Information Studies, University of California, Los Angeles. He has written widely in the area of revolutionary critical pedagogy and critical social theory.

Gregory Martin is a Lecturer in the Faculty of Arts and Social Sciences, University of Technology, Sydney. His research interests include critical theories and pedagogies, social movements and participatory activist research.

Mr Sean Mitchell is an undergraduate student in Medicine at the University of Queensland.

Olli-Pekka Moisio, University of Jyväskylä, Finland, has written numerous articles on critical theory, Karl Marx, ethics, critical pedagogy, and critical philosophy of education. He is an editor of several books including a book on the Frankfurt School (in Finnish) and Theodor W. Adorno (in Finnish), and a book entitled *Education and the Spirit of Time* (with Juha Suoranta).

Dr. Shauneen Pete is from Little Pine First Nations, SK. An educator for over 20 years, she is currently working at First Nations University of Canada as the VP Academic.

Dr. Alison Sammel works at Griffith University on the Gold Coast in Australia. Ali's research and teaching focus includes the teaching and learning of science with particular interest in social, environmental justice and political issues, and the impacts of White privilege in education. She explores the world through the lenses of critical pedagogy and feminist poststructuralism.

Dr Norm Sheehan is a Senior Lecturer with Aboriginal and Torres Strait Islander Studies Unit, University of Queensland. He has completed an ARC Discovery Indigenous Research Development project Testing Ground: Investigating Indigenous Knowledge Programs and Indigenous Research Methodologies in Higher Education and has recently accepted a Postdoctoral Fellowship with the School of Psychiatry at The University of Queensland to work with mental health and Indigenous health experts in the formation of a framework for social and emotional wellbeing in rural and remote Aboriginal communities in Queensland.

Juha Suoranta grew up in a working-class family in the working-class city of Tampere, Finland. Currently he is tenured Professor of Adult Education at the University of Tampere. His research interests relate to working-class studies, radical adult education, critical pedagogy, and critique of political economy of education.

Olli Tammilehto is a free lance writer and researcher. His fields of interest are, among other things, environmental philosophy, societal and ideological causes of the global ecological crisis, energy policy, globalization, poverty, criticism of the prevailing economical and political thinking, social change and social movements, Russia and stateless peoples outside civilizations. Besides numerous articles Tammilehto has written following books and studies: The Environment and War (1980), Ecological Philosophy, Alternative Movements and Nuclear Power (1982, only in Finnish), When Representatives Aren't Enough: A Guide to Social Activism (1988, only in Finnish), The Collected Explanations for The State of The World (1998, only in Finnish), The Effects of the Production and Consumption Patterns of Industrialized Countries on the Environment in the South (1999), Globalisation and Dimensions of Poverty (2003). He has co-edited the book Outside the Imperium: Development-Critical Discussions (1991, only in Finnish) and the report Indigenous Peoples and Oil (2001). Tammilehto has given lectures in the universities of Helsinki, Oulu and Riga on enviroanmental philosophy, on understanding of the ecological crisis and on ideological discourses. He has been active to a varying degree in various environmental and solidarity organizations.

Annette Woods is Senior Lecturer within the Faculty of Education at Queensland University of Technology. Her work spans the fields of literacy, assessment and accountability, curriculum, social justice and diversity. She has edited two anthologies and is published in national and international scholarly journals. She is currently writing a joint authored (with Allan Luke and Katie Weir) book Entitled Curriculum, Syllabus Design And Equity: A Primer And Model, and her recent work in the literacy field is published in the Handbook of Adolescent Literacy Research (Luke & Woods in Christenbury, Bomer, & Smagorinsky, 2009); The Journal of Early Childhood Literacy (Woods & Henderson, 2008); Iskolakultural (School Culture) (Woods, 2008) and Curriculum Perspectives, (Woods, 2007). She was integral to a large-scale curriculum reform movement in Solomon Islands in 2001–2004 and brings this practical experience and fieldwork to her theoretical understandings of curriculum and syllabus design.

CPSIA information can be obtained at www.ICGtesting.com
259897BV00004B/19/P

9 789460 911118